Women & Gender

Economics and Finance

Women & Gender
Economics and Finance

Siddhartha Sarkar

KALPAZ

ISBN : 978-93-532-4041-7

First Published, 2019

Published by

Kalpaz Publications
C-30, Satyawati Nagar,
Delhi – 110052
Ph.: 011-47034999, 9811692060
www.kalpazpublications.com
E-mail: kalpaz@hotmail.com

Printed at: G. Print Process, Delhi

Contents

Preface

Most of the latest literature on the economics of gender equality starts from the proposition that men and women are not fundamentally different and that women should become equal to men in all socio-economic spheres. The aim is to bridge the gender gaps in education, employment and pay, as well as equalizing the percentage of women and men on powerful positions on the market and in governmental institutions. The emphasis is thus not only on equality in starting positions, but rather on equality in terms of outcomes. The efficiency gains are mainly related to economic growth. The efficiency argument emphasizes the importance of socio-economic equality between men and women – a higher employment rate widens the human capital base, increases economic competitiveness, broadens the tax base, and promotes social inclusion.

The evidence on gender differences in preferences is used to make the argument that women, precisely because they are different, should have a more equal position in the boardroom to counterbalance the riskier and daring male decision making.

The emphasis on a more equal economic role of men and women has had a major impact on the female educational level and employment rate.

There has been a strong debate about the one-sidedness of the 'efficiency-of-equality approach' if this implies women becoming equal to men. For example, it is by no means obvious that women's positions are strengthened by having to work as many hours in paid employment as men. In addition, the efficiency argument, based on the untapped potential, may not be entirely valid in the sense that the inactive population may in fact be very active in terms of unpaid and care work.

The economic crisis has also raised some doubts about the notion of full time employment and the emphasis on increasing the labour supply of both men and women. If the future economy is based on a different organisation of paid and unpaid work, with less emphasis on long working hours, the efficiency argument for increasing the labour supply becomes less clear. By implication, we not only have to redefine the concept of gender equality, but also the concept of full employment and the concept of efficiency. An efficient and resilient economy may be a gender-smart economy, using the full potential of both men and women in a differentiated way, by investing in a supportive infrastructure. In the long run, however, the policy emphasis may not be at closing the gender gaps at the level of paid work but rather at facilitating the working population to participate in unpaid work.

For generations, there has been widespread prevalence of economic and social barriers that inhibit empowerment and economic inclusion of women in the global economy. There is extensive number of literature that discusses different challenges women face in their quest for equality particularly in terms of access to finance irrespective of their socio-economic, demographic, and geographical circumstances. In the pursuit of sustainable financial inclusion, addressing this gender gap in terms of access and usage of financial services is one of the key priority areas amongst policymakers. Currently, there are over one billion women globally who are financially excluded from the formal financial system. Thus, the only way to have a genuine inclusive financial system is to incorporate gender dimension to financial inclusion strategies and goals. Therefore, one thing is clear is that advancing the agenda of gender finance will require a multi-stakeholder approach with women being at the helm of this movement. Moving forward, innovation would be a key in supporting women to proactively grasp their full economic potential. A better comprehension of gender and finance would allow professionals in the area to offer more suitable products and advice to clients. Investments programs based on gender can produce better investment results. It is also of great importance for policy- makers, business leaders and researches to explore the issue in order to develop approaches to close the gender gap in wealth, income and financial knowledge.

Siddhartha Sarkar

1

Gender Inequality and Economic Growth

Kiriti-Nganga, T.W. *University of Nairobi*

Introduction

Kenya's gross domestic product (GDP) grew at an annual average of 6.6% from 1963 to 1973. Between 1974 and 1990, however, Kenya's economic performance declined. From 1991 to 1993, Kenya had its worst economic performance since independence. From 1994-1996, Kenya's real GDP growth rate averaged just over 4% a year. Its economic growth rate declined from 1.4% in 1998 to a negative 0.3% in 2001. In 2000, GDP growth was negative, but improved slightly in 2001. Economic growth continued to improve slightly in 2002 and reached 1.4% in 2003; it was 4.3% in 2004, 5.8% in 2005 and 6.1 in 2006 (Table 1).

Kenya's population was estimated to be 35.5 million in the year 2005 with a growth rate of 2.4 percent per annum. Its economic performance in the last two decades has been far below its potential. Its income per capita in constant 1982 prices declined from US dollar 271 in 1990 to 239 in 2002 and rising to 481 in 2004. However, it fell to 464 in 2005 (UNDP 2006). Unemployment stands at close to 15 percent of the labour force and youth unemployment accounts for 45 percent of this total. The deterioration in Kenya's economic performance has aggravated the problem of poverty that is estimated to have an incidence of 56 percent (Republic of Kenya 2003).

The incidence of poverty varies from one province to another. In 1994, the North Eastern Province recorded the highest level at 58 per cent; the Eastern had 57 per cent followed by the Coast province 55 per cent and Nyanza 42 per cent while Central recorded the lowest level of 32 per cent. By 1997, poverty had increased rapidly and its distribution pattern changed with Nyanza recording the highest level 63 per cent, followed by the Coast 62 per cent, Western and Eastern 59 percent, Rift Valley 50 percent and Central 31 per cent. In 2005.

Central still recorded the lowest poverty at 30.4 percent, Coast at 69.7 percent; Eastern at 50.9 percent; North Eastern at 73.9 percent, Nyanza at 47.6 percent; Rift Valley at 49.0 percent and Western at 52.2 percent.

The incidence of poverty also varies from rural to urban areas. In 1997, it was estimated that 75 percent to 80 percent of the poor live in the rural areas. In the rural areas, food poverty was estimated at 51 percent while absolute poverty was 53 percent. In urban areas, food poverty was estimated at 38 percent while the absolute poverty was 49 percent. The overall national incidence of poverty stood at 56 percent. In urban areas, Kisumu recorded the highest 63 percent, followed by Nairobi 50 percent, Nakuru 41 percent and Mombasa 38 percent. In 2005, rural poverty stood at 49.1 percent while food poverty was 47.2 percent. In Urban areas, absolute poverty stood at 33.7 percent while food poverty stood at 40.5 percent (Republic of Kenya various issues). The number of poor increased from 3.7 million in 1972-73 to 11.5 million in 1994. Thereafter, numbers increased to 12.5 million in 1997 and in 2005 the number of poor people living below the poverty line reached some 16.7 million.

The poor are identified to include the aged, pastoralists, physically challenged persons, female-headed households, child-headed households, casual labourers, AIDS orphans, street children, slum dwellers and the unemployed youth. Among the poor persons, women are more vulnerable to poverty than men. For instance, 69 per cent of the active female population work as subsistence farmers compared to 43 per cent of men. The high incidence of poverty is explained by factors such as the declining economic growth, which contracted to negative -0.2 percent in the year 2000, gender disparities, bad governance, corruption, inefficient delivery of services, HIV/AIDS, environmental factors, and the adverse effects of structural adjustment programmes (Republic of Kenya 2003).

Table 1: GDP Growth Rate 1963-2006

Year	*Growth Rate*
1963-1973	6.6
1990	1.4
1994-1996	4
1998	1.4
2000	-0.2
2001	1.2
2002	1.1
2003	1.0
2004	4.9
2005	5.8
2006	6.1

Source: UNDP: Human Development Report [Various Issues]

According to UNDP (1995), poverty has a woman's face with over 70 percent of the poorest people in the world being women. It is also asserted that poverty among women is rising faster than poverty among men. Between 1965 and 70 and the mid-1980s, the number of rural women living in poverty increased by 48 percent, while the number of rural men living in poverty increased by 30 percent in the same period. Women constitute 52 percent of Kenya's population, but the majority of them are between the illiterate and poor in the country (United Nations Economic and Social Council 1998).

A third of rural households are female-headed, and as many as 60 percent of these have no male support. In the World Bank sponsored Participatory Poverty Assessment, communities interviewed classified 44 percent of the female-headed households as 'very poor' compared to 21 percent of the male-headed households. Ownership and access to land is a critical factor. Sixty percent of the people asked how they would sub-divide land said that they would give all their land to their sons. Another 8 percent said they would give more land to their sons. Married women enjoy usufructuary rights to land but widowhood brings uncertainty and upon divorce or separation, many assets including land, become the sole property of the man. Destitute women often migrate to urban slums where they remain poor. Women have a heavier burden of work, which cuts into their rest (World Bank 1996).

Studies in Kenya indicate that women are more vulnerable to poverty than men. For instance, as mentioned above, 69 percent of the active female population work as subsistence farmers compared to 43 percent of men. Given that subsistence farmers are among the very poor, this relative dependence of women upon subsistence farming explains the extreme vulnerability of women. These problems are most severe in arid and semi-arid areas where women spend a great portion of their time searching for water and fuel. The release of women's productive potential and increasing their economic potential through financial and economic empowerment are pivotal to breaking the cycle of poverty so that they can share fully in the benefits of development and in the products of their own labour. In the urban areas, the proportion of poor female-headed households was higher than male-headed households in 1997. Both rural and urban women in 1997 were severely affected by poverty. This means that women are affected more by the development process and the area of residence plays a major role in poverty status of women (Republic of Kenya 2000). Their exclusion from decision-making structures, itself due to institutional biases, in turns limits their capacity to influence rules, norms and practices which would bring about more gender equitable policies and practices for poverty reduction.

Reducing poverty, advancing human development and increasing the rate of economic growth by 10% per annum is the vision and agenda for the Kenya Government to join the ranks of middle-income countries by 2030. In the

Kenya Vision 2030 the Kenya Government would like to increase the per capita GDP from the current US$464 to US$3,065 by the year 2030. This vision is envisaged to be inclusive, one that all Kenyan's can identify with. However, certain constraints my hinder the achievement of this vision one of them being gender inequality that is pervasive in Kenya. A country cannot grow if over half of its population is denied access to productive resources and is not allowed to participate fully in the society.

Gender

Gender can refer to the biological condition of being male or female. Since the 1950s the term gender has been increasingly used to distinguish a social role (gender role)/or personal identity (gender identity) distinct from biological sex. Gender and particularly the role of women are widely recognized as vitally important to development issues. This not only means a focus on gender-equality, ensuring participation, but also includes an understanding of the different roles and expectations of the genders within the community. Gender inequality exists in most parts of the world, Kenya included. However, inequality between women and men can take very many different forms. Indeed, gender inequality is not one homogeneous phenomenon, but a collection of disparate and interlinked problems (Sen 2001). Sen identifies various forms of gender inequality such as:

Mortality Inequality

In some regions of the world, inequality between women and men directly involves matters of life and death, and takes the brutal form of unusually high mortality rates of women and a consequent preponderance of men in the total population, as opposed to the preponderance of women found in societies with little or no gender bias in health care and nutrition. Mortality inequality has been observed extensively in North Africa and in Asia, including China and South Asia.

Natality Inequality

Given a preference for boys over girls that many male-dominated societies have, gender inequality can manifest itself in the form of the parents wanting the newborn to be a boy rather than a girl. There was a time when this could be no more than a wish (a daydream or a nightmare, depending on one's perspective), but with the availability of modern techniques to determine the gender of the foetus, sex-selective abortion has become common in many countries. Kiriti and Tisdell (2005) in their study of Nyeri district found that chid gender preference is very common in Kenya.

Basic Facility Inequality

Even when demographic characteristics do not show much of any anti-female bias, there are other ways in which women can have less than a square deal. Afghanistan may be the only country in the world the government of which is keen on actively excluding girls from schooling (it combines this with other features of massive gender inequality), but there are many countries in Asia and Africa, and also in Latin America, where girls have far less opportunity of schooling than boys do. There are other deficiencies in basic facilities available to women, varying from encouragement to cultivate one's natural talents to fair participation in rewarding social functions of the community.

Special Opportunity Inequality

Even when there is relatively little difference in basic facilities including schooling, the opportunities of higher education may be far fewer for young women than for young men.

Professional inequality

In terms of employment as well as promotion in work and occupation, women often face greater handicap than men. A country like Japan may be quite egalitarian in matters of demography or basic facilities, and even, to a great extent, in higher education, and yet progress to elevated levels of employment and occupation seems to be much more problematic for women than for men.

Ownership Inequality

In many societies the ownership of property can also be very unequal. Even basic assets such as homes and land may be very asymmetrically shared. The absence of claims to property can not only reduce the voice of women, but also make it harder for women to enter and flourish in commercial, economic and even some social activities.

Household Inequality

There are often enough, basic inequalities in gender relations within the family or the household, which can take many different forms. Even in cases in which there are no overt signs of anti-female bias in, say, survival or son-preference or education, or even in promotion to higher executive positions, the family arrangements can be quite unequal in terms of sharing the burden of housework and child care. It is, for example, quite common in many societies to take it for granted that while men will naturally work outside the home, women could do it if and only if they could combine it with various inescapable and unequally shared household duties. This is sometimes called 'division of labour', though women could be forgiven for seeing it as 'accumulation of labour'. The reach of this inequality includes not only unequal relations within the family, but also derivative inequalities in employment and recognition in the outside world. Also, the established fixity of this type of division or accumulation of labour can also have far-reaching effects on the knowledge and understanding of different types of work in professional circles (Sen 2001).

Evidence of Gender Inequality in Kenya

Although there is a dearth of data and statistics on gender inequality, one can look at various indicators to make a conclusion as to whether gender inequality exists. One can look at the differences in hours of work or time burden, poverty levels, allocation of and access to resources and farm inputs, literacy and illiteracy levels, ownership of land and access, life expectancy, employment in terms of labour force participation rates, trends in employment, maternal mortality rates, HIV/AIDS and nutrition, participation in governance and human rights.

Time and Work Burden

Employment and national accounts data do not capture non-market activities (where women predominate) and therefore fail to demonstrate the full contribution of women to the household economy and the extent of the female work burden as shown in Table 2.

Table 2: Gender, Work and Time Allocation in Kenya

Year/ Region	*Total Work Time (Hours, and Minutes per Day*		*Female Work Time (% of Male)*	*Total Work Time*		*Time Allocation*			
						Time Spent by Women		*Time Spent by Men*	
				Market Acti-vities	*Non Market Acti-vities*	*Market Acti-vities*	*Non Market Acti-vities*	*Market Acti-vities*	*Non Market Acti-vities*
Urban	Women	Men							
1986	9.50	9.32	103	46	54	41	59	79	21
Rural									
1988	11.16	8.20	135	56	44	42	58	76	24

Source: UNDP: Human Development Report [2005]

On average, women work longer hours (12.9 hours per day) compared to men (8.2 hours), yet they earn less since more of these hours are not remunerated. Women in Kenya constitute 60.8 percent of unpaid family workers (Saito and Spurling 1994).

Elson and Elvers (1997) compared the female and male hours of work in market and non-market activities and found that in total women worked 11.3 hours per day compared to men's 8.3 hours for both market and non-market activities. This is shown in Table 3.

Table 3: Kenya: Comparison by Gender of Work Hours in Marketed and Non-marketed Activities; Shares of Marketed /Non-marketed in Total Work

System	*Female*		*Male*		*Total*
	Hours per day	*(%)*	*Hours per day*	*(%)*	*in %*
Marketed Activities	5.7	42	6.3	76	56
Non- marketed activities	6.6	58	2.0	24	44
Total	11.3	100	8.3	100	100

Source: Elson and Evers [1997].

In addition to their prominence in agriculture, women bear the brunt of domestic tasks: processing food crops, providing water and firewood, and caring for the elderly and the sick. The time and effort required for these tasks, in the almost total absence of even rudimentary domestic technology, is staggering. Yet this productive work is largely invisible, unrecorded and not included in national accounts.

In 1990, Kenya's GDP was US$8,533.2 and out of this, women's share amounted to 45.4 percent (www.genderstats.worldbank.org). This share would have been much higher had the non-marketed activities been included in the GDP. Women in Kenya work 50 percent more hours than men on agricultural tasks. They work half as many hours again as men when agricultural and non-agricultural tasks are combined. The disproportionate cost born by women in terms of reproductive work in the household economy limits the time women can spend on economic activities hence subjecting them to poverty and contributing negatively to economic growth.

Poverty Levels

Women and men experience poverty differently, and different aspects of poverty (deprivation, powerlessness, vulnerability, its seasonality) have gender dimensions (World Bank 1996). Vulnerability reflects the dynamic nature of poverty such as defencelessness, insecurity and exposure to risk. Vulnerability is a function of assets. The more assets people have, the less vulnerable they are. Assets include stores, concrete productive investments, human investments, collective assets and claims on others for assistance. Both absolute and food poverty are associated with lack of physical and human assets (World Bank 1997). Women are more vulnerable because tradition usually gives them less decision-making power over assets than men, while at the same time their opportunities to engage in remunerated activities, and therefore to acquire their own assets, are more limited (Blackden and Bhanu 1999, World Bank 1995 & 1996). Greer and Thorbecke (1986), Collier and Lal (1980) and Republic of Kenya (1991 and 1998) showed that food poverty and absolute poverty occur mainly among female-headed households.

Quisumbing *et al.* (2001) found that women are disproportionately represented among the poor. The World Bank's (1995) Participatory Poverty Assessment for Kenya shows that while 25 percent of the study population was categorised as very poor, there were nearly twice as many female-headed households (44 percent) as male-headed households (21 percent) in that category. The remaining 35 percent represented male-headed with no wife present. Greer and Thorbecke (1986), Collier and Lal (1980), and Republic of Kenya (1991 and1998) also find that female-headed households account for the high proportion of the poor in Kenya. Mwabu *et al.* (2000) using the cost of basic needs (CBN) and food energy intake (FEI) approaches in computing poverty rates for Kenya, found that poverty rates were marginally higher in female-headed households (41 percent) than in male-headed households (38 percent) where husband and wife live together.

The World Bank's (1995) Participatory Poverty Assessment for Kenya found that to cope with increased levels of poverty, female heads of households in Kenya consistently limit the number of meals eaten. They found that one third of the female-headed households had only one meal per day while the rest had two meals. Some women resort to begging for food, others rely on brewing alcohol despite being harassed by police.

Apart from lack of physical and human assets, women are generally immobile because of greater responsibilities for childcare, household provisioning, doing household chores and home-based agricultural activities. The cultural norms are such that women find it hard to venture out to look for work or in certain traditions, to mix with men. This prevents them from gathering information on job opportunities. They are cut off from channels of communication, or the information they receive is filtered through the (male) head of household or community leaders.

Poverty rates generally decline as the level of education increases (Mwabu *et al.* 2000, Schultz 1960). Education and training reduce the chances of falling back into poverty. Females in Kenya generally have lower levels of education compared to males. A long-term remedy to alleviate poverty would be to invest in poor people, especially women, particularly in their education and training, and to bring them into the mainstream of development.

Women not only suffer from income poverty but also human poverty. Human poverty means that opportunities and choices most basic to human development are denied. Human poverty is more than income poverty. It involves the denial of choices and opportunities most basic to human development to lead a long, healthy, creative life, acquire knowledge, and enjoy a decent standard of living, freedom, dignity, self-esteem and the respect of others (UNDP 1998).

One way of measuring human poverty, although it is far from adequate, is by using the human poverty index (HPI) introduced by UNDP in the Human

Development Report of 1997. The HPI is a composite index of different features of deprivation in the quality of life that helps to judge the extent of poverty in a community. HPI-1 measures human poverty in developing countries. The variables used are: (1) The percentage of people expected to die before age 40; (2) the percentage of adults who are illiterate; and (3) deprivation in overall economic provisioning measured by: (a) the percentage of people without access to health services and safe water and (b) the percentage of underweight children under five. The HPI is constructed by taking a simple average of the three variables.

The trend in the HPI for Kenya between 1997 and 2006 is evident from Table 4. This table shows that the value of the HPI for Kenya has been rising and the poverty ranking of Kenya increased compared to other developing nations. Table 4 also shows that the percentage of people living below the poverty line rose from 42 percent in 1992 to 56 percent in 2001 implying that over half the population in Kenya was living below the poverty line in 2001. The HPI for Kenya in 2004 was 35.5, ranking it 60th among 102 developing countries for which the index was calculated. Between 1997 and 2004, a span of 7 years, human poverty in Kenya had increased by 8.4 percent and the population living below the poverty line increased by 10 percent and of course this affected females most although the data is not disaggregated according to gender.

Table 4: Human Poverty Index for Kenya: 1992-2006

Year	*Human poverty index*		*Population below absolute national poverty line*
	Rank among developing countries	*Value (%)*	
1992	Na	Na	42.0
1997	35	27.1	Na
1998	49	28.2	47.0
1999	51	29.5	42.0
2000	49	31.9	50.0
2001	63	37.8	56.0
2002	63	37.5	52.0
2003	60	35.5	52.0
2004	60	35.5	52.0
2006	NA	NA	45.9

Source. UNDP: Human Development Report [Various Issues].

However, Mwabu *et al.* (2005) estimated that in 1997, the proportion of rural male-headed households living below the poverty line was 52.50 while that of female-headed households was 54.10. They also predicted that in 2000, the proportion of rural male headed households living in poverty would be 59.08 compared to 60.88 percent of rural female headed households a clear indication that females suffer more poverty than males. In 2005, the proportion of rural male-headed household living below the poverty line was 48.8 percent while that of rural female-headed households was 50 percent. However, rural male-headed households contributed to 72 percent of overall rural poverty compared with 28 percent from rural female households.

HDI, GDI and GEM

Other measures of gender inequality are Gender-related Development Index (GDI), the Gender Empowerment Measure (GEM) and the Human Development Index (HDI). The GDI and the GEM can be used to rank countries in order of achievements on gender equality, rather than just on human development as with the HDI. Table 5 shows the HDI for Kenya from 1975 to 2004.

Table 5: Human Development Indices for Kenya: 1994 - 2004

Year	*HDI Rank (among UN member countries)*	*HDI Value*
1975	134	0.445
1980	134	0.490
1985	134	0.515
1990	113	0.540
1995	137	0.524
1999	123	0.514
2000	134	0.496
2002	148	0.488
2003	154	0.474
2004	152	0.491

Source: UNDP: Human Development Report [Various Issues]

Table 6 shows that the HDI for Kenya has been deteriorating over the years and even in terms of ranking, it has moved from position 134 in 1975 to 152 in 2004. The HDI may not show the inequalities in achievements between males and females. Table 6 shows the GDI for Kenya from 1995 to 2004.

Table 6: Kenya's Gender Related Development Index: 1995-2004

Year	*GDI*	*Rank*	*Share of Earned Income*	
			Males	*Females*
1995	0.459	122	58.22	41.78
1997	0.517	113	57.4	42.6
1998	0.508	115	61.0	39.0
1999	0.511	145	52.7	47.3
2000	0.512	110	52.3	47.7
2001	0.488	112	52.6	47.4
2002	0.486	114	52.6	47.4
2003	0.472	117	51.9	48.1
2004	0.487	111	54.5	45.5

Source: UNDP: Human Development Report [Various Issues]

Table 6 shows that the GDI fell from 0.517 in 1997 to 0.487 in 2004 showing that the situation of women deteriorated during that period. The share of earned income also shows females earn less than males and this gap increased in 2006.It can also be seen that in 1998, women only earned 39 percent of total earnings compared to men's 61 percent. One may be mislead in thinking that the gap is not significant but this share of earned income reflects mainly the experience of women in full-time formal employment in larger workplaces and do not consider the majority of women who work in part-time or informal employment in small scale places of work or at home.

The other evidence of gender inequality is the Gender Empowerment Measure (GEM) but Kenya is not ranked by the Human Development Reports due to lack of data.

Education/Literacy Level

Literacy is a powerful determinant of an individual's life choices and opportunities. Shortcomings in literacy skills limit the opportunities of a large proportion of the people living in developing countries. Illiteracy is defined as the percentage of people without a minimum of four years of schooling (UNDP 1998).

Among the developing world's 900 million illiterate people, women outnumber men two to one. And girls constitute the majority of the 130 million children without access to primary school. In sub-Saharan Africa (SSA) the average number of years of schooling for the female adult population in 1960 was only 1.1 years, which was barely half of the schooling achievement by men. Females in SSA experienced the lowest average annual growth of total years of schooling between 1960 and 1990 of all regions (an annual increase of 0.04 years rising the average years of schooling of the adult female population by only 1.2 years between 1960 and 1990). The female-male ratio in the growth of total years of schooling was only 0.89 meaning that females experienced a slower expansion in educational achievement than males (Blackden and Bhanu 1999).

In 1992, Kenya's adult literacy rate was 70.5 percent while the mean years of schooling was 2.3. In 1994, the adult literacy rate was 77 percent and the gross enrolment ratio was 55 percent. The adult literacy rate in 1995 was 78.1 percent. The gross enrolment ratio was only 52 per cent. This was as a result of a decrease in per capita expenditure on education, health and other social services due to pressure from the World Bank and the IMF. The adult literacy rate for females in 1995 and 1997 was 70.02 and 71.8 respectively, compared to 86.3 and 86.9 for males for the same years, while the gross enrolment ratio was 51 for females and 52 for males (UNDP 1996). This shows that there exists a gender gap in adult literacy of well over 15 points in both 1995 and 1997.

The need to undergo fiscal adjustment because of unsustainable fiscal deficits and mounting payment obligations on its external debt constrained the government's ability to increase the education budget. Attempts to solve the resource shortage by shifting costs to families and communities ran into difficulties. The extremely low per capita incomes limited the ability of communities and households to contribute more to education of their children. The additional burden on low-income households may have had a negative effect on school enrolment, especially enrolment of girls, as the demand for education is price sensitive in low-income households (Kabubo and Kiriti-Nganga 2001). However, the National Rainbow Coalition (NARC) government started offering free primary schooling in 2003.

Table 7 shows the education enrolments by gender in Kenya from the year 2000 to 2005.

Table 7: Enrolment in Pre-primary, Primary and Secondary Schools in Kenya (2000-2005) ***(000's)***

Year	*Pre-Primary*		*Primary*		*Secondary*		*University*	
	Male	*Female*	*Male*	*Female*	*Male*	*Female*	*Male*	*Female*
2000	636.8	609.8	306.5	301.4	40.3	35.7	37.4	21.8
2001	674.6	648.9	300.3	293.9	40.3	36.0	43.7	27.6
2002	742.8	712.9	307.4	298.9	41.2	36.7	51.1	29.9
2003	816.6	785.7	367.4	348.5	45.9	42.4	51.5	30.6
2004	823.4	804.3	381.6	357.9	48.9	43.4	57.9	33.6
2005	830.8	812.3	390.3	368.9	49.4	44.0	58.8	33.5
2006	846.4	825.9	389.7	373.6	54.6	48.4	68.3	43.9

Source: Republic of Kenya: Economic Survey [Various Issues]

Table 7 shows that enrolments in primary school increased by 19.5 percent for males and 16.6 percent for females between 2000 and 2005. One would have expected parity in enrolments in primary school. Other levels of education including tertiary have to be met by the parents although at the University level, students are entitled to a loan from the Higher Education Loans Board (HELB). Nevertheless, there are glaring inequalities in literacy rates and enrolments at all levels.

Costs are the most common cause for girls dropping out of school. Generally when the cost of education increases at the household level, families tend to prefer school for boys and even where places in school are limited and resources are scarce, girls are at a particular disadvantage. Parents may prefer to educate sons, both because expected benefits are higher due to better job prospects for sons and dependence on sons in old life (Kiriti-Nganga and

Tisdell 2005), and costs are lower because of the low opportunity cost of their time in terms of help in the household (Mincer and Polachek 1974). Other factors such as teenage pregnancy and early marriages lead to lower transition rates to secondary and tertiary education for girls. Girls also face greater burdens of domestic tasks compared to boys when they arrive home.

The gender gap in primary school enrolments is measured as the ratio of female to male enrolment at this level times 100. The gender gap in secondary school enrolment is measured as the ratio of female to male enrolment at this level times 100. These two are measures of women's status as far as education in early years is concerned. Table 8 shows gross enrolment ratios by gender in Kenya from 1991 to 1998.

Table 8: Gross Enrolment Ratios for Primary and Secondary Levels of Education for Kenya by Gender: 1991-1998

Year	*Primary enrolment*				*Secondary enrolment*			
	Total	*Male*	*Female*	*Gap*	*Total*	*Male*	*Female*	*Gap*
1991	93.0	94.5	91.5	3.0	27.9	31.5	24.4	7.1
1992	91.7	92.9	90.5	2.4	27.3	30.7	23.9	6.8
1993	90.5	91.1	89.8	1.3	25.7	28.5	22.8	5.7
1994	86.9	87.1	86.6	0.5	24.8	27.0	22.6	4.4
1995	84.9	84.9	83.2	1.7	24.8	26.4	22.4	4.0
1998	90.7	91.4	90.0	1.4	29.9	31.5	28.2	3.3

Source: UNFPA [2005]

As Table 8 shows, the enrolment ratios of females in both primary and secondary schools are lower than that of males. However, the gender gap, though exhibiting a declining trend in both primary and secondary school levels, is much wider in secondary schools. The data indicate that although enrolment levels are high for both girls and boys in primary schools (although enrolment ratios for females are lower than those of males), there is a higher dropout of female students than of male students and enrolment ratios are much higher for males than for females in secondary school. This shows that a huge percentage of girls do not make it to tertiary level reducing their chances of better opportunities in employment and earning power.

The gender gap in adult illiteracy is measured as the percentage of illiterate females in the 15 years and above age group minus the percentage of illiterate males in the same age group. Adult illiteracy rates are largely a reflection of historical trends in primary school enrolment. A higher gender gap is a reflection of women's lower status since literacy is the forerunner to a host of expanded opportunities for women including earning power, control over health and child-bearing, political and legal rights and so on. Table 9 shows the adult illiteracy rates for Kenya by gender for a selected number of years where data were available.

Table 9: Adult Illiteracy Rates for Kenya by Gender (Adults above 15 years of Age)

Year	*Adult Illiteracy*			
	Total	*Male*	*Female*	*Gap*
1970	55.0	44.0	74.0	30.0
1980	43.9	30.1	57.3	27.2
1985	36.2	24.3	48.0	23.7
1990	29.2	19.1	39.2	20.1
1995	23.0	14.8	31.1	16.4
1999	17.6	11.1	24.0	12.9
2000	17.6	11.1	24.0	12.9
2003	14.9	9.40	20.3	10.9

Source: UNFPA [2005]

Table 9 shows that in 1970, 74 percent of the adult female population was illiterate compared to 44 percent of adult males. By 1999, 24 percent of the adult female population remained illiterate compared to 11.1 percent of the adult male population. Table 9 also shows that there exists a gender gap in adult illiteracy in Kenya although it seems to be declining but at a very slow pace. For example, between 1970 and 2003, a duration of 33 years, the illiteracy gap declined by only 19.1 percent. Low enrolment ratios for females in institutions of higher learning and high illiteracy rates means that women cannot participate effectively in decision-making institutions.

Gender disparities in education also affect women's labour force participation and their ability to acquire the skills needed to start and grow business. Women's lower levels of education result in lower labour participation as well as higher fertility rates and lower levels of skills for them as entrepreneurs.

Female/Male Ratios in Decision-making Institutions

The majority of women in formal sector employment are concentrated in semi-skilled and non-skilled jobs that are also low paying. Women's representation in technical and professional fields is still limited. Their representation in decision-making positions is also extremely limited. There are various reasons that account for this situation. First, early socialisation practices emphasise the primary role of women as mothers and wives influence girls' total expectations for future participation in the labour force and the choice of clear career paths. Second, women's overall limited educational attainments as well as the types of curricula used in schools that emphasise stereotypic role for women create further barriers. Career guidance and counselling likewise tends to channel girls into traditional female fields such as nursing, teaching and home economics. Third, women's multiple responsibilities as mothers, wives, employees and employers create role conflicts that at times could result in compromises in careers. Women's careers tend to be interrupted during their childbearing years, resulting in loss of seniority. In addition, as women are usually expected to move with their husbands, the interrupted career syndrome further compromises their career progression. Fourth, organisational policies and procedures are often influenced by cultural perceptions of women's roles and capabilities. This leads to women being discriminated against in recruitment, to be promoted to senior positions and benefits as it is assumed that women lack the qualities essential for successful managerial careers (Mincer and Polachek 1974).

African culture is a barrier to growth and development to the extent that it perpetuates culturally sanctioned biases against women and provides excuses for men. Cultural biases operate at all levels ranging from national institutional level, government policy, community level, household and individual levels (Kiriti-Nganga *et al.* 2003). In Africa, women's participation at all levels of decision making is low. In parliament, the highest level of decision-making, women are under represented. In 1995, at the time of the Beijing Platform for Action, only 10 percent of the members of legislative bodies were women. In 1998, this had increased to 12 percent, which is still a very low percentage. The UNDP in its Human Development Report of 1995 states that there should be a target of 30 percent of women in all spheres of political and social life for an impact to be felt.

United Nations (1995) states that women's equal participation in political life play a pivotal role in the general process of the advancement of women. Without the active participation of women and the incorporation of women's perspectives at all levels of decision-making, the goals of growth, equality, development and peace cannot be achieved. Incorporation would ensure women's equal access to and full participation in power structures and decision-making. It would also increase women's capacity to participate in decision-making and leadership. However, twelve years later many of the injunctions in the Beijing Platform for Action still remain agendas for the future and there are even some issues that some governments, have refused outright to take into account saying that they go against their cultures. For example, the proposed new constitution was rejected although it had good laws that would have protected the rights of women and society in general.

According to the United Nations Division for the Advancement of Women (UNDAW 1996) the percentage of women in both ministerial and sub-ministerial levels ranges from zero percent (in about 15 countries), to 30 percent in 2 countries. Only 3.5 percent of the world's cabinet ministers are women, and women hold no ministerial positions in 93 countries of the world. Before the NARC government came to power, most women in high government positions were in such ministries as education, culture, social welfare, women affairs and so on. Women in Kenya rarely achieve elective office, and are severely under-represented at top positions in political parties. Table 10 shows the distribution of national assembly members by gender from 1969 to 2002.

Table 10: Distribution of National Assembly Members by Gender 1969- 2002

Year	Elected Members			Nominated Members			National Assembly		
	Men	Women	% Women	Men	Women	% Women	Men	Women	% Women
1969	154	1	0.7	11	1	8.3	165	2	1.2
1974	152	5	3.2	10	2	16.7	162	7	4.1
1979	155	3	1.9	11	1	8.3	166	4	2.4
1983	157	1	0.6	10	2	16.7	167	3	1.8
1988	186	2	1.1	11	1	8.3	197	3	1.5
1992	182	6	3.2	11	1	8.3	193	7	3.5
1997	206	4	1.9	7	5	41.7	213	9	4.1
2002	201	9	4.3	4	8	66.7	205	17	7.7

Source: Republic of Kenya: Economic Survey [2004]

Out of a total of 200 seats in parliament women occupied only 7 seats after the 1992 first multi-party elections. These increased to 17 in the 2002 elections out of 222 seats. In Kenya women are under represented in the judiciary, in local authorities (Table 11) and even in government administration.

Table 11: Percentage of Women in Local Authorities Membership in Kenya: 1992

Local Authority	*Percentage of Women representatives*
City Councils	7.3
Municipal Councils	4.2
Urban Councils	1.2
Town Councils	2.2
County Councils	2.3
Total	2.7

Source: United Nations [1995]

The above statistics show that despite the fact that many governments have adopted and adapted affirmative action measures and the rhetoric of gender equality, the figures still indicate that globally, despite the fact that women are half of the population, they constitute nowhere near half of the personnel in decision-making structures. The threshold of 30 percent advocated by the UNDP Human Development Report (1995), as a prelude to the 50 percent is still a dream for most women.

Female lecturers in public universities and institutions of higher learning represent only a very small percent of the total teaching staff as shown in Table 12 for the University of Nairobi. Gender stereotypes, attitudes, perceptions, customs and norms make it difficult to achieve gender equality in these institutions. For example, some male students doing art subjects usually threaten their girlfriends who may be doing engineering courses with ending relationships if they do not drop out of the engineering courses (a sample of engineering students interviewed by the author attested to this). Some girls even try not to be competitive with men especially if the males are their boyfriends.

The department of engineering at the University of Nairobi does not even have women's toilets because at inception, it was designed as a men's only department. The secretaries have to go to other departments to use the bathrooms. It has 92 percent male students and only 8% female. The department of economics also has skewed representation in the teaching fraternity. For so many years, there were no female lecturers until the early 1990s. Now it has 7 female lecturers and 28 male lecturers. A gender analysis of the staff and student population at the University of Nairobi is shown in Table 12.

Table 12: Gender Analysis of the Staff and Student Population (2005)

Category	*Female (Number)*	*Proportion (%)*	*Total*
Management Staff*	29	25.0	116
Academic Staff*	275	20.3	1,355
Other Staff			
A-F	668	45.8	1,458
I-IV	377	28.1	1341
Undergraduate Students			
Module 1	4,621	34.6	13,357
Module 2	2,157	36.6	5,890
Postgraduate Students			
Module 1	535	31.4	1,704
Module 2	**1,805**	**42.4**	**4,258**

*Note that the categories management staff and academic staff are overlapping because senior management staff is selected from among academic staff.

Table 12 shows significant gender disparities at the University of Nairobi. Among the management staff there are 87 male (75 percent) and 29 female (25 percent). Among the academic staff, there are 1,355 members of staff consisting of 275 female (20.3 percent) and 1080 male members. The proportion of female academics is largest at the lecturer level and decreases at each higher step. For example, in the College of Humanities and Social Sciences, female lecturers and senior lecturers constitute only 24.8 and 26.2 percent of their respective groups, but female professors are only 11.5 percent of their total.

Grade I-IV includes cleaners, messengers, clerks, machine operators, kitchen staff, security guards and so on. Current staffing is 28.1 percent female overall, but a closer examination reveals that many jobs at this level appear to be allocated based on prevailing gender stereotypes of appropriate work for men and women. For example, the security and transport section workers include only 1.8 percent and 4.3 percent women respectively.

Grades A-F includes technicians, secretaries, and librarians and so on. Staffing in these areas is nearly balanced overall, with women comprising 45.8 percent of the workers. There are however some notable disparities as, for example, in several departments, technicians of grades A-F workers are all male.

A gender analysis of student's enrolment also shows that most students are enrolled in the art based faculties and colleges such as humanities and social sciences as shown in Table 13.

Table 13: Total Female Undergraduate Enrolment by Module and Colleges (2004-2005)

College	*Module 1*			*Module 2*			*Total*		
	Total	*No. of Females*	*%*	*Total*	*No. of Females*	*%*	*Total*	*No. of Females*	*%*
CAE	1823	277	15.2	195	24	12.3	2018	301	14.9
CAVS	1177	285	24.2	69	21	30.4	1246	306	24.6
CBPS	1945	611	26.3	269	56	20.8	2214	567	25.6
CEES	1598	651	40.7	3408	1210	35.5	5006	1861	37.2
CHS	1109	393	35.4	380	154	28.8	1489	547	36.7
CHSS	5705	2504	43.8	1569	692	44.1	7274	3196	43.9
Total	13,357	4,621	34.6	5890	2157	36.6	19247	6778	35.2

CAE : College of Architecture and Engineering
CAVS: College of Agriculture and Veterinary Services
CBPS : College of Biological and Physical Sciences
CEES : College of Education and External Studies
CHS : College of Health Sciences
CHSS: College of Humanities and Social Sciences

Table 13 shows that among the undergraduate students, there were 12,469 male (64.8 percent) and 6,778 female (35.2 percent). Module 1 is 34.6 percent female, while module 2 is only slightly higher at 36.6 percent female. It worth noting that in module 1, the government gives loans to needy students and parents pay the rest. It shows that when money is scarce, parents are more willing to educate male children than female children. In module 2, these are mainly older students who pay for themselves and it can be seen that the proportion of female students is slightly higher.

Table 13 also shows that most of the female students enrol in the education and arts. This is mainly due to socialisation and the curriculum that mainly depicts females as teachers and social workers and nurses. Most female students imagine that courses like mechanical engineering involves wearing greasy overalls and electrical engineering involving climbing electrical posts which to them is not feminine. Mechanical engineering has the smallest female enrolment at 8% while Nursing has the highest at 49 percent. Apart from that it can also be seen that in the academic year 2004-2005, female students were only 34.6 percent of the total student population.

Among the postgraduate students, there are 3,622 male (60.8 percent) and 2,340 female (39.2 percent). Module 1 is 31.4 percent female, while module 2 is 42.4 percent female.

Women and girls also face gender violence in terms of sexual abuse, battering, assault and so on. Table 14 shows the reported cases of rape, attempted rape, assault and battering from 2000 to 2005.

Table 14: Reported Cases of Rape, Attempted Rape, Assault and Battering on Women between 2000 and 2005

Offence	*Year*					
	2000	*2001*	*2002*	*2003*	*2004*	*2005*
Rape and attempted Rape	883	933	984	1126	1419	1451
Defilement/ Incest	752	1094	1021	1182	1489	1416
Assaults and Battering	6255	6648	7896	8544	8950	9169
Total	7890	8635	9901	10852	11867	12036

Source: Republic of Kenya: Economic Survey [2006]

This is a serious problem, which creates insecurity among women and girls, traumatises them and acts as an obstacle from realising their potential in productive activities.

Gender Inequality and Economic Growth

Economic growth is the increase in value of the goods and services produced by an economy. It is conventionally measured as the percent rate of increase in real gross domestic product or GDP. The real GDP per capita of an economy is often used as an indicator of the average standard of living of individuals in that country, and economic growth is therefore often seen as indicating an increase in the average standard of living. Economic growth is determined by various factors among them land, capital, labour, technology, human capital, institutions, culture, geographical location and so on. For economic growth or national output to increase, resources need to be allocated equally among the various players especially among men and women. However, gender inequality in Kenya is evident in various forms as discussed above and may act as a constraint to growth.

Use of gender for the assignment of adult roles and responsibilities in the society is often seen as wasting the potential of half the population. Of key concern are inequalities in the division of responsibilities, and access to and control over resources. Gender relations within the household are an important mediator of women's life outcomes, as are gender relations within other institutions such as the community, market, and the state.

Gender inequality starts right at the household level and right up to the high echelons of society and this produces inequalities in outcomes between men and women. This is mainly influenced by institutions and culture and assigns roles and responsibilities according to gender. In 2006, Mr. David Nalo, the permanent secretary in the Ministry of Trade and Industry was quoted as saying that 'gender inequality is a serious economic issue in Kenya. Addressing this will lead to improved outcomes not only for women themselves but also for families and society as a whole (IFC, Foreign Investment Advisory Services and World Bank 2006).

Gender equality is good for economic growth. Where gender inequalities constitute barriers to women entering or participating fully in markets, economic growth and private sector development will be constrained with less investment, less competition and lower productivity (Blackden and Bhanu 1999). Gender inequalities can also adversely affect the outcome of trade and macroeconomic policy reforms and their ability to translate incentives into economic development.

The empirical literature clearly shows that human capital stock is an important determinant of the growth prospects of an economy (Klasen 2002, Knowles *et al.* 2002). In an economy where there is inequality in girls' education, the average level of human capital is likely to be low, resulting in lower returns to investment and economic growth. Empirical calculations and simulations (using coefficient on human capital from Mankiew *et al.* (1992) suggest that this gender inequality in girls' education could depress the *per capita* growth rate by 0.3 percentage points per year in a country characterized by levels of gender inequality similar to those observed in Kenya.

Total labour force in Kenya has been increasing from 7 million in 1980 to 14 million in 2004. However, the proportion of women in this labour force has declined from 46 percent in 1980 to 44 percent in 2004 (ww.genderstats.worldbank.org). Klassen (1999) showed that the female share of the working age population in the formal sector has a statistically significant and positive correlation with economic growth. Such biases imply that norms and prejudices rather than efficiency determine labour supply and demand in the economy. The resulting of misallocation of labour means that competent females worker may be overlooked because of their gender.

To work out the relationship between economic growth and gender inequality, one needs to examine the impact of economic growth on patterns of employment and wage rates across gender lines. The way in which economic growth affects these patterns depends on the character of growth itself and relative share of the fruits of such growth in industry, agriculture, formal and informal sector and services. Women, tend to be concentrated in the agricultural

Table 15: Formal Sector Wage Employment by Industry and Sex: 2004-2006

Industry	*2004*					*2005*					*2006*				
	Males		*Females*		*Total*	*Males*		*Females*		*Total*	*Males*		*Females*		*Total*
	1000s	*% of total*	*1000s*	*% of total*	*1000s*	*1000s*	*% of total*	*1000s*	*% of total*	*1000s*	*1000s*	*% of total*	*1000s*	*% of total*	*1000s*
Agriculture & forestry	241.0	75	79.6	25	320.6	246.1	75.1	81.3	24.9	327.4	248.8	74.4	85.8	25.6	334.6
Mining and quarrying	4.3	78	1.2	22	5.5	4.5	78.9	1.2	21.1	5.7	4.7	78.3	1..3	21.7	6.0
Manufacture	199.8	83	42.2	17	242.0	204.3	82.5	43.2	17.5	247.5	208.1	82	45.7	18	253.8
Electricity and water	17 1	82	3.8	18	20.9	16.7	82.3	3.6	17.7	20.3	15.9	81.5	3.6	18.5	19.5
Building and construction	72 4	94	4.9	6	77.3	73.2	93.6	5.0	6.4	78.2	74.6	93.4	5..3	6.6	79.9
Trade, restaurants and hotels	123.0	73	45.0	27	168.0	128.6	73.2	47.1	26.8	175.7	134.5	72.4	51.4	27.6	185.9
Transport & Communication	78.4	80	19.9	20	98.3	91.6	79.7	23.3	20.3	114.9	105.1	79.1	27.8	20.9	132.9
Finance, Insurance, real estate and business Services	63.3	74	22.1	26	85.2	64.7	74.1	22.6	25.9	87.3	66.2	73.2	24.2	26.8	90.4
Community, Social and Personal services *such as*	443.3	59	302.6	41	745.9	431.1	59.3	319.7	40.7	749.8	438.3	58.0	317.1	42	755.4
Public administration	95.7	63	56.5	37	152.2	87.1	62.8	56.2	37.2	143.4	84.6	61.6	52.7	38.4	137.3
Educational Services	188.1	57	143.3	43	331.4	185.7	56.7	152.7	43.3	338.4	188.7	55.3	152.4	44.7	341.1
Domestic services	59.8	60	39.6	40	99.4	58.5	60.2	42.0	39.8	100.5	60.9	59.0	42.4	41	103.3
Other services	99.7	61	63.2	39	162.9	99.8	61.2	68.8	38.8	168.6	104.1	59.9	69.6	40.1	173.7
Total of which	1242.4	70	521.3	30	1763.7	1260.8	70.6	547.0	29.4	1807.8	1296.2	69.7	562.2	30.3	1858.4
Regular	995.8	72	394.7	28	1390.5	995.8	71.6	394.7	28.4	1390.5	1033.5	69.2	405.7	28.2	1439.2
Casual	246.6	66	126.6	34	373.2	265.0	66.6	152.3	33.4	417.3	262.7	62.7	156.5	37.3	419.2

Source: Republic of Kenya: Economic Survey [2005-2007]

sector and informal sectors where the rate of growth and the potential for growth are relatively low. In the industrial and service sector, where the rates are much higher, the majority of women are concentrated in the unskilled or semi-skilled categories, and hence have limited access to the opportunities and benefits of economic growth.

In Kenya, women are major players in the economy particularly in agriculture and the informal sector while men tend to dominate the formal sector. Republic of Kenya (2005 and 2006) reports that most women, (58 percent, as shown in Table 15) employed in the formal sector are employed in service industries such as education and that they mainly occupy the lower paid jobs.

As Table 15 shows, the number of female employees in formal sector employment rose from 521.2 thousand in 2004 to 532.3 thousand in 2005 representing only 29.4 per cent in wage employment compared to 70.6 percent males. The Table also shows that education services, followed by agriculture and forestry remained the major female employer. Majority of the females employed in the formal sector (40.7 percent) were working in the community, social and personal services in 2005.

The Kenyan economy is mainly reliant on agriculture as its mainstay. Arable land in Kenya is in short supply. Only 20 percent of the country's land is arable with the remainder of it being classified as arid and semi arid. 75 percent of Kenya's population live on this 20 percent. Agriculture continues to be the major sector in Kenya's economy although its contribution to GDP has declined from 35 percent in 1963 to 27 percent in 2001, 25.6 percent in 2002, 25.3 percent in 2003, 24.3 percent in 2004 and 24.2 percent in 2005. However, it employs about 62 percent of the overall employment, is a major foreign exchange earner contributing over 50 percent of total export revenues and provides nearly all the food requirements for the nations (Republic of Kenya Various Issues).

Women represent the majority of the labour force in Agriculture in Kenya, while men represent the majority in manufacturing and services sectors. Women are a major force in the agricultural sector constituting over 70 percent of all agricultural workers but in most cases, they operate as unpaid workers. They provide over 80 percent of the labour in subsistence production and 50 percent in cash crop production (Republic of Kenya 2000). Men and women have distinct roles within the agricultural sector. Women concentrate on the production of food crops, mainly for family consumption, while simultaneously providing much of the labour for cash crop production. In livestock production, women concentrate on poultry and small ruminants such as goats, sheep, and rabbits while men concentrate on large livestock such as horses, cattle, donkeys and camels. In non-farm production, men predominate. The above analysis implies that women are less predominant in formal sector employment and tend to have lower wages than men. Although most women dominate the agricultural sector they lack security of tenure. Women supply over 70 percent of labour in the agricultural sector yet they only hold 1 percent of registered land titles in Kenya, with around 5 to 6 percent of registered titles in joint names. Insecure land rights limit women from making the necessary investments into their land to increase its productivity and economic value. Studies in different parts of developing countries have found that secure title to land is positively correlated with agricultural investments and outputs (Republic of Kenya 2005). A study in Thailand found that gaining title to land induced higher investment in faming capital and as a result, output was 14 to 15 percent higher on titled land than on untitled land of equal quality (Besley 1995, Feder 1988, Jacoby *et al.* 2002). 'Lack of title to land' means that women cannot use the land as security for loan for buying farm inputs, access cooperative membership and so on which lower their productivity. Saito *et al.* (1994) found that the gross value of output per hectare from male managed plots was 8 percent higher than on female managed plots. On the other hand Moock (1976) found that if female farm managers had the same access as men to extension services and productive inputs, then their yields would be between 7 and 9 percent higher. There is also evidence that the average production per farmer tends to be lower in countries in which women represent a larger share of the agricultural labour force than men. In Kenya, women are particularly disadvantaged because they often have smaller plots of land and with uncertain tenure. This therefore means that reducing gender inequalities in access to inputs will therefore increase productivity. Quisumbing (1996) contends that in Kenya, increasing access to agricultural inputs to the same levels as male farmers could increase yields by as much as 22 percent. Given the importance of agriculture in Kenya's GDP, this would translate to a one off doubling in Kenya's growth rate from 4.8 percent to 8.92 percent (In 2004, Kenya's real production of crops and horticulture was Ksh.19554 0million in 2001 prices. Real GDP was Ksh.1107715million in the same year, up from Ksh.1056454m in 2003, a growth of 4.8 percent. A 22 percent increase in yields in 2004 would have implied crop and horticultural production of Ksh.238558.8m increasing real GDGP in the same year to Ksh.1150733.8 an increase of 8.92 percent).

Under most customary law systems in Kenya, a woman's property rights are often through a man hence a married woman may use matrimonial property but she cannot dispose of it without her husband's consent meaning that married women in Kenya lack control over property and most communities in Kenya are governed by customary law.

Customary law also makes it impossible for women to inherit their parents or their husband's property and since family land is usually registered in the husband's name, this puts the wife in a difficult situation in case of death of husband (Kiriti-Nganga 2006). It also means that in certain situations the husband can dispose of the land without the wife's consent. These disparities between men and women's status, access to resources, control of assets and decision-making powers persist and these undermine sustainable growth and development (World Bank 1995). If Kenya's mainstay is agriculture and yet resources are unequally allocated to the majority of the very people who are involved in production, then output may not grow as expected hence leading to slow or even negative economic growth. Although the Kenya Government's Agricultural Productivity Project is aimed at increasing agricultural production and to improve farming methods men control most of the resources and proceeds from the sector.

Kiriti-Nganga (2003) found that commercialisation has increased gender inequality in Kenya since men control the cash from cash crops although it is women who provide the labour in cash crop production. The author also found that female-headed households have less acreage, have less capital equipment than male-headed households a finding that concurred with World Bank (2001). United States Agency for International Development (United Nations Programs for AIDS 2002) also found that women lack appropriate technology for processing and storage, which acts as a major constraint in increasing productivity in the agricultural sector. Thus, while women in Kenya have the potential to become more efficient, they lack the complementary inputs that would increase their productivity.

In the agricultural sector, training and extension services, and the use of female field extension workers are important factors in training female farm productivity. However, only 7 percent of agricultural extension services are directed towards female farmers and only about 11 percent of all extension workers are female (FAO 1989). Kiriti-Nganga (2003) also found that most extension officers in Kenya target male farmers who usually do not pass the information to female farmers. Field trips to model farms are usually by male farmers or male village elders who leave the females at home to look after children. This information and learning is not transmitted to the female farmers and especially those who head their own households. FAO (1998) found that women in Kenya receive only 1 percent of the total amount of credit directed to agriculture.

Kenya has considerable resources that could allow it to grow at a significantly greater rate than it has over the last decade but these are unequally allocated among the actors in the economy. The World Bank (2003) suggests that the Kenya's long run growth of 2 percent per capita; translating to 4.5 percent is low. This is due to various factors among them the high burden of disease especially HIV/AIDS, high fertility rate, gender violence, gender inequality in access in education and other forms of inequality. HIV is estimated to result in a 1.3% reduction in annual economic growth (United Nations Programs for AIDS 2002).

The prevalence of HIV/AIDS in Kenya is higher for women than for men as shown in Table 16.

Table 16: People Living with HIV/AIDS in Kenya

Year	*Total Adults and Children*	*Adults (millions)*	*Adult rate (%)*	*Women 15-49yrs*	*Men 15-49 yrs*	*Children <15 yrs*	*Orphaned due to AIDS <15 yrs*
End 1999	2.1m	2.0	10	1.1m	0.9m	0.078m	NA
End 2001	2.5m	2.3	NA	1.4m	0.9m	0.22m	0.890m
End 2003	1.2m	1.1	7	0.720m	0.380m	0.100m	0.650m
End 2005	1.3m	1.2	9	0.740m	0.460m	0.150m	1.1m

Source: United Nations Programs for AIDS [2005].

In Kenya 1.4 million women in the age bracket 15-49 years were HIV-positive compared to 0.9 million men in the same category by the end of 2001.Women and girls are more vulnerable to HIV because of their limited access to economic and educational opportunities, and the multiple household and community roles they are responsible for. Also women and girls are subject to social norms that deny them sexual health knowledge and practices that prevent them from controlling their bodies. The gender division of labour and male urban migration keeps men away from their wives for long periods leading to promiscuity and the spread of HIV.

Women in the rural areas may also find themselves discriminated against when trying to access care and support when they are HIV-positive. United Nations Programs for AIDS (2002) reports that in Kenya, women who are HIV-infected are divorced even when it is their husbands who have infected them. Family resources are more likely to be devoted to buying medication and arranging care for ill males than females. Because of lack of hospital facilities in rural areas and lack of income, those in rural areas affected by AIDS may find it difficult if not impossible, to obtain hospital care. Therefore, they mostly have to be cared for at home. Generally this is the burden of females (Kiriti-Nganga and Tisdell 2005). USAID (2002) says that the increasing number of widows and orphans resulting from the high number of HIV/AIDS cases has significantly increased women's workload and their financial responsibilities. Conventional economic indicators hide this transfer of cost or financial responsibilities in terms of women's time and efforts. It is women who bear the real costs of the spread of HIV/AIDS as they take on the increasing burden of care, first for the sick and dying and then for the orphaned children. As soon as the care economy grows, it remains invisible and unrecorded, supported by billions of additional hours of wage less labour that appear nowhere in indices of GDP and figure nowhere in calculations of the need for international aid or debt relief.

As the country loses young productive people to AIDS, the effects have an influence on all sectors of the economy. The loss of income of the breadwinner, increased medical expenses and increased time taking care of the sick persons may lead to reduced agricultural output. Households fall into deeper poverty and women are left bearing even larger burdens as workers, educators, mothers, and ultimately as caregivers, as the burden of caring for the ill family members rests mostly with women and girls. Of HIV-positive pregnant women in Kenya, 30 percent give birth to HIV-positive babies who are likely to die before 5 years of age increasing the child mortality rate. HIV/AIDS has led to a decrease in life expectancy in Kenya as shown in Table 17.

Table 17: Life Expectancy in Kenya in Years: 1970-2004

Year	*Life expectancy at birth*	*Female*	*Male*	*Female less male*
1970	50.5	52	48	6
1980	54.9	57	53	4
1990	58.3	59	55	4
1995	53.8	53	52	1
1997	52	53.0	51.1	1.9
1998	51.3	52.2	50.5	1.7
1999	50.8	48	47	1
2000	47	47	47	0
2001	47	47	46	1
2002	45.5	46.4	44	-2.4
2003	47.2	46.1	48.1	-2
2004	47.5	46.5	48.5	-2

Source: UNDP: Human Development Report [Various Issues]

Table 17 shows that life expectancy in Kenya has been on the decline from a high of 58 years in 1990, reaching a bottom in 2002 with a life expectancy of 45.5 years. This decline was brought about by the HIV/AIDS epidemic, which started around 1994. This decline in life expectancy is worse for women than men as shown in the Table 17. Normally females are expected to live longer than males and this is evident from the Table. However the gap between the life expectancy has been narrowing from a high of 6 in 1970 to -2.4 years in 2002 and seems to have stabilized at -2 since 2003. The Table implies that female infants are dying at a higher rate than male infants though the data for infant and child mortality is not disaggregated in terms of gender. The Table also means that women are dying earlier than men mainly due to HIV/AIDS, which has affected more women than men. Considering that women are the caregivers, agricultural producers, factory workers, service providers, this decrease in life expectancy has also affected the level and rate of economic growth.

Sala-I-Martin and Barro (1995) found a strong and positive relationship between life expectancy and economic growth; a 13-year increase in life expectancy is estimated to raise the annual growth by 1.4 percentage points. Croix and Licandro (1999) argue that there are several channels through which life expectancy affects economic growth directly, for instance, when the probability of dying young is high, the shortened time horizon makes it optimal for people to start working early in their life and not to stay at school for too long. Moreover, when life expectancy is short, the depreciation rate of human capital is high, making its accumulation more difficult. Since the human capital accumulated in school is an important engine of growth, we should thus expect a country's growth rate to depend upon life expectancy.

Development economics literature shows that an increase in economic growth is associated with a higher life expectancy due to better nutrition, reduced infant mortality rates and improved medical care. Life expectancy for both men and women in the world's richest countries is about 80 years, which is almost twice that in the world's poorest countries of 45 years (UNDP 1998). The problem here however, is of deciding what the causal is and what the dependent factor is; a kind of mutual causation problem or 'chicken and egg problem' exists.

When Kenya attained independence in 1963, life expectancy was only 44.7 years. It rose to 50.5 years in 1970, increasing life expectancy coinciding with a growth in GDP of 6.5 percent between 1963 and 1974, and subsequently to 58.3 years in 1990. However, this fell to 45.5 years in 2002. Kenya started implementing structural adjustments programs in 1994. These reduced government expenditure in such sectors as health, education, transport, social services and so on. This meant shifting the cost of consultation and drugs to households. Considering their already low per capita incomes, most sick people avoid medical facilities thereby raising morbidity rates and the mortality rate. This contributed to the decline in the life expectancy for both males and females to less than 50 years. The female life expectancy in 1980 was 57 years compared to 53 years for males. In 2000, it was 47 years for both females and males.

Apart from HIV/AIDS, another reason for declining life expectancy is that Kenya had been relying on donor aid to fund various programs in its health sector. For along time Kenya was cut off as a donor aid recipient due to its non compliance with conditions given by the World Bank, IMF and other bilateral aid agencies. This resulted in some doctors moving to Southern Africa and to other more developed countries worsening the situation in Kenya (Kiriti-Nganga 2003).

As mentioned earlier, life expectancy for both men and women in the world's richest countries is almost twice that in the worlds poorest. Much of this differential is due to very high infant mortality rates in low-income countries, which is in turn due to the gap in living standards, particularly nutritional status and medical care. In most of the world, women have a longer life expectancy than men, but differentials are narrower in developing than in developed countries, and in some cases reversed from the norm. In the developed countries, women's life expectancy is on average six to seven years longer than men's. But in most developing countries the gap narrows to three years or less (UNDP 1995). For example, in Kenya the differential was only four years in 1980 and it fell to -2.4 years in 2002. On the whole, the trend in the differential has been downward since 1970 reflecting retrogression in socio-economic conditions in Kenya. The life expectancy gap reflects patterns of discrimination, which give preference to male over female infants and children early in life in nutrition, in medical care, in the mother's scarce time, and so on; discrimination that often continues into adulthood (Kiriti-Nganga and Tisdell 2005).

Child and infant mortality rates may also exhibit signs of inequality in nutrition, medical care and so on. With a high infant and child mortality rate, mothers are inclined to increase the number of children born in their lifetime with the hope that some will survive. Table 18 shows the fertility, infant and child mortality rates in Kenya from 1970 to 2004. The Table shows that the child and infant mortality rates for Kenya have been rising since the country started implementing structural adjustment programmes in 1994. In addition, it is found that the child mortality rates for female children rose by 15.2 percent between 1997 and 2000 compared to 9.1 percent for male children. Consequently, in 2000 female mortality rate of children under 5 years exceeded that of males. However, disaggregated data by gender for the other years was not available.

Table 18: Child Mortality Rates per 1000 Live Births for Kenya: 1970-2004

Year	*Total Fertility Rate*	*Infants 0-1 years*	*Children under 5 years*	*Mortality rate (children under 5 years)*	
				Male	*Female*
1970	8	102	156	-	-
1980	7.4	73	115	-	-
1990	5.8	64	97	-	-
1991	-	62	96	-	-
1995	-	73	111	-	-
1997	-	74	112	33	33
1998	-	76	124	-	-
1999	5	76	118	-	-
2000	5	77	120	-	38
2002	-	78	122.0	-	-
2004	5	79	120	-	-

Source: World Bank [2005a] and Population Reference Bureau [2006]

A high population growth rate and increased fertility rates may translate to low per capita food availability not only at the national level but also at the household level, as average family sizes of 5 are also quite large. Gender inequality in the provision of education, preference for male children and use of child labour may be some of the factors that have contributed to the large family sizes and hence rising population in the rural areas. Increased family sizes and declining agricultural output may contribute to low standards of living not only now but also in the future (Kiriti-Nganga and Tisdell 2005).

Differences in fertility levels between regions are strongly related to differences in levels of income and women's education. Little education, less economic opportunities and lack of control of resources has an immediate effect on children's nutritional status, health and development of the mother and on the size of the family (Kiriti-Nganga 2003).

The decrease in adult life expectancy, increase in child mortality rates, the narrowing of the difference between female and male life expectancy and the increase in the child mortality rates for female children presents a worrying trend for Kenya. For Kenya to succeed in Vision 2030, gender inequality needs to be addressed.

As mentioned above, gender inequality in the provision of education contributes to high fertility rates and constrains productivity and output. Klassen (1999) asserts that gender inequalities have a significant and adverse impact on economic growth rates. The author uses education spending as a share of GDP, initial fertility levels and changes in these instruments for levels of and changes in the female to male ratio of years of education. For Kenya, Klassen shows that because women during the 1960-1992 period did not complete as many years of schooling on average as men, this accounts for almost a percentage difference between the long-run growth potential of Kenya when compared to high performing Asian economies (Klassen 2002). Shultz (1991) also shows that private rates of return to additional schooling for women are at least as large as that for men and often higher. This implies potentially higher marginal returns of increased investment in female education in Kenya. Dollar and Gatti (1999) found that an increase in one percentage point for the share of adult women with secondary schooling increases per capita income growth, on average by 0.3 percentage points. This means that for Kenya this would imply a year-on-year increase in GDP growth of 3.5 percent if female secondary education enrolment was brought up to the level of male secondary enrolment.

The IFC, Foreign Investment Advisory Service and World Bank (2006) conclude that gender inequality is a powerful constraint to economic growth. They contend that if Kenya eliminated gender based inequalities in education and access to inputs, the country could gain from a one off increase in GDP growth by as much as 4.3 percent followed by a sustained increase in GDP growth of 2.0 and 3.5 percent. Removing gender-based barriers to growth will thus make Kenya realise its growth potential and achieve its vision 2030.

Conclusion

My analysis has shown that gender inequality exists in Kenya and I have also shown that micro and macro studies confirm that gender inequality acts as powerful constraint to productivity and economic growth. This gender inequality directly and indirectly limits economic growth in Kenya, and diminishes the effectiveness of poverty reduction efforts.

This implies that removing gender inequality in whatever form would go a long way in helping Kenya realise its growth potential and achieve its goals for the Kenya Vision 2030.

Women are not well represented in decision-making institutions. This means that pro-active measures are needed to ensure inclusive participation and the formulation of inclusive policies and programs.

Since women and men differ in their access to and control over, productive assets, economic capacities and incentives are strongly gender-differentiated in ways, which affect supply response, resource allocation within the household, labour productivity, and general welfare. These differences have implications for the flexibility, responsiveness, and dynamism of the economy, and directly limit economic growth.

I have shown that since most women do not have titles for the land they use, they cannot use it for access to loans and most have been relying on microfinance which Kiriti-Nganga (2007) found ends up impoverishing the poorest of the women borrowers. Therefore microfinance institutions should provide complementary services such as business training and market advice and not merely provide loans. The risks associated with microfinance need more recognition as especially since they affect the assets of these poor women.

If men and women make approximately equal contributions to total measured economic production, the same cannot be said of their contributions to the household economy. I have shown how time allocation data reveal an unequal burden on women's labour time in the non-marketed or household economy, while they still have to contribute time to the marketed economy and especially in this era of globalisation. Moreover, these tasks are not captured in the systems of national accounts. Increases in women's productivity may therefore not be recorded at all or even acknowledged at all. It is therefore important that whenever new policies are proposed or implemented there should always be a gender perspective of the policies' impact. Policy makers should be trained to look at economic issues from a gender perspective and engendering economic analysis. Attention must be given to urgent issues of how to integrate a gender perspective into the national budget, into taxation and investment, into financial and credit markets, into export policies and employment generation, into agricultural and land policies.

Compared with men, women operate under severe time constraints, which limit their options and their flexibility to respond to changing economic opportunities. Time constraints induce allocative inefficiency. These inefficiencies may be a key source of female poverty, as well as a contributor to the overall poverty of the household. Moreover, the non-substitutability of male and female labour time in specific activities, especially in household tasks, reduces the ability of women to reallocate their time in accordance with changes in market and non-market opportunities. The government must also remove policy biases that undervalue women's work while promoting growth in dynamic economic sectors in which women are concentrated. Although we may pride ourselves that jobs have been created in the informal sector, we should also be thinking of the decency and dignity of the work place.

Property rights for women especially title to land must be given priority if we have to increase agricultural productivity. Extension services and training must be directed to women farmers and affirmative action taken during field trips to model farms so that women farmers also benefit.

Empowerment for women especially through education, training and appointment of women to positions of decision-making would go along way in eradicating gender inequality in Kenya. This can be done through affirmative action, for example reserving a certain percentage of seats in national schools for girls, providing bursaries and scholarships to girls especially from the marginalised areas, making it illegal for girls to marry below the age of 21years, educating society on the benefits of gender equality, and doing away with those aspects of customary law that propagate gender inequality. This would reduce gender stereotypes at all levels. School syllabus should also be gender neutral to avoid socialising girls from thinking that only certain careers are good for them.

Education inequality, life expectancy gap, HIV/AIDS, fertility rates, gender violence, assets inequality and so on all indicate that there is a strong connection between gender inequality and economic growth. It is therefore upon the Government of Kenya to come up with growth enhancing and poverty reducing policies that take account of these gender based influences and constraints to growth. These policies must strive to end these inequalities and to promote equity and justice, promote economic growth and also promote efficiency. Gender mainstreaming must be seen to be tackling these gender inequalities at all levels to promote efficiency and to help women realise their potential and to participate actively in economic development. Promoting gender equality is not a favour to women but for the whole nation.

Gender inequality in earnings should be eliminated and employment should be based on qualifications and not on gender. Sexual harassment, assault and battering of women should be outlawed and there should be concerted efforts by both the government and other stakeholders in educating women on their legal rights regarding seeking redress and succession.

Apart from legislating laws, enforcements of these laws should be enhanced and made easier. For example, it takes 360 days on average to enforce a contract in Kenya and it is generally very costly (World Bank 2005b) and most women cannot afford these.

Kenya should adopt a policy such that 30% of members of each and every committee are women for women's voices to be heard. So far the Gender Commission does not look as if it is doing much and for it to be noticed and have increased funding, it should be de-linked from the sports and culture. Gender should have a whole ministry by itself.

We should not just have gender desks (that is what they are, just desks) in ministries. These should be fully-fledged departments with secretariats, research departments and all that if we are serious about promoting women's ability and capacity in contributing to economic growth. There should be collaboration among government ministries and between government and Non-Governmental Organisations in addressing gender issues in Kenya. The Ministry of Planning and National Development and also the Ministry of finance should play a leading role in addressing gender issues and especially gender dimensions of economic growth. The role of women in contributing to private sector led growth should be fully acknowledged, encouraged, and acted upon. The ongoing land reform should ensure that it helps empower women in legally owning tilted land. These policy recommendations, if implemented, should go along way in having a real impact on policy development and implementation and eventual realisation of the Kenya Vision 2030.

References

Besley, T. (1995), Property Rights and Investment Incentives: Theory and Evidence from Ghana, *Journal of Political Economy*, 103(5): 903-937.

Blackden, C. M. and Bhanu, C. (1999), *Gender, Growth and Poverty Reduction: Special Program for Assistance for Africa, 1998: Status Report on Poverty in Sub-Saharan Africa*, World Bank Technical Paper No. 428, World Bank, Washington DC.

Collier, P. and Lal, D. (1980), *Poverty and Growth in Kenya*, World Bank Staff Working Paper, World Bank, Washington DC.

Croix, D. and Licandro, O. (1999), Life Expectancy and Endogenous Growth, *Economics Letters*, 65(2): 255-263.

Dollar, D. and Gatti, R. (1999), *Gender Inequality, Income and Growth: Are Good Times Good for Women?* World Bank Paper, World Bank, Washington DC.

Elson, D. and Evers, B. (1997), *Gender-aware Country Economic Reports,* Working Paper No. 2, Prepared for DAC/WID Task Force on Program Aid and other Forms of Economic Policy-Related Assistance, OECD, Paris.

FAO (1989), *Report on the Global Consultation on Agricultural Extension*, Food and Agriculture Organisation of the United Nations, Rome.

FAO (1998), *Rural Women and Food Security: Current Situations and Perspectives,* Food and Agriculture Organisation of the United Nations, Rome.

Feder, G. (1988), *Land Policies and Farm Productivity in Thailand*, The John Hopkins University Press, Baltimore and London.

Greer, J. and Thorbecke, E. (1986), A Methodology for Measuring Food Poverty Applied to Kenya, *Journal of Development Economics*, 24: 59-74.

IFC, Foreign Investment Advisory Services and World Bank (2006), *Kenya Gender and Economic Growth Assessment*, Washington DC.

Jacoby, H. G., Li, G. and Rozzelle, S. (2002), Hazards of Expropriation: Tenure Insecurity and Investments in Rural China, *American Economic Review*, 92(5): 1420-1447.

Kabubo, J. and Kiriti-Nganga, T. (2001), Macroeconomic Adjustment, Poverty and Economic Growth: An Analysis for Kenya, *African Journal of Economic Policy*, 8(1): 42-58.

Kiriti-Nganga, T. (2003), *Gender Inequality in Agricultural Households in Kenya: An Economic Analysis*, Unpublished PhD Thesis, University of Queensland.

Kiriti-Nganga, T. and Tisdell, C. (2005), Family Size, Economics and Child Gender Preference: A Case Study of Nyeri District of Kenya, *International Journal of Social Economics*, 32(6): 492-509.

Kiriti-Nganga, T., Tisdell, C. and Roy, K. (2003), Female Participation in Decision-making in Agricultural Households in Kenya: Empirical Findings, *International Journal of Agricultural Resources, Governance and Ecology*, 2(2): 103-124.

Kiriti-Nganga, T. (2006), Economic Growth and Poverty in Kenya: Will the Poverty Reduction Strategy Paper Help? *Indian Development Review*, 4(2): 323-338.

Kiriti-Nganga, T. (2007), Micro-finance and Poverty Alleviation: How Effective is it in Alleviating Gender Based Poverty? In: Clem Tisdell (ed.), *Poverty, Poverty Alleviation and Social Disadvantage: Analysis, Case Studies and Policies*, Serials Publications, New Delhi.

Klassen, S. (1999), *Does Gender Inequality Reduce Growth and Development? Evidence Form Cross Country Regressions*, World Bank Paper, World Bank, Washington DC.

Klassen, S. (2002), Low Schooling for Girls, Slower Growth for All? Cross Country Evidence on the Effect of Gender Inequality in Education on Economic Development, *World Bank Economic Review*, 16(3): 345-373.

Knowles, S., Lorgelly, P. and Owen, P. (2002), Are Educational Gender Gaps a Break on Economic Development? Some Cross Country Empirical Evidence, *Oxford Economic Papers*, 54(1): 118-149.

Mankiew, N., Romer, D. and Weil, D. (1992), Contribution to Empirics of Economic Growth, *Quarterly Journal of Economics*, 107(2): 407-437.

Mincer, J. and Polachek, S. (1974), Family Investment in Human Capital: Earnings of Women, *Journal of Political Economy*, Part 2, 82(2): S76-S108.

Moock, P. (1976), The Efficiency of Women as Farm Managers: Kenya, *Journal of Agricultural Economics,* 58(5): 831-835.

Mwabu, G. *et al.* (2000), *Poverty in Kenya: Profiles and Determinants*, A Joint Research Project by the Department of Economics, University of Nairobi and the Ministry of Planning and National Development, African Economic Research Consortium, Nairobi.

Mwabu, G. *et al.* (2005), Predicting Rural Household Poverty: Methodological Issues and the PRSP Process in Kenya, In: Frank Ellis and H. Ade Freeman (eds.), *Rural Livelihoods and Poverty Reduction Policies,* Routledge, Tylor and Francis Group London and New York.

Population Reference Bureau (2006), *World Population Data Sheet*, Washington DC.

Quisumbing, A. (1996), Male-female Differences in Agricultural Productivity: Methodological Issues and Empirical Evidence, *World Development*, 24:1579-1595.

Quisumbing, A., Haddad, L. and Pena, C. (2001), Are Women Over Represented among the Poor? Analysis of Poverty in Ten Developing Countries, *Journal of Development Economics*, 66(1): 225-269.

Republic of Kenya (Various Issue), *Economic Survey*, Government Printer, Nairobi.

Saito, K., Mekonnen, H. and Spurling, D. (1994), *Raising the Productivity of Women Farmers in Sub-Saharan Africa*, World Bank Discussion Paper No. 230, World Bank, Washington DC.

Sala-i-Martin, X. and Barro, R. J. (1995), *Economic Growth*, McGraw Hill, New York.

Schultz, T. (1991), Research in Population Economics, JAI Press, Greenwich, Conn. and London.

Schultz, T. W. (1960), Human Capital Formation by Education, *Journal of Political Economy*, 68(6): 571-583.

Sen, A. (2001), Many Faces of Gender Inequality, *India's National Magazine*, 18(22): 35-40.

United Nations (1995), *Platform for Action and the Beijing Declaration,* United Nations Department of Public Information, New York.

United Nations Division for the Advancement of Women (1996), *Women and Decision-making: Percentage of Women in Government 1996*, United Nations Secretariat, Bethesda.

UNDP (Various Issue), *Human Development Report*, Oxford University Press, New York.

United Nations Economic Council (1998), *Assessing the Political Empowerment of Women*, Available at www.uneca.org/eca_programmes/acgd/publications

UNFPA (2005), *State of World Population 2005: The Promise of Equality, Gender Equity, Reproductive Health and MDGs,* UNESCO Data Sets, Available at www.unfpa.org/swp/2005/presskit/factsheets/facts_gender.htm

United Nations Programs on Aids (2002), *Conceptual Framework Basis for Action: HIV/AIDS Stigma and Discrimination,* UNAIDS, Geneva.

United Nations Programs on Aids (2005), *AIDS: from Crisis Management to Sustained Strategic Response*, UNAIDS, Geneva.

USAID (2002), *A Review of Gender Issues in the USAID/Kenya Integrated Strategic Plan (ISP) 2001-2005*, Women in Development Technical Assistance Project, USAID, Nairobi.

World Bank (1995), *Kenya Poverty Assessment*, Report No. 13152-KE, World Bank, Washington DC.

World Bank (1996), *The World Bank Annual Report*, World Bank, Washington DC.

World Bank (1997), *The World Development Report: The State in a Changing World*, World Bank, Washington DC.

World Bank (2001), *World Development Report 2000/2001: Attacking Poverty*, Oxford University Press, Oxford.

World Bank (2003), *Gender and Growth in Kenya: A Review of Evidence and Issues for the 2003 CEM*, World Bank, Washington DC.

World Bank (2005a), *World Development Indicators Database*, World Bank, Washington DC.

World Bank (2005b), *Doing Business in 2005*, World Bank, Washington DC.

2

Women Participation in Economy

Rena, R. *Eritrea Institute of Technology*
Narayana, N. *University of Botswana*

Introduction

Fruits of development should reach all sections of the society particularly to women. Social scientists believe that real development lies in the empowerment of women. Employment for women is an important issue in empowering women. It is believed that unemployment for women implies not only deterioration in their living standards but also an increase in their dependence on men and loss of autonomy as well as security (Sen 1989). Moreover, the fact is that earnings of women unlike men are spent entirely on welfare of the family members particularly on children. The levels of health and education of mothers are closely related to children's survival and quality of life (World Bank 1993).

In spite of women empowerment measures, women have less access to resources as men. In many societies women are not fully economically dependent. Women came to be regarded as primarily dependent on men, making it unnecessary to plan and provide for their needs. They have to work in the fields and home to produce food and other crops to support their men who are employed or engaged in different productive activities. Among the majority of rural and low-income urban dwellers, women perform all domestic tasks, while many also farm and trade. They are responsible for the care of children, the sick and the elderly, in addition to performing essential social functions within their communities.

The main objective of this paper is to understand the status of women in Africa and to analyze the level of participation of women workers in the national economy of Eritrea. The issue of women empowerment is viewed as important in the present set up as women, by and large, has lower levels of education and health. Education and employment are the two issues, which have been analyzed here in the context of women of Eritrea. The emergence of women as a work force in the traditional patriarchal society is a new dimension after the Independence of Eritrea (Government of Eretria 2003a).

Women Empowerment in Africa

African women's fundamental contributions in their households, food production systems and national economies are increasingly acknowledged, within Africa and by the international community (World Bank 2005). But women in Africa continue to face enormous obstacles. The growing recognition of their contributions has not translated into significantly improved access to resources or increased decision-making powers.

Women shared initially in the promises of independence and saw gains in their access to education, formal sector employment, health care and nutritional profiles. Their life expectancy at birth rose from 37 to 50 years by the end of the 1960s. But development plans in African countries continued to be formulated and implemented without an adequate understanding of women's contributions to African economies.

Women provide the backbone of the rural economy in much of sub-Saharan Africa. About 80 per cent of the economically active female labour force is employed in agriculture and women comprise about 47 per cent of the total agricultural labour force (UNDP 2005). Food production is the major activity of rural women and their responsibilities and labour inputs often exceed those of men in most areas in Africa. Women also provide much of the labour for men's cultivation of export crops, from which women derive little direct benefit. Women's contribution to the production of food crops ranges from 30 per cent in Sudan to 80 per cent in the Republic of Congo, with estimates for other countries tending toward the higher end of the scale. Women are responsible for 70 per cent of food production, 50 per cent of domestic food storage, 100 per cent of food processing, 50 per cent of animal husbandry and 60 per cent of agricultural marketing (FAO 2004). The fact remains that o develop a more productive, sustainable, and equitable agricultural sector in Africa, it cannot afford to neglect women and constraints that women face must be addressed if agriculture is to be the engine of economic growth.

Constraints to Women Empowerment

The following are some of the constraints for empowerment of women in Africa. They are mostly in terms of access to resources and labour market imperfections and limited jobs outside household activities.

Access to Land

The first of these constraints is access to land. Across Africa, agricultural intensification, population growth and economic change have led to substantive shifts from common property systems of tenure towards more centralized resource control. In the process, women and poorer people generally have lost out. Women rarely own land and even when they own, their holdings tend to be smaller and less fertile than those of men (FAO 2004).

Where land reform schemes have been introduced in many countries, they often have displaced complex systems of land use and tenure in which women had certain rights in common law and local practice, if not in legislation. New land titles usually have been registered in the name of a male household head regardless of women's economic contribution to the household and their customary rights or the increasing number of female-headed households.

Labour Bottleneck

Labour is also a bottleneck for female farmers in Africa, as men have left rural economies in search of more viable livelihoods and women have lost access to male help on farms or the money they may have previously provided. In countries like Lesotho, Botswana and Burkina Faso, the out-migration of adult males is very high, influencing the sexual division of labour for those left behind (World Bank 2005). The only means for most women to increase their yields is through hard work, using more labour-intensive methods to maintain soil regeneration and fertility. Where technical innovations such as irrigation techniques have made more than one cropping season possible, increased women's labour has been crucial in meeting the intensified work demands.

Women's Employment

Analysis of women's employment in Africa indicates that the ongoing economic crises and the gulf between job creation and the growth in the numbers of job seekers have worsened the employment situation for women. Women also face greater vulnerabilities in the labour market because of their relative lack of education and training. In addition, the tendency to channel women into certain occupations, continuous heavy burdens of unpaid domestic work and child-bearing and child-care which restrict women their time and energy available for income-earning activities.

Formal Sector

Women are two-thirds less likely than men to get waged employment, while only 3 out of 10 women in the labour force in sub-Saharan Africa are paid employees. In 2000, about 5 per cent of the female labour force worked in industry, 20 per cent in services, 23 per cent in sales, and only 6 per cent in professional, technical, administrative or managerial positions (UNDP 2004).

Employees in both the public and private sectors earn steady but low incomes. The self-employed are more insecure who often must make substantial investments in time and energy. Despite International Labour Organization (ILO) conventions, to which many African countries are signatories, there are significant income disparities, with women earning half or less of the incomes of men in some countries. Many women also do not benefit in practice from formal laws and policies guaranteeing maternity protection or equal pay for equal work.

Data from the ILO (2004) and other sources suggest that women's formal sector participation rates dropped from 57 per cent in 1970 to 33 per cent in 2000, with 3.5 million women losing their jobs between 1985 and 2000. In Benin, to cite just one example, women accounted for 26 per cent of retrenched workers, although they were only 6 per cent of formal sector workers. Women had predominated in the lower echelons of the social services sector, which faced the heaviest budget cuts. Many of such retrenched women have relocated to the informal sector.

Informal Sector

The non-agricultural informal sector employs about 25 per cent of the female labour force, mainly in petty trading and home-based processing and manufacturing, where they have little access to official sources of credit or information. Congestion and lack of water and sanitation create a hazardous environment for both the women and the children they must take with them to work (because no other childcare is available). These women workers also do not benefit from minimum wage and social security provisions and have to provide for their own health and retirement needs. Many are subject to harassment and exploitation from municipal authorities.

With the contraction of formal sector jobs, the informal sector has become a safe haven for both men and women because of its low capital requirements and ease of entry. For the majority of women, participation in the informal sector is a survival strategy as they take over aspects of household maintenance that men can no longer afford, although they tend to face stiff competition from new entrants, including men who have lost or cannot obtain formal sector employment. Many girls have been withdrawn from school to assist their mothers or guardians in informal sector activities.

The informal sector has shown some dynamism in creating new jobs. In Zimbabwe, for example, it is estimated that job creation in the informal sector may average 25,000 to 35,000 a year (ILO 2004). The sector also provides needed linkages among small-scale manufacturers, promotes labour-intensive production processes and integrates local and regional markets. Informal sector workers have built associations to protect their interests and mobilized traditional savings and credit schemes to offer sources of capital for women. In places like Nairobi, Kisangani and Accra, rich women traders have used their profits to build houses to rent out; a few have crossed over into the formal sector, in importing, manufacturing and commerce (ILO 2004).

In general, however, women's lack of access to affordable credit, information, technical advice and services prevents them from expanding their enterprises. The sector is characterized by low productivity and disguised unemployment.

Providing credit, information, services and infrastructure to the informal sector would enhance its productivity, thus supporting women's efforts to maintain their families and provide services to farmers, artisans and other producers.

Education and Training

Lack of access to formal education and training has been identified as a key barrier to women's employment and advancement in society. In Africa, female illiteracy rates were over 55 per cent in 2000, compared to 41 per cent for men. Certain countries have extremely high rates: Burkina Faso at 91.1 per cent, Sierra Leone at 88.7 per cent, Chad at 82.1 per cent and Guinea at 86.6 per cent (World Bank 2004). Literacy classes for women appear to have limited impact, while programmes linked to income generating activities have been most successful.

In many African countries, parents still prefer to send boys to school, seeing little need for education for girls. In addition, factors such as adolescent pregnancy, early marriage and girls' greater burden of household labour act as obstacles to their schooling. While most girls do not go beyond primary education, school curricula have not been guided by this reality and their content is not geared to helping girls acquire basic life skills. The curriculum also is suffused with gender biases and leads girls into stereotypical feminine jobs in teaching, nursing and clerical work. Few women are found in scientific or technical education where they could develop better skills to secure better paying jobs.

There have been improvements in the net enrolment of girls at primary levels, but disparities persist in comparison with the enrolment of boys. Female enrolment numbers decrease as girls move up the education ladder. Exceptionally, in Southern Africa, the out-migration of men has led to a very different pattern of gender representation in the education system. Botswana and Lesotho provides the most striking case, with females accounting for more than fifty percent of students, even in higher education.

Prospects for increasing the access of women and girls to education have been undermined by economic crisis, budgetary cuts, and debt servicing burdens. Cuts in state spending on education have led to a slower rate of increase in gross enrolment rates, while dropout rates for girls have risen, as they have been withdrawn from school in response to new fees and cost recovery and other economic factors.

The teaching profession shows a similar level of female participation. In 2000, women accounted for 30 per cent or less of primary teaching staff in 13 African countries, while their proportions in secondary schools remained at 33 per cent in sub-Saharan Africa between 1985 and 2000 (UNDP 2002). Women are largely absent in technical fields, with the exception of home economics and secretarial courses, depriving girls of needed role models.

It is evident that a woman's education beyond primary school is a reliable route to economic empowerment and long-term change in the status quo, as well as a determinant of a family's health and nutrition. Education beyond ten or more years of school is also a reliable predictor of lower fertility, improved infant survival, reduced maternal mortality and enhanced levels of infant and child development and educational attainment. However, the current economic and policy situation, combined with socio-cultural factors, threaten any real advances in the education of women and girls. Training programmes are needed to help women develop their technical competence, to enable them to be better informed, better infiltrate the political and economic structures and help them gain the maximum competence and means.

An important issue raised in the Beijing Platform for Action is equality of responsibility between men and women for gender equality to become a reality (Government of Eretria 2004a). In order for more women to reach the same high positions as men in various fields, more focused education and socialization are needed for better burden-sharing and a fairer division of labour between the sexes in the home and society. Not only should governments' macroeconomic policies incorporate gender perspectives in their design, they also need to take into account intra-household differences in resource use and control, recognizing that improvements in women's incomes promote equity as well as child welfare.

Most economic programmes in Africa tend to overlook the unpaid economy, where women predominate. They also assume that males and females respond to incentives in the same way, thereby ignoring gender and power relations within households and communities. But gender biases and rigidities may strongly affect women's access to productive resources and markets, ultimately frustrating economic reform policies.

Women in Eretraian Economy

Women play an important role in the war-ravaged Eritrean economy. Many enterprises are owned and run by women, and women make up 30 percent of the workforce in manufacturing, services, and trade. It is to be noted that a legal framework for gender equality and equity is in place. Eritrea's 1997 Constitution prohibits the violation of the human rights of women and mandates the Legislature to enact laws designed to eliminate inequalities in the Eritrean society because of gender discrimination. Laws forbid the kidnapping of women and the exchange of dowries upon marriage, and women now can initiate divorce. Women gain the right to access land for housing and farming at the age of 18 (UNO 2001). Women ex-combatants have found it difficult to return to their home communities and therefore stayed in towns where they tried to make a living without the traditional support provided by their families. Some of these women acquired skills during the war that could be helpful in running a micro-enterprise in peacetime, such as metal welding and machine operation. It is to be noted that, after independence the women fighters (from rural areas) settled in towns after demobilization rather than returning to their home villages because of their employment and other responsibility. Besides, better facilities motivated them to settle in towns than in villages (Rena 2006; Ruth 1995).

An examination of Eritrean society reveals a more traditional picture, however. Nearly 70 percent of Eritreans live below the poverty line; this pattern is particularly acute among the major percent of households that are headed by women. Women are concentrated in low-skill, low-paying jobs and earn only 50-80 percent of what their male colleagues earn (UNO 2001). In addition, women's enterprises are concentrated in areas with limited growth, such as simple food processing and small tailor workshops (Rena 2006).

Thus, political and economic gender equality is still weak in Eritrea despite the enactment of mechanisms to empower women and to inform them of their rights. One reason is the lack of organizations to mobilize and support women. Only one women's organization i.e. National Union of Eritrean Women (NUEW) is involved in advocacy and education on key women's issues, including health, education, micro-finance, and human rights (Amrit 1989; UNO 2001).

The gender gap is prevalent in the area of basic education. Household responsibilities, early marriage, and economic and cultural factors hamper girls' access to education. At the primary school level, girls have lower enrollment rates and higher-grade repetition rates than do boys, and only 13 percent of eligible girls attend secondary school. The low education level among girls and women inevitably has a negative influence on their income-earning capabilities and on their access to economic opportunities (Rena 2005).

Although the end of the Eritrean/Ethiopian war is welcome and likely have a negative effect on the economic participation of women because male workers tend to be the first to be employed in post-war jobs and enterprises. Improvement in the availability and efficiency of the economic activities of women, and in turn their well being, therefore is critical (Amrit 1991;Connell 1997). Since many men were mobilized for the war, a large number of women are now de facto heads of households and of their husbands' businesses. For example, many women also occupy jobs that were previously held by men in construction sector.

Following the war, many Eritreans returned to their native country from abroad, where they had acquired skills and business experience. About 100,000 Eritreans were expelled from Ethiopia alone, many of whom have experience in managing restaurants, hotels, taxis, and other services. The newly created enterprises of this group have been witnessing many problems because of hostile economic situation in the country (Connell 1997).

Eritrea is a country located at extreme North East of Africa. It is a young nation as it has got its independence in the year 1991, 24 May. Total land area of Eritrea is about 125000 Square Kilometers (Government of Eretria 2003b). Eritrea lies in between 12° and 18° North latitude and 36° and 44 ° East longitudes. The country is having more than 1000 Kilometers of coastal line along the Red Sea with about 350 off shore islands. Besides Red Sea, which is located east and north-east side of Eritrea, it shares boundaries with Sudan in the north and west and Ethiopia and Djibouti in the south. The population is estimated to be 4.5 million, including about a half a million refugees in Sudan. With about 70 per cent of its population dependent on agriculture, it is producing only 16 per cent of GDP in 2005-06 (Rena 2005).

Table 1 gives the picture of Eritrea in terms of socio-economic conditions of the people of Eritrea.

Table 1: Socio-Economic Indicators of Eritrea

Item	*Particulars*
Population (millions)	
a. 1975	2.1
b. 2002	4.0
c. 2015 (estimate)	5.9
Annual growth rate of Population (%)	
a. 1975 - 2002	2.4
b. 2002 – 2015 (estimate)	3.0
Urban Population (% of total)	
a. 1975	12.7
b. 2002	19.5
c. 2015 (estimate)	26.5
Illiteracy (% of people15 years & above)	
a. Male	42 (1990) 33 (2000)
b. Female	72 (1990) 61 (2000)
Population with sustainable access to improved sanitation (%)	
a. 2000 year	13
Population with sustainable access to an Improved water resource	
a. 2000 year	46
GDP (US billions $)	
a. 2002 year	0.6
b. 2003 year	0.9

(Contd...)

GDP per Capita (US $) a. 2002 b. 2003	 150 190
GDP (% growth 2002-03)	3.0
GDP (per Capita % growth 2002-03)	0.8

Source: Compiled from UNDP [2004] and World Bank [2005]

Women Education in Eritrea

It is generally accepted that economic and social factors are the major causes of girls' low participation, retention, and achievement rates in education. The Educational statistics published by the Eritrean Ministry of Education (2003b) reveals that enrollment of female students has increased by 2.32 times from 1991-92 to 2002-03 against 2.67 times increase in male students. The details are presented in the Table 2.

Although enrollment levels of female students have increased, but the rate of increase has not been significant. In the home arena, factors affecting girls' education include attitudes toward women's limited roles due to early marriage and heavy domestic responsibilities.

The Ministry of Education has tried to address these factors through the enforcement of marriage law and projects to help reduce domestic chores (such as water and fuel wood collection) and by the establishment of schools closer to local communities and resources. The United Nations International Children's Emergency Fund (UNICEF) also addresses the problem of physical distance from schools by building hostels and dormitories for girls at the secondary level (Gruber 1998; Stefanos 1997).

Table 2: Enrolment of Female Students from Elementary Level up to Technical & Vocational Level (1991/92- 2002/03)

Year	*Female*	*Total*
1991/92	96,131	208,162
1992/93	110,899	247,567
1993/94	120,626	274,723
1994/95	130,786	298,741
1995/96	141,900	321,256
1996/97	145,663	329,696
1997/98	152,657	347,150
1998/99	165,644	377,896
1999/00	188,698	431,508
2000/01	193,532	442,033
2001/02	206,501	484,357
2002/03	223,119	522,099

Source: Ministry of Education [2003c]

On the other hand, with respect to female teachers, the statistics show that at different levels of education, number of teachers has increased overwhelmingly over a period of 11 years (Table 3).

Table 3: Number of Female Teachers- 1991/92 – 2002/03

Academic Year	*Level of Education*					
	1-5 Grade		*6-7 Grade*		*8-11 Grade*	
	Total	*Female Teachers*	*Total*	*Female Teachers*	*Total*	*Female Teachers*
1991/92	3,647	1,411	783	139	758	67
1992/93	4,978	1,849	855	143	905	93
1993/94	5,272	1,865	978	140	1,015	104
1994/95	5,583	1,974	948	139	1,081	108
1995/96	5,828	2,025	992	156	1,039	103
1996/97	5,476	1,977	1,017	170	942	106
1997/98	5,799	1,893	1,162	170	959	113
1998/99	5,576	1,951	1,208	149	982	112
1999/00	6,229	2,330	1,312	167	1,047	109
2000/01	6,668	2,710	1,377	160	1,188	115
2001/02	7,498	2,873	1,529	177	1,419	145
2002/03	7,692	2,754	1,614	178	1,277	140

Source: Ministry of Education [2003c]

Women Participation in Eritrean Economy

Participation of women in all spheres of life enhances their role in economic development process. It is to be noted that the Fourth World Conference on Women held in Beijing in the year 1995 declared to develop the fullest potential of girls and women of all ages, ensure their full and equal participation in building a better world for all and enhance their role in the development process. Beijing declaration further stressed to promote women's economic independence and empowerment by enhancing opportunities of employment to women and eradicating persistent and increasing burden of poverty on women. Besides this, the declaration stated for equal access and equal treatment of women and men in education (UNO 1995).

After independence of Eritrea in 1991, Government of Eritrea took all-round measures for its development. Education is the initial step for development because without human resource development no development can take place.

Women also make up a major part of the large-manufacturing workforce especially in the garments, leather, and tobacco industries. This participation probably increased during the war with Ethiopia as a result of the military mobilization of a large proportion of the male workforce. Women make up 50 percent of the workforce in the public sector, compared with 22 percent in the private sector. About 80 percent of the workforce in women-owned enterprises is female (Gerde 2001). The average age of women factory workers is 35 years. About 12 percent of the women workers, mainly those in public factories, are older than 50 years of age. Many of the women workers started working in these factories when they were very young (National Union of Eritrean Women 2004).

According to the survey carried out by the Ministry of Trade and Industry, total number of Medium and Large Scale Manufacturing Establishments (MLSMEs) were 276 in 2004. The number of MLSMEs has increased substantially for last several years as indicated in the Table 4.

Women are engaged primarily as unskilled labor in the production process. Skilled women represent a very small percentage (7.4 percent) of employment in large enterprises. In both public and private sector offices, women do predominantly secretarial work, with little participation in management (Gerde 2001).

Table 4: Major Economic Indicators of MLSMEs (2002-2004)

Indicators	*2002*	*2003*	*2004*
Number of establishments	250	252	276
Number of persons engaged	13,431	13,842	14,818
Number of employees	13,084	13,528	14,485
Compensation of employees ('000 Nakfa)	132,485	154,230	187,896
Gross Output ('000 Nakfa)	1,755,108	2,194,459	2,766,612
Gross Input ('000 Nakfa)	1,133,345	1,393,476	1,824,479

Source: Ministry of Trade & Industry [2004b]

Composition of the employees in manufacturing sector as shown in the Table 5 indicates that there is a high rate of women participation in the manufacturing sector. According to 2004 census, women employees comprise about 46.5 per cent of the total number of persons engaged in medium and large establishments. This rate varies widely between manufacturing groups. The high rate of women participation is due to large number of women enrolled in textile industry. In 2004, the number of women employees engaged in textile industry was 2,342, which constitute 34 per cent of the total employees. The next higher participation of female employees is in the food industry accounting for 21.6 per cent of the total number of women employees (Government of Eritrea 2004b).

In the same year, (2004) foreign employees engaged in the MLSMEs were only 15 per cent of the total number of persons engaged. Most of them were engaged in manufacturing of finished textiles and non-refractory clay and ceramic products.

Table 5: Composition of Paid and Unpaid Workers in Eretria

Employees	*2003*			*2004*		
	Total No. of Unpaid Workers	*Total no. of Paid Workers*	*Total Workers (Paid& Unpaid)*	*Total No. of Unpaid Workers*	*Total No. of Paid Workers*	*Total Workers (Paid& Unpaid)*
Eritrean Male	216	6960	7176	254	7478	7732
Eritrean Female	85	6401	6486	73	6784	6857
Total	301	13361	13662	327	14262	14589
Non-Eritrean Male	8	140	148	3	193	196
Non-Eritrean Female	5	27	32	3	30	33
Total	13	167	180	6	223	229
Total Male	224	7100	7324	257	7671	7928
Total Female	90	6428	6518	76	6814	6890
Grand Total	314	13528	13842	333	14485	14818

Source: Ministry of Trade & Industry [2004b]

Compensation Paid to Employees

As shown in the Table 6, compensation paid to employees consists of two types – wage/salary and benefits. Total compensation paid to employees in 2004 was about Nakfa 188 million, of which about Nakfa 171 million was paid as wages and salaries, and remaining Nakfa 17 million was paid for different types of benefits. This includes commission, bonus, professional hardship allowances, pension, life and causality insurance scheme, etc.

The annual compensation of employees varies from one industrial group to another. Data relating to the compensation paid per employee shows variation in payments among the industrial groups.

Table 6: Compensation per Employee by Industry Type (In '000 Nakfa)

Type of Industry	*2003*			*2004*		
	Total No. of Workers	*Compen-sation*	*Compen-sation per Worker*	*Total No. of Workers*	*Compen sation*	*Compen-sation per Worker*
Food	2,472	24,180	9.782	2,627	28,860	*10.986*
Beverages & Alcoholic Drinks	1,083	17,147	15.833	1,321	25,645	*19.413*
Tobacco	49	2,065	42.143	44	2,065	*46.932*
Textile	2,924	28,130	9.620	2,991	26,596	*8.892*
Leather & Shoe	974	10,104	10.374	934	10,087	*10.800*
Paper and Printing	517	6,326	12.236	556	8,897	*16.002*
Chemical Products	542	7,315	13.496	585	9,284	*15.870*
Rubber& Plastic Products	578	4,414	7.637	582	5,689	*9.775*
Non-Metallic Mineral Products	1,952	21,011	10.764	2,233	27,202	*12.182*
Metal Products	1,083	12,788	11.808	1,088	15,754	14.480
Furniture	1,354	20,749	15.324	1,524	27,817	18.253
TOTAL	13,528	154,230	11.401	14,485	187,896	12.972

Source: Ministry of Trade & Industry [2004b]

It is evident from the table 6 that the annual compensation of employees in 2004 ranges from the lowest ratio of Nakfa 8.892 per employee in Textile Industry to the highest ratio of Nakfa 46.932 per worker in Tobacco Industry. In general the compensation per worker in 2004 has increased in all industrial groups (except in Textile Industry) as compared to 2003. The payment in tobacco industry is higher than the other Industrial groups due to higher salary scales for administration and technical employees. The compensation paid per worker in the manufacturing of Beverage and Alcoholic drinks and Furniture stands second and third respectively. Compensation of employees in general is low in Textile, Rubber and Plastic products (People's front for Democracy and Justice 2006).

Participation of Women in Transport Sector

In recent years, women participation in transport sector has increased in Eritrea, especially driving of commercial vehicles. Those who are trained by the National Union of Eritrean Women (NUEW) and the defense forces and other organizations now working as professional drivers constitute a substantial number. It is now common to see women driving government or commercial vehicles such as buses as well as heavy vehicles used in the construction industry of Eritrea.

It is after 2000 that the number of women drivers started to show a rapid increase. Out of 1,772 drivers' license issued in 2000, 638 were given to females, only 2.8% of which were third grade licenses authorizing the holders to drive commercial vehicles. In the following year the number of women obtained licenses was lower but the percentage of third grade license holders was 4.3%. During the period 2000-2005 29,926 licenses were issued, 3,490 or 12% were issued to females (People's front for Democracy and Justice 2006).

The government garages, which operate 200 vehicles serving different government departments, employ the largest number of women drivers. The garage has 160 drivers 60 of which are women. Most of these women work in cities. Each woman drives an average of 80kms per day. It is believed that the women acquire necessary skills and turn out to be better drivers than men. They tend to show appropriate respect for traffic rules and are generally more disciplined drivers. In general, they have a better driving record and the accidents they cause are generally minor and thus cost less.

It is reported that during the last 10 years (1996-2006) no major accident resulting in serious damage has been caused by women drivers. Accidents involving women drivers are usually minor such as those causing slight damage to fenders. Women tend to be careful drivers, this attests to the superiority of women drivers. Women drivers have implications on saving life and protecting property and it therefore something, which goes beyond the principle of women's equality. Various studies show that women are more careful drivers than men. Women drivers do not display 'macho' characteristics while men do and this leads to avoidable accidents. The participation of Eritrean women in all spheres of activity has been demonstrated in practical terms (People's front for Democracy and Justice 2006).

Appropriate measures have to be taken to protect women workers in order to ensure their participation in the economic development of Eritrea. It is important to develop confidence in women and raise their level of consciousness so as to safeguard their rights in the political and legal systems. What is essential is equal access to education and employment opportunities, equal pay for equal work and equal rights to skills development to promotion, eradication of harmful traditional practices that endanger women's health and well-being and reduction of poverty for Eritrean women and their families.

Access to Resources

Government of Eritrea and local authorities must demonstrate commitment to removing legal impediments and socio-cultural obstacles against women, especially in the rural areas where the majority of women live and are economically active. The constraints on women's access to land, credit, extension services, inputs and new technologies must be removed, and opportunities should be created for their enterprise. Measures to improve women's access through institutional reforms must be pursued and monitored for effectiveness.

Reducing Labour Time

Appropriate technologies for household chores, food processing, preservation and storage are needed. Farm tools that are appropriate for women, including small transportation equipment that will free women from head loading must be provided. The increased provision of potable water and cheap and reliable energy sources are also needed to reduce the long hours that women work and to remove the drudgery from their lives.

Improving Education and Health

Gender biases in the educational system, training and employment must be consistently eliminated to give women new opportunities for achievement, while school curricula must incorporate concepts of gender equality and peace at all levels, so that students will incorporate them throughout their lives. Young women need role models to motivate them and must be given a usable education and skills to play meaningful roles in society and to safeguard them from harmful practices, which mortgage their health and lives.

It is critically important for policy-makers to listen to and work with women to improve their positions and thereby accelerate economic development. A comprehensive approach must be taken up by the government of Eritrea in conjunction with development agencies and women themselves to remove the social, economic and legal constraints on women.

Conclusion

Women play an important role in African economies in general and the war-ravaged Eritrean economy in particular. The participation of Eritrean women in all spheres of activity has been demonstrated in practical terms. Government and the private sector throughout Eritrea have to commit to achieving gender equity. The translation of this commitment into reality is, however, limited by factors such as differences in terms of educational and economic status in the towns and cities on one hand and rural areas on the other and a lack of experience with the implementation of gender policies. In addition, women can play a crucial role in Eritrea's socio-economic development if they are recognized as vital resource and given opportunities to participate. This includes women completing their national service and engaging actively in the formal economy.

Since women participation in the employment is found to be low in Eritrean economy, the government should make efforts by bringing necessary changes in the system by taking measures in providing equal access higher education and health needs, food security, enterprise development etc. In each of these areas, attention to gender-based opportunities could lead to stronger and more positive support to achieve gender equity goals of the Eritrean people. Every organization should recruit the women and give importance to the women workers to develop the organization and thus develop its economy. As it is well known, anything that is anti-woman represents socio-economic backwardness. It therefore makes economic sense to take into account gender biases and tailor planned interventions to improve women's ability to take advantage of incentives, thus enhancing overall economic efficiency.

References

Amrit, W. (1989), *Eritrean Women and Struggle*. London Printing Press, London.

Amrit, W. (1991), *Women and the Eritrean Revolution*. Red Sea Press, Trenton, New Jersey.

Connell, D. (1997), *Against All Odds: A Chronicle of the Eritrean Revolution*. Red Sea Press, Trenton, New Jersey.

FAO (2004), *Agricultural Investment and Productivity in Developing Countries*. FAO, Rome.

Gerde, H. (2001), *Women's Employment and Microenterprise Development in Eritrea: Development Alternatives*. USAID, Washington DC.

Gruber, J. (1998), *Report on Gender Situation Analysis in Eritrea*. UNICEF, New York.

Government of Eretria (2003a), *Eritrea Demographic and Health Survey (EDHS) 2002*. National Statistics Office, the Government of the State of Eritrea, Asmara.

Government of Eretria (2003b), *Eritrea: A Land of Diversity, Excitement and Endless Adventures.* Ministry of Tourism, Asmara, Eritrea.

Government of Eretria (2003c), *Eritrea: Essential Education Indicators 2002/03.* Ministry of Education, Asmara, Eritrea.

ILO (2004), *World Employment Report.* ILO, Geneva.

National Union of Eritrean Women (2004), *Eritrean Women and Economy.* 25th Anniversary of NUEW, Asmara, Eritrea.

Government of Eritrea (2004a), *Report on the Implementation of the Beijing Platform for Action and the Outcome of the Twenty-Third Special Session of the General Assembly.* Asmara, Eritrea.

Government of Eritrea (2004b), *Report on Census of Manufacturing Establishments.* Ministry of Trade & Industry, Asmara, Eritrea.

Rena, Ravinder (2005), Gender Disparity in Education: An Eritrean Perspective. *The Global Child Journal,* 2 (1): 43-49.

Rena, Ravinder (2006), *A Hand Book on the Eritrean Economy: Problems and Prospects for Development.* New Africa Press, Dar es Salaam, Tanzania.

Ruth Iyob (1995), *The Eritrean Struggle for Independence.* Cambridge University Press, Cambridge.

Sen, A. (1989), *Hunger and Public Action.* Clarendon Press, Oxford.

Stefanos, A. (1997), Women and Education in Eritrea: A Historical and Contemporary Analysis. *Harvard Educational Review*, 67(4): 658-688.

UNDP (2002,2004 and 2005), *Human Development Report.* Oxford University Press, New York.

UNO (1995), *The Beijing Declaration and the Platform for Action.* Fourth World Conference on Women (September), United Nations, New York.

UNO (2001), *Common Country Assessment (CCA): Volume I.* GSE, United Nations, New York.

World Bank (1993), *Investing in Health.* World Development Report, Washington DC.

World Bank (2004), *Making Services Work For Poor People.* World Development Report, Washington DC.

World Bank (2005), *A Better Investment Climate for Everyone.* World Development Report, Washington DC.

People's front for Democracy and Justice (2006), *Women Economic Participation: Beyond Equality.* Available at www.shaebia.com

3

Women in Agriculture

Imasiku, E.N. S. *University of Zambia*
Nyoni, F. *University of Zambia*

Introduction

Boserup (1983) argues that the dependency ratio and the structure of the households influence women's productivity by their effects on the selection of productive activities. Infants and young children demand a great deal of time, but older children can substitute for a mother a number of tasks and expand the family labour force. Despite the modern techniques where agriculture becomes less dependent on human muscular power in some cycles, men still "monopolize the use of new equipment and modern methods" (Boserup 1983:168). Thus, women are not dominant in agricultural development, as the playing field is not leveled. They are still disadvantaged by their lack of equal access to resources such as information, credit facilities, inputs, land, technology and decision making power as compared to their male counterpart.

In subsistence or small-scale commercial farming, family labour forms the main source of labour input and is segregated by gender. Women contribute higher labour input than their husbands or children, working longer hours on both family and independent plots. Women are estimated to perform 50 to 75 percent of all agricultural labour and virtually all of the daily household chores (Loxley 1990). Women's labour tend to be concentrated in the areas of weeding, harvesting, transporting and marketing while men tend to concentrate more on soil preparation, fertilizing and pest control. Women perform virtually all-household chores, while men provide most of the labour for non-household employment, hunting and gathering. Loxley (1990) further argues that the patterns of gender segregation of labour are reproduced among children, with girls performing three to seven times as many hours of household chores as boys and less time on leisure and education.

Men control women's labour through marriage, and the high incidence of polygamy among small-scale farmers attests to the high female labour input in family enterprises. Women are perceived as cheaper, more reliable and a more permanent source of labour than hired labour or kin and female headed rural households often face severe labour problems.

Technologies are needed which can reduce the burden on women of weeding, transplanting, harvesting, food processing/ preservation and water carrying. These are needed not solely to raise output but also to allow women more time for leisure activities and education.

Credit, which is closely associated with technical advancement, is crucial for small-scale farmers attempting to grow cash crops, which need investment in inputs in the form of seeds, fertilizers and labour, as well as transportation costs. However the evidence suggests that it is only families who are already relatively rich who receive credit and the poor families are virtually excluded. It is estimated that only about "10 percent of rural households benefit from credit" (Loxley 1990:73). Women face severe constraints in attempting to gain access to credit, in particular they face challenges in the areas of security, access and socio-cultural attitudes.

Zambian Women's Marginalization in Agriculture

The Ministry of Agriculture and Cooperative's extension system not only has problems of under funding and inefficiency, but it also fails to cater for the needs of women farmers even though they are the major food producers in Zambia. The extension services are directed primarily at men and especially to the emergent, commercial farmers rather than peasants and small-scale farmers. The focus on single production units means that the extension system is biased against women. Many extension officers fail to take seriously the needs, as well as the importance, of women farmers, and women may be inhibited from talking to a male stranger. Often the only training offered to women concentrates on home economics and household management. It is clear that more female extension officers are needed to help raise the productivity of female headed households in particular and women farmers in general.

The failure to provide extension services means that women are disadvantaged to access improved agricultural inputs such as fertilizers, pesticides, hybrid seeds, among others, which are crucial to improving productivity. Gender-differentiated access to farm equipment, particularly modern implements, contributes to the differentiation in resources available to female and male-headed households. "Women often spend long hours doing arduous agricultural tasks which could be relieved by access to farm implements" (ZARD 1985:91).

The low educational attainment of rural women means that the majority of rural women in Zambia are illiterate and thus disadvantaged in the learning of modern productive skills. The government's functional literacy programme, which uses maize cultivation as a teaching tool, is intended to assist women to increase yields from their lands and to learn a few basic skills in arithmetic - but coverage is not widespread. "Wives may also face opposition from husbands who do not wish them to attend courses" (Roelofs 1988:33).

The status of women has continued to be suppressed as their ability to control important decisions in their lives or freedom from control by others is reduced by their male counterpart and systems in many agricultural institutions. As a result women in terms of participation across all sectors remains low, hence there is little progress that "can be made on the poverty traps that are found in every country" (Boulding et al. 1976: 23).

Women have critical roles, which need consideration in order for development and eradication of poverty to be achieved. It is suggested that this significant role of women can be attained if women's autonomy is considered in such arrangements as out grower schemes, where firms provide extension services to farmers and sell inputs on loan that can be repaid at the time of harvest.

Land Gender-based Constraints in Agriculture

Ordinarily Zambian women do not own land in their own right. They only access the use of land through marriage, relatives or village headmen. Married women generally work on family plots which have been allocated to male heads of household. If they wish to have an independent field, they must obtain use-rights by virtue of a relationship with a man - mostly their husband, but occasionally a relation. Widows and divorcees typically have no further claim on land obtained through a husband and must rely on claims to land under the control of their own relatives. Unmarried women are especially disadvantaged in that they have no claims to land and can only be given use of land by relatives. With increasing commercialization of land and crops, women's traditional rights to use land and control the products of the land may be further threatened.

Married women are obliged to work first on family plots, their husbands control the income from which, and which are generally bigger than their own independent plots. Women's independent plots vary between less than a hectare to approximately three hectares, and widows have in general less acreage than divorced women. The land granted for women's use often has problems of quality and location. The result of poor, unirrigated land or scattered and small plots means that women are unable to use more efficient cropping measures, thus limiting their productivity (ZARD 1985).

Background of Cotton out Grower System in Zambia

The Zambian cotton sector was heavily regulated from 1977 to 1994;

cotton marketing was controlled by Lint Company of Zambia (Lintco) a parastatal organization. In 1994 comprehensive cotton reforms began to take place in line with the liberalization policy which expanded market opportunities and induced the entry of private ginners among them Dunavant Zambia Limited in 2000. Dunavant has established several ginneries in Zambia among them in Katete. Dunavant operates an out grower scheme through the farmer group system and the farmer distributor system by providing loans to farmers that are repaid at harvest time (Porto 2005).

Study Area

The research was carried out in Katete district, which is situated in the Eastern Province of Zambia. Katete lies at longitude 31° and 33° E, latitude 14° and 15° S. The district covers an area of approximately 10,834 Km². It is bordered by Mambwe district in the North, Mozambique in the South, Petauke in the West and Chipata district to the north-east (Simute et al. 1998).

The Eastern province has approximately 3.8 million hectares of arable land (out of 6.9 million total hectares) although only 35% of the arable land is currently utilized. Almost 75% of the total labor force in the province is involved in agriculture a bigger percentage being women, while others are in forestry and fishing (Peterson 1999). The main agriculture products include maize, cotton, groundnuts, tobacco, sunflower, and livestock. Peterson (1999) further states that about 905 of the farmers earn their living from subsistence agriculture. Part-time work and major off-season activities include black smith lumber jacks (though on a small scale), basket making, reed mat production, beer brewing, carpentry, charcoal production and gardening.

Methodology

Katete Dunavant operation area is divided into seven zones; Masala, Mphangwe, Katete, Chanida, Vulamkoko, Msoro and Chadiza zones. One of these zones (Mphangwe) was chosen as the study area. A manageable sample size of 50 was randomly chosen out of 1,395 female farmers from various settlements in Mphangwe zone. This was due to resource and time constraints.

Structured interviews were used to get information directly from the women cotton growers taking into account the fact that the majority of rural women have a low educational background. Issues that were considered included:

- The performance of women cotton growers in the last three years
- The benefits realized from cotton growing
- Problems they encountered as women cotton growers

Direct observation was also used to collect the needed information. This method was useful when touring the cotton fields as it helped to ascertain the size of the fields. It also helped to ascertain investments made from money realized from cotton sales such as houses with iron sheets, cattle in the kraal and spraying machines used during spraying. This helped to verify data obtained through the interviews.

Interviews administered to the Dunavant Officers at the ginnery; zone coordinators and the District Agricultural Coordinators office also helped to enrich the data that was collected. Issues investigated included:

- The general performance of women in agriculture
- Policy on women by Dunavant Zambia Limited
- Dunavant involvement in women groups
- Type of assistance Dunavant is giving women cotton growers
- Problems encountered by female cotton growers

The data obtained was processed manually through the evaluation of the interview schedules mainly because the data collected was qualitative. The data was then qualitatively analyzed. The percentages of various responses were presented using tables or pie charts, to enhance a high visual presentation thereby making it easy for people to understand the presented data.

Results

The study revealed that none of the respondents attended tertiary (college) education. Those who had not attended any formal school were 21 (42%), 8 (16%) attended only lower primary (grade 1 – 4), 15 (30%) upper primary (grade 5 – 7), only 1 (2%) attended Junior Secondary and 5 (10%) attended Senior Secondary (grade 10 – 12).

The survey showed that 14 (28%) became members during the 2000/2001 growing season, 9 (18%) during the 2001/2002 growing season, 8 (16%) during 2002/2003 growing season, 9 (18%) during the 2003/2004 growing season and 10 (20%) during the 2004/2005 growing season (See Table 1).

Table 1: Membership Information

Year (growing season)	*Number of women*	*Percentage (%)*
2000/2001	14	28
2001/2002	9	18
2002/2003	8	16
2003/2004	9	18
2004/2005	10	20
TOTAL	50	100

Source: Field Data [2006]

All respondents interviewed indicated that they depended on agriculture only as their main source of income even before they engaged in cotton growing.

Table 2 shows the performance of women in three growing seasons (2002/2003 to 2004/2005). In 2002/2003, there were 23 (46%) that produced and sold less than five bales of cotton each weighing an average of 90 kg. Then 21 (42%) produced and sold 5 to 10 bales of cotton, 2 (4%) produced and sold between 11 – 15 bales, and three (6%) produced and sold 6 to 20 bales of cotton.

In the 2003/2004 season, 15 (30%) produced and sold less than five bales, 17 (34%) had 5 – 10 bales, 11 (22%) had 11 – 15 bales, 4(8%) had 16 – 20 bales while 3(6%) produced and sold more than 20 bales. In 2004/ 2005 season, 12 (24%) produced and sold less than five bales, 26 (52%) had 5 – 10 bales, 7 (14%) had 11 – 15 bales, 2 (4%) had 16 – 20 bales and 3 (6%) produced and sold more than 20 bales of cotton.

Table 2: Production Performance of Women in the Last Three Years

Number of Bales	*2002 – 2003 season*	*2003 – 2004 season*	*2004 – 2005 season*
Less than 5	23	15	12
5 – 10	21	17	26
11 – 15	2	11	7
16 – 20	3	4	2
More than 20	1	3	3
TOTAL	50	50	50

Source: Field Data [2006]

In 2002/2003 season, Dunavant was buying cotton at ZMK970.00 per kilogram, in 2003/2004 season it was ZMK1, 420.00 and in the 2004/2005 one, it was ZMK1, 220.00 Table 3 shows that in 2003, the majority 23 (46%) earned up to ZMK436,500.00, 21 (42%) between ZMK436,500.00 and ZMK873,000.00, 2 (4%) earned between ZMK874,000.00 and ZMK1, 309,500.00, 3 (6%) earned between ZMK1,310,500.00 and ZMK1,746,000.00 and only 1 (2%) earned above ZMK1,746,000.00.

Table 4 shows that in 2004, the majority, 17 (34%) earned between ZMK689,000.00 and ZMK1,279,000.00, 15 (30%) earned less than ZMK 639,000.00, 11 (22%) earned between ZMK1,280,000.00 and ZMK 1,917,000.00, 4 (8%) between ZMK1,918,000.00 and ZMK2,556,000.00, and 3 (6%) earned more than ZMK2,556,000.00.

Table 3: Income Earned from Cotton Sales in 2003

Income (ZMK)	*Number of women*	*Percentage (%)*
Less than 436,500.00	23	46
436,500.00 – 873,000.00	21	42
874,000.00–1,309,500.00	2	4
1,310,500.00– 1,746,000.00	3	6
Above 1,746,000.00	1	2
TOTAL	50	100

Source: Field Data [2006]

Table 4: Income Earned from Cotton Sales in 2004

Income (ZMK)	*Number of women*	*Percentage (%)*
Less than 639,000.00	15	30
639,000.00 – 1,278,000.00	17	34
1,279,000.00 - 1,917,000.00	11	22
1,918,000.00 – 2,556,000.00	4	8
Above 2,556,000.00	3	6
TOTAL	50	100

Source: Field Data [2006]

Table 5 shows that the majority26 (52%) earned between ZMK549,000.00 and ZMK1,098,000.00, 12 (24%) earned less than ZMK550,000.00, 7 (14%) earned between ZMK1,099,000.00 and ZMK1,647,000.00, 2 (4%) between ZMK1,648,000.00 and ZMK2,196,000.00 and 3 (6%) earned more than ZMK2,196,000.00.

Table 5: Income Earned from Cotton Sales in 2005

Income (ZMK)	*Number of women*	*Percentage (%)*
Less than 549,000	12	24
549,000 – 1,098,000	26	52
1,099,000 – 1,647,000	7	14
1,648,000 – 2,196,000	2	4
Above 2,196,000	3	6
TOTAL	50	100

Source: Field Data [2006]

Table 6 shows the amount of land they cultivated for cotton during the 2005/2006 growing season. Half of the respondents, 25 (50%) cultivated an estimated area of one hectare, 18 (36%) cultivated an area of about 2 hectares, 6 (12%) cultivated about 3 hectares and only 1 (2%) cultivated about 10 hectares (15kg of seed covers about 1 hectare of land).

Table 6: Amount of Area Cultivated 2005-2006

Amount of seed planted	*Estimated cultivated area*	*Number of women*	*Percentage (%)*
15Kg	1 hectare	25	50
30Kg	2 hectares	18	36
45Kg	3 hectares	6	12
Above 45Kg	Above 3 hectares	1	2
TOTAL		50	100

Source: Field Data [2006]

Only 5 (10%) indicated that they were failing to pay back the loan while the rest 45 (90%) were paying back successfully.

Table 7 shows that the women had diversified to avoid a complete loss due to crop failure and also to ensure household food security. All the respondents, 50 (100%) grew maize alongside cotton, 6 (12%) grew beans, only 2 (4%) grew sorghum, and 2 (4%) cultivated cassava. Only 14 (28%) cultivated groundnuts and 20 (40%) of the women cultivated sunflower. Plate 1 shows a woman in a field of maize and sunflower in addition to cotton.

Table 7: Other Crops Grown

Name of a Crop	*Number of women(out of 50)*	*Percentage (%)*
Maize	50	100
Beans	6	12
Sorghum	2	4
Cassava	2	4
Groundnuts	14	28
Sunflower	20	40

Source: Field Data [2006]

All the women 50 (100%) practiced conservation farming while none used irrigation in cotton growing. More than half (76%) of the women interviewed used ox-drawn implements to cultivate the land while 12 (24%) used hand tools to cultivate cotton. Most of them, 49 (98%) of the women interviewed depended on household labour during the cultivation of cotton while only 1 (2%) hired labour throughout the cultivation process. Only 11 (22%) indicated that they grew seed cotton while 39 (78%) did not.

All the women 50 (100%) indicated that they grew food crops specifically for household consumption.

Most of the respondents (86%) indicated that there was a difference in terms of their standard of living from the time they started growing cotton and only 7 (14%) indicated that there was no change in their standard of living (see Table 8). The results also revealed that most (88%) of the respondents had an increase in their income due to cotton growing while 6(12%) did not. More than three quarters of them (76%) indicated that they had invested in ventures they failed before while 12 (24%) indicated they did not afford to invest. Only 8 (16%) indicated that cotton growing helped them to save some money for future use while 42 (84%) did not save with any bank.

Table 8: Difference in Standard of Living of theRespondents

Difference in well being	*Number of women*	*Percentage (100%)*
Yes	43	86
No	7	14
Total	50	100

Source: Field Data [2006]

Table 9 shows how the women used the income realized from cotton growing. More than half (68%) of them bought cattle, 21 (42%) built brick houses, 6 (12%) bought solar panels, 6 (12%) bought television sets, 36 (72%) were paying school fees for their children, 46 (92%) used the money for fertilizers either as down payment under fertilizer support programme or paid cash for it. More than three quarters of them (78%) used the money on household food security, 42 (84%) bought bicycles and all of them (100%) used the money on household needs.

Table 9: Use of Income from Cotton

How income was used	*Number of women*	*Percentage (100%)*
Buying cattle	43	68
Brick houses	21	42
Solar panels	6	12
Television sets	6	12
Children's school fees	36	72
Inputs (fertilizers etc.)	46	92
Food security	39	78
Household needs	50	100
Buying a Bicycle	42	84

Source: Field Data [2006]

Table 10 shows challenges which the respondents faced as cotton growers. Most of them (92%) lacked finances and labour while 46 (92%) lacked labour. All of the women (100%) were neither happy with the price of cotton nor aware of the effects of the chemicals to their health. Most of them (86%) complained that the spraying machines were heavy to carry on the back, 10(20%) indicated that they wanted to have independent fields from their husbands and 16 (32%) expressed lack of support from their husbands.

Table 10: Challenges Faced by Female Cotton Growers

Nature of challenge	*Number of women*	*Percentage (%)*
Lack of labour	45	90
Lack of finances	46	92
Low price of cotton	50	100
Effects of chemicals on human health	50	100
Spraying machines are too heavy	43	86
Women to have independent fields from their husbands	10	20
Lack of support from husbands	16	32

Source: Field Data [2006]

All (100%) of the respondents indicated that taking up cotton growing could be one way in which rural women can help meet costs of household needs. The majority of the women (66%) further indicated that they had adopted cotton growing, as a strategy in meeting some of their household needs, as it was their main source of household income. On the contrary, 17 (34%) indicated that they had not adopted it as a strategy in meeting household needs.

Conclusion

More than a quarter (28%) of the respondents became members of the out grower scheme during the 2000/2001 farming season, 9 (18%) during 2001/2002 season, 8 (16%) during the 2003/2004 season and 10 (20%) during the 2004/2005 growing season. Though more women take up cotton growing each season, the 2000/2001 season had the highest number of women joining the out grower scheme. This was a year after the Ginnery was established. It can be argued that more women adopted cotton growing in order to diversify and move away from traditional cash crop and food crop maize, which was increasingly becoming difficult to grow because of the prices of inputs as well as the unreliable liberalized market system. Since all the respondents indicated that they depended on agriculture only as their main source of income, there was the need for them to grow a cash crop that did not require the use of organic fertilizers but with a ready market, as an alternative to maize. In addition cotton is much more drought tolerant than maize.

Half (50%) of the respondents just cultivated 1 hectare while only 1 cultivated above 3 hectares in the 2005/2006. This shows that nearly all the respondents' fields were small. Close to half (46%) of the respondents produced less than five (5) bales of cotton in the 2002/2003 growing season, 15 (30%) in the 2003/2004 season and only 12 (24%) in the 2004/2005 season. There was a steady reduction in the number of respondents producing less than five (5) bales of cotton. This could be attributed to the fact that they were somehow gaining experience on how to grow cotton. In 2002/2003 growing season only one produced more than 20 bales of cotton, while the 2003/2004 and 2004/2005 seasons, had 3 women each. The amount of money earned despite producing the same number of bales of cotton each season has not been the same due to the variation in the price of cotton each season. In 2003, it was ZMK970.00 per kilogram and in 2004 it increased to ZMK1, 420.00. The price reduced to ZMK1, 220.00 in 2005 and further reduced to ZMK840.00 per kilogram in 2006. During the 2002/2003 season, the highest number of respondents (46%) earned less than ZMK436, 500.00 each whereas during the 2003/2004 those who earned between ZMK639, 000.00 and ZMK1, 278,000.00 had an increase income. More than half of the respondents (52%) earned between K549, 000.00 and K1, 098,000.00 during the 2004/2005 season.

Apart from producing cotton for Dunavant Ginnery women have also diversified by growing other crops to avoid a complete loss due to crop failure and to boost household food security. They grow beans, maize, sorghum, cassava, groundnuts, and sunflower

The respondents indicated that there were benefits in cotton growing. Most of the respondents, 44 (88%) indicated an increase in household income and 43 (86%) indicated that there was a difference in terms of their standard of living. About three quarters (76%) had new investments such as ox-drawn farming implements which they previously had been failing to do due to lack of resources whereas only 8(16%) were now able to save money for future use. Those who bought cattle from the season's sales were able to increase their yields in the following seasons due to the use of ox-drawn farming implements which can plough larger areas as opposed to hand tools that hindered them from expanding their fields. Despite the low levels of education on the part of the respondents, 72% of them were able to use the money earned from cotton growing to send their children and dependants to school. Thus out grower schemes still remains a plausible strategy for poverty reduction if well designed (The Post Newspaper 2006).

The study revealed that female cotton growers faced several challenges. One of these challenges was the lack of resources to hire labour during planting, thinning, spraying and harvesting time. Another challenge faced by women was the weight of the spraying machines. Most of the women interviewed (86%) complained that the spraying machines were too heavy to carry on their backs, which affected their frequency of use at the scheduled time always. This in the long run affected their yields. Nearly all (98%) of them depended on household labour. This means that even school going children were made to abscond classes to spray the fields. This action has a negative effect on the children's education. The low producer price for cotton is another challenge, which the respondents faced. There was declining trend in the pricing of cotton. The pricing of the produce by the buyer, puts the buyer at an advantage over the poor farmer who is greatly exploited in the process. The farmer in trying to avoid living in abject poverty usually succumbs to the pressure of having their produce bought at low prices. The respondents' lack of protection from the chemicals used to spray cotton has been another problem faced by female cotton growers. All the respondents expressed concern about the effects of the chemicals used to kill pests on the cotton to human health. Dunavant's non-provision of protective clothing such as overalls, masks, glasses, and gum boots for use during spraying was said to have resulted into the farmers' being exposed to several health risks as chemicals used in cotton farming are usually harmful to human health.

Some women indicated that another challenge they faced was their husbands. Some of them 10 (20%) clearly expressed the desire for women to have independent fields which would give them an independent income. This could help them to directly meet household needs. They argued that their husbands usually spent their money on alcohol and other activities that did not benefit the entire household. They further complained that because of high illiteracy levels among the women, they usually sold the cotton in the names of their husbands. Since the cheques were prepared in their husbands' names, there were cases where husbands after cashing the cheques stayed away from home or even spent all the money without the consent of their wives.

Although the out grower scheme has some accomplishments; more needs to be done in order for farmers to fully enjoy the benefits. There is the need for a legal framework to regulate funding and selection of out grower scheme promoters. A policy framework to monitor the management of the out grower scheme fund ought to be put in place. In the absence of strong commodity – based funds given to the ginnery, farmers are not capable of negotiating for better inputs and producer prices. If the government does not put in place a single policy on cotton growing in Zambia, farmers may continue to produce cotton under low producer prices and health risks due to non-availability of protective gear.

References

Boserup, S. (1983), Factors Influencing Women's Participation and Productivity, In: B.L, Greenshields and A. M., Bellamy (eds.), *Rural Development: Growth and Inequality*, Gower Publishing Limited, Aldershot.

Boulding, E., Nuss, S. A., Carson, D. L. and Greenstein, M. A. (1976), *Handbook of International Data on Women*, Halsted Press Inc., New York.

Government of the Republic of Zambia {GRZ} (2000), *National Gender Policy*, Government Printers, Lusaka.

Loxley, J. (1990), *Structural Adjustment and Rural Labour Markets in Zambia*, World Employment Programme, Rural Employment Policy Research Programme Working Paper 104, ILO, Geneva.

Peterson, J.R. (1999), *Deforestation in Zimbabwe Problems and Prospects*, University of Zimbabwe, Salisbury.

Porto, G. (2005), *Farm Productivity and Market Structure: Evidence from Cotton Reforms in Zambia*, Yale University Press, New Haven.

Roelofs, K. P. (1988), *Women and Food Production in Zambia, World Employment Programme*, Southern African Team for Employment Promotion (SATEP), ILO, Lusaka.

Simute, S., Phiti, C.L. and Oegnas, B. (1998), *Agro Forestry Extensional Manual for Eastern Zambia*, Regional Land Management Unit, Nairobi.

Zambia Association for Research and Development (ZARD) (1985), *An Annotated Bibliography of Research on Zambian Women*, Lusaka.

4

Gender Impact Assessment in Black Economy

Sarkar, S. *A.C.College of Commerce*

Introduction

Existing literature on the black or shadow economy distinguishes the divisions of the total economy activities in several forms such as official-unofficial, formal-informal, registered-unregistered, observed-unobserved, formal-shadow, formal-underground, formal-subterranean, official-parallel, unhidden-hidden, regular-irregular, etc. A very convenient and simple definition of the total economic activities put forward by Smith (1986) and also adopted by Fagan (1997). According to Smith (1986), total economic activities comprise all production of goods and services whether sold in markets or not. The formal economy is that portion of total economic activity, which appears in official estimates of national income. It includes both recorded market activity and non-market activity such as public administration and various imputations (e.g. rent on owner-occupied housing. According to Smith (1986), the shadow economy comprises that part of the total economic activity, which is excluded from the official measurement process. Some items are excluded for conceptual reasons (e.g., home production and gardening). However, other components are not recorded because of the desire of participants to conceal their activities (e.g., crime or tax evasion). Smith (1986) defines this component of the shadow economy as the black economy. He also defines the black economic activities in a broader framework, that these activities include various components of individual or corporate incomes, which are not reported to the authorities in order to evade taxation.

The informal economy is interacting with different forms of formal order viz., the financial/economic order (formal economy), the social order (national and city politics) and the criminal justice system. In some areas there is no clear dividing streak between formal and informal. Work typically done in the catering and leisure sectors in bars, cafes etc. is casual work, lowly paid, sometimes with the employer paying taxes and obeying health and safety or employment regulations (formal economy), sometimes not (informal economy). Equally, the dividing line between the informal economy sometimes called the 'grey' economy and the shadow (criminal) economy is also often blurred. Street trading of counterfeit or stolen goods, prostitution and dealing in drugs overlap the line between informal work (part-time prostitution by housewives, supplying drugs to friends) and organized crime. These fuzzy lines contribute to the difficulty there has been in providing adequate definitions and boundaries to the informal and shadow economies and hence, the formal economy which works across economic, sociological and social order/criminal justice discourses.

Some factors affecting the emergence and prevalence of particular forms of the informal economy are predominant. One is the kinds of opportunities which the geographical and trade situation of that city has encouraged and so which are available to people. To take a simple example, seasonal casual work picking fruit and vegetables can only exist where there is such agriculture and for crops where mechanized picking is either difficult to develop or very expensive (for example, apples). Street robbery is not very profitable in villages or residential neighbourhoods where there are few strangers and little passing pedestrian traffic. Drugs trading routes lead from producers to distributors to consumers, like any other commodity. Another factor is whether particular opportunities have been taken over by particular groups, to which entry is difficult. So, for example, the opportunities or the techniques may have been monopolized within ethnic groups, within cultural groups or by certain families. For example, prostitution on the street may be open to any women though being economically successful at prostitution tends to require youth and either attractiveness or technique. However, prostitution tends to occur in certain cities areas, which remain red light areas for many years. Having a 'patch' of pavement from which to operate in a city may sometimes be difficult to acquire. The regulars may not look kindly on newcomers or there may be more or less organized attempts to secure particular patches for particular women. Nonetheless, newcomers in cities of developed countries are usually able to start prostitution on. Yet another factor is the extent to which seizing the opportunity requires acquiring skills and techniques and how these may be acquired. For example, some credit and cheque card fraud requires equipment and limited skill although much of this equipment is more available than many will realize. Other forms of fraud may require nerve or bravado, but hardly technical expertise. Equally, if the opportunity results in non-legitimate property, the person will need to convert the property into cash or legitimately held property. This is the market for stolen goods. If it results in lots of illegitimately acquired cash, the authorities are increasingly looking out for people depositing suitcases of grubby notes - there is now a market for stolen cash as well, which requires more specialized knowledge. The lack of trust in the legal system and the possibility for people to have influence on it in a non-transparent way are major issues. It is very difficult to get precise information in this area but it is obvious that petty corruption of law enforcement officials is widespread in the poorer countries of South Asia.

While the divergence between informal and hidden activities is the subtlest, it is also imperative to discriminate between other forms of non-measured, non-taxed, and/or non-regulated activities. Several scholars have argued that a distinction can be made between households, informal, underground and illegal activities (ILO 1993; Thomas 1992). In fact, as much of the research in developing countries has revealed there is a continuum, not only between informal and formal activities, but also between household, informal, underground and illegal activities. However, for policy, measurement and analytical purposes it is important to distinguish between them. Initiating with the household sector, the informal sector could be defined as the set of activities, enterprises, income or persons, which satisfy certain characteristics and which are by definition, not part of the household sector, and so on (Sarkar 2006a; 2006b).

Thus the concept of the informal sector has sufficient flexibility and content to provide a suitable framework of analysis for the non-formal sector. In developing countries the debate on the informal sector has been mainly conceptual while in developed countries; it has been methodological, focusing principally on measurement techniques. Moreover, whereas in developing countries there is disagreement over what constitutes the informal sector, but agreement over what to call it, in developed countries there is general agreement over what it is but absolutely no agreement over what to call it. Thus the term informal economy has been used to fundamentally describe income or production, which escapes taxation and/or gross domestic product estimates (Sarkar 2005).

The diversity in definitions of the informal sector is a result of the fact that different units of observation and different criteria of informality have been used. Four main units of observation namely, enterprises, activities, income and people can be identified. Similarly, three main criteria used to determine informality such as registration (mainly for tax and social security purposes), measurement in GDP statistics and regulation; mainly labour regulation could also be recognized. The informal sector has been defined by any combination of the above units and criteria. Thus, for instance, it has been defined as the set of all income that escapes measurement, all enterprises that escape registration, all activities that escape regulation, all income that escapes registration, all people whose work escapes registration, all enterprises that escape regulation, and so forth. Although these concepts are related, they do not necessarily define the same thing. For instance, the 'registration' and 'measurement' criteria are often assumed to delineate the same group of observations (Kaufmann and Kaliberda 1996). However, activities that escape taxation are not necessarily activities that escape measurement of GDP. Moreover, only productive activities are included in GDP, whereas certain activities such as illegally exporting capital or concealing income on capital gains, are considered tax evasion but are not productive activities and therefore are not considered to be unmeasured GDP. Similarly, household activities such as agricultural production for own-consumption should be included in GDP, and would therefore be included in measures of the underground economy based on the measurement criterion, but are not considered part of tax evasion. In the same way, using income or productive activities as units does not necessarily measure the same thing, as certain taxable income is generated by non-productive activities such as capital gains. None of these criteria or units of observation are preferable to the others per se. Different units and criteria may be used depending on the aim of the research. However, it is important to make a conceptual distinction between those unmeasured, and/or unregistered and/or unregulated activities (income, enterprises, or people) whose primary purpose is to meet basic needs, from those, which are deliberately concealed to avoid taxes or regulations. This is particularly important in transition countries where, despite the focus of both policy and academic research on tax evasion, money laundering and corruption, there is increasing evidence of the existence and growth of an informal sector in the 'developing country' sense, as people turn to small-scale income and employment generating activities to generate livelihoods in the absence of sufficiently remunerated formal employment and social security (Anderson 1998; Bernabè 2002). By distinguishing between these two concepts, it is possible to analyze the extent to which these 'informal' income-generating activities provide a social-safety net, and the extent to which they undermine government revenue. This information will be critical for public policy, as it will allow the benefits of an increase in government revenue to be weighed against the risk of an increase in poverty, which would result from an attempt to 'tax' or 'eradicate' some of these income-generating activities without providing any other form of social security. The call to distinguish between the informal and the underground/hidden/unofficial sector or economy is not new. Thomas (1992; 1995) suggests that informal enterprises can be distinguished from irregular ones in that the latter involve the production of legal goods and services, but are illegal in the production or distribution process (because they evade taxes, social security contributions, or infringe other regulations), while the former involve legal goods and services and are 'quasi-legal' in their production or distribution process. They are 'quasi-legal' in that they are undertaken 'not to evade taxes, since their earnings are unlikely to be large enough to attract the tax collector, but because the authorities do not formally encourage such activities' (Thomas 1995).

Similarly, the Organization for Economic Cooperation and Development (OECD), the System of National Accounts (SNA) and the International Labour Office (ILO) suggest that 'activities performed by production units of the informal sector are not necessarily performed with the deliberate intention of evading the payment of taxes or social security contributions, or infringing labour or other legislations or administrative provisions. Accordingly, the concept of informal sector activities is separated from the concept of the hidden or underground economic activities (ILO 1993; OECD 1997; SNA 1993). However, the argument given is for a distinction between informal economic activities, and underground economic activities, irrespective of the type of enterprise in which they take place, whereas the ILO and OECD distinguish between activities that take place in informal enterprises and underground activities. The European Bank for Reconstruction and Development (EBRD) also differentiates between 'informal work undertaken to maintain subsistence levels' and 'informal labour motivated by market incentives such as tax evasion or the business environment' (EBRD 2000). It suggests that informal work has played a crucial role in the provision of employment and earnings for many people during the transition period but that the driving forces have differed across regions, with the poorer countries motivated by the lack of formal opportunities and a need to survive while in the more advanced countries the motivation has been more market-related including tax evasion and avoidance of bureaucratic delays and impediments (EBRD 2000). Finally, it is important to note that the use of motive (or intent) to differentiate between activities is common practice in both law and economics. As Cowell (1990) points out, from a legal perspective the distinction between (illegal) evasion and (legal but questionable) avoidance relies on the judge's perception of the intentions underlying the taxpayer's actions.

The Genesis

The term 'hidden economy' refers to the output from all productive activities, enterprises, income or people, which are unmeasured in gross domestic product and/or untaxed and/or unregulated. Thus the hidden economy comprises a wide range of productive activities from housework to organized crime. These can be grouped into four main categories namely, the household sector, the informal sector, the underground sector and the illegal sector. Add to, the household sector as the set of household productive economic activities that produce goods and services for own consumption within the same household and which are unmeasured and/or untaxed and/or unregulated because they are outside the SNA production boundary. The household sector includes those activities that fall within the general production boundary but not within the SNA production boundary. Some scholars have argued for the inclusion of non-quantitatively significant household activities in the SNA, particularly in developing countries where they may contribute considerably to livelihoods. In developing and transition countries where social services are extremely limited and incomes are very low, household activities are an important source of income and employment for a significant share of the population.

The informal sector is defined as the set of productive economic activities, which fall within the SNA (1993) production boundary and are unmeasured untaxed and/or unregulated, not because of deliberate attempts to evade the payment of taxes or infringe labour or other legislation, but because they are undertaken to meet basic needs. The ILO (1993) and SNA (1993) also argue for the need to distinguish informal sector activities from underground activities on the basis that the former are not necessarily performed with the deliberate intention of avoiding the payment of taxes, social security contributions or complying with certain legal standards, while the latter are. The ILO (1993) defines the informal sector as the set of units engaged in the production of goods or services with the primary objective of generating employment and incomes to the persons concerned. Production units of the informal sector are defined as a subset of household unincorporated enterprises. Household enterprises are units engaged in the production of goods or services which are not constituted as separate legal entities independently of the households or household members that own them, and for which no complete set of accounts are available which would permit a clear distinction of the production activities of the enterprises from the other activities of their owners and the identification of any flows of income and capital between the enterprise and the owners. Indeed, since its conception the informal sector has been of interest in developing countries because it is an important source of income and employment for the poor. It is a survival strategy in countries where there is insufficient formal employment opportunities, where wages may be too low to cover the cost of living and where social safety nets such as unemployment or pension benefits are either lacking or also insufficient to cover the cost of living. As such, it should include all productive activities, which generate income and employment for the poor, and not just those that take place in household enterprises with certain characteristics.

The concepts of underground and illegal production as defined in the SNA (1993) consists of legal productive economic activities that are part of the production boundary and are unmeasured and/or untaxed and or unregulated because they are deliberately concealed from public authorities for the following kind of reasons to avoid the payment of income, value added or other taxes; to avoid the payment of social security contributions; to avoid having to meet certain legal standards such as minimum wages, maximum hours, safety or health standards, etc. to avoid complying with certain administrative procedures such as completing statistical questionnaires or other administrative forms. The illegal sector consists of productive activities that generate goods and services forbidden by law or that are unlawful when carried out by unauthorized producers. There are two types of illegal activities: those that produce goods and services whose sale, distribution or possession is forbidden by law, and activities which are usually legal, but become illegal when carried out by unauthorized producers (SNA 1993). Furthermore illegal activities are included in the SNA production boundary if the transactions involved are based on mutual consent.

Studying the literature on the hidden economy soon makes it evident that there is no uniform conceptual framework covering the subject. A wide variety of terms are used for numerous definitions or less accurate descriptions of the phenomenon. Terms and definitions do not always correspond. Sometimes the same term is used for different concepts and sometimes several terms describe the same concept. Various methods of research have been used to obtain information on different concepts of the hidden economy. The choice of methodology often determines which part of the hidden economy can be covered. This explains why institutions or researchers interested in a specific definition and a specific coverage of the hidden economy tend to use related methodology. Statistical bureaus, which produce national accounts, for example, use discrepancy methods to deduce which part of published national income can be attributed to hidden activities. An interdisciplinary analysis of the causes of the increase of the shadow economy seems to be necessary as the economic factors can partly explain this increase. Micro-sociological and psychological approaches can provide very interesting additional insights in individuals' decision process choosing to work in the underground. In almost all studies, the rise of the tax and social security contribution burdens is one of the most important causes of the growth of the shadow-economy. Since taxes affect labour-leisure choices and stimulate labour supply in the shadow economy, or the untaxed sector of the economy, the distorting effect of this choice is a major concern of economists. The bigger the difference between the total cost of labour in the official economy and the after-tax earnings from work, the greater the incentive to avoid this difference and to work in the shadow economy. Since this difference depends largely on the social security system and the overall tax burden, they are key factors of the existence and the growth of the shadow economy.

Studies trying to measure the shadow economy first face the difficulty of defining it. For instance, one commonly used definition is the shadow economy includes all currently economic activities, which contribute to the officially calculated or observed GNP. However, Smith (1994) defines it as market-based production of goods and services, whether legal or illegal, that escapes detection in the official estimates of GDP. In general, a precise definition seems quite difficult, if not impossible, as the shadow economy develops all the time according to the 'principle of running water' – it adjusts to changes in taxes, to sanctions from the tax authorities and to general moral attitudes etc. (Mogensen *et al.* 1995).

The informal economy poses considerable concerns and threats, which have been documented in some previous research. In relation to the fiscal order, informal activities do not contribute in tax. Should they be taxed (prostitution is currently one of the main problematic areas)? What form of taxation might be appropriate – a tax burden falling on workers (income tax or VAT), a tax burden falling upon those who supply premises for the activity (property taxes), or a tax burden falling upon the more organized and possibly more profitable forms of the activity (company taxes)? Each form of taxation will target different aspects of the informal economic activity and differentially advantage particular forms. It will have the effect of discouraging certain forms and, consequently, seeming to advantage other forms, with allied social effects. High property taxes on brothels, for example, may increase street prostitution, which has unfortunate consequent effects upon others using the streets, including other women and children. The overall tax burden on the different forms of the informal economy can be termed the fiscal order. The fiscal order tends to be set at a national level, with only minor variations between cities or regions. The fiscal order is not the same as the economic order. The economic order concerns the economic effects of the informal economy.

In several countries, certain economic sectors are to some degree reliant on the low wages and lack of regulation characteristic of the informal economy. The agricultural, catering and tourism sectors are the most obvious, with seasonal work being common in the agricultural sector and now resulting in relatively organized forms bringing in seasonal workers from other parts of the country or even other countries, used to lower wages. Catering is increasingly regulated on hygiene grounds, but bar staff are still often casual workers. The economic order is far more differentiated geographically than the fiscal order, with different regions and cities having varying dependence on tourism or agriculture. Therefore, fiscal preferences for taxing also immediately pose problems of whether so doing implies condoning the threats to the social order posed by the same activities, which may breach city-wide policies for control of their symptoms, designed to promote social order (zoning, environmental policies, health and safety, employment law). Not only is there a regulatory question about the balance to be struck between tolerance and control (as well as one about the often conflicting demands between different population groups - for example, in relation to prostitution, residents and curb crawlers), but also one about the criminal justice order and the extent of policing. The preventive approach adopted by regulators to the kinds of work places typical of the informal economy (trying to improve workers' conditions) comes up against the retributive approach of traditional policing (prosecute them for currently illegal activity) and the exclusionary approach of immigration regulation (deportation etc.). From a bottom-up perspective of those seeking employment, however, the informal economy provides opportunities, albeit accompanied by potential threats–the impossibility of complaining about conditions, illegal activities etc. It is important to explore the choices available in the employment market for different kinds of people in the city. These will be linked to the population groups, the raw materials available (tourists etc.), formal employment opportunities (minimum wage thresholds, etc.), general economic conditions and cultural factors. Though the criminal justice order is often a national one though there are often significant regional variations, social order is normally governed by citywide policies for regulation, planning, community safety and economic regeneration. Those most likely to work in the informal economy tend to come from poorer sectors of the community and their employment opportunity horizons are citywide, rather than national. Though informal social control operates at a much more localized level than cities (neighbourhoods, streets, clusters of houses, tenements), yet it is affected by citywide policing cultures. The framework for the exploratory work hence involved consideration of different forms of the informal economy, and their links with the formal and shadow economies. Both threats and opportunities needed to be taken into account, so that it is possible to consider both the control environment and employment structures. The field needs to be dominated by multi-disciplinary, comparative focus.

The essence of an informal economy is to escape from being measured and captured; therefore both definition and methodologies shall be treated only as a way of approximation more than elsewhere in the economy in general. The informal economy is particularly flexible in reacting to changes in the regulatory framework - every new prohibition or regulation widens its scope and size. The informal economy exists in all countries, although those, which are in a process on transition, provide additional space for its existence. From the perspectives of policy decision-making finding measures that would make informal business activity less attractive is crucial. For the shadow sector to contract and, more importantly, for the formal economy to expand, it is essential to have:

- Minimum taxes and regulations, including legal provisions on starting a business, employment regulations, licensing rules etc.;
- Simple and efficient administration;
- Equal and transparent rules (e.g., no tax exemptions, minimal discretionary powers of public officials to interpret and apply legal provisions) and small bureaucracy;
- Clear procedures for settling tax and other business disputes;
- Reasonable fines;
- Property and business security (e.g., law enforcement);
- Stability of the legal system;

- Corporate development (more companies investing in brand name, publicity, etc.);
- Adequate general level of income.

Revisiting Underground Work

The shadow or underground economy represents all economic activity, which is not subject to direct taxation. It arises exclusively from government intervention, i.e. regulation and taxation. Such a policy intervention has side effects. Many empirical studies show that the size of the shadow economy has been most spectacular in the planned socialistic economies with maximum governmental intervention. However, Giles (1999) suggests that the size of the shadow economy has been growing over the past two or three decades in almost all of the countries for which comparative data have been assembled. According to Giles, growth in the underground economy is associated with increases in the actual or perceived tax burden but also with the degree of economic regulation. The view is shared by Thomas (1999) who describes that a growing shadow economy may be an indication of over-taxation and over-regulation. He also suggests that at least some part of the shadow economy may be social security fraud, making unemployment less bad as it looks. Schneider (2000) gives a concerned note by suggesting that under a growing or substantial shadow economy, policy is based on mistaken official indicators. In addition, he suggests that a growing shadow economy attracts workers to work in shadow economy and to work less in the official economy. Giles and Caragata (1999) are concerned that unpaid tax in hidden economy or loopholes allowing abusive avoidance in the existing tax system create a deadweight loss on the economy. These will, in turn, undermine taxation equity by shifting tax burden in the direction of honest, socially responsible individuals and corporations. Accordingly, part of the hidden economy is learned response to changing opportunities and constraints in fiscal policy, but on the other hand, there is a threshold level of underground activity that will sustain.

Theoretical attempts to analyze the shadow economy include Cowell (1989) who asks how far should taxation authorities go in pursuit of the missing income. Johnson et al. (1997) propose that supply of public goods tends to result in increasing returns in private firms, leading to multiple equilibria. Data on transition economies suggests that market-supporting institutions are critical for a successful transition. Friedman *et al.* (2000) suggest that the incentive to go underground to dodge higher tax rates is outweighed by the benefits of remaining official. Dabla-Norris and Feltenstein (2003) apply an inter-temporal general equilibrium model to explore the link between tax rates, access to credit and the size of the underground economy. Simulation results for Pakistan demonstrate that entry into underground economy can have a cyclical nature. Moreover, the share of underground activity will decline over time and sectors gradually move back into legal economy. With low taxes, there is no underground economy, but due to high budget and trade deficit the low tax regime is not sustainable over time. Thus an economy may have to accept some underground activity as part of an otherwise acceptable tax program. Research on the shadow economy focuses on the aspects of driving force in dealing with illicit work is the fact that these illegal and semi-legal activities are undesirable to official institutions. A growing shadow economy can be seen as the reaction of individuals who feel overburdened by the state and who choose the exit option rather than the voice option. If the increase of the shadow economy is caused by a rise in the overall tax and social security burden together with institutional sclerosis then the consecutive flight into the underground may erode the tax and social security bases. The result can be a vicious circle of additional increase of budget deficit or tax rates, further growth of the shadow economy and gradual weakening of the economic and social fundament of collective arrangements. In addition, the effects of the shadow economy on the official one should also be taken into consideration because illicit work can be a source of allocation distortions, since resources and production factors are not used in the most efficient way. On the one hand, a growing shadow economy may attract workers away from the official labour market and create competition for official firms. On the other hand, at least two-thirds of the income earned in the shadow economy is spent in the official economy, thereby having a positive and stimulating effect on the official economy. Furthermore, a prospering shadow economy may cause severe difficulties for politicians because official indicators, e.g. on unemployment, labour force, income, GDP and consumption, are distorted. Policy based on erroneous indicators is likely to be ineffective, or even worse. Therefore, the reciprocal effects between the shadow and the official economy have to be considered when planning measures of economic policy, especially fiscal policy. The shadow economy is foremost a challenge both for economic theory and economic policy as answers have to be found to questions, such as why people work illicitly, why transactions are made in the shadow economy and what are the effects resulting from this behaviour. Currently, there are theoretical approaches in different social sciences, which concentrate on individual aspects of this complex phenomenon. As a coherent, integrative and interdisciplinary approach for the analysis of the causes is missing, however, it is necessary to develop a basic systematic model. Empirical studies have to test the methods for measuring the size and conceptualizing the development of the shadow economy, the theoretically derived causes and consequences of shadow-economic activities have to be verified; reverse effects on the official economy as well as the interaction between the two sectors have to be analyzed. The most difficult task for economic policy analysts is to convey the often not very much appreciated results of their work to politicians and to convince them that the findings are correct and relevant. But our suggestions with regard to specific economic policies are based on an analysis of the relationship between the causes and the effects of the shadow economy.

The general view in the literature is that the shadow economy is a manifestation of some kind of crisis (Weiss 1987) that is of the malfunctioning of an economic system. Excessive taxes, increases in social security contribution burdens and regulations are generally held responsible for the existence as well as for the growing size of the shadow economy. Unemployed are assumed to have an even higher incentive to work in the shadow economy due to their reduced income, plenty of leisure time, and clear disincentives to report their part-time work to the authorities because of an implicit marginal tax rate of nearly cent percent. Another factor receiving more and more attention in the shadow economy literature are moral considerations, e.g. civic attitudes, tax morals etc.

Analyzing the literature on the underground economy, it quickly becomes apparent that the principal focus has been upon estimating its magnitude and how this varies either spatially or socially (Feige 1999). Taking as the starting point the marginality thesis that views underground work to be concentrated amongst marginalized groups and areas most studies have done little more than attempt to either corroborate or falsify this thesis (Williams and Windebank 1998). Although the steadfast popular belief in most western economies is that underground work is concentrated in marginalized populations, namely in deprived inner city localities (Blair and Endres 1994) and poorer peripheral regions (Button 1984), the vast majority of empirical studies show that this is not always the case and that it is frequently concentrated in affluent populations. Turning to why people engage in underground work, the predominant belief is that underground work is conducted under market-like work relations for profit-motivated purposes; it is a form of employment that people use and supply in order to make/save money. Such a market-centered reading pertains both amongst those accepting the tenets of the marginality thesis which views such work to be conducted by marginalized populations (Blair and Endres 1994; Button 1984; Portes 1994) and those who recognize that it is more concentrated in affluent areas. This market-centered reading even predominates when multiple types of underground work are recognized ranging from its organized forms where such work is conducted for formal or informal businesses to its autonomous forms where it is undertaken on a self-employed basis. Consequently, even if underground work is no longer always viewed solely as an exploitative form of low-paid employment sitting at the bottom of a hierarchy of types of formal employment, but as a heterogeneous labour market with a hierarchy of its own, all such work remains widely viewed as market-like and profit-motivated, as displayed by the fact that this sector has been often discussed as a segmented informal labour market. More pertinently, such a market-centered reading also prevails when studies consider the geographical variations in the nature of underground work. This is the case whether underground work is seen to be composed mostly of exploitative organized forms of employment concentrated in deprived areas or a more refined approach is adopted that views residents in affluent areas as engaged in higher-quality underground work of the well-paid self-employed autonomous variety and the populations of deprived areas in lower-quality work of the poorer paid organized kind (Williams and Windebank 1998).

There is a vast verbal literature on the possible determinants and consequences of the shadow economy. Obviously, as a sub-group of the shadow economy, the black economic activities are determined by almost the same determinants and have almost the same implications. In general, there are two major causes distinguished, as put forward by Gutmann (1977) and Tanzi (1980) namely, taxes and regulations. Gutmann (1977) argues that the government and its rules are the major reason for the existence of subterranean economy. According to Tanzi (1980), both of these factors can bring about an underground economy. Tanzi (1980) argues moreover that all kind of taxes causes some degree of underground activities. He also argues that if there were no taxes, there would still be underground economy because of various governmental restrictions on the activities of economic agents. The restrictions are imposed either because of inherently criminal or illegal reasons or for socioeconomic reasons. As these activities still use resources and generate incomes, they inevitably bring into existence the underground economy. Even some restrictions on legal activities cause the underground economy to some degree, in the form of underpayment of taxes or welfare payments, paying wages below the legal minimum etc. Frey *et al.* (1983) argue that factors such as tax morality, the vote of unemployment and the level development of an economy also be included as the consequences of the shadow economy. They argue that an individual feels that the government spends the taxes inadequately or as the unemployment level increases or economic development level is low, then there will be incentive for the individuals to participate in the shadow economy. Tanzi (1980) argues that the existence of a substantial underground economy would have important and, at times, disturbing implications for the measurement of macroeconomic variables, the pursuit of economic policy and the efficient functioning of the economy. For example, employment statistics may overestimate unemployment rates as a result of the underground economy. He also argued that the prices were likely to be lower in the shadow economy because of lower costs due to not paying taxes or not buying licenses to operate businesses; therefore the growth of the actual economy would be higher than the measured growth. Of course, as a result of these biased measurements in the crucial macroeconomic variables, the efficiency of monetary and fiscal policies will be adversely affected. The growth of the shadow economy has been caused by many different factors but the most important and most often cited ones are:

- The rise of the burden of taxes and social security contributions combined with the increase in the density and intensity of regulations in the official economy, especially on labour markets;

- The (forced) reduction of weekly working time, the early retirement and the growing unemployment rate, and
- The long-term decline of civic virtue and loyalty towards public institutions combined with a declining tax morale.

An interdisciplinary analysis of the causes of the increase of the shadow economy seems to be necessary as the economic factors can partly explain this increase. Micro-sociological and psychological approaches can provide very interesting additional insights in individuals' decision process choosing to work in the underground. In almost all studies, the rise of the tax and social security contribution burdens is one of the most important causes of the growth of the shadow-economy. Since taxes affect labour-leisure choices and stimulate labour supply in the shadow economy, or the untaxed sector of the economy, the distorting effect of this choice is a major concern of economists. The bigger the difference between the total cost of labour in the official economy and the after-tax earnings from work, the greater the incentive to avoid this difference and to work in the shadow economy. Since this difference depends largely on the social security system and the overall tax burden, they are key factors of the existence and the growth of the shadow economy.

A macroeconomic analysis of some of the causes for the increase of the shadow economic activities is given by Loayza (1996). He presents a simple macroeconomic endogenous growth model in which production technology depends on congestable public services. The determinants and effects of excessive taxes and regulations on the informal sector are studied; in the model the government lacks the capability to enforce compliance. The estimated coefficient of the independent variable, the direct tax burden (including social security payments), has the biggest influence, followed by the intensity of regulation and the complexity of the tax system.

The increase of the intensity of regulations, often measured by the number of laws and regulations, such as licenses requirements, is another important factor, which limits the freedom of choice for individuals engaged in the official economy. In this context one can think of labour market regulations, trade barriers and labour restrictions for foreigners. The influence of labour regulations on the shadow economy has also been analyzed in various studies. Regulations lead to a substantial increase in labour costs in the official economy. Since most of these costs can be shifted to the employees, these costs provide another incentive to work in the shadow economy, where it is possible to avoid them.

The numerous regulations on the official labour market and the total wage costs also represent driving forces for the shadow economy. Two main factors namely, the effects of the reduction in official working hours and the influence of the unemployment rate on the increase of the shadow economy.

The growth of the shadow economy leads to reduced state revenues, which, in turn, reduces the quality, and quantity of publicly provided goods and services. Ultimately, this can lead to an increase of the tax rates for firms and individuals in the official sector, quite often combined with a deterioration in the quality of the public goods (such as the public infrastructure) and of the administration, with the consequence of even stronger incentives to participate in the shadow economy. In a good number of countries the public sector is facing the challenge to impose substantial reforms of the social security and tax systems in order to prevent the total defeat of the protective welfare state, because the vicious circle of high tax and regulation burdens causes growth of the shadow economy, additional pressure on public finance resulting in higher tax rates, which, in turn, increase the incentives to evade taxes and to escape in the shadow economy and so on.

Research on the shadow economy focuses on three of its major aspects. In economic and social policy, the driving force in dealing with illicit work is the fact that these illegal and semi-legal activities are undesirable to official institutions. A growing shadow economy can be seen as the reaction of individuals who feel overburdened by the state and who choose the exit option rather than the voice option. If the increase of the shadow economy is caused by a rise in the overall tax and social security burden together with institutional sclerosis, then the consecutive flight into the underground may erode the tax and social security bases. The result can be a vicious circle of additional increase of budget deficit or tax rates, further growth of the shadow economy and gradual weakening of the economic and social fundament of collective arrangements.

In addition, the effects of the shadow economy on the official one should also be taken into consideration because illicit work can be a source of allocation distortions, since resources and production factors are not used in the most efficient way. On the one hand, a growing shadow economy may attract workers away from the official labour market and create competition for official firms. On the other hand, at least two-thirds of the income earned in the shadow economy is spent in the official economy, thereby having a positive and stimulating effect on the official economy. Furthermore, a prospering shadow economy may cause severe difficulties for politicians because official indicators, e.g. on unemployment, labour force, income, GDP and consumption are distorted. In social sciences, the shadow economy is foremost a challenge both for economic theory and economic policy as answers have to be found to questions, such as why people work illicitly, why transactions are made in the shadow economy and what are the effects resulting from this behaviour. Currently, there are theoretical approaches in different social sciences, which concentrate on individual aspects of this complex phenomenon. As a coherent, integrative and interdisciplinary approach for the analysis of the causes is missing, however, it is necessary to develop a basic systematic model. The most difficult task for economic policy analysts is to convey the often not very much appreciated results of their work to politicians and to convince them that the findings are correct and relevant.

Instead, reforms of the tax system and the social security system are necessary to improve the dynamics of the official economy and make the official institutions more competitive within the different institutional arrangements at national and international level. The discussion about adequate economic policies is often influenced by various ideological preferences. One can come across contradictory arguments ranging from a forced denial of the phenomenon shadow economy to imaginative exaggerations of its size and impact. The starting point of nearly all controversies is the different estimates of the size of the shadow economy, which makes the assessment of the validity of the findings really hard. Due to this attitude, unfortunately, research efforts are fixated on questions, such as which is the best method to estimate the extent of the shadow economy, how large is the shadow economy labour force and how it changes over time. But the analysis of the causes and consequences of the increase of the shadow economic activities is much more important. Knowledge of these causes and effects on resource allocation, income distribution and stabilization policies as well as on the official economy in general provides the foundations for proposals for policy change on treating illicit work as an economic and social challenge.

Attention is drawn to the shadow economy due to the dramatically rising unemployment and the financing problems of public expenditure, as well as the rising vexation and disappointment with economic and social policies. Studies trying to measure the shadow economy first face the difficulty of defining it. For instance, one commonly used definition is the shadow economy includes all currently economic activities, which contribute to the officially calculated (or observed) GNP. However, Smith (1994) defines it as market-based production of goods and services, whether legal or illegal, that escapes detection in the official estimates of GDP. As these definitions leave open a lot of questions, Table 1 may be helpful for developing a better feeling for what could be a reasonable consensus definition of the legal and illegal underground or shadow economy.

There is a widespread feeling that a substantial and increasing share of activities takes place outside the formal economy. This holds, in particular, for developing and transition but also for high-income economies. Such activities are unrecorded by the system of national income accounting, which has become the accepted standard in all countries of the world. The existence and increase of an underground economy gives rise to three major sets of concerns. The economic and social conditions of individuals, household and countries are evaluated in a biased way if one relies on the official statistics. Thus, the official number of unemployed persons may hide that an (unknown) share of them actually work and receive wage income. As a consequence, the macro economic policies are likely to be too expansionary and social policy too excessive. A second concern is the loss of tax revenue as underground activities escape taxation. A third concern interprets the underground economy as an indicator of an unhealthy state between citizens and government. The taxpayers are dissatisfied with what public services they get for their contributions and seek to re-stress the balance by evading to the underground economy. It is feared that such reaction makes government unable to finance the public goods necessary for an economy and society. In contrast, opponents of government welcome such a development.

The phenomenon is known, and has been discussed in the literature, under many different names such as informal, unofficial, irregular, parallel second underground, subterranean, hidden, invisible, unrecorded and shadow economy or moonlighting. In several languages the term most often used is black economy. No single definition exists but it depends on the purpose. The most precise and predominantly used definition seeks to relate the underground economy to officially measured national income. It comprises all presently not recorded productive (i.e. value-adding) activities, which should be in the national product (GNP). This definition allows to compare and to add the underground economy to GNP. This definition excludes two major activities namely, production that by convention is not part of GNP, in particular private household activities and tax evasion is not value adding but redistribution and is therefore not included as such in the above definition (e.g. when taxes on interest payments are evaded). However, in general, no taxes are paid on underground activities (such as moonlighting for house building), which are value-adding. Thus, underground activities and tax evasion are related but certainly not identical.

The underground economy should neither be identified with illegality. Some activities are perfectly legal but are not subject to taxes (e.g. because of their small size), and therefore escape measurement in official statistics. Other activities are legal as such, but taxes are evaded. Finally, on illegal activities (such as drug production and distribution) no taxes are paid. Broader definitions of the informal and shadow economy, depending on their purpose, include private household production and redistribution activities.

The major emphasis of economists has been to measure the size of the shadow economy relative to official GNP; its size compared to other countries and its development over time. Three general sets of measurement approaches may be distinguished.

An obvious way to analyze the shadow economy is to undertake surveys among (supposed) suppliers and demanders of such services. This method allows to gather a detailed picture of the structure of this sector. However, because a substantial part of these activities is illegal, the interviewees may not be prepared to disclose their involvement. Somewhat surprisingly, research has shown this is no serious problem. Typically, men are more involved than women, the young more than the old, people without work more than employed ones, and the most prominent sectors are construction and all kinds of services. In contrast, where substantial capital assets (which are visible) are needed, less underground activity is observed.

A second direct approach is based on auditing of tax returns undertaken by tax collection and social security administrations. A sample of taxpayers is scrutinized in depth and under threats of sanctions for failing collaboration. This approach provides detailed information on the strongest evaders, in particular the self-employed who have better opportunities for concealment. Capital income lends also easier to evasion than labour income. Tax audits have proved unable to reveal all tax evasion, and are limited to taxable activities. As a large part of tax evasion is redistribution, that part is not relevant to the narrow definition of the underground economy. A disadvantage of the two direct methods (surveys and tax auditing) is that they lead only to point estimates. Moreover, it is unlikely that they capture all shadow activities, so they can be seen as providing lower bound estimates. They are unable (at least at present) to provide estimates of the development and growth of the shadow economy over a long period of time. They have, however at least one considerable advantage - they can provide detailed information about shadow economy activities and the structure and composition of those who work in the shadow economy.

The shadow economy is reflected in discrepancies showing in various markets. Persons working in the unofficial sector are able to spend more than their officially recorded income. The discrepancy between the two may be observed at the level of individual households as well as in the aggregate national accounts. This approach is questionable as this expenditure income discrepancy may either be due to measurement errors (which is indeed often the case) or to reasons unrelated with the underground economy (e.g. the use of credits or reductions in wealth). Another discrepancy may be observable in the labour market. A decline in official participation rates, or a low participation rate compared to other countries, may be an indication of unofficial work. But again, the discrepancy may be related to other factors. Moreover, this approach is unable to isolate those persons who are at the same time active in the official and the unofficial economy (which is often the case). A third discrepancy may be visible in the monetary market. The dominant approach starts from the assumption that underground transactions are paid in cash in order to make detection more unlikely. The size of the underground economy is reflected in the amount of cash used in a country beyond that used for official transactions. This approach is elegant and easily applicable because the amount of currency is well documented.

Add to the model approach focuses on the causes and effects of the underground economy. By constructing a model, it seeks to identify the unobserved sector in-between. Three sets of factors are taken to be the main motivators of whether to engage in the unofficial economy: incentives to exit the official economy are the burden of taxation and of social security contributions, as well as government regulations. The latter hinder or even prohibit activities in the official economy (e.g. because of a lack in work permit, especially for foreigners), which provides an incentive to undertake them unofficially. This holds, of course, also for illegal activities such as the production and distribution of drugs. An important reason to exit the official sector is the restrictions imposed on working time. Low work hours, long holidays, early retirement, and above all unemployment are important reasons for moonlighting. Disincentives to be active in the underground economy are the expected punishment of doing so. It is composed of the probability to be caught and the size of punishment. For persons outside the established society (for example for illegal immigrants), or being self-employed, expected punishment is lower than for other persons, and therefore a higher rate of participation in the underground sector is likely. Another disincentive to be active in the underground economy is the moral costs entailed. A good citizen has moral qualms to undertake a forbidden activity. These moral costs are closely related to tax morale, which motivates citizens to pay their dues to the state. The effects of the underground economy are reflected in the traces visible in the labour, money and product markets discussed above. A specific econometric technique called unobservable variables allows to estimate the size of the underground economy lying between the causes and effects. This approach is the most comprehensive and builds on a well-structured behavioral model but it requires a large amount of data. As these are often not available (in particular not for developing and transition economies) this approach is not generally applicable. The estimation technique moreover tends not to be statistically robust.

Tackling in Underprivileged

Men and women work in both official-unofficial sectors. However, there is a gender division of labour across them, and it is mainly women's time that is stretched between work in the unpaid economy and the two sectors of the paid economy. When a person takes a job, some quantity of that person's time moves between the two economies, from the unpaid economy to the paid economy. However, although the amount of time gained for the paid economy is usually specified in the labour contract, how much time is lost from the unpaid sector depends on what that person was previously doing. For this reason, women tend to make employment decisions on a different basis from men. In general, men's decisions about employment roughly conform to economic theory's representation of the issue, in which wages are simply payment for loss of leisure time. For many women, the situation is more complicated. The net financial gain to a woman of employment is often less than her wage, since she may have to spend some of her earnings on providing substitutes for her own unpaid caring labor. Correspondingly, if she does find substitutes for most of her previous work, the net effect on her leisure time of taking employment will be smaller than on a man's. This explains the wellknown result that the wage elasticity of women's labour supplies is generally greater than that of men's. For the wage rate is crucial to a woman with caring responsibilities in deciding how many hours of paid work to take on or even whether she should take a job at all, since the loss of her caring work from the unpaid economy creates a real cost that has to be paid.

There is a bustling and shadowy world where jobs, services, and business transactions are conducted by word of mouth and paid for in cash to avoid scrutiny by government officials. It is called the 'underground economy', which is as old as government itself. It springs from human nature that makes man choose between given alternatives. Facing the agents of government and their exactions, man will weigh the alternatives and may choose to go 'underground'. Man has again become a subject under the watchful eye of government. Guided by ancient notions and prejudices he depends on his rulers for mandates and directives. When government intervention fails to satisfy him, or even works evil, he is slow to relinquish his notions and prejudices. He may cling to them with tenacity and perseverance, but may seek to avoid the ill effects through circumvention, evasion, and escape. He may find his way to the 'black market', where economic transactions take place in violation of price control and ration laws. Or he may descend to the underground where political edicts are ignored and exactions avoided through word-of- mouth dealings and cash transactions. The underground economy must be distinguished clearly and unmistakably from the criminal activities of the underworld. Government officials and agents are ever eager to lump both together, the criminals and their organization with the producers in the underground. Both groups are knowingly violating laws and regulations and defying political authority. But they differ radically in the role they play in society. The underworld comprises criminals who are committing acts of bribery, fraud, and racketeering, and willfully inflicting wrongs on society. The underground economy involves otherwise law-abiding citizens who are seeking refuge from the wrongs inflicted on them by government. They are employers and employees who are rendering valuable services without a license or inspection sticker, or failing to report their productive activities to the political authorities.

Analyzing literature on the underground economy, it quickly becomes apparent that the principal focus has been upon estimating its magnitude and how this varies either spatially or socially (Feige 1999; Leonard 1998; Renooy 1990; Thomas 1992; Williams and Windebank 2001a, 2001b). Taking as the starting point the 'marginality thesis' that views underground work to be concentrated amongst marginalized groups and areas (Castells and Portes 1989; De Soto 1989), most studies have done little more than attempt to either corroborate or falsify this thesis (Williams and Windebank 1998). Although the steadfast popular belief in most western economies is that underground work is concentrated in marginalized populations, namely in deprived inner city localities (Blair and Endres 1994) and poorer peripheral regions (Button 1984), the vast majority of empirical studies show that this is not always the case and that it is frequently concentrated in affluent populations (Renooy 1990; Williams and Windebank, 1998). Turning to why people engage in underground work, the predominant belief is that underground work is conducted under market-like work relations for profit-motivated purposes; it is a form of employment that people use and supply in order to make/save money. Such a market-centered reading pertains both amongst those accepting the tenets of the 'marginality thesis' which views such work to be conducted by marginalized populations (Blair and Endres 1994; Button 1984; Castells and Portes, 1989; Portes, 1994) and those who recognize that it is more concentrated in affluent areas (Jensen *et al.*, 1995; Pahl 1984; Renooy 1990; Williams and Windebank 1998). This market-centered reading even predominates when multiple types of underground work are recognized ranging from its 'organized' forms where such work is conducted for formal or informal businesses to its 'autonomous' forms where it is undertaken on a self-employed basis (Jensen *et al.* 1995; Leonard 1994, 1998; MacDonald 1994; Pahl 1984; Renooy 1990; Williams and Windebank 1998). Consequently, even if underground work is no longer always viewed solely as an exploitative form of low-paid employment sitting at the bottom of a hierarchy of types of formal employment, but as a heterogeneous labour market with a hierarchy of its own, all such work remains widely viewed as market-like and profit-motivated, as displayed by the fact that this sector has been often discussed as a 'segmented informal labour market' (Williams and Windebank 1998). More pertinently, such a market-centered reading also prevails when studies consider the geographical variations in the nature of underground work. This is the case whether underground work is seen to be composed mostly of exploitative organized forms of employment concentrated in deprived areas or a more refined approach is adopted that views residents in affluent areas as engaged in higher-quality underground work of the well paid self-employed autonomous variety and the populations of deprived areas in lower-quality work of the poorer paid organized kind (Pahl 1984; Renooy 1990; Williams and Windebank 1998).

In consequence, and based on this widespread view that such work is conducted for unadulterated economic reasons, the near universal pubic policy response has been to seek to ensure that the expected cost of being caught and punished is greater than the economic benefit of participating in such activity. To do this, stringent regulations and punitive measures have been adopted so as to change the cost-benefit calculation of participants and thus dissuade participation in underground work.

As long as people can profit by not declaring their work, it will be impossible entirely to eradicate the hidden economy. Therefore, the most effective way of tackling the problem is significantly to improve the likelihood of detecting and penalizing offenders. Grabiner (2000) thus recommended the following measures to dissuade engagement in underground work:

- To provide incentives to join the legitimate economy, a confidential phone line should be launched to enable advice to be given on how people can put their affairs in order;
- To prevent identity fraud, procedures should be tightened for issuing National Insurance numbers and better controls introduced on the issue and use of birth certificates, to prevent their use as proof of identity by third parties;
- To improve the rate of detection and the effectiveness of punishment, it recommended that the Government should: consider ways to use information from private sector sources as a cross-check on the details people provide to departments; give investigators the power to make routine 'reverse searches' of the telephone directory to find names and addresses of people who advertise businesses giving only a telephone number; build on the inter-departmental work already begun by setting up a specific government function to detect and investigate informal businesses, and; agree common guidelines for staff about what data sharing is legally permissible and how it should be carried out in practice. In particular, it advocated a central point of contact to co-ordinate the exercise and monitors its effectiveness;
- To increase punishment through: requiring people suspected of working while claiming that they are unemployed to attend the Jobcentre more frequently, and at unpredictable times, as a condition of receiving their benefit; make more use of a warning procedure such as to employers reasonably suspected of colluding with fraudulent benefit claims, that if they do not clean up their act, they will expose themselves to more detailed investigation and possible prosecution; if other measures fail to work, consider the option of punishing persistent fraudsters by removing, or heavily reducing, their right to benefit for a specific period; and carry out research into the sentences imposed for benefit fraud and particularly into variation in the sentencing of persistent offenders. To resolve the inequities in prosecution rates between 'ghosts' and those 'working whilst claiming', meanwhile, it advocated the introduction of a new statutory offence of fraudulently evading income tax to be tried in the magistrates' court;

- To use publicity as a deterrent, the incentives available to people to take formal jobs and the costs of being informal should be advertised, and it also advocated the use of advertising as a tool for changing attitudes regarding the social acceptability of underground work. It is clear therefore that the overarching policy thrust suggested is one of increasing both the probability of detection and the punishments for those caught so as to deter people from engaging in such work.

Conclusion

The informality could exacerbate poverty, either directly or indirectly, through increasing inequality in the access to services and opportunities, increased vulnerability, and human abuse. It is an important coping mechanism when formal systems have collapsed or are under immense stress. Informality comes at a cost – the inability to use government and some private sector services available to firms that fully comply with regulations. Many transition economies have experienced surging share of entrepreneurial activity in the informal sector. People recognize that informality is harmful to their standards of living and to the distribution of income in general, but in most cases they have no choice because there are no viable formal alternatives. In some cases, however, there is a perception that through informal means it may be possible to get better deals by playing on connections or just by appealing directly for the understanding of the service provider. Indeed, in countries where formal cost recovery for services has been imposed to try and reduce under-the-table payments, it is not clear that the poor have been made better off. Regardless of this, informal payments are very important as a coping mechanism for the poor. In the poorer South Asian countries informality as a coping mechanism is prevalent due to a number of very straightforward factors. The lack of fiscal capacity of governments, which has many consequences i.e., social benefits are too low to survive on; in some cases they are lower than the poverty line. Health and education are insufficiently provided and staff employed in the social services is underpaid, which stimulates informal payments. Second, the lack of capacity of state institutions, where capability to target benefits is low in part because of the large-scale informal sector but also because the capacity for outreach and support is limited. Consequently, it is very difficult for the state to target subsidies for the poor and to introduce users' fees for the wealthy. Moreover, nongovernmental organizations and civil society in the region are also weak and not sufficiently organized to carry out the sort of support and outreach. Third, the lack of formal organizations to support trade and economic activity i.e., private sector activities are limited while the poor are numerous. This is both a cause and a consequence of poverty. Regional imbalances have increased dramatically with the transition to a market economy, mostly because the substantial subsidies supporting poor and isolated regions were sharply reduced.

Add to, the shadow economy can be regarded as part of an evolutionary process, making economic and societal development increasingly dynamic. On the one hand, the societal pressure on deregulation and tax reduction is increased and, on the other hand, new innovative forms of living together and economizing outside the restrictions are fashioned which could be regarded as a test for the official sector. The growth of the shadow economy over the last decades and its effect on the official economy both in general perception and scholarly research has prevailingly been evaluated as a negative development which should be counteracted. It has also been noticed that many developing and transition economies would break down or function at a much lower level of production and welfare if the shadow economy did not exist. Estimates of the shadow economy can also be based on the discrepancy between income declared for tax purposes and that measured by selective checks. Fiscal auditing programs have been particularly effective in this regard. Designed to measure the amount of undeclared taxable income, they have been used to calculate the shadow economy in several countries. The analysis of the effects of a growing shadow economy is quite difficult and comprehensive empirical evidence is not available. Most studies focus on the influence on allocation of resources and the loss of revenue for the state. But the impact on the official institutions, norms and rules is even more important. The shadow economy can be seen as an indicator of a serious deficit of legitimacy of the present social order and the existing rules of official economic activities. Failing economic policy was confirmed as the most important cause for the burly increase in shadow-economic activities. Not only the rising tax burden and regulation density are important factors for the migration into the hidden economy, but also the defensive labour-market policy directed at a re-distribution of working hours. In addition, the lack of clear and stable institutions in transition countries is a driving force of informal economic activities. The tax deficit and evasion of social security contributions is the main arguments, with which the state wishes to substantiate its fight against the shadow economy. In combination with a reduced tax moral and less loyalty to the government, the potential of these factors will be exploited increasingly, which leads to the causes of the phenomenon call for to be addressed scientifically.

References

Anderson, J. H. (1998), *The Size, Origins, and Character of Mongolia's Informal Sector During Transition*. World Bank, Washington, DC.

Bernabè, S. (2002), *A Profile of the Labour Market in Georgia*. ILO/UNDP.

Blair, J.P. and Endres, C.R. (1994), Hidden Economic Development Assets. *Economic Development Quarterly*, 8(3): 286-291.

Button, K. (1984), Regional Variations in the Irregular Economy: A Study of Possible Trends. *Regional Studies*, 18: 385-392.

Castells, M. and Portes, A. (1989), World Underneath: the Origins, Dynamics and Effects of the Informal Economy. In A. Portes, M. Castells and L.A. Benton (eds.). *The Informal Economy: Studies in Advanced and Less Developing Countries*. John Hopkins University Press, Baltimore.

Cowell, F.A. (1989), Honesty is Sometimes a Best Policy. *European Economic Review*, 33: 605-617.

Cowell, F. A. (1990), *Cheating the Government: The Economics of Evasion*. Massachusetts MIT Press, Cambridge.

Dabla-Norris, E. and Feltenstein, A. (2003), *An Analysis of the Underground Economy and Its Macroeconomic Consequences*. IMF Working Paper, 23/03.

De Soto, H. (1989), *The Other Path*. Harper and Row, London.

EBRD (2000), *Transition Report*. European Bank for Reconstruction and Development, London.

Fagan, P.G. (1997), The Black Economy in Ireland. *Irish Banking Review,* Summer: 19-25.

Feige, E.L. (1999), Underground Economies in Transition: Non-compliance and Institutional Change. In E.L. Feige and K. Ott (eds.). *Underground Economies in Transition: Unrecorded Activity, Tax Evasion, Corruption and Organized Crime*. Ashgate, Aldershot.

Frey, S.B. and Weck, H. (1983), Estimating thc Shadow Economy: A Naive Approach. *Oxford Economic Papers*, 41: 23-44.

Friedman, E et al. (1999), *Dodging the Grabbing Hand: The Determinants of Unofficial Activity in 69 Countries*. World Bank Discussion Paper, Washington, D.C.

Giles, D. E. A. (1999), Measuring the Hidden Economy: Implications for Econometric Modeling. *The Economic Journal*, 109: F370-F380.

Giles, D.E. A. and Caragara, P. J. (1999), *The Learning Path of the Hidden Economy*. Econometrics Working Papers 9904, Department of Economics, University of Victoria.

Grabiner, L. (2000), *The Informal Economy*. HM Treasury, London.

Gutmann, P.M. (1977), The Subterranean Economy. *Financial Analysts Journal*, 33: 26-28.

ILO (1993), *Resolution Concerning Statistics of Employment in the Informal Sector*. Geneva.

Jensen, L., Cornwell, G.T. and Findeis, J.L. (1995), Informal Work in Non-metropolitan Pennsylvania. *Rural Sociology*, 60(1): 91-107.

Johnson, S., and Kaufman, D., Shleifer A., Goldman, M. I., and Weitzman, M. L. (1997), The Unofficial Economy in Transition. *Brookings Papers on Economic Activity*, (2): 159-239.

Kaufmann, D. and Kaliberda, A. (1996), *An Unofficial Analysis of Economies in Transition: An Empirical Framework and Lessons for Policy*. Harvard Institute for International Development, Cambridge.

Leonard, M. (1998), *Invisible Work, Invisible Workers: the Informal Economy in Europe and the US*. Macmillan, London.

Loayza, Norman V. (1996), The Economics of the Informal Sector: A Simple Model and Some Empirical Evidence from Latin America. *Carnegie-Rochester Conference Series on Public Policy*, 45: 129-162.

MacDonald, R. (1994), Fiddly Jobs, Underground Working and the Something for Nothing Society. *Work, Employment and Society*, 8(4): 507-530.

Mogensen, G.V. *et al.* (1995), *The Shadow Economy in Denmark 1994: Measurement and Results*. Study No. 3, The Rockwell Foundation Research Unit, Copenhagen.

OECD (1997), *Framework for the Measurement of Unrecorded Economic Activities in Transition Economies*. OECD, Paris.

Pahl, R.E. (1984), *Divisions of Labour*. Blackwell, Oxford.

Portes, A. (1994), The Informal Economy and Its Paradoxes. In N.J. Smelser and R. Swedberg (eds.). *The Handbook of Economic Sociology*. Princeton University Press, Princeton, NJ.

Renooy, P.H. (1990), *The Informal Economy: Meaning, Measurement and Social Significance*. Netherlands Geographical Studies, Amsterdam.

Sarkar, S. (2005), The Conceptual and Theoretical Framework of Informal Economy: A Review of Literature in Developed and Developing Countries. *Journal of Social and Economic Policy,* 2(2): 187-205.

Sarkar, S. (2006a), *Theorising Informal Economy*. Abhijeet Publications, Delhi.

Sarkar, S. (2006b), *Women Struggle for Sustainability*. Serials Publications, New Delhi.

Schneider, F. (2000), *The Increase of the Size of the Shadow Economy*. CESIfo Working Paper 306.

Smith, P. (1994), Assessing the Size of the Underground Economy: The Canadian Statistical Perspectives. *Canadian Economic Observer,* Catalogue No. 11-010, 3.16-33 at 3.18.

Smith, P. M. (1997), Assessing the Size of the Underground Economy: The Statistics Canada Perspective. In Lippert, Owen and Michael Walker (eds). *The Underground Economy: Global Evidences of Its Size and Impact*. Fraser Institute, Vancouver, B.C.

Smith, S. (1986), *Britain's Shadow Economy*. Clarendon Press, Oxford.

System of National Accounts (1993), *System of National Accounts 1993.* World Bank, Washington, DC.

Tanzi, V. (1980), The Underground Economy in the United States: Estimates and Implications. *Banca Nazionale Del Iavaro Quarterly Review*, 33: 427-453.

Thomas, J.J. (1992), *Informal Economic Activity*. Harvester Wheatsheaf, Hemel Hempstead.

Thomas, J.J. (1995), *Surviving in the City: The Urban Informal Sector in Latin America*. Pluto Press, East Haven: CT.

Thomas, J. (1999), Quantifying the Black Economy: Measurement without Theory yet Again? *The Economic Journal*, 109: F381-F389.

Weiss, L. (1987), Explaining the Underground Economy. *British Journal of Sociology*, 38: 216-234.

Williams, C.C. and Windebank, J. (1998), *Informal Employment in the Advanced Economies: Implications for Work and Welfare*. Routledge, London.

Williams, C.C. and Windebank, J. (2001a), Beyond Profit-motivated Exchange: Some Lessons from the Study of Paid Informal Work. *European Urban and Regional Studies,* 8(1): 49-61.

Williams, C.C. and Windebank, J. (2001b), Reconceptualising Paid Informal Exchange: Some Lessons from English Cities. *Environment and Planning,* 33(1): 121-140.

5

Farmers' Income and its Determinants

Acheampong, I. K. *University of Cape Coast*
Anoff, J. *University of Cape Coast*

Introduction

The paper examines the distribution of income accruing from farming activities and its determinants in the Assin Foso district in the Central region of Ghana in order to unravel the determinants of incomes accruing to farmers to unearth the mechanisms through which incomes of farmers can be improved to minimize poverty afflicting the poor farmers. Even though attempts continue to be made to reduce poverty and inequality in Ghana, the evidence shows that poverty is pervasive and endemic in Ghana (Ghana Statistical Service 2000).

Standard Surveys (GLSS 1-4) show that over 30% the population is poor, with poverty being predominant in the rural areas. In the rural sector poverty is rife among rural farmers especially food crop farmers (Ghana Statistical Service 1995a, 1995b, 2000). Even though Ghana's Poverty Reduction Strategy (Republic of Ghana 2003) intends to focus on rural development and agricultural modernization in order to raise agricultural productivity and incomes, there is a dearth of studies that attempt to track the variations in the distribution and the determinants of farm incomes in the various districts in Ghana. In order to increase the incomes of farmers in rural communities there is the need to examine the distribution of income accruing from farming activities and also to track down the factors influencing farmers' income in the various districts. The identification of the determinants of farmers' income across the various districts in Ghana will aid policy in terms of locality specific policy interventions that will be needed to accelerate poverty reduction in rural agricultural communities. In this regard, it is increasingly important to undertake studies on the distribution and determinants of farm income in order to unearth the mechanisms through which incomes of farmers can be improved to minimize poverty afflicting the poor farmers in Ghana. This study makes a modest contribution in that regard by examining the distribution and determinants of farmers income in Assin Foso District in the Central Region of Ghana. There is no doubt that the understanding of the distribution and determinants of rural income can be a powerful guide in designing effective interventions to accelerate rural income growth in order to reduce the incidence of poverty in the future.

The rest of the paper is outlined as follows. The next section focuses on the discussion on theoretical issues relating to the pattern of income distribution and a review of the empirical literature. This is followed by a discussion on the methodology adopted for the study and profile of the respondents, then follows the presentation of the results of the study and its implications.

Theoretical Issues on the Pattern of Income Distribution

Economists have attempted to explain the pattern of income distribution. Theoretically, three paradigms attempt to explain income distribution in terms of exploitation, productivity and appropriation (Samuels and Kelsey 1991). The classical economists explained inequality in terms of separate social classes owing particular factors of production, notably landlords and workers. Modern distribution theory, as postulated by Marshall (1920), is based on the marginal productivity of productive factors. Factor prices and employment levels therefore determine incomes. The Appropriation theory, on the other hand, attempts to explain income distribution in terms of the actual factors that are actually at work such as policy effects, land ownership and employment.

Traditionally, the analysis of income distribution has been looked at from the functional distribution of income. This perspective looks at income inequality from the viewpoint of factors of production, especially labour and capital. Individuals are classified into workers and capitalists, with the vulnerable group being workers. Since this approach to the analysis of income distribution and equity issues does not reflect much on how the household or the farmer is worse off, most researchers tend to look at income inequality from the perspective of interpersonal distribution of income or consumption. Owing to differences in factor ownership and imperfections in factor pricing, incomes tend not to be equitably distributed.

In conclusion, we observe that it is the interplay of the various strands of arguments advanced by the three schools of thought that tend to influence the distribution of income in a farming setting in a rural community like that of ours.

Empirical Literature Review

There is scant literature on the distribution and determinants of farm income in the rural setting. We review the few studies that we were able to lay hands on including those connected with the issue of household income determination.

Gardner (1969) examines the determinants of farm family income in the United States agriculture using cross-sectional regression analysis from 1949 to 1959. He finds that labour market adjustments, increasing capital labour ratio, average level of schooling, research and extension account for income inequality in the United States.

Jones *et al.* (1995) analyse various aspects of farming in Rondonia, in the United States of America. The aspect that is of particular relevance to this study is that on determinants of farm income. They find possible evidence of overuse of land and under-investment or de-capitalization of farms over time, overpopulation, and a trade-off between children and capital accumulation.

Sanchez (2005) examines, among other things, the distribution and the factors influencing household income. They show that approximately 42% of total income is derived from agricultural production and 11% from agricultural wages. In terms of the distribution of income for the highest quartile, 32% of income comes from non-agricultural wage employment. On the other hand, the share of income for the lowest quartile is heavily dependent upon agriculture, which accounts for 55% of the earnings followed by 15% of unearned sources, 13% from non-agricultural self-employment and 8% from non-agricultural wage income. Using ordinary least squares regression he finds agricultural income, education, distance from the market and having additional adult member in the household to be the major determinants of household income.

Meng and Wu (1998) examine income determination and regional income differential in rural China using ordinary least squares. They find, among other things, that education, average market experience, ratio of female labour over total household labour have positive and significant impact on rural household income.

Tschirley and Weber (1994) use household survey data from northern rural Mozambique to examine the factors associated with higher incomes and improved rural household food security for small farm holders. In relation to the focus of this study household incomes were found to be low in terms of Sub-Saharan African's standards. However, incomes within each district were found to be strongly and positively associated with land holdings. They maintained that land holdings would continue to be key determinants of household income and consumption in the foreseeable future.

Benin *et al.* (2004) examines the economic determinants of cereal crop diversity on farms in the Ethiopian highlands. We throw light on the relevant segments of the study that are relevant for this study. They find that farm physical features and household characteristics such as wealth and labour stocks have large and significant effects on both the diversity among and within cereal crops, varying among crops. Younger households and education positively influence crop diversity.

Ministry of Agriculture (1992) has examined the determinants of household income and consumption in Rural Nampula Province in Mozambique using a survey of 343 smallholders. In relation to the focus of this study they find that incomes are low and variable in each district, and highly correlated with land holdings. The evidence also indicates clearly that many households are constrained in their access to land.

Walker *et al.* (2004), have examined the determinants of rural income, poverty, and perceived well being in Mozambique in 2001-2002. They estimate the mean household annual income to be $280 per household and $65 per capita during 2001-2002 and this in their estimation is low. They find that household asset base plays an important role in household income. Both land area owned and number of fields is positively associated with income. Irrigation is also strongly correlates with income however; agricultural extension has no measurable impact on either net crop income or livestock sales.

The empirical literature review shows that incomes of farmers are low and tend to fall below Sub Saharan Africans standard. Furthermore, the relevant factors that explain farmers' income are capital, labour utilization, land, education and irrigation.

Methodology

This segment throws light on the Gini coefficient, which is used as a measure of inequality of income and describes the econometric model used to track the parameters of farm income, data collection procedures and estimation technique used for estimating the parameters of the farm income econometric model.

The Gini Coefficient

There are various measures of inequality in the literature. However, in this paper we will employ the Gini Coefficient in the analysis of income distribution or inequality. The ramifications of the Gini Coefficient are explained below.

The Lorenz Curve

The Lorenz Curve shows the relationship between the cumulative percentage of income received by the cumulative percentage of households or recipients. A Lorenz curve is constructed by plotting the graph of these data with the cumulative percentage of the recipients (population), P%, on the horizontal axis and the cumulative percentage of income (Y), Y%, on the vertical axis. The Lorenz curve also helps to determine, deciles or quintile distribution of income. A Lorenz curve is depicted in Figure 1 showing the percentage of total income received by any given cumulative percentage of the population.

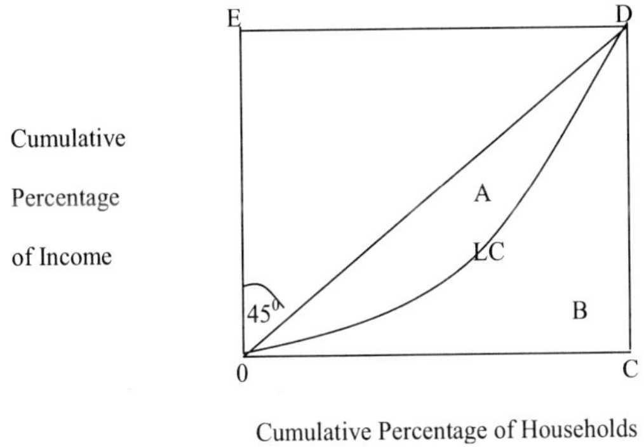

Figure 1: The Lorenz Curve

From Figure 1 the area denoted A, between the LC and the 45 degree line, relative to the entire area of the right angled triangle, A+B, is used to measure the degree of inequality. The statistic used to measure inequality is the Gini coefficient and given the Lorenz curve, it can be defined as follows:

$G = A/(A+B)$ where $0 \leq G \leq 1$

Where
G is the Gini coefficient
A is the area between the Lorenz curve and the diagonal
A+B is the total area under the diagonal.

The shape of the Lorenz curve throws light on the degree of income inequality in a given country or area. For instance, should the Lorenz curve be the 45 degrees line, then it will indicate perfect equality or complete egalitarianism, whereby say 10% of the population receives 10% of the total income or whereby say 30% of the population receives 30% of the total income, or say 75% of the population receives 75% of the income, or 92% of the population receives 92% of the income and so on.

The actual Lorenz curve of a country or an area, however tends to correspond more closely to the bulging curve shown in figure 1 as LC which reflects the actual pattern of a country's income distribution. It shows that income is not distributed equally across the population, that is, the poorest 40% of the population, say, might be receiving only about10% of the income.

The closer the LC curve is to the 45 degree line the, the greater the degree of income equality and the more the LC curve gets away from the 45 degrees line, the greater the degree of income inequality.

The Gini Coefficient is a statistic that measures the relative inequality in the distribution of income. The computation of the Gini Coefficient is based on the cumulative percentages of households and the corresponding percentages of the total income accruing to them. It must be emphasized that the Gini

Coefficient is not able to show whether the income level is high or low. However, changes in income thresholds could either induce a decrease or increase in the Gini coefficient (Sadoulet and Janvry 1995:20-23)

The Gini coefficient (G) is defined statistically as follows:

$$G = 1 - \sum_{i=0}^{n-1} (F_{i+1} - F_i)(H_{i+1} + H_i)$$

Where

n = number of households.

F_i = Cumulative population shares corresponding to household, and

H_i = Cumulative expenditure shares corresponding to household

The Gini Coefficient ranges from zero (when incomes are equal) to one (when incomes are extremely unequal). Thus, each inequality measure is scaled to lie between zero (prefect equality) and one (perfect inequality). The Gini coefficient is more sensitive to measuring changes in the middle range of an expenditure distribution (Tsakloglou 1993).

Theoretically, the Gini coefficient ranges between 0 (perfect equality) and 1 (absolute inequality). The Gini Coefficient may be seen to range from zero (0) when incomes are equal and to one (1) when inequality is worse. As a rule of thumb a Gini coefficient of 0.4 and less is said to reflect low inequality in income distribution. While that of the order greater than 0.5 depicts a high inequality in income distribution (Sadoulet and Janvry 1995:20-23).

Modelling Determinants of Farm Income

The empirical model for the study which is specified in double log form after the results of the Pearson bivariate correlation matrix and various diagnostic testing is follows:

$$LNY = \beta_0 + \beta_1 LNC + \beta_2 LNL + \beta_3 LNI + \beta_4 LNA + U \quad \text{.............} [1]$$

The apriori expected sign are as follows:

$$\beta_0 > 0 \, or < 0; \; \beta_1 > 0, \beta_2 > 0, \beta_3 > 0, \beta_4 > 0$$

Where,

LN = Natural log (that is log to base e, where e = 2.718)

Y = Gross farm income.

C = Capital measured by the sum total of annual charge of machinery and implements.

L = Farm labour utilization which covers both household and hired labour in man-days.

I = Insecticide used in kilograms

A= Farm size in acres.

β_1= Elasticity of farm income with respect to labour utilization.

β_2= Elasticity of income with respect to annual capital charge.

β_3= Elasticity of income with respect to insecticide use.

β_4= Elasticity of income with respect to farm size in acreage.

All the $\beta's$ are expected to be positively related to farm income as noted in the apriori expected signs below the model formulated in the equation [1].

Data Collection

The study is based on a survey of small scale farmers in the Assin Foso District of Ghana based on multi-staged sampling procedure, which was collected in the year 2000 using structured questionnaire and interview schedule. Data was gathered on the production of various agricultural products, capital, both household and hired labour, farm inputs comprising planting materials or seeds, fertilizers, pesticides and herbicides, and acreage of agricultural land farmed, among other things.

Data used for this study is based on a cross sectional survey conducted in 2000. A multi-stage sampling procedure was adopted in the data collection with the frontline staff of the Ministry of Food and Agriculture working in the area, the district assembly representatives and the district council, the district council office staff and opinion leaders. The target population for the study was small-scale farmers within the Assin district. Data was collected on the following: output, capital, labour input, farm inputs comprising planting materials or seeds, fertilizers, pesticides and herbicide, acreage of agricultural land farmed.

Preliminary Survey

This phase involved a three-week long visit to the study area. The purpose of the reconnaissance survey was to collect primary and secondary information to develop the survey interview schedules, finding out the feasibility of getting a good sample for the study and to book appointments for the main study. The preliminary survey afforded us the opportunity to interact with the communities and establish good and sound rapport. During the preliminary survey farmers were interviewed relating to their current agricultural production practices, cost involved, quantity of product obtained, quantity of product sold, returns (money) obtained from products sold, source and regularity of inputs supply, credit, labour, marketing and other supporting services (infrastructure) available to assist in their productive activities.

Sample Selection of Settlements and Households

The target population for the study was all small-scale farmers within the

Assin district. The Assin District was selected as the study area because it is located in the tropical rainforest zone. Furthermore, this zone is the largest district in the Central Region and a major belt for producing cocoa and oil palm fruit in Ghana and also major producers of food crop.

In the planning of a sample survey, a stage is always reached at which a decision must be made about the size of the sample. This decision is very important. Too large a sample implies a waste of resources, and too small a sample diminishes the utility of the results. This decision cannot always be absolutely satisfactorily; often we do not posses enough information to be sure that our choice at sample size is the best one (Cochran 1997).

The level of precision desired might be made by giving the amount of error that we are willing to tolerate in the sample estimates. This amount is determined, in the light of uses to which the sample results are to be put (Cochran 1997).

In the process for estimating sample size when proportions are involved, the units are classified into two classes, C and C' while P is the proportion of elements in in the population. Some margin of error in the estimated proportion of units has been agreed on, and there is a small risk that we are willing to incur that the actual error is larger than ; that is, we want

$$\Pr\left(|p-P| \geq e\right) = \alpha$$

Hence, the formula that connects 'n' with the desired degree of precision using the formula in Sproull (1988) is as follows:

$$n = \frac{(p)(1-p)}{e^2.(p)(1-p)}$$

Where N = size of the population

z = number of standard errors for a specified confidence level

p = proportion of incidence of the variable in the population

e = proportion of tolerable error

n = sample size

The population of the Assin District was 193,888 by the 2000 census report. In the 2000 population census, there were 95,798 males and 98,090 females. In the 1984 Population Census, the Assin District was 123,564. The farmers, in the economically active, population were represented by 43,851(44.17%). With that representation the population could be imputed as 85,640 in the 2000 Population Census, comprising of 42,314 males and 43,326 females. Using above equation for the estimation, and a tolerable error of 5% the sample size came to 160.

Design and Administration of the Research Instrument

The research instrument used for farmers consisted of a structured interview schedule used to collect farm data. Data was based on the normal year of production. The selected farmers were interviewed and their responses entered separately on each interview schedule. In addition to the study of farmers, agricultural extension staff in the study area whose work mandate covered both food crops and export crops were also included in the study in order to capture their technical expertise relating to the research.

Estimation Technique

The ordinary least squares technique is used to estimate the parameters of the model. The Microfit econometric software package was used to estimate the model and the variety of diagnostic tests in the software were used to assess the goodness of the estimated model as demonstrated in the presentation of the regression results (Pesaran and Pesaran 1997:347-353).

Profile of Respondents

This section reports on the profile of respondents and their farms. We first report on the sex of the head of the household.

(a) Sex Distribution

Table 1: Sex Distribution of Head of Household

Sex	*Frequency*	*Percent*
Male	133	83.1
Female	27	16.9
Total	160	100.0

Source: Field Survey [2000]

The sample of 160 respondents consisted of 133 (83.1%) males and 27 (16.9%) females giving a sex ratio of 1:5 as shown in Table 1

(b) Age Distribution

The mean age of the respondents is about 51 years from Table 2 and the range is 60.This is an indication that most farmers are aging and therefore there was the need to encourage the younger generation to get actively involved in the farming enterprise in order to take over from the aged.

Table 2: Age Distribution of Head of Household

Years	*Frequency*	*Percent*
26 – 35	13	8.1
36 – 45	50	31.2

(Contd...)

46 – 55	47	29.7
56 – 65	24	15.1
66 – 75	23	14.4
76 – 85	3	1.8
Total	160	100.0

Source: Field Survey [2000]

(c) Education

Table 3: Educational Attainment of Head of Household

Level	*Frequency*	*Percent*	*Cumulative Percent*
None	48	30.0	30.0
Primary	88	55.0	85.0
Secondary/Commercial	17	10.6	95.6
Vocational/Technical	4	2.5	98.1
Teacher Training	3	1.9	100.0
Total	160	100.0	

Source: Field Survey [2000]

Table 3 shows that the most frequent educational attainment is primary education and accounts for 88(55.0%) while those who have never attended schooling accounts for 48(30.0%). This is followed by secondary/commercial 17(10.6%) with vocational/technical making 4(2.5%) and teacher training 3(1.9%). The educational profile of the farmers is low.

(d) Experience in Farming

Table 4: Number of Years of Experience in Farming

Years	*Frequency*	*Percent*	*Cumulative Percent*
0 – 9	10	6.2	6.2
11 – 19	82	51.4	57.6
21 – 29	33	20.7	78.3
31 – 39	23	14.5	92.8
41 – 49	9	5.6	98.4
51 – 59	3	1.8	100.0
Total	160	100.0	

Source: Field Survey [2000]

The number of years that the respondents have been farming, which is used as proxy for experience, is summarized in Table 4. The average number of years of experience is about 24 years with a range of 56 years. This outcome is indicative of long farming experience.

(e) Household Labour

The labour force used in farming consists of family and hire labour.

Family labour plays an important role in agrarian communities where hired labour is relatively scarce and mechanized farming is not popular.

Table 5 shows the size and structure of households with the mean household size of about 8.4, which is far above the national average of about 6.

Table 6 shows the total household labour capacity in the district with a mean of about 5.57 (The labour utilization capacity factor, males and children up to 16years = 1, females=0.75, children 7-15 years=0.5, and children less than 7years=0).

Table 7 reveals the distribution of household labour availability in man-days.

Table 5: Size and Structure of Household

Household size	*Frequency*	*Percent*	*Cumulative percent*
1 – 5	39	24.4	24.4
6 – 10	89	55.6	80.0
11 – 15	17	10.6	90.6
16 – 20	11	6.9	97.5
21 – 25	3	1.8	99.3
26 – 30	1	0.6	100.0
Total	160	100.0	

Source: Field Survey [2000]

Table 6: Total Household Labour Capacity

Labour Capacity	*Frequency*	*Percent*	*Cumulative percent*
0.6 – 4.5	74	46.3	46.3
4.6 – 8.5	62	38.8	85.1
8.6 – 12.5	17	10.6	95.7
12.6 – 16.5	5	3.1	98.8
16.6 – 20.5	1	0.6	99.4
20.6 – 24.5	1	0.6	100.0
Total	160	100.0	

Source: Field Survey [2000]

The mean household farm labour available amounts to 460 man-days, with a median of 200 and a range of 4600 man-days. It is clear from the Table that majority of the households require household farm labour greater than 400 man-days. Family labour was popular in farms less than 2-acres.

Table 7: Household Farm Labour Availability (Man-days)

Man-days	*Household*	*Percent*	*Cumulative percent*
0 – 500	121	75.6	75.6
501– 1000	24	15.0	90.6
1001 – 1500	9	5.6	96.2
1501 – 2000	4	2.5	98.7
2001 –2500	0	0.0	98.7
2501 – 5000	2	1.3	100.0
Total	160	100.0	

Source: Field Survey [2000]

(f) Hired Labour

An alternative way of securing labour is for a farmer to give an agreed amount of money to people to help him on his farm. The use of this form of labour is limited because of the cash payment involved and the scarcity of surplus labour.

Table 8 shows the distribution of hired labour employment. The mean size of hired labour employed is 370 man-days with a median of 72 and a range of 5010 man-days. Majority of farmers 142 (88.9%) employ less than 500 man-days of hired labour. Family labour play a major role relative to hired labour in farming as shown in Tables 7 and 8, respectively.

Table 8: Hired Labour Employment

Man-days	*Household*	*Percent*	*Cumulative percent*
0 – 500	142	88.9	88.9
501– 1000	13	8.1	97.0
1001 – 1500	1	0.6	97.6
1501 – 2000	1	0.6	98.2
2001 – 5500	3	1.9	100.0
Total	160	100.0	

Source: Field Survey [2000]

(g) Land Acquisition

Five basic categories of tenure have been identified in Ghana (Benneh 1985; Ewusi 1983). These are: the allodial title (an absolute ownership right), which is supposed to be the highest grant or right in land; the customary freeholds; the leasehold (usufructuary right for an agreed period in exchange for an initial agreed payment); the abusa, abunu and abehyem share cropping tenures; and nto, a cash rental tenure.

Table 9 shows the responses made by household heads on land acquisition. It is clear that 48.4 percent of the respondents inherited the land, while 33 percent rented their land holding (abusa and abunu categories). Those who purchased land outright constituted 2.5 percent and wife's land constituted only 0.8 percent.

The average amount of land purchased was about ¢11,000. On the other hand, the average amount of rent paid for the cultivation on the fields per annum stood at ¢143,000.

Table 10 depicts the distribution of the size of farm holdings. The average size of holdings was 4.7 hectares 4.78 hectares with the corresponding standard deviations of 2.75.

Table 9: Land Acquisition

Category	*Fields*					*Total*	*Percent*
	1	*2*	*3*	*4*	*5*		
Not applicable	0	0	4	30	89	123	15.4
Land inherited	83	79	75	68	39	344	43.0
Land rented	60	61	64	52	27	264	33.0
Land purchased	4	6	6	3	1	20	2.5
Land as gift	12	13	9	6	3	43	5.4
Wife's land	1	1	2	1	1	6	0.8

Source: Field Survey [2000]

Table 10: Size of Farm Holdings

Hectares	*Frequency*	*Percent*
1-4	64	40.0
5 – 8	82	51.3
9 – 12	13	8.1
13 – 16	1	0.6
17– 20	0	0.0
Total	160	

Source: Field Survey [2000]

(h) Crops Cultivated

Table 11 shows the distribution of crops grown in the study area. It is clear that cocoa, maize, cassava, oil palm and plantain claim a greater share of the land area. The last column of the Table reveals the average acreage of crops cultivated by a typical household. It can be realized from the Table that the average size varies between about one and two hectares.

Table 11: The Distribution of Crops Cultivated

Type of crop	*Total Hectares*	*Percent*	*Total Household*	*Percent*	*Average Hectares per Household*
Cocoa	272	35	125	78.1	2
Maize	143.2	19	160	100	0.8
Cassava	130.4	17	160	100	0.8
Oil palm	92.4	12	63	39.3	1.6
Plantain	66.8	9	96	60.0	0.8
Citrus	28	4	15	9.4	2.0
Rice	15.6	2	13	8.1	1.2
Cocoyam	14.4	2	20	12.5	0.8
Yam	6.0	1	10	6.3	0.8
Tomatoes	5.2	1	11	6.9	0.4
Total	734				

Source: Field Survey [2000]

Discussion of Results

Before we proceed to the empirical estimates of the determinants of farm income, we shall discuss issues related to distribution of farm income in terms of frequency tables and the Gini coefficient before we proceed to the discussion of the correlation matrix on farm income and its determinants which is then followed by the discussion on the econometric estimates of the determinants of farm income.

Income Analysis

Income analysis is undertaken to determine the relative well being of the surveyed farmers. One of the most important yardsticks for measuring the well being of a given population is income per head and this index is employed as a measure of well-being whereas the Gini coefficient is used to determine the degree of inequality in the size distribution of income.

Table 12: The Distribution of Household Income

Income ¢'000	*No. of Households*	*%*	*Cumulative %*	*Average Income*	*Total Income ¢'000*	*%*	*Cumulative %*
0-3000	59	36.9	36.9	1500	88500	14.2	14.2
3001-6000	57	35.6	72.5	4500	256500	41.2	55.4
6001-9000	22	13.8	86.3	7500	16500	2.7	58.1
9001-12000	13	8.1	94.4	10500	136500	21.9	80.0
12001-15000	8	5.0	99.4	13500	108000	17.3	97.3
15001-18000	1	0.6	100.0	16500	16500	2.7	100.0
Total	160	100.0			622500	100.0	

Computed Gini = 0.3374

Source: Field Survey [2000]

Household income is used for the analysis and it consists of both farm and non-farm incomes that were reported by household heads during the survey. Table 12 shows the distribution of gross household income for both farming and non-farming activities. The mean household income that was computed was ¢4,818,750 with a range of ¢17,543,873 and standard deviation of ¢3,522,385.Given an average household size of eight people as revealed by the survey, the income per head amounts to ¢602,344. This figure is rather low when compared to the national average of ¢2,600,000 (US $370) per capita income at the time of the survey. In terms of household income distribution Table 12 reveals that 99 percent of the households receive about 97 percent of the total income. This implies that the distribution of income is near perfect equality and this is confirmed by the computed Gini coefficient of 0.3374. This magnitude of Gini coefficient reinforces the fact that there is a moderate inequality in the distribution of household income.

Table 13 depicts the distribution of the estimated gross farm income in the sample survey. The average amount of income amounted to ¢1,556,250 and this is even far below the mean for total household income. Just like the distribution of total household income, the distribution of farm income is equally even given a Gini coefficient of 0.3279

The major concern here is that both household and farm incomes are low and these results conform to the work of Tschirely and Weber (1994) and the Ministry of Agriculture (1992) for Mozambique as shown by our literature review.

Table 13: The Distribution of Farm Income

Income ¢'000	*No. of House holds*	*Per cent*	*Cumul ative %*	*Average Income*	*Total Income ¢'000*	*Per cent*	*Cumulative %*
0 - 2000	138	86.3	86.3	1000	138000	55.4	55.4
2001 - 4000	12	7.5	93.8	3000.5	36006	14.5	69.9
4001 - 6000	6	3.8	97.6	5000.5	30003	12.1	81.9
6001-8000	2	1.3	98.9	7000.5	14001	5.6	87.6
8001 -10000	1	0.6	99.5	9000.5	9000.5	3.6	91.2
10001-12000	0	0	99.5	11000.5	0	0	91.2
12001 -32000	1	0.6	100.1	22000.5	22000.5	8.8	100
Total	160	100		58003	249011	100	
Computed Gini = 0.3279							

Source: Field Survey [2000].

Correlation Matrix Results

The Person correlation matrix for farm income and an array of its determinants are shown in the equation [1]. The results reveal that farm income is positively and significantly related to farm size in acreage, age of household heads, annual capital charge, years of experience in farming, insecticide use and farm labour utilization. On the basis of the correlation results, the econometric model was formulated to capture those variables in equation [1] and we now report on the estimated results.

The estimated results of the double log farm income model gives good results as shown by the summary statistics and diagnostic tests in Table 14 except that there are estimation problems with respect to autocorrelation and serial correlation. Using the summary statistics, it can be observed that the F statistic is significant at less than 1% level thereby rejecting the null hypothesis that all the coefficients are equal to zero. This by implication means that all the estimated parameters jointly explain farm income.

Regression Results

The estimated regression results are presented in Tables 14 and 15, respectively.

Table 14: Ordinary Least Squares Estimation

Dependent variable is LNGFY
160 observations used for estimation from 1 to 160

Regressor	Coefficient	Standard Error	T-Ratio[Prob]
K	5.1940	1.7346	2.9944[.003]
LNACAP	.53521	.17556	3.0486[.003]
LNLABCAP	.45417	.19292	2.3541[.020]
LNACREAGE	.49144	.21793	2.2551[.026]
INSEC	.086910	.025022	3.4733[.001]

R-Squared	.32684	R-Bar-Squared	.30947
S.E. of Regression	1.2274	F-stat. F (4, 155)	18.8143[.000]
Mean of Dependent Variable	13.0358	S.D. of Dependent Variable	1.4771
Residual Sum of Squares	233.5192	Equation Log-likelihood	-257.2774
Akaike Info. Criterion	-262.2774	Schwarz Bayesian Criterion	-269.9653
DW-statistic	1.6815		

Diagnostic Tests

* Test Statistics * LM Version * F Version *

*A: Serial Correlation*CHSQ (1)=4.1166[.042]*F (1, 154) = 4.0669[.045]*

* B: Functional Form *CHSQ (1)= .23739[.626]*F (1, 154)= .22883[.633]*

* C: Normality *CHSQ (2)= 37.6528[.000]* Not applicable *

* D: Heteroscedasticity*CHSQ (1)= .27886[.597]*F (1, 158)= .27586[.600]*

A: LaGrange multiplier test of residual serial correlation
B: Ramsey's RESET test using the square of the fitted values
C: Based on a test of skewness and kurtosis of residuals
D: Based on the regression of squared residuals on squared fitted values

The adjusted R squared shows that approximately 31% of the variation in farm income is explained by the regression and this is satisfactory for regression based on cross-sectional data. The Durbin-Watson statistic of 1.6 accepts the hypothesis of auto-correlation. Further from the diagnostic tests, the Lagrange multiplier test of serial correlation is significant thereby accepting the presence of serial correlation. The Ramsey's reset test for the functional form is also not significant implying that the functional form is satisfactory. The normality test for the distribution of the residuals based on the test of skewness and kurtosis of residuals is significant implying that the residuals are not normally distributed. The test for Heteroskedastic errors based on the regression of squared residuals on squared fitted values rejects the presence of heteroskedasticity. However, because of the problems associated with autocorrelation and serial correlation and normality assumption, we applied the Cochrane Orcutt iterative procedure to clear the problems, which converged with two iterations, and the results are reported in Table 15 (Pesaran and Pesaran 1997:371-372).

Table 15: Cochrane-Orcutt Method AR (2) Converged after 2 Iterations

Dependent variable is LNGFY			
160 observations used for estimation from 1 to 160			
Regressor	Coefficient	Standard Error	T-Ratio [Prob]
K	4.7434	1.7146	2.7664[.006]
LNACAP	.58753	.17639	3.3308[.001]
LNLABCAP	.51939	.19145	2.7129[.007]
LNACREAGE	.40838	.22406	1.8227[.070]
INSEC	.083465	.025139	3.3201[.001]
R-Squared	.34987	R-Bar-Squared	.32404
S.E. of Regression	1.2194	F-stat. F (6, 151)	13.5438 [.000]
Mean of Dependent Variable	13.0358	S.D. of Dependent Variable	1.4771
Residual Sum of Squares	224.5417	Equation Log-likelihood	-251.9581
Akaike Info. Criterion	-258.9581	Schwarz Bayesian Criterion	-269.7212
DW-statistic	2.0024		
Parameters of the Autoregressive Error Specification			
U= .18307*U(-1)+ -.098441*U(-2)+E			
(2.2174)[.028] (-1 1757)[.242]			
T-ratio(s) based on asymptotic standard errors in brackets			

From Table 15 it can be observed that the summary statistics obtained are not indicative of any estimation problem. The adjusted R-square of 0.32 was obtained and this means that the estimated regression line explains about 32% of the variation in farm income which is satisfactory for cross sectional data and an improvement over the figure in Table 3. The F-statistic, which shows the joint significance of the explanatory variables, is significant at less than one percent level. This by implication means that the regressors together explain variations in farm income significantly at less than one percent significance level. The Durbin-Watson statistic of approximately 2.0 implies that there is the absence of autocorrelation in the estimated parameters.

With respect to the individual regressors, it can be observed that the log of annual capital charge, farm labour utilization, farm size in acreage and insecticides use are able to explain farm income at less than one percent significance level while insecticide explains farm income at less than seven percent probability level. The constant also explains the dependent variable at less than 1% probability level.

Since the farm income model is a double logged, the estimated parameters can be interpreted as elasticities. Thus the estimated parameter for capital is 0.6 and this is less than one implying that farm income is less responsive to annual capital charge. This implies that if capital increases by 100% farm income will increase by 60%. The estimated parameter for farm labour utilization is about 0.5. This implies that if farm labour utilization increases by 100% farm income will increase by 50%. The estimated parameter for farm size in acreage is about 0.4 and this implies that if the farm size in acreage increases by 100%, farm income will increase by 40%.

From the results, it can be inferred generally that farm income is less responsive to the parameters in the model. The constant has a significant positive coefficient implying that the parameters featured in our model are not exhaustive. As can be observed from the correlation matrix in Appendix, not all the factors were able to explain farm income statistically due to the sheer absence of certain facilities in the study area. For example, field observation shows that the availability of irrigation facility, the use of fertilizers, agricultural extension, and agricultural credit are more likely to enhance productivity and for that matter farm income but they do not feature significantly in the activities of the farmers in the study area as our field observation shows. The mere absence of these support systems account for low farm output and for that matter incomes and are indeed relevant in formulating policies to bail out farmers from low incomes and poverty.

We observe that the outcome of our study synchronizes with the empirical literature review that was undertaken earlier on in this paper. To be specific, these results conform to the work of Meng and Wu (1998), Ministry of Agriculture (1992) and Walker *et al.* (2004) in terms of labour utilization and Tschirely and Weber (1994) in terms of land and labour.

Conclusion

The study set itself to examine the distribution and determinants of farm income using frequency tables, the Gini coefficient and regression analysis. The results show that average income is low when compared to the national average and this is worrying. In terms the distribution of income the results show that there is moderate inequality in the distribution of household income as well as farm income. Both household and farm income are evenly distributed with Gini coefficients of 0.34 and 0.33 respectively and that there is no cause for alarm as far as the distribution of income is concerned. The correlation results reveal that farm income is positively and significantly related to farm size, age of household heads, annual capital charge, years of experience in farming, insecticide use and farm labour utilization. On the other hand, the regression results revealed that annual capital charge, farm labour utilization, farm size and insecticides use are able to explain farm income at the acceptable level. The regression results correspond to the variables in the correlation results except the age of household head and years of experience in farming.

The regression results show that generally farm income is less responsive to the parameters in the model. The constant has a significant positive coefficient implying that the parameters featured in our model are not exhaustive. From field observation and survey results there is near absence of support systems in terms of irrigation facility, the use of fertilizers, agricultural extension, and agricultural credit. But the provision of these support systems are more likely to enhance productivity and for that matter farm income.

The implications of the results of the study therefore are that farmers need to be provided with training to adopt good husbandry practices and this should go in tandem with the provision of adequate support systems such as farm inputs, irrigation facilities or dams, credit facilities. The expansion of the farm size should be encouraged in order to raise the incomes of farmers to offset poverty in the short term but intensive agriculture should be encouraged in the longer term perspective. In order for all these to be realized agricultural extension in the district needs to be strengthened. These support systems are critical in formulating policies to bail out farmers from low incomes and poverty on sustainable basis.

References

Benin, S., Smale, P. M., Gebremedhind, B. and S. Ehui. S. (2004), The Economic Determinants of Cereal Crop Diversity on Farms in the Ethiopian Highlands. *Journal of Agricultural Economics,* 31: 197-208

Benneh, G. (1985), *Dynamics of Land Tenure and Agrarian Systems in Africa: Case Study.* Mimeograph, Ghana Publishing, Accra.

Cochran, W.G. (1997), *Sampling Techniques*. John Wiley & Sons Inc., USA.

Ewusi, K. (1983), *The Dynamics of Rural Poverty in Ghana and its Alleviation*. WCARRD Follow-up Programme, In-depth Studies No. 8, Food and Agriculture Organization, Mimeo, Rome.

Gardner, B. L. (1969), Determinants of Farm Family Income Inequality. *American Journal of Agricultural Economics*, 51(4): 753-769.

Ghana Statistical Service (1995a), *The Pattern of Poverty in Ghana 1988-1992: A Case Study based on the Ghana Living Standards Survey.* Commercial Associates Ltd., Accra.

Ghana Statistical Service (1995b), *The Pattern of Poverty in Ghana 1988-1992.* Commercial Associates Ltd., Accra.

Ghana Statistical Service (2000), *Poverty Trends in Ghana in the 1990's.* Ghana Statistical Service, Accra.

Jones, D. W. *et al.* (1995), Farming in Rondonia. *Resource and Energy Economics*, 17:155-188.

Marshall, A. (1920), *Principles of Economics.* Macmillan Company Ltd., London.

Meng, X. and Wu, H. X. (1998), Household Income Determination and Regional Income Differential in Rural China. *Asian Economic Journal*, 12(1): 65-88.

Ministry of Agriculture (1992), *The Determinants of Household Income and Consumption in Rural Nampula Province: Implications for Food Security and Agricultural Policy Reform.* Working Paper No. 6, National Directorate of Agricultural Economics, Mozambique.

Pesaran, M. H. and Pesaran, B. (1997), *Microfit 4.0.* Oxford University Press, Oxford.

Republic of Ghana (2003), *Ghana Poverty Reduction Strategy 2003-2005: An Agenda for Growth and Prosperity.* Ghana Publishing Corporation, Accra.

Sadoulet, E and de Janvry, A. (1995), *Quantitative Development Policy Analysis.* The Johns Hopkins University Press, Baltimore.

Samuels, W. J. and Kelsey, T. W. (1991), Some Fundamental Considerations on the Positive Theory of Income Distribution. In: W. L. M. Adriaansen and J. T. J. M. van der Linden (eds.). *Post-Keynesian Thought in Perspective.* Wolters Noordhoff, Groningen.

Sanchez, V. (2005), *The Determinants of Rural Non-Farm Employment and Incomes in Bolivia.* Unpublished M A Thesis, Michigan State University.

Sproull, N. L. (1988), *Handbook of Research Methods.* The Scarecrow Press Inc., Metuehen, New Jersey & London.

Tschirley, D. L. and Weber, M. T. (1994), Food Security Strategies Under Extremely Adverse Conditions: The Determinants of Household Income and Consumption in Rural Mozambique. *World Development,* 22 (2): 159-173.

Tsakloglou, P. (1993), Aspects of Income Inequality in Greece: Measurement, Decomposition, and Inter-temporal Change. *Journal of Development Economics*, 40: 53-74.

Walker, T. *et al.* (2004), *Determinants of Rural Income, Poverty, and Perceived Well-being in Mozambique in 2001-2002.* Research Report No 57 E, May 2004, Ministry of Food and Rural Development, Mozambique.

Appendix: Correlation Matrix

	CAPITAL	*ACREAGE*	*CREDIT*	*EDUCATION*	*EXPERIENCE*	*INCOME*	*INSECTICIDE*	*LABOUR*	*EXTENSION*	*PLANTING MATERIALS*	*SEX*
CAPITAL	1	.423(**)	.146	.027	.220(**)	.469(**)	.404(**)	.323(**)	.235(**)	.049	.122
	.	.000	.065	.731	.005	.000	.000	.000	.003	.538	.123
ACREAGE	.423(**)	1	.063	.081	.266(**)	.303(**)	.375(**)	.336(**)	.170(*)	.145	.270(**)
	.000	.	.431	.306	.001	.000	.000	.000	.032	.067	.001
CREDIT	.146	.063	1	.030	-.027	-.005	.141	.069	.011	-.048	-.066
	.065	.431	.	.703	.733	.953	.075	.385	.888	.546	.410
EDUCATION	.027	.081	.030	1	-.334(**)	-.066	.022	-.093	.143	.017	.054
	.731	.306	.703	.	.000	.406	.779	.241	.072	.835	.499
EXPERIENCE	.220(**)	.266(**)	-.027	-.334(**)	1	.252(**)	.338(**)	.375(**)	-.032	.095	-.002
	.005	.001	.733	.000	.	.001	.000	.000	.692	.234	.975
INCOME	.469(**)	.303(**)	-.005	-.066	.252(**)	1	.309(**)	.322(**)	.115	.057	.070
	.000	.000	.953	.406	.001	.	.000	.000	.148	.476	.381
INSECTICIDE	.404(**)	.375(**)	.141	.022	.338(**)	.309(**)	1	.250(**)	.177(*)	-.107	-.038
	.000	.000	.075	.779	.000	.000	.	.001	.025	.178	.633
LABOUR	.323(**)	.336(**)	.069	-.093	.375(**)	.322(**)	.250(**)	1	.202(*)	.180(*)	.109
	.000	.000	.385	.241	.000	.000	.001	.	.011	.023	.169
EXTENSION	.235(**)	.170(*)	.011	.143	-.032	.115	.177(*)	.202(*)	1	.290(**)	.112
	.003	.032	.888	.072	.692	.148	.025	.011	.	.000	.160
PLANTING MATERIALS	.049	.145	-.048	.017	.095	.057	-.107	.180(*)	.290(**)	1	.166(*)
	.538	.067	.546	.835	.234	.476	.178	.023	.000	.	.035
SEX	.122	.270(**)	-.066	.054	-.002	.070	-.038	.109	.112	.166(*)	1
	.123	.001	.410	.499	.975	.381	.633	.169	.160	.035	.

Notes: ** Correlation is significant at the 0.01 level (2-tailed).
*Correlation is significant at the 0.05 level (2-tailed).

6

Gender Disparity in Agriculture Commercialisation

Kiriti-Nganga, T. W. *University of Nairobi*

Introduction

The main objective of this study is to examine the effects of commercialisation of agriculture on land use and work patterns by means of a case study in the Nyeri district in Kenya. Commercialisation of subsistence agriculture can take different forms. It can occur not only on the output side of production with increased marketing of agricultural surpluses, but also on the input side with increased use of purchased inputs. In this study, we concentrate on sales of output rather than purchases of inputs as an indicator of commercialisation.

Generally, cash crops can be defined as crops for sale. Commercialisation is not restricted to just non-food cash crops. Traditional food crops are also sometimes marketed to a considerable extent, and some cash crops are retained, to a substantial extent, on the farm for home consumption. Commercialisation can also be enforced by direct government action, namely, by various forms of compulsion related to the establishment of plantations, execution of certain management practices and input use, or forced procurement of produce (McComb *et al.* 1994).

In many developing countries, much land and other resources are devoted to the production of agricultural crops for export. Davison (1988) contends that as more land is converted to cash crop production, land scarcity becomes a pressing reality, and women's obligation to produce food for their families is at risk. The author found that smallholders with more land tend to allocate relatively more of it to cash value crops and conversely, those with less land tend to allocate relatively more of it to food production. Besteman (1995a and 1995b) and Goheen (1991) also argue that commercialisation of agriculture decreases women's access to land. Fortmann (1982) found that in Tanzania, commercialisation contributed to land shortages, and men tend to be the recipients of land rights. Julin (1993) contends that commercialisation results in a decreased demand for male labour while at the same time increasing the demand for female labour.

Does non-cash food production suffer in the process of commercialisation? How are fixed resources, like land and labour, reallocated to cater for commercialisation? To what extent are resources for non-food cash crop production drawn from non-cash food production? Do women devote their time to non-cash food crop production while men spend their time on non-food cash crop production? Do men spend fewer hours than women on non-food cash crop farming in the Nyeri district?

This article provides a historical review of agricultural commercialisation in Kenya first. This is followed by a review of literature relevant to commercialisation of agriculture and changes in land use patterns. Section four presents information about the study site and data collection methodology. Section five uses descriptive statistics to present and discuss the main survey results. These results are then analysed in section six by applying multiple regression analysis and section seven concludes.

Commercialisation of Agriculture in Kenya: A Review

During the early 20th century, colonial policies restricted land use mainly in two ways: the establishment of reserved areas for Europeans and legislation against African cash crop production. This resulted in a sharply dualistic agricultural system in Kenya. The strategy of commercialising agricultural and overall rural development in Kenya was started early in the colonial era. Starting around 1910 in most areas, export cropping took off in earnest after the Second World War with the rapid expansion of cropped area per agricultural worker following the expansion of cash cropping for export. In the 1950s African farmers in Kenya were subsistence-oriented and generally had smallholdings. The African farmers produced only 20 percent of the marketed production. European settlers cultivated large holdings of about 800 hectares on average, produced cash crops and were dependent on hired African labour.

The Swynnerton Plan of 1954 for Kenya led to the consolidation and registration of land holdings and title deeds granted to individual African male household heads who were encouraged to produce cash-value crops for export which further marginalised the labour of women in food production. The plan set a precedent for male African domination of income-producing agriculture and transformed land from a source of family food to a commercial asset, from an abundant resource valued for its ability to provide food to a scarce commodity having cash-value (Nasimiyu 1985).

The Swynnerton Plan meant a change in the colonial agricultural policies and attitudes towards agricultural development. African smallholders were allowed to produce some cash crops and land registration paved the way for long term-investments by small holders. The major impact of the Swynnerton plan was to provide more favourable conditions for a market-oriented development in agriculture on a widespread scale.

Land policies since Kenya's independence in 1963 have continued the trend first established by the Sywnnerton Plan. By 1978, 7.6 million hectares had been registered in the names of African males (Barnes 1983). In addition, technical inputs and agricultural extension services promoted by transnational and national donor agencies to increase production of smallholders have continued to favour male rather than female producers (Staudt 1987).

At independence in 1963, the government of Kenya lifted completely colonial restrictions on cash crop growing by Africans. In the 1960s and the first half of the 1970s, cash crop production on small-holdings provided farmers with substantial incomes, and provided the state with foreign exchange. However, in the last half of the 1970s, coffee began to lose its attraction for smallholder producers. State corruption swallowed sales income and farmers were not being paid fairly and promptly. The 'hey day' of cash crop expansion continued throughout the 1960s as world commodity prices rose until the first oil shock in 1973. It was also a time when many African small holders first obtained access to cropping opportunities previously reserved for colonial farmers (Heyer, Maitha and Senga 1975).

The commercialisation of agriculture, particularly of crops for export, was adopted as a growth strategy, consistent with the then prevailing view that growth and development were synonymous and that the binding constraint on growth was lack of foreign exchange. It was also consistent with the prevailing view at the time that the role of agriculture in economic development was a source of resources for industrialisation.

In order to achieve the post colonial commercial objective of promoting agricultural production for exports, the Kenyan Government put emphasis on the development of exportable agricultural commodities by providing supporting agricultural loans, technical inputs and extension services. Subsistence crops were generally neglected in the provision of extension services and credit and this forced most farmers to shift to the production of cash crops. This emphasis was reflected in the export bias in the allocation of land resources, resulting in structural distortions of the pattern of agricultural production. Government policies tend to encourage the production of export cash crops because in the process, the government earns foreign exchange; charges export taxes whose incidence falls directly on the producer. At the same time, food price policies that are pursued through state interventions in food marketing keep prices paid to farmers low in the interest of urban consumers.

The second oil shock of 1979 drove up the cost of production of oil dependent cash crops. Between 1980 and 1990 real international prices for Africa's coffee exports fell by 70 percent (World Bank 1994). Most farmers in Kenya's Central Province uprooted their coffee and replaced it by maize, beans and other horticultural crops. In 1986, the Government of Kenya accepted an International Monetary Fund program, which featured export crop expansion and privatisation. In response to lower coffee export earnings, the World Bank and the International Monetary Fund provided funds to increase coffee production. At the same time, the government's adoption of IMF recommended policies for cost sharing in health and education between citizens and the state created a greater need amongst producers for cash. This need constituted a coercive incentive to farmers to concentrate on the production of cash crops at a time when most farmers were abandoning coffee production. Apart from introducing cost sharing in health and education, peasant farmers are also put under pressure to grow cash crops to meet cash obligations such as to buy salt, sugar, cooking oil, cost of transport, purchase of clothing and so on.

In 1996, the International Monetary Fund loaned 12 billion shillings (US960m) to the Kenyan Government earmarked to support the full commercialisation of agriculture with emphasis on export crops (Kimenia 1996).

Overview of Relevant Literature

Besteman (1995a) notes that the commercialisation and mechanisation of agriculture leading to increased production of cash crops, has had both positive and negative consequences for women of the Third World. The benefits lie primarily in enabling them to earn cash income in an increasingly cash-based economy. Yet, as more productive land is dedicated to cash crop production, which is often controlled by male farmers, women are left with less land and with increasingly marginal land. In Africa, commercialisation has been a major factor in shifting land tenure systems from use rights on community land to the individualisation and consolidation of land rights. In this process, women lose their traditional use rights. In Asia, increased commercialisation by large plantations has led to a large class of landless women working as agricultural wage labourers. Where women do retain access to land, their choices of which crops to grow are often constrained since men make many of the decisions regarding agriculture (Kiriti, Tisdell and Roy 2003).

Women in developing countries are often considered responsible for feeding the family. Where wives and husbands keep separate fields, as is frequently so in Africa, men have traditionally had more options for moving into cash cropping on their own fields and leaving the production of subsistence crops to their wives. With this increased responsibility for family subsistence, women often do not have adequate land, labour and time to produce their own cash crops. Furthermore, in most cases, wives work as unpaid family labourers in their husband's cash crop fields. Men are not necessarily under any obligation to share the proceeds from their fields with their wives (Kiriti, Tisdell and Roy 2003).

Charlton, Everett and Staudt (1989) claim that Third World countries have been increasingly drawn into the international trade in foodstuffs, because many governments actively encourage the production of crops that can be sold for badly needed foreign currencies. Women are most disadvantaged by this policy when they have no choice but to continue working in the subsistence economy with few resources and no institutional support. Worldwide, men are often in better positions to exploit new cash crops, and thus women become increasingly responsible for food crop production (Safilios-Rothschild 1988). Changes in production strategies seem to have resulted in increased work and decreased access to cash for women in many developing countries.

Davison (1987) found that in Africa food crops were commonly cultivated and harvested exclusively by women with the help of their children. In 27 percent of the households surveyed the entire family performed the cultivation tasks of crop for cash, though women did most of the weeding. In 23 percent of the compounds, adult members of both sexes performed the tasks. There were no cases where men were the sole producers of cash crops. Thus, women continue to be identified culturally with the production of food crops in Africa, while cash crop production is largely a family affair, often though not always orchestrated by male household heads, as their work is mainly supervisory. An exception to this pattern is the female-headed compound where women bear the major responsibility for agricultural tasks regardless of gender norms.

Davison (1988) found that in Mutira location, more land had been converted to cash crop production and women's obligation to produce food for their families was at risk. She also found that smallholders with less land tended to allocate more of it to food production, and conversely, those with more land assign a larger percentage to the production of cash value crops. Davison's survey found that the more land an owner had, the more he allocated to cash crop production relative to household food production. Of 30 small-holder households in Mutira location in Kenya, small-holders with one to 3 acres of land allocated 44.3 percent of cultivated land to food crop production, while small holders with 4-6 acres only allocated 33.2 percent of their cultivated land to the growing of food crops, and small holders with 7-8 acres reserved even less land for food production (27.8 percent).

Davison also found that in Mutira location, women spend the bulk of their time cultivating and harvesting tea yet it is the owner (the husband) of the land and tea crop who largely benefits from production. Her findings imply that cash cropping and increased income does not necessarily lead to increased welfare for women and children. These findings are also supported by Fortmann (1982) who after examining the effect of Tanzania's national agricultural policy on the nation's women found that agricultural policies had reduced their income and their families' well being.

The competition for arable land between cash crops and food crops means that women depend increasingly upon cash to buy food they no longer produce themselves. Because cash is necessary to buy commodities not produced at home and is necessary for children's school fees, women farmers are allocating more of their labour time to the production of crops that bring a cash-value (Davison 1988).

Julin (1993) contends that modernisation efforts in the Kenyan agricultural sector have been directed towards cash crop production and introduction of modern technologies, areas that are traditionally dominated by men. Men's productivity has therefore increased resulting in decreased demand for male labour, while the demand for female labour by men has increased due to the larger land areas prepared by men and the increase in the number of crops. Women's ability to produce their own food and cash crops has diminished due to lack of time. Women work as unpaid family workers on their husband's fields and have no control of the profit from this work. This view supports that of Davison (1988).

According to Gladwin *et al.* (1991), Structural Adjustments Programs (SAPS) designed to stimulate cash crop production benefit men more than women. Women often have little access to the vital agricultural inputs necessary to increase production. SAPS that focus on those factors, without also focusing on increasing their availability to women, do not benefit women directly and may serve to decrease food availability as prices rise and supplies diminish.

Women are the major food producers for families in many developing countries. At the same time, they increasingly have a need to generate cash income for commodities and services such as education and the health services required by their children, that they cannot directly provide. In areas where a cash economy has taken hold, women's agricultural labour at the compound-household level is likely to be under-compensated or not compensated at all (Safilios-Rothschild 1988). This view agrees with that of Angelique (1995) who found that in Kenya the people who really pick the coffee are not men, it is the women and children. But when time comes for the payment, the people who actually collect the money are men, not women. The labour is for the wife and the children, but the money is for the husband. The state and transnational corporations continue to regulate women's labour by giving credit to male title deed-holders to encourage horticulture. This is a labour intensive and chemically dependent type of export production.

The consequences of commercialisation are reflected in changes in time allocation of men and women and control over household resources. Women may also find that their decision-making role is reduced significantly with cash crop farming. Commercialisation may affect differently the welfare of various members, depending on how work and responsibilities and control over income within a household change (Von Braun, de Haen and Blanken 1991, Kaiser and Dewey 1991, Julin 1993, Angelique 1995).

Study Site and Data Collection Methodology

Kenya has a total land area of 580,367 km$^{2.}$ Only about 20 percent of Kenya's land is considered to have high or medium potential for farming or intensive livestock production. Another 10 percent of the land is categorised as marginal for agriculture, while the remaining 70 percent is used for extensive grazing or taken up by national parks and forests. With a population of about 28.7 million (1999 census), Kenya has one of the highest agricultural population densities in the world when its agro-climatic potential is taken into consideration. Central Province has a population of 3.7 million people.

Kenya has since independence relied heavily on the agricultural sector as the base for its economic growth, employment creation, and foreign exchange generation. The sector contributes to the country's food security and a source of off-farm employment (Government of Kenya 1997). Approximately 80 percent of Kenyans live in rural areas and depend on agriculture for their livelihood.

This study is based on data collected in Nyeri district in Central Kenya. The Kikuyu, who are Kenya's largest ethnic group and account for over half the province's population, mainly inhabit Central Kenya. Nyeri district is bordered by Mount Kenya to the East and the Aberdare ranges to the West. The Western part is relatively flat while to the south and east the topography is characterised by steep ridges and valleys. Rainfall varies from 750 millimetres in the central-northern part of the district to 1750 millimetres in the southwestern and northeastern parts of the district. The long rains normally begin in March and end in May, while the short rains begin in October and end in December.

Nyeri district has a very high population density with some areas of high agricultural potential, such as Tetu division, having more than 400 persons per km^2, whereas new settlement areas such as Kieni West have 100 persons per km^2. The infrastructure in the district is better developed than in other rural districts of Kenya. The principal town is Nyeri with a population of about 50,000 persons and it is also the provincial headquarters.

Six divisions were selected for the study. These divisions were selected because of their differences in ecology and levels of commercialisation. The divisions are Nyeri, Othaya, Tetu, Mukurweini, Mathira and Kieni. In these divisions, farmers produce subsistence foods mostly for home consumption and some for sale, as well as cash crops such as tea, coffee, pyrethrum and tobacco for sale in the international market.

We used the Kenya Central Bureau of Statistics Welfare Monitoring Sampling Frame to randomly select our sample. The data were collected in the months of December 2000 and January 2001.

A random sample of 330 households was selected but due to death, migration, absentees and non-responses we ended up with 185 households with 235 respondents. The sample consisted of 98 male respondents, 63 wives staying with their husbands, 26 wives staying alone as their husbands were working in the urban areas, and 48 unmarried women who were heads of their households.

A questionnaire was administered to collect information on the various products households produce, size of farm, labour and other inputs for the previous season, fertiliser and agro-chemicals, contact with extension officers, use and availability of credit, education, age and so on. Usually, the harvest months are September and October. This therefore means that the recall period was quite short and for this reason, we assume the data is reasonably correct and quite representative of agricultural production in Nyeri district.

Subsistence crops in Nyeri include maize, beans, bananas, cassava, onions, tomatoes, carrots and potatoes. Additionally, garden vegetables such as cabbages and kale are also grown. Coffee, tea, pyrethrum, tobacco and wheat are grown as cash crops.

The distinction between cash crops and subsistence crops is an arbitrary one in some cases. For example, in Nyeri the farmers grow maize and beans, carrots and so on, which they concurrently sell and use for their own consumption. Further, what is a subsistence crop at one point in time may become a cash commodity at another as the economic needs of each household fluctuate. In our study, subsistence crops are referred to as non-cash food crops; semi-subsistence crops as food cash crops; and cash crops as non-food cash crops.

Non-food Cash Crop Farming, Non-cash Food Production and Allocation of Resources in Nyeri District: Summary Statistics

Commercialisation of agriculture has had a profound effect on the production priorities of households. As more land is converted to cash crop production, land scarcity becomes a pressing reality and households' food security can fall.

Specific characteristics of non-food cash crops may imply certain household food security and nutritional effects. For example, if a cash crop that is also a food is introduced, has several products, has a short maturation period, fits into existing cropping patterns, women have a role in farm decision-making and marketing systems are efficient, the crop may have a positive impact on food security and nutrition. On the other hand if a cash crop introduced is a non-food, is backed up with a comprehensive research, extension and marketing service which ignores all the food crops, inputs may be subsidised to the exclusion of the staple crops, has a long maturation period, revenues from it are lumpy and is controlled by men, does not fit with the existing cropping patterns, it may have a negative impact on food security and nutrition (Longhurst 1988).

The technical characteristics of crops impinge on the ability of farm households to respond to changing price ratios in the short run. The characteristics of perennials such as coffee and tea production give less ability in the short run to respond to price changes than is the case for annual crops such as carrots, potatoes, maize and beans. Coffee and tea represent a semi-fixed factor situation to a farmer who has switched to these. If after the switch is made and investments are made, the terms of trade between coffee and a competing crop (say maize) shift in favour of the competing crop, then moving out of coffee is constrained in the short run. Production of tea and coffee will continue as long as variable costs are covered (Islam 1994).

Although many authors agree that women's role as food producers has been marginalised by the introduction of cash cropping (Boserup 1970; Safilios-Rothschild 1982, Barnes 1983; Guyer 1984; Nasimiyu 1985), others find that women producers in some areas of West Africa, in particular, have actually benefited from the introduction of cash cropping and the commercialisation of land (Berry 1975; Okali 1983; Afonja 1986).

According to Afonja (1986), Yoruba wives of cash crop farmers in Nigeria were initially compensated by their husbands in gifts and later in cash for their labour in cash crop production (Afonja 1986: 131). Additionally, the increase of individual private property ownership in connection with cash crop production means that some Yoruba women in bilaterally organised kin groups who customarily inherited land, subsequently gained access to cash crop producing farms or inherited uncultivated land on which they began to grow cocoa (Afonja 1986: 131). Consequently, where commercialisation has intruded on subsistence forms of production, its impact is experienced differently depending upon pre-existing and changing forms of production and exchange, kinship patterns of inheritance and land use practices.

Women's food production in Kenya is directly affected by the amount of land their husbands are willing to assign to them for the production of food crops. Besteman (1995b) claims that as more productive land are dedicated to cash crop production, which is often controlled by male farmers or by agribusinesses, women are left with less land and with increasingly marginal land. Is this the case in Nyeri district? Table 1 shows how women perceive the quality of the land on which they practice farming.

Table 1: Land Quality of their Farms as Perceived by Women in the Nyeri District According to the Marital Status

Quality of land → / *Marital status* ↓	*N*	*Above Average (%)*	*Average (%)*	*Below Average*	*Total Percentage*
Married women living with husbands	63	17.5	66.7	15.9	100
Married women living alone	26	26.9	61.5	11.5	100
Unmarried women	48	27.1	70.8	2.1	100
Total	137				

Table 1 shows that the largest percentage of land in Nyeri district is perceived to be of average quality and only a very small percentage is of poor quality. But how much of this good quality land is allocated to non-cash food production? This question will be answered in the next section.

How do the farmers in Nyeri district allocate the land between subsistence and cash crops? Table 2 shows the percentage allocation of land between uncultivated land, non-cash crops, food-cash crops and non-food cash crops by marital status.

Table 2: Average Farm Size, Average Percentage Allocation of Land to Crops for Home Consumption and for Cash in Nyeri District

Marital Status	*N*	*Average Farm Size (acres)*	*% Fallow (a)*	*% Non-cash Crops (b)*	*% Food Cash Crops (c)*	*% Non-food Cash Crops (d)*	*Total*
Married women living with husbands	63	2.25	16.24	48.73	7.08	27.87	100
Married women living alone	26	1.65	15.19	55.65	4.00	25.00	100
Unmarried women	48	2.70	14.58	52.29	7.21	25.92	100
Total	137						

Table 2 shows that on farms where married women live with husbands a higher percentage of the land is allocated to non-food cash crops than on farms headed by unmarried women and those where the husband has migrated. Unmarried women have the biggest farms and they allocate slightly over 50 percent of the farm to non-cash farming and slightly over 25 percent to non-food cash crops. When unmarried women head households they allocate the lowest percentage of their farm to uncultivated land. Married women living alone on average allocate the highest percentage of their land (56 percent) to non-cash farming and almost 26 percent for non-food cash crops. None of the households entirely specialise in cash cropping. All households had some subsistence food production.

Does non-cash food output decline with commercialisation in Nyeri district? Table 3 shows the production of non-cash food crops, food cash crops and non-food cash crops by marital status. This output is attributable to the whole farm. In male-headed households, husbands generally control cultivation of non-food cash crops while their wives manage cultivation of non-cash food crops. However, married women living with husbands are expected to work on their husband's fields (cash crop fields) if they are not working on their own fields. On the other hand, the female-headed households (households headed by single mothers, divorced or widowed and those women whose husbands have deserted them and those headed by women whose husbands are away working as migrant workers in urban areas) have greater choice.

Table 3: Production of Non-cash Food Crops, Food Cash Crops and Non-food Cash Crops by Women's Marital Status for one Season

Marital status	*N*	*% Land for food cash and non-food cash crops*	*Non-cash food output (kg)*	*Food cash output (kg)*	*Non-food cash output (kg)*	*Total output (kg)*
Married living along	26	29	107.73	71.92	90.46	270.11
Married living with husband	63	34.95	103.78	101.02	79.08	283.88
Unmarried women	48	33.13	95.53	29.71	98.29	223.53
Total	137					

Table 3 shows that although all women in Nyeri district practise non-cash crop farming, unmarried women produce the lowest amount of non-cash food crops and the highest amount of non-food cash crops. They also produce the lowest output of food cash crops. On those farms where married women live with their husbands, the lowest output of non-food cash crops is produced and the highest output of food cash crops. Married women living alone produce the highest output of non-cash food crops.

Do households spend less time on non-cash food crops and allocate more time to non-food cash crops? Von Braun and Kennedy (1994) found that in general, women work less on the more commercialised crops than do men or hired labourers, who are also mostly men. They contend that women generally spend more time working on subsistence crops than they do on commercial crops. Table 4 shows allocation of time between non-cash food crops and non-food cash crops by marital status of women in our sample. The hours spent on non-food cash crops are inclusive of the hours spent on food cash crops.

Table 4: Allocation of Time per Week between Non-Cash Food Crops and Non-Food Cash Crops by Gender and Marital Status

Marital Status	*N*	*Hours Spent on Non-cash Food Crops*	*Hours Spent on Non-food Cash Crops*	*Total Hours Spent*
Married women living with husbands	63	17.73	13.52	31.25
Married men living with Wives	73	16.71	10.75	27.46
Married women living alone	26	17.38	10.19	27.57
Unmarried women	48	14.32	11.53	25.85
Total	210			
Missing	25			

Table 4 shows that hours spent on non-cash food production are generally higher than the hours spent on non-food cash crops in all cases. However, married women living with husbands and unmarried women work longer than men on non-food cash crops. This table also indicates that women living with their husbands generally work more hours than all the other women. They spend on average 31.25 hours working on the farm. Their husbands work equally hard on both non-cash food crops and non-food cash crops. Although not shown, these women also spend their time preparing food, collecting firewood and water, looking after children, and so on implying that women in Nyeri district work harder than men, findings that concur with those of Funk (1988) in her study in Guinea Bissau. This author found that although men spend more hours per day in field labour, if we count the total work hours including food gathering, processing and domestic work, women clearly work more hours per day than men.

The above results imply that commercialisation leads to an increased workload for women for jointly managed households. Also married women living with husbands still work more hours than their husbands. Julin (1993) contends that commercialisation results in decreased demand for male labour, while demand for female labour increases due to the larger land areas prepared by men and the increase in the number of crops. Our results suggest that demand for female labour increases with commercialisation when husbands are present in a household. This is consistent with Julin's hypothesis. However, it is not clear that the demand for male labour declines with commercialisation.

According to Gladwin *et al.* (1991), Structural Adjustments Programs (SAPS) designed to stimulate cash crop production benefit men more than women. Women often have little access to the vital agricultural inputs necessary to increase production. Extension services are not generally offered for food crops since their economic returns are very low yet these are the crops controlled by women, which provide households with the main source of income and food security. From our Nyeri sample we found that extension officers had visited only 12.4 percent of the 137 women farmers. We also found that only 13.9 percent of the women had attended training on good farming techniques. This would imply that the women farmers could be using outdated and crude methods of cultivation since they lack the knowledge, which they could gain if extension officers visited them, or they attended seminars and training on good farming techniques.

Efficient cultivation of land requires investment. Land titles enable land to be used as collateral to obtain credit from financial institutions. Although land titles are not essential prerequisites for investment in agriculture they are necessary. With land titles, women can have greater access to technology and information on productivity increasing agricultural practices and inputs. However, in our Nyeri sample, 74.5 percent of all female farmers did not own the farms they cultivated implying that they did not have titles to the land.

To be able to improve farm output, a farmer can borrow money or hire farm materials such as tractors, water pumps, wheelbarrows, fertilisers, seeds and so on, from the local cooperative society. They can repay through monthly deductions from their sale proceeds. From our female sub-sample, only 5.8 percent had borrowed money from the cooperative society, 7.3 percent had borrowed money from moneylenders while 86.9 percent had not borrowed at all due to various reasons one of them being lack of title deeds. On the other hand, 38 percent of the women had borrowed farm materials from the cooperative society.

Lack of credit, lack of visits by extension officers and lack of knowledge on good farming techniques could be some of the factors that may have contributed to the decline in non-cash food production in Nyeri district.

Smallholders that have adopted coffee production in Kenya have been experiencing returns to coffee that are not competitive with crops such as potatoes and cereals. Legal regulations do not permit them to completely abandon the coffee and convert to subsistence farming. As mentioned before, coffee prices have been declining over the years and this, coupled with corruption in cooperatives and allegedly in the Coffee Board of Kenya has meant that most farmers have lost confidence in coffee growing and started paying attention to food cash crops. The farmers who grew coffee had not been paid by December 2000 for coffee delivered to the factories in early 1999. It is worth noting that men seem to be spending more hours on food crops than on cash crops. This may be due to the poor prices that cash crops have been fetching and therefore men have moved to the production of subsistence crops, since compared to cash crops the terms of trade are much better. Falls in prices of traditional export crops is affecting the food sector in particular and attracting males to commercial food crops such as maize, beans and horticulture, traditionally controlled by women. The results imply that since cash crops like coffee (a man's crop) have lost favour in terms of cash value, the men have now turned to growing food crops (a woman's crop) for cash and this explains their increased participation in food crops as shown by the many hours they devote to food production. Our results concur with those of Nasimiyu (1985); Okali (1983); Davison (1987) who contend that as selected crops become commoditised for export production, women's control over all aspects of production and allocation continues for some food crops, while for others that obtain a cash value, women's control becomes increasingly limited to allocated labour tasks such as hoeing, weeding, harvesting and processing. Men largely pre-empt women's allocation rights over crops grown for a cash value. Cowen (1986) also observes that when maize is grown for cash and has an exchange value, men cultivate it, but when it has subsistence value only women cultivate it. When maize loses its commercial value, the crop tends to revert to female production (1986:367). It has also been found (for example in Nigeria, Afonja 1986) that if a woman's crop starts to increase in value due to, for example, changed price policies, men begin to take over the cultivation from the women and soon dominate the former female activity.

Do women lose their power of decision-making with cash crop farming? Decision-making in the context of land and production refers to decisions regarding the transfer (including inheritance, sales) of land and its use as an agricultural resource. Allocation of resources means the right to loan, pledge or sell a tract of land; access to and control over improvements to land; and control over products harvested from that land, including processing, distribution and income generated (Davison 1988). Boserup (1970: 53-57) points to the introduction of cash cropping with its attendant emphasis upon male-controlled agricultural intensification as a primary determinant of women's loss of status and power in African agriculture. The introduction of cash crops has meant that male rather than female producers more often control intra-family decisions related to agricultural production (Staudt 1982; Fortmann 1984; Kennedy and Cogill 1985; Cowen 1986).

Capitalisation of land and production in Kenya means that although women have continued to play a major role in subsistence food production, men exercise an increasingly dominant role in the management of resources (including agricultural inputs), control of land, and the distribution of goods and services. As a result women experience a greater loss of socio-economic power (Boserup 1970, Staudt 1982, Nasimiyu 1985).

In our study only 12.5 percent of the wives reported having made the decision regarding the acreage of the cash crop. For those who did not make the decision about the acreage of the cash crop, 69.8 percent said their husbands made the decision, 14.6 percent reported that their fathers-in-law made it, 14.6 percent attributed the decision to their mothers-in-law while 2.1 percent reported that their brothers-in-law decided on the acreage of the cash crop.

This shows that most wives are presented with a fait accompli by their husbands in terms of decisions regarding cash crops.

Only 25.8 percent of the wives reported making decisions regarding acreage of non-cash food crops, 28.1 percent made decisions regarding how much fertiliser and pesticide to use on food crops and only 18.8 percent of the wives made decisions regarding how much fertiliser and pesticide to use on non-food cash crops. On the other hand, only 26.1 percent of the wives made decisions on when to direct labour to cash crops, 32.9 percent made decisions on how much to use at home and how much to sell. Our findings support those of Boserup (1970), Staudt (1982), Nasimiyu (1985), Cowen (1986), Fortmann (1984), Kennedy and Cogill (1985).

Tisdell *et al.* (2001) found that whereas the wife has control over the food that she grows for the family, she has little or no control over cash. It is generally contended that non-cash food production is under the control of the wife and directly used for family nutrition. However, cash income is not, and it is considered that husbands are less likely to use cash for the welfare of wives and children (Kaiser and Dewey 1991). Our results show that only 13.5 percent of the wives make decisions on household spending. However, only 16.5 percent of the wives keep the cash after sale of crops compared to 83.5 percent of husbands. About 60 percent of the husbands keep the money in their own individual accounts while 40 percent keep it in a joint account. Thus, in the Kenyan case, women appear to have very little say in decisions on cash crops but they seem to have more leeway in matters concerning food crops. In other words, women appear to lose their ability to make decisions with increased commercialisation and this may impact negatively not only on food availability in general but also on the nutrition of children. Our results also support Von Braun, de Haen and Blanken (1991), Kaiser and Dewey (1991).

Many women do not directly benefit from their increased work efforts or efficiency as individuals. Instead, men control the incomes (Julin 1993). Women work as unpaid family workers on their husband's fields and have no control of the profit from this work. Muntemba (1982:99) gives the example of an old Zambian woman farmer who said, 'Now a woman is like a slave. She works hard .... At the end of the year, the family sells one hundred bags of maize. The man gives her 20 Kwacha. The following year the family sells three hundred bags. He still gives her 20 Kwacha. What is that but slavery?' However, husbands' payments to wives for work on their fields have been documented in some cases in Nigeria (Galtetti *et al.* 1956). In Ghana male cocoa farmers prefer wives' labour because they can delay wage payment (Okali 1983), and payments occur in the Gambia (Dey 1982) and in Cameroon (Guyer 1984 and Jones 1983). In our study, 93.8 percent of the wives said they and the children are not paid for work done on the cash crop plot and gave various reasons for this state of affairs. Our results support those of Julin (1993), Muntemba (1982),

Safilios-Rothschild (1988), and Angelique (1995). Introduction of cash cropping has brought about greater gender segregation in labour tasks with men increasingly becoming agricultural managers.

Asked whether their husbands would like to grow less or more cash crops, 37.5 percent of the married women living with their husbands said their husbands would like to grow more cash crops, 25 percent said less while 37.5 percent thought their husbands think the percentage is just correct. On the whole, husbands would like more cash cropping.

Multiple Regression Analysis: Influences of Allocation of Household Land and Amount Produced of Non-cash Food and Non-food Cash Crops

To explain what determines the allocation of household land between non-food cash crops (the amount of food cash crops is included in the total for non-food cash crops for ease of analysis) and non-cash food crops and the amount of output from either, non-cash food crops and non-food cash crops, we estimate separate multiple regression models. The amount of land allocated to various crops can be expressed as a function of the proportion of income out of total crop revenue of a particular crop, the return of the particular crop per unit of land allocated to that crop, the amount of land the household has, the quality of land, age of the household head, the number of children in the family and earnings from outside employment. On the other hand, the amount of output from a particular crop is assumed to be a function of the amount of land the household has, the amount of output produced of the competing crop, quality of land, the proportion of household needs met by sale of the crop, hours of work devoted to that particular crop, hours of work devoted to the competing crop, visits by extension officers, attendance of training on good farming techniques, and so on. However, a the return to land of a particular crop, outside employment, visits by extension officers and training were dropped out of the model as they were found to be superfluous and added no value to the model. The model was expressed as follows.

$$\text{SUBSIST} = \alpha_0 + \beta_1\text{SUBREV3} + \beta_2\text{TOTFMSZ} + \beta_3\text{LANDQUAL} + \beta_4\text{Age} + \beta_4\text{NOCHILD} \quad \text{(Equation 1)}$$

$$\text{CASH} = \alpha_0 + \beta 1\text{CASHREV3} + \beta 2\text{TOTFMSZ} + \beta 3\text{LANDQUAL} + \beta 4\text{Age} + \beta 4\text{NOCHILD} \quad \text{(Equation 2)}$$

We also estimate the determinants of the amount of land for food cash crops and for the land left fallow making a total of 4 equations. On the other hand, the amount of output from each type of crop can de determined by the following:

$$\text{TOUPTHC} = \alpha_0 + \beta_1\text{TOTFMSZ} + \beta_2\text{TOTOSALE} + \beta_3\text{LANDQUAL} + \beta_4\text{HHNEEDS} + \beta_5\text{HOURSFC} + \beta_6\text{HOURSCC} \quad \text{(Equation 3)}$$

$$\text{TOTOSALE} = \alpha_0 + \beta_1\text{TOUPTHC} + \beta_2\text{TOTFMSZ} + \beta_3\text{LANDQUAL} + \beta_4\text{HHNEEDS} + \beta_5\text{HOURSFC} + \beta_6\text{HOURSCC} \quad \text{(Equation 4)}$$

Where:

Subsist = Absolute amount of land allocated for non-cash food crops

Cash = Absolute amount of land allocated for non-food cash crops

Semisub = Absolute amount of land allocated for food cash crops

Fallow = Absolute amount of land left uncultivated

Totfmsz = Total amount of land a household has

Landqual = Quality of land

Age = Age of woman

Nochild = Number of children in the family

Subsrev3 = Proportion of food cash income out of total revenue

Cashrev3 = Proportion of non-food cash crop income out of total revenue

Hhneeds = Percentage of household needs met by sale of non-food cash crops

Totosale = Total output sold and is equal to the output from food cash crops and from non-food cash crops.

Hoursfc = Number of hours spent on non-cash food crops

Hourscc = Number of hours spent on non-food cash crops

Toupthc = Total output for home consumption

α_0 = constant

β_i = regression coefficients

The results of the regression analysis are found in Appendices A, B and C. Appendix A provides information on those women who are married but living alone as their husbands have migrated. Table A1 shows the means and standard deviations of the variables used in the analysis while Tables A2 through to A7 show the results of the analysis for these women. Appendix B contains information on those women who live with their husbands. Table B1 shows the descriptive statistics for these women while Tables B2 through to B7 show the results of the regression analysis for them. On the other hand, Appendix C is for those women who are unmarried and table C1 shows the descriptive statistics of the variables used in the regression analysis whose results are shown in Tables C2 through to C7.

Regression Result with Discussion

As shown in Table 1, most agricultural land in Nyeri district is of average quality and only a very small percentage is of poor quality. But how much of this good quality land is allocated to non-cash food production? Are non-food cash crops grown on good quality land while non-cash food crops are grown on poor quality land? Tables A2, B2 and C2, show that quality of farm land in

Nyeri district is negatively related to the amount of land allocated to non-cash food production. This means that farmers with poorer quality land, non-cash food crop production is relatively more important as Tables A4, B4 and C4 show that quality of farm land is positively related to the amount of land allocated for non-food cash crop production. However, quality of land is not significant in explaining the amount of land allocated to both non-cash food crop production or even non-food cash crop production except in the case of married women living with husbands, where quality of land is statistically significant at the 5 percent level in explaining the amount of land allocated to non-food cash crop production. This means that where husbands are present, non-food cash crop production is relatively more important than non-cash food production.

There is a negative relationship between the quality of land and the amount of land allocated for food cash crops for married women living alone. This means that for these types of households food cash crops are not very important in their land allocation patterns as opposed to the unmarried women and the married women living with their husbands, where the amount of land allocated for food cash crops is positively related to the quality of land.

Married women living with their husbands also leave part of the poor quality land uncultivated as quality of land is negatively related to uncultivated land (Table B5). However, for the married women living alone and the unmarried ones, there is a positive relationship between the amount of land left uncultivated and the quality of land. It is hard to understand why these women would leave part of the good quality land uncultivated. A possible explanation would be that on a farm, not all land is of equal quality. Hence, even on farms with good quality land on average, some of it would be poor and left uncultivated.

Besteman (1995a) contends that smallholders with less land tend to allocate more of it to food production, and those with more land assign a larger percentage to the production of cash value crops. This also accords with the findings of Davison (1988). However, our findings contradict those of Besteman and Davison in that as total amount of land rises, the amount of land allocated to non-cash food crop production rises and this relationship is highly statistically significant at the 1 percent level for all women (Tables A2, B2, and C2). Also, as farm size increases, the amount of land allocated to non-food cash crop production rises for all women and farm size is also statistically significant at the 1 percent (Tables A4, B4 and C4). The amount of uncultivated land also rises with total farm size for all women and farm size is also statistically significant at the 1 percent level.

Von Braun, Bouis and Kennedy (1994) contend that the proportion of income out of total crop revenue derived either from food crops or non-food cash crop can also determine how the land as a resource will be allocated between non-cash food crops and non-food cash crops. If the proportion of income out of total crop revenue derived from food cash crops is very low, we would expect the relationship between the amount of land allocated to food crops and the proportion of income out of total crop revenue derived from food crops to be negative and vice versa. On the other hand, if the proportion of income derived from non-food cash crops out of total crop revenue is high, we would expect the relationship between the amount of land allocated for non-food cash crops and the proportion of income out of total crop revenue derived from non-food cash crops to be positive and vice versa. Our results show that there is a positive relationship between the amount of land allocated for non-cash food crops and the amount of income arising from sale of food crops for all women and the variable (SUBSREV3) is statistically significant at the 1 percent level for married women living with their husbands and 10 percent level for the unmarried women (Tables B2 and C2).

On the other hand, the proportion of income derived from non-food cash crops is negatively related to the amount of land allocated for non-food cash crops. The variable, (CASHREV3) is statistically significant at the 10 percent level for married women living alone (Table A4). These findings imply that non-food cash cropping is not bringing revenue commensurate with the amount of land allocated to it. This means that food cash crops are bringing in more revenue compared to non-food cash crops. A possible reason for these findings could be the declining prices of the major cash crops such as coffee, pyrethrum, tobacco and to a certain extent tea which are the crops grown in Nyeri district. Also, forceful deductions of cash, corruption and mismanagement of marketing cooperatives may have contributed to the low income from cash crops received by the farmers.

Sharma (2000) concurs that agricultural commercialisation does not reduce food availability. Khandker's (1988) basic finding in Bangladesh differs from that of Sharma because he believes it is possible that women may become worse off as a result of cash cropping. He also found that commercialisation increased intra-household inequality in terms of access and control over household resources. His views are also supported by Tisdell *et al.* (2001) in relation to West Bengal.

Does increase in non-food cash crop farming lead to a reduction in non cash food production? Tables A6 and A7 show that for married women living alone, as non-food cash crop production rises, the amount of non-cash food crop production falls, findings Sharma (2000). However, non-food cash crop production is not statistically significant in explaining the variations in the production of non-cash food production. The small sample size for these women may explain this negative relationship. On the other hand, Tables B6, B7 and C6 and C7 show that for married women living with their husbands and the unmarried women, non-food cash crop production and non-cash food production are positively related and this relationship is statistically significant at the 10 percent level. This means that non-cash food production and non-food cash crop production rise together, findings that support of Sharma (2000).

So how do we explain the fall in non-cash food output? Our results show that the amount of non-food cash crop production is negatively related to the number of hours all women spend on non-cash food production and this is statistically significant at the 1percent level for married women living alone and 10 percent level for married women living with husbands and the unmarried women (Tables A6, B6 and C6). This may explain the fall in non-cash food crop production in Nyeri district, findings that accord with those of critics of commercialisation such as Gross and Underwood (1971), Longhurst (1988).

The trend toward increased export crop production means that less emphasis is placed upon non-cash food production, which in turn affects the nutritional status of women and their children (Davison 1988). Schoepf and Schoepf (1988) argue that land expropriation for cash crop production has had a pronounced effect on peasant women's ability to provide a balanced diet for their families, leading often to advanced cases of nutritional deficiency. Schoepf (1982) found that in the Kabare Zone, South Kivu had one of the highest rates of malnutrition, including kwashiorkor among women and children, because large plantations growing export crops occupied much of the cultivable land, thus reducing the area available for peasant cultivation.

Conclusion

In summary, it can be seen that commercialisation has led to a decline in non-cash food production in Nyeri district. Resources, such as good quality land, labour and time have disproportionately been allocated to non-food cash crops leading to a reduction in non-cash food crops and exposing a lot of households to famine. Women also lack other resources like credit, are not visited by extension officers, and the majority of them have never obtained any training on good farming techniques.

Our results contradict those of Davison (1988) in showing that non-food cash cropping and increased allocation of land for non-food cash crops have moved in tandem with non-cash food production.

Our findings also contradict those of Julin (1993) in that in our case, the demand for male labour has not declined with commercialisation. There is also evidence to show that women living with husbands work more hours than those married but living alone and also the unmarried women who are household heads.

Also, we have seen that women seem to lose their decision-making ability with commercialisation, as husbands make most decisions to do with non-food cash crops. This includes handling of cash income, which as Kaiser and Dewey (1991) contend, husbands are less likely to use for the welfare of wives and children due to their different expenditure patterns. Our results also accord with those of Fortmann (1982). Women in Nyeri district have little or no power to change the way land and their labour is allocated for food and non-food cash crop production. This implies that commercialisation impacts negatively on women, food availability and indirectly on the nutrition of children. Prices that these smallholder farmers have been receiving for the non-food cash crops fluctuate with world market prices and recently prices have declined making non-food cash crop production unprofitable while the revenue derived from food cash crops has been rising. Due to the deteriorating terms of trade for non-food cash crops, men have started cultivation of food cash crops with the potential of crowding out women.

In our study, there were no households that were exclusive non-food cash crop producers or exclusive non-cash food producers. Smallholder producers make a conscious effort to maintain non-cash food production along side the new cash crops. This reliance on food from own production, under household control is a response to market, employment, and production risks and can be viewed as an insurance policy by farm households in a risky income environment. Farmers choose non-cash food production for home consumption because it is subjectively the best option given all constraints.

Although commercialisation may provide much needed cash income, rural households are forced to maintain non-cash food production for several reasons. These include: (1) poor economic conditions, poor terms of trade for cash crops, corruption and mismanagement of cooperatives and lack of insurance services making farmers have limited ability to cope with increased risks associated with commercial production; (2) transaction and marketing costs are tremendously high due to limited markets and lack of infrastructure. Under these circumstances as noted by Von Braun and Kennedy (1994), maintenance of their own food supplies is perhaps the only feasible and economically efficient strategy available to small farmers in developing countries.

References

Afonja, S. (1986), Changing Modes of Production and the Sexual Division of Labour Among the Yoruba, In: Eleanor Leacock and Hellen I. Safa (eds.), *Women's Work*, Bergin and Garvey Publishers, South Hadley, MA.

Angelique, H. (1995), *The Culture of Politics in Modern Kenya*, Cambridge University Press, New York.

Barnes, C. (1983), Differentiation by Sex Among Small Scale Farming Households in Kenya, *Rural Africana*, 15(16): 41-63.

Berry, S. (1975), *Cocoa, Custom and Socio-Economic Change in Rural Western Nigeria*, Clarendon Press, London.

Besteman, C. (1995a), Income Generation, In: Henderson, H. Kreider and Hansen Ellen (eds.), *Gender and Agricultural Development: Surveying the Field*, University of Arizona Press, Tuscon.

Besteman, C. (1995b), Agricultural Extension, In: Henderson, H. Kreider and Hansen Ellen (eds.), *Gender and Agricultural Development: Surveying the Field*, University of Arizona Press, Tuscon.

Boserup, E. (1970), *Woman's Role in Economic Development*, St. Martin's Press, New York.

Charlton, S., Everett, J., and Staudt, K. (1989), *Women, the State and Development*, State University of New York Press, Albany.

Cowen, M. (1986), Change in State Power, International Conditions and Peasant Producers, *The Journal of Development Studies*, 22(23): 55-84.

Davison, J. (1987), Without Land We are Nothing: The Effect of Land Tenure Policies and Practices Upon Rural Women in Kenya, *Rural Africana*, 27:19-33.

Davison, J. (1988), Who Owns What? Land Registration and Tensions in Gender Relations of Production in Kenya, In: Jean Davison (ed.), *Agriculture, Women, and Land: The African Experience*, Westview Press, Boulder and London.

Dey, J. (1982), Development Planning in The Gambia: The Gap Between Planners and Farmers' Expectations and Objectives, *World Development*, 10(2): 377-396.

Fortmann, L. (1982), Women's Work in a Communal Setting: The Tanzanian Policy of Ujamaa, In: Bay Edna (ed.), *Women and Work in Africa*, Westview Press, Boulder, Colombia.

Fortmann, L. (1984), Economic Status and Women's Participation in Agriculture: A Botswana Case Study, *Rural Sociology*, 49(3): 452-464.

Funk, U. (1988), Land Tenure, Agriculture, and Gender in Guinea-Bissau, In: Jean Davison (ed.), *Agriculture, Women, and Land: The African Experience*, Westview Press, Boulder and London.

Gladwin, C., Staudt, K., and Mcmillan, D. (1991), Reaffirming the Agricultural Role of African Women: One Solution to the Coming Food Crisis, *Journal of African Studies*, 10(2): 123-134.

Goheen, M. (1991), The Ideology and Political Economy of Gender: Women and Land in Nso, Cameroon, In: Gladwin and Christina (eds.), *Structural Adjustment and African Women Farmers*, Centre for African Studies. University of Florida Press, Gainesville.

Government of Kenya (1997), *National Development Plan*, Government Printers, Nairobi.

Gross, D. and Underwood, B. (1971), Technological Change and Calorie Costs: Sisal Agriculture in Northern Brazil, *American Anthropologist*, 73:725-740.

Guyer, J. (1984), *Family and Farm in Southern Cameroon*, Boston University Press, Boston.

Heyer, J., Maitha, J. K. and Senga, W. M. (1975), *Agricultural Development in Kenya: An Economic Assessment*, Oxford University Press, Nairobi.

Islam, N. (1994), Commercialisation of Agriculture and Food Security: Development Strategy and Trade Policy Issues, In: J. Von Braun and E. Kennedy (eds.), *Agricultural Commercialisation, Economic Development, and Nutrition*, International Food Policy Research Institute, Johns Hopkins University Press, Baltimore and London.

Julin, E. (1993), *Structural Change in Rural Kenya*, Unpublished PhD Thesis, University of Gotenborg, Sweden.

Jones, C. (1983), The Mobilisation of Women's Labour for Cash Crop Production: A Game Theoretic Approach, *American Journal of Agricultural Economics*, 65(5): 1049-1054.

Kaiser, L. and Dewey, K. (1991), Household Economic Strategies and Food Expenditure Patterns in Rural Mexico: Impact on Nutritional Status of Pre-school Children, *Ecology of Food and Nutrition*, 25:147-168.

Khandker, S. R. (1988), Determinants of Women's Time Allocation in Rural Bangladesh, *Economic Development and Cultural Change*, 37(1): 111-126.

Kimenia, M. (1996), Saitoti on SAPs: They Tap Economic Potential, *Daily Nation*, 17th October 1996, Nairobi.

Kiriti, T., Tisdell, C., and Roy, K. (2003), Female Participation in Decision-making in Agricultural Households in Kenya: Empirical Findings, *International Journal of Agricultural Resources, Governance and Ecology*, 2(2): 103-124.

Longhurst, R. (1988), Cash Crops, Household Food Security, and Nutrition, *IDS Bulletin*, 19(2): 28-36.

McComb, J. R., Finlayson, M. O., Hardaker, J. B., and Heywood, P. F. (1994), The Effect of a Short-Lived Plantation on Income, Consumption, and Nutrition: An Example from Papua New Guinea, In: J. Von Braun and E. Kennedy (eds.), *Agricultural Commercialisation, Economic Development, and Nutrition*, International Food Policy Research Institute, Johns Hopkins University Press, Baltimore and London.

Muntemba, M. S. (1982), Women and Agricultural Change in the Railway Region of Zambia: Dispossession and Counter-strategies, 1930-1970, In: Edna Bay (ed.), *Women and Work in Africa,* Westview Press, Boulder, Colombia.

Nasimiyu, R. (1985), Women in the Colonial Economy of Bungoma: Role of Women in Agriculture, 1902-1960, In: G. S. Were (ed.), *Women and Development in Africa*, Gideon Were Press, Nairobi.

Okali, C. (1983), *Cocoa and Kinship in Ghana*, Kegan Paul, London.

Safilios-Rothschild, C. (1982), *The Persistence of Women's Invisibility in Agriculture: Theoretical and Policy Lessons from Lesotho and Sierra Leone*, Centre for Policy Studies, The Population Council, New York.

Safilios-Rothschild, C. (1988), The Impact of Agrarian Reform on Men's and Women's Incomes in Rural Honduras, In D. Dwyer and J. Bruce (eds.), *A Home Divided: Women and Income in the Third World*, Stanford University Press Stanford.

Schoepf, C. (1982), *Results of Base-line Survey in Four Localities Near INERA Mulungu Station, Kivu Province*, Report for USAID/Zaire.

Schoepf, G. B. and Schoepf, C. (1988), Land, Gender, and Food Security in Eastern Kivu, Zaire, In: Jean Davison (ed.), *Agriculture, Women, and Land: The African Experience*, Westview Press, Boulder and London.

Sharma, K. R. (2000), Farm Commercialisation and Nutritional status of Children: The Case of Vegetables, Fruits and Cash Crops (VFC) Program in Western Nepal, *Mimeo*, University of Hawaii.

Staudt, K. (1982), Women Farmers and Inequities in Agricultural Services, In: Edna G. Bay (ed.), *Women and Work in Africa*, Westview Press, Boulder.

Staudt, K. (1987), Uncaptured or Unmotivated? Women and the Food Crisis in Africa, *Rural Sociology*, 52(4): 37-55.

Swynnerton, R. J. M. (1954), *A Plan to Intensify the Development of African Agriculture in Kenya,* Government Printers, Nairobi.

Tisdell, C *et al.* (2001), Socio-economic Determinants of the Intra-Family Status of Wives in Rural India: Analysis and Empirical Evidence, *Gender Issues*, 19(3): 41-60.

Von Braun, J., Bouis, H. and Kennedy, E. (1994), Conceptual Framework, In: J. Von Braun and E. Kennedy (eds.), *Agricultural Commercialisation, Economic Development, and Nutrition*, International Food Policy Research Institute, Johns Hopkins University Press, Baltimore and London.

Von Braun, J., de Haen, H., and Blanken, J. (1991), *Commercialisation of Agriculture under Population Pressure: Effects on Production, Consumption, and Nutrition in Rwanda,* Research Report No. 85, International Food Policy Research Institute: Washington DC.

Von Braun, J. and Kennedy, E. (1994), *Agricultural Commercialisation, Economic Development, and Nutrition*, International Food Policy Research Institute, Johns Hopkins University Press, Baltimore and London.

World Bank (1994), *Adjustment in Africa: Reforms, Results and the Road Ahead*, Washington DC.

APPENDIX A: Married Women Living Alone

Table A1: Mean and Standard Deviations of Variables used in Analysis

Variable	*Mean*	*Standard Deviation*	*N*
Subsist	0.9182	1.7180	26
Totfmsz	1.650	3.20	26
Landqual	1.85	0.61	26
Age	38.31	14.35	26
Nochild	4.31	2.60	26
Semisub	0.066	0.6149	26
Cash	0.4125	1.3534	26
Fallow	0.2506	0.6661	26
Hhneeds	1.65	1.06	26
Totosale	90.46	136.30	26
Hoursfc	17.38	14.24	26
Hourscc	10.19	12.00	26
Toupthc	107.73	57.46	26
Subsrev3	0.9198	0.1159	26

Table A2: Determinants of Amount of Land for Non-Cash Food Crops

Variable	*β Coefficient*	*Standard Error*	*t-statistic*
Constant	-0.523	1.566	-0.334
Totfmsz	0.469	0.057	8.274***
Landqual	-0.319	0.327	-0.973
Age	1.034×10^{-3}	0.018	-0.057
Nochild	-0.117	0.098	-0.191
Subsrev3	1.692	1.730	0.978
R^2	0.782		
Adj R^2	0.728		
F stat	14.354		

Table A3: Determinants of Amount of Land for Food Cash Crops

Variable	*β Coefficient*	*Standard Error*	*t-statistic*
Constant	1.226	0.462	2.655**
Totfmsz	3.666×10^{-2}	0.036	1.019
Landqual	-0.395	0.189	-2.089*
Age	-1.124×10^{-2}	0.011	-0.981
Nochild	1.969×10^{-3}	0.063	-.031
R^2	0.268		
Adj R^2	0.128		
F stat	1.919		

Table A4: Determinants of Amount of Land for Non-Food Cash Crops

Variable	*β Coefficient*	*Standard Error*	*t-statistic*
Constant	-0.646	0.562	-1.150***
Totfmsz	0.379	0.040	9.444***
Landqual	6.702×10^{-2}	0.232	0.289
Age	8.246×10^{-3}	0.012	0.661
Nochild	5.029×10^{-2}	0.070	0.723
Cashrev3	-2.957	1.274	-2.322*
R^2	0.839		
Adj R^2	0.796		
F stat	19.755		

Table A5: Determinants of Amount of Uncultivated Land

Variable	*β Coefficient*	*Standard Error*	*t-statistic*
Constant	-0.811	0.363	-2.233*
Totfmsz	0.141	0.028	4.980***
Landqual	0.247	0.149	1.660
Age	7.441×10^{-3}	0.009	0.826
Nochild	3.587×10^{-2}	0.049	0.726
R^2	0.614		
Adj R^2	0.540		
F stat	8.336		

Table A6: Determinants of Amount of Non-Food Cash Crop Production

Variable	*β Coefficient*	*Standard Error*	*t-statistic*
Constant	81.427	94.577	0.861
Totfmsz	19.713	10.030	1.965*
Landqual	28.243	38.625	0.731
Hhneeds	-21.346	22.005	-0.970
Hoursfc	-5.387	1.595	-3.377***

(Contd...)

Hourscc	4.051	2.370	1.709
Toupthc	-8.613×10^{-2}	0.524	-0.164
R^2	0.569		
Adj R^2	0.433		
F stat	4.185		

Table A7: Determinants of Amount of Non-Cash Food Crop Production

Variable	*β Coefficient*	*Standard Error*	*t-statistic*
Constant	94.578	36.170	2.615**
Totfmsz	12.621	3.846	3.282***
Landqual	-20.562	16.473	-1.248
Hhneeds	12.452	9.441	1.319
Hoursfc	0.138	0.882	0.156
Hourscc	-0.476	1.108	-0.429
Toupthc	-1.649×10^{-2}	0.100	-0.164
R^2	0.536		
Adj R^2	0.389		
F stat	3.658		

APPENDIX B: Married Women Living with Husbands

Table B1: Mean and Standard Deviations of Variables used in Analysis

Variable	*Mean*	*Standard Deviation*	*N*
Subsist	0.8267	0.6210	63
Totfmsz	2.25	2.12	63
Landqual	1.98	0.58	63
Age	38.73	12.00	63
Nochild	4.54	2.49	63
Semisub	0.1929	0.5839	63
Cash	0.7659	1.1224	63
Fallow	0.4649	0.7602	63
Hhneeds	1.52	1.06	63
Totosale	79.08	108.45	63
Hoursfc	17.73	14.19	63
Hourscc	13.52	12.45	63
Toupthc	103.78	50.80	63
Cashland	34.9524	26.0993	63
Subsrev3	0.8751	0.1869	63
Cashrev3	0.1235	0.1857	63

Table B2: Determinants of Amount of Land for Non-Cash Food Crops

Variable	*β Coefficient*	*Standard Error*	*t-statistic*
Constant	-0.349	0.388	-0.900
Totfmsz	0.204	0.032	6.448***
Landqual	-0.110	0.105	-1.046
Age	-5.44 x 10^{-3}	0.007	-0.732
Nochild	-1.64 x 10^{-2}	0.036	-0.456
Subsrev3	1.380	0.337	4.093***
R^2	0.470		
Adj R^2	0.422		
F stat	9.920		

Table B3: Determinants of Amount of Land for Food Cash Crops

Variable	*β Coefficient*	*Standard Error*	*t-statistic*
Constant	0.358	0.310	1.153
Totfmsz	0.114	0.035	3.302**
Landqual	-0.208	0.117	-1.780
Age	-2.539 x 10^{-3}	0.008	-0.305
Nochild	1.947 x 10^{-2}	0.040	0.482
R^2	0.228		
Adj R^2	0.175		
F stat	4.294		

Table B4: Determinants of Amount of Land for Non-Food Cash Crops

Variable	*β Coefficient*	*Standard Error*	*t-statistic*
Constant	-1.270	0.366	-3.474***
Totfmsz	0.416	0.041	10.155***
Landqual	0.426	0.135	3.151**
Age	3.715 x 10^{-2}	0.010	0.389
Nochild	2.721 x 10^{-2}	0.046	0.588
Cashrev3	-0.107	0.434	-0.246
R^2	0.730		
Adj R^2	0.706		
F stat	30.774		

Table B5: Determinants of Amount of Uncultivated Land

Variable	*β Coefficient*	*Standard Error*	*t-statistic*
Constant	0.141	0.257	0.550
Totfmsz	0.301	0.029	10.505***
Landqual	-0.174	0.097	-1.804

(Contd...)

Age	3.593×10^{-3}	0.007	0.522
Nochild	-3.226×10^{-2}	0.033	-0.966
R^2	0.689		
Adj R^2	0.667		
F stat	32.056		

Table B6: Determinants of Amount of Non-Food Cash Crop Production

Variable	β Coefficient	Standard Error	t-statistic
Constant	-4.893	55.002	-0.089
Totfmsz	17.124	6.499	2.635**
Landqual	30.297	22.087	1.372
Hhneeds	-9.943	12.739	-0.781
Hoursfc	-2.469	1.031	-2.394*
Hourscc	2.621	1.222	2.145*
Toupthc	8.478×10^{-2}	0.253	0.335
R^2	0.263		
Adj R^2	0.184		
F stat	3.338		

Table B7: Determinants of Amount of Non-Cash Food Crop Production

Variable	*β Coefficient*	*Standard Error*	*t-statistic*
Constant	83.549	21.164	3.948***
Cashland	-1.508	0.270	-5.585***
Landqual	16.107	9.525	1.691
Hhneeds	10.531	5.815	1.811
Hoursfc	-0.551	0.448	-1.232
Hourscc	1.680	0.535	3.138**
Totosale	0.152	0.058	2.613**
R^2	0.400		
Adj R^2	0.336		
F stat	6.218		

APPENDIX C: Unmarried Women

Table C1: Mean and Standard Deviations of Variables used in Analysis

Variable	*Mean*	*Standard Deviation*	*N*
Subsist	0.9776	1.5555	48
Totfmsz	2.70	5.43	48
Landqual	1.75	0.48	48
Age	55.08	13.40	48
Nochild	5.48	2.85	48

(Contd...)

Semisub	0.1446	0.4498	48
Cash	1.1921	3.3093	48
Fallow	0.3877	0.6745	48
Hhneeds	1.40	1.23	48
Totosale	83.60	137.40	48
Hoursfc	13.38	9.37	48
Hourscc	9.85	12.11	48
Toupthc	90.02	71.66	48
Subsrev3	0.9025	0.1701	48
Cashrev3	0.009748	0.1701	48

Table C2: Determinants of Amount of Land for Non-Cash Food Crops

Variable	*β Coefficient*	*Standard Error*	*t-statistic*
Constant	-0.285	0.649	-0.440
Totfmsz	0.272	0.014	19.401***
Landqual	-0.227	0.159	-1.438
Age	1.364×10^{-3}	0.006	0.239
Nochild	-1.08×10^{-2}	0.028	-0.382
Subrev3	1.020	0.462	2.209*
R^2	0.916		
Adj R^2	0.906		
F stat	101.590		

Table C3: Determinants of Amount of Land for Food Cash Crops

Variable	*β Coefficient*	*Standard Error*	*t-statistic*
Constant	-0.338	0.322	-1.050
Totfmsz	1.152×10^{-2}	0.012	0.934
Landqual	0.183	0.135	1.353
Age	-3.63×10^{-3}	0.005	-0.664
Nochild	3.041×10^{-2}	0.024	1.292
Hhneeds	0.118	0.057	2.079*
R^2	0.113		
Adj R^2	0.031		
F stat	2.049		

Table C4: Determinants of Amount of Land for Non-Food Cash Crops

Variable	*β Coefficient*	*Standard Error*	*t-statistic*
Constant	-0.699	0.343	-2.037
Totfmsz	0.607	0.013	47.027***
Landqual	6.893×10^{-2}	0.146	0.473
Age	3.784×10^{-3}	0.005	0.720

(Contd...)

Nochild	-1.358 x 10^{-2}	0.026	-0.052
Cashrev3	-0.820	0.426	-1.926
R^2	0.984		
Adj R^2	0.982		
F stat	512.733		

Table C5: Determinants of Amount of Uncultivated Land

Variable	*β Coefficient*	*Standard Error*	*t-statistic*
Constant	5.469 x 10^{-2}	0.255	0.214
Totfmsz	0.106	0.010	10.858
Landqual	5.091 x 10^{-2}	0.107	0.477
Age	-2.917 x 10^{-3}	0.004	-0.749
Nochild	2.136 x 10^{-2}	0.019	1.142
R^2	0.769		
Adj R^2	0.747		
F stat	35.756		

TableC6: Determinants of Amount of Non-Food Cash Crop Production

Variable	*β Coefficient*	*Standard Error*	*t-statistic*
Constant	-56.085	59.499	-0.943
Totfmsz	10.295	3.593	2.865**
Landqual	37.414	29.329	1.276
Hhneeds	1.792	12.092	0.148
Hoursfc	-3.231	1.663	-1.944*
Hourscc	3.145	1.315	2.391*
Toupthc	0.634	0.270	2.352*
R^2	0.590		
Adj R^2	0.528		
F stat	9.584		

Table C7: Determinants of Amount of Non-Cash Food Crop Production

Variable	*β Coefficient*	*Standard Error*	*t-statistic*
Constant	45.262	32.268	1.403
Totfmsz	5.662	1.974	2.868**
Landqual	-1.152	16.438	-0.070
Hhneeds	1.991	6.638	0.300
Hoursfc	1.522	0.925	1.646
Hourscc	-0.734	0.764	-0.962
Totosale	0.192	0.081	2.352*
R^2	0.545		
Adj R^2	0.476		
F stat	7.976		

Notes: *** Significant at the 1% level; ** Significant at the 5% level; * Significant at the 10% level

7

Women Participation in Labour Market

Okurut, F. N. *University of Botswana*

Ssewanyana, S. *Economic Policy Research Centre, Kampala*

Introduction

Uganda has been implementing economic and institutional reforms since the mid1980s, which include liberalization of agricultural output marketing, financial sector liberalization, privatization of state enterprises, decentralization, civil service reforms and deregulation of labour markets. The reforms were adopted so as to eliminate the distortions in the factor and product markets so as to enhance the market mechanisms in the mobilization and allocation of resources to promote sustainable economic growth (Bigsten and Kayizzi-Mugerwa 1999; Deininger and Okidi 2003; Sharer *et al.* 1995). The labour market reforms were expected to result in free movement of labour across the various sectors where it gets the highest return, with the real wages determined by market forces of demand and supply. The limited empirical analysis of women participation of the extent of female participation in Uganda's labour over the economic period motivated this study. The rationale is that labour market participation is closely linked to women economic empowerment. Sudan (2006) observed that women's work tends to range from wage employment to self-employment and unpaid family (including child bearing, child rearing and domestic chores). This study investigates the trends in female labour market participation rates and the factors that influenced them over the reform era using descriptive statistics.

Labour Market Participation

Lanot and Muller (1997) observed that in Cameroon, the probability of female participation in formal labour markets is positively and significantly influenced by age, education level, being married, and having substitutes for domestic work. However, the probability of female participation in formal labour markets is negatively and significantly influenced by the husband's age, and number of small children. The positive and significant coefficient of education level was interpreted in terms of higher returns to education in the formal labour market. The negative and significant coefficient of husband's age was related to the traditional mentality of the household head where women were expected to stay at home and not participate in the labour market. The presence of children had a negative and significant effect on the probability of female participation in the formal labour market, which was explained in terms of caring for children at home by mothers. Female participation in the informal labour market was only positively and significantly influenced by age.

Fallon and Riveros (1989) had similar results where they noted that female labour force participation rates in Tunisia, Israel, and Korea is influenced by their educational attainment. The female participation rate was observed to grow with increase in secondary education. This is almost similar with the argument by Matshe and Young (2004) that education and gender are very important individual characteristics that determine labour allocations.

Education level in turn influences both the choice of activity combination (farming, wage work or own family business) and earnings. Wambugu (2003) observed that in Kenya as education level increases from primary to secondary, the probability of generating income from a combination of economic activities also increases. However, higher levels of education (tertiary or university) increase the probability of generating income from only wage employment. The results suggested that more educated households have higher total earnings both in the rural and urban areas, which underscores the correlation between labour market participation and education.

Bigsten and Kayizzi-Mugerwa (1999) estimated separate models for urban and rural labour market participation rates in Uganda. Male participation in the formal urban labour markets was positively and significantly influenced by secondary education, and being household head, while negatively influenced by income of other household members. In comparison with female participation in the formal urban labour markets was positively and significantly influenced by post secondary education and being household head. However, education level was found to be insignificant in explaining labour market participation in the urban informal sector. While being household head and being a public service employee positively influenced participation in the urban informal sector, it was negatively influenced by age. The positive coefficient for being household head was explained by the fact that the heads were under pressure to earn more income for the household. The significant coefficient for being a public service employee was accounted for by the fact that public servants who were under pressure to supplement their meagre incomes were using their official positions to provide business opportunities. The negative coefficient for age was due to the fact that much of the informal sector business was the hawking type, which needed more physical resilience. Participation in formal employment in the rural sector was also observed to be positively and significantly influenced by secondary and post-secondary education.

Data

The data are from a series of nationally representative cross-section household surveys conducted by Uganda Bureau of Statistics. Although the Bureau has conducted eight rounds of such surveys, we focus on the 1992-93, 1999-2000 and 2002-03 survey rounds (hereafter 1992, 1999 and 2002, respectively). The 1992 round were conducted from March 1992 to February 1993, covering 9,923 households with 46,107 individuals. The 1999 round were conducted from August 1999-July 2000 covering 10,696 households with 55,617 individuals. However, some four districts including Kitgum, Gulu, Kasese and Bundibugyo were excluded from the survey because of insurgences at the time of the survey. The latest survey at the time of this study is the 2002 round that was conducted from May 2002 to April 2003, covering 9,711 households with 48,560 individuals. However, Pader district (which was part of Kitgum district) was not covered. Consequently, to make our results comparable over time, we omit all the five districts (Pader, Gulu, Kitgum, Kasese and Bundibugyo) from our analysis.

Empirical Results

Structure of the Labour Market and Trends

The labour market is characterized by high rates of population growth (3.3% per annum) and labour force growth. Table 1 presents the evolution of the labour force for individuals aged 15 to 64 years in Uganda since 1992. The labour force growth rates were three percent during the 1990s and about 4.4 percent between 1999 and 2002. For the entire period of study, labour force grew by 3.4 percent.

The distribution of the labour force by gender displays a higher proportion of females than of males, a pattern consistent as that observed elsewhere in developing countries. With regard to educational attainment, the Ugandan labour force has become more educated, both for females and males. There have been significant drops in the proportion of individuals with no formal education especially for females, followed by increases in those with completed primary and above. By contrast, the proportion of females with some primary education increased against a falling trend for males at the same level. The improvements in the primary education are partly attributed to Universal Primary Education (UPE). The increases in the proportions with some secondary education were comparable between females and males, 4.9 and 4.1 percentage points between 1999 and 2002. The proportion of the female labour force with completed secondary education increased by 0.8 percentage points, a change comparable to that of males of 0.43 over the same period. In other words, the labour force in Uganda experienced a gender pattern of the changes in education composition over the entire period. Like for the entire

Table 1: Labour Force of Persons Aged 15-64 Years, 1992-2002

Uganda	*1992/93*		*1999/00*		*2002/03*		*Annualized growth rates (%)*		
	Persons	***Share (%)***	***Persons***	***Share (%)***	***Persons***	***Share (%)***	***92-99***	***99-02***	***92-02***
	7,680,442		***9,544,099***		***10,776,671***		***3.0***	***4.4***	***3.4***
Place of residence:									
Rural	6,605,282	86.0	8,050,858	84.4	8,980,438	83.3	2.7	4.0	3.0
Urban	1,075,160	14.0	1,493,241	15.7	1,796,233	16.7	4.5	6.7	5.1
Region:									
Central	2,346,923	30.6	2,847,836	29.8	3,573,894	33.2	2.6	8.3	4.2
Eastern	2,174,418	28.3	2,444,040	25.6	3,025,478	28.1	1.6	7.8	3.3
Northern	1,315,495	17.1	1,800,772	18.9	1,581,617	14.7	4.3	-4.7	1.8
Western	1,843,606	24.0	2,451,451	25.7	2,595,682	24.1	3.9	2.1	3.4
Education level:									
No formal education	2,246,095	29.2	2,289,115	24.0	1,783,110	16.6	0.3	-9.1	-2.3
Some Primary	3,443,991	44.8	4,187,763	43.9	4,618,566	42.9	2.7	3.6	2.9
Completed primary	816,190	10.6	1,140,932	12.0	1,526,304	14.2	4.6	10.6	6.2
Some secondary	565,557	7.4	901,438	9.4	1,504,410	14.0	6.4	18.6	9.7
Completed secondary	275,302	3.6	373,099	3.9	489,111	4.5	4.1	9.8	5.7
Post secondary	332,891	4.3	604,936	6.3	794,285	7.4	8.1	9.9	8.6
Education missing	416	0.0	46,816	0.5	52,219	0.5			
Gender:									
Female	4,034,841	52.5	5,061,977	53.0	5,688,718	52.8	3.1	4.2	3.4
Male	3,645,601	47.5	4,482,122	47.0	5,087,953	47.2	2.8	4.6	3.3
Marital status:									
Female unmarried	811,598	10.6	1,211,960	12.7	1,330,059	12.4	5.5	3.4	4.9
Female married	2,652,630	34.5	3,111,541	32.6	3,506,105	32.5	2.2	4.3	2.8
Female divorced	256,489	3.3	322,486	3.4	437,133	4.1	3.1	11.1	5.3
Female widowed	314,124	4.1	415,990	4.4	412,204	3.8	3.8	-0.3	2.7
Male	3,645,601	47.5	4,482,122	47.0	5,087,953	47.2	2.8	4.6	3.3

(Contd...)

Age cohort:									
15 - 19	1,594,411	20.8	2,142,450	22.5	2,317,693	21.5	4.0	2.9	3.7
20 - 24	1,366,131	17.8	1,465,403	15.4	1,901,401	17.6	1.0	9.5	3.3
25 - 29	1,238,536	16.1	1,376,474	14.4	1,770,591	16.4	1.4	9.2	3.5
30 - 34	931,213	12.1	1,140,475	12.0	1,381,509	12.8	2.8	7.0	3.9
35 - 39	678,932	8.8	1,013,270	10.6	1,077,019	10.0	5.5	2.2	4.6
40 - 44	494,528	6.4	699,002	7.3	759,794	7.1	4.7	3.0	4.3
45 - 49	432,982	5.6	585,314	6.1	600,219	5.6	4.1	0.9	3.2
50 - 54	414,753	5.4	447,379	4.7	427,833	4.0	1.0	-1.6	0.3
55 - 59	276,593	3.6	339,114	3.6	286,113	2.7	2.8	-6.2	0.3
60 - 64	252,363	3.3	335,218	3.5	254,499	2.4	3.9	-10.0	0.1

Source: Authors' calculations based on household surveys 1992, 1999 and 2002.
Notes: (i) Estimates exclude the districts of Gulu, Pader, Kitgum, Kasese and Bundibugyo.

labour force, there have been changes in the education composition of the youth defined as those aged 25-29 years. The results reveal that between 1992 and 1999 the proportion with some secondary education increased by 1.6 and 0.5 percentage points to 4.4 and 3.4 points between 1999 and 2002 for females and males respectively.

With regard to location, the urban areas experienced higher growth in the labour force compared to rural areas. This is largely explained by the rural-urban migration. On the other hands, labour force growth has a regional dimension especially after 1999. The negative growth in the Northern region is explained by the insurgence that has persisted in the area since the late 1980s. Worth mentioning, is the result suggesting that the labour force is skewed towards the young generation. Uganda has nearly a fifth of its child population in the age group 15-19 years in the labour force, and the trend increased up to 1999 before declining in 2002.

The indicator of labour market participation used in this study is the employment-to-population ratio (EPR). EPR is defined as total employment of the population 15-64 years as a percentage of the total population in the same age group. This ratio indicates the extent to which the population is involved in productive labour market activities. Total employment increased from about 6 million in 1992 to nearly 8 million persons in 2002. Table 2 presents EPR as related to age, education, gender, marital status and geographical location. It also presents growth rates in the number of employed population. Broadly speaking, EPRs have declined from nearly 78 percent in 1992 and stabilized around 77 percent thereafter.

Disaggregating the population by gender suggests that though the male participation rates always exceeded those of female, the rates by age groups for both tended to follow a similar trend for the entire period. As a whole, the average annual growth rate of female workforce was 3.5 per cent compared to that of male of 1.9 percent between 1992 and 1999; and for the entire period was 3.6 for female and 2.7 percent for male workforce. In other words, the female employment grew faster than that of the male; and there has been a definite trend towards a narrowing gender gap in EPR, with female rate becoming increasing closer to that of male.

A regional dimension in EPR is observed with the Central region recording the lowest rate and the highest rates are observed in the Northern region. It is only the Northern regions that recorded an increase in the EPR by 3.5 percentage points. The high education participation rates in the Central region partly explain the lower EPR. The same explanation holds for the decline observed in the rural areas. By extension, the urban areas have higher numbers of children and adults attending educational institutions and hence the explanation for the lower rates compared to rural areas.

Age composition is an important determinant of labour participation. As expected, the EPR rates by age show an inverted U shape pattern, suggesting relatively low rates, with the rates reaching the peak among 30-34, and then starting to decline among the older segments. The results also suggest high participation in the higher age groups. We observe a declining growth for individuals 50-64 years old in the last period. Although not presented in Table 2, the participation of older individuals outside the workforce (65 years plus) increased drastically between 1992 and 1999 before declining again in the last period. The participation of the elderly population in the workforce is not surprising in a country like Uganda where there no such social systems to assist such a group. By extension, the AIDS pandemic that affected mostly the productive population might have transferred much of the burden to the elderly population. Thus, explaining their high participation rates in the labour market.

Turning to educational attainment, the EPR increased for all levels between 1992 and 1999 with the exception of those individuals with completed primary education. Worth noting is the declining numbers of those individuals with no formal education, representing a negative growth of about 2 percent per annum over the entire period. Despite of the education expansion, the bulk of the workers still have low educational levels.

In sum, the results reveal increased female participation in the labour market, which may be explained by the UPE policy that enabled the girl child to have increased access to education (Bategeka *et al.* 2004). This has been reinforced by the deliberate policy of encouraging female education in public universities by giving them extra 1.5 points for entry.

Table 2: Employment-to-Population and Growth Rates (%)

	Employment-to-population			*Employment growth rates*		
	1992	***1999***	***2002***	***1992-99***	***1999-02***	***1992-02***
Uganda	78.3	76.8	76.5	2.7	4.3	3.1
Place of residence:						
Rural	80.5	79.4	78.8	2.5	3.7	2.8
Urban	64.8	63.3	65.0	4.2	7.7	5.1
Region:						
Central	71.7	73.9	72.7	3.0	7.7	4.3
Eastern	81.6	77.3	77.9	0.9	8.0	2.8
Northern	76.8	77.5	80.3	4.4	-3.4	2.3
Western	83.7	79.3	77.8	3.2	1.4	2.7
Education level:						
No formal education	87.3	89.8	89.4	0.7	-9.3	-2.1
Some Primary	76.5	74.8	76.5	2.4	4.4	2.9
Completed primary	77.8	77.8	79.9	4.6	11.6	6.5
Some secondary	56.6	54.2	58.1	5.7	21.1	9.9
Completed secondary	72.6	68.6	77.7	3.4	14.4	6.4

(Contd...)

Post secondary	78.6	78.4	75.7	8.1	8.6	8.3
Education missing	0.0	82.9	86.6			
Gender:						
Female	75.1	77.1	76.5	3.5	3.9	3.6
Male	81.8	76.5	76.6	1.9	4.6	2.7
Age cohort:						
15 – 19	46.6	33.9	31.3	-0.3	-0.1	-0.3
20 – 24	75.5	74.2	76.5	0.7	10.6	3.4
25 – 29	86.1	89.4	90.1	2.0	9.4	4.0
30 – 34	92.1	93.3	94.2	2.9	7.3	4.1
35 – 39	91.9	94.9	94.6	5.9	2.1	4.9
40 – 44	92.9	95.8	95.2	5.1	2.8	4.5
45 – 49	90.9	94.5	94.2	4.6	0.8	3.6
50 – 54	90.5	96.0	91.9	1.8	-3.2	0.5
55 – 59	89.1	90.6	89.9	3.0	-6.5	0.4
60 – 64	84.6	90.5	83.1	4.8	-13.1	-0.1
Marital status:						
Female unmarried	51.4	40.0	37.2	2.1	0.8	1.7
Female married	80.2	88.3	88.4	3.5	4.4	3.7
Female divorced	83.3	91.8	87.8	4.5	9.4	5.8
Female widowed	86.8	90.0	90.2	4.3	-0.3	3.1
Male	81.8	76.5	76.6	1.9	4.6	2.7
Uganda ('000)	6,011.6	7,334.0	8,245.2			

Source: Authors' calculations based on household surveys 1992, 1999 and 2002.
Notes: (i) Estimates exclude the districts of Gulu, Pader, Kitgum, Kasese and Bundibugyo. (ii) Estimates based on main activity status during the last 12 months prior to the surveys.

Employment Status by Sector and Social Grouping

The sectoral decomposition is in three broad groups, namely agriculture, industry and services. Agriculture includes crop and non-crop agriculture; industry includes mining & quarrying, manufacturing, public utilities and construction; and services include trade, hotels, transport/communication, miscellaneous and public services. Employment status is broadly categorized into two broad groups, namely self-employed and paid employees. The self-employed include employers, who could create jobs for others; own account workers, and unpaid family workers who assist in the household enterprises. The paid employees include those working for a wage/salary either in the public or private sector.

The results of employment status (see table 3) suggest that though males' dominate in all employment groupings except self-employment in agriculture, their shares are falling with increasing participation of females. Worth noting is the increase of females in the self-employment in non-agricultural activities from nearly 38 percent in 1992 to about 45 percent in 1999 before falling to 43 percent in 2002. The increased female participation in non-agricultural activities may be explained by the emergence of micro-finance institutions that provided collateral free loans especially to women (Okurut 2005).

Table 3: Share of Employment Status within Each Sector by Social Grouping

	1992/93				*1999/00*				*2002/03*			
	Self		*Paid*		*Self*		*Paid*		*Self*		*Paid*	
	Agriculture	*Non-agric*	*Public*	*Private*	*Agriculture*	*Non-agric*	*Public*	*Private*	*Agriculture*	*Non-agric*	*Public*	*Private*
Gender:												
Female	57.7	37.6	26.8	17.6	59.7	45.1	24.6	23.4	62.0	42.6	29.3	26.1
Male	42.3	62.4	73.2	82.4	40.3	54.9	75.4	76.6	38.0	57.4	70.7	73.9
Age cohort:												
15 - 19	13.8	5.0	0.6	13.7	10.8	5.5	0.2	11.8	10.2	3.9	0.0	12.1
20 - 24	17.5	14.8	9.0	20.7	14.7	15.0	4.1	18.9	13.0	16.7	7.6	20.7
25 - 29	16.8	22.0	22.2	18.8	15.5	21.1	19.5	20.6	17.3	22.9	19.2	24.1
30 - 34	12.6	24.0	21.7	15.3	13.4	18.3	20.0	17.0	14.6	18.8	23.8	14.9
35 - 39	9.8	14.2	14.9	9.5	12.4	16.2	22.7	11.8	11.7	15.0	18.6	9.7
40 - 44	7.5	6.5	11.8	7.2	9.4	8.3	12.8	6.7	8.9	9.5	9.2	6.5
45 - 49	6.9	5.4	7.2	4.5	7.9	7.1	9.6	4.9	7.1	6.3	9.6	5.5
50 - 54	6.5	4.0	7.4	5.2	6.4	3.7	6.7	4.2	5.2	3.7	6.7	3.4
55 - 59	4.6	2.2	3.1	2.4	4.8	2.7	2.5	2.0	3.8	1.9	3.5	1.6
60 - 64	4.0	1.9	2.1	2.6	4.8	2.2	1.8	2.2	3.2	1.4	1.9	1.5
Education level:												
No formal education	38.3	13.2	4.4	20.4	33.4	11.7	2.6	14.3	24.6	8.8	3.0	13.2
Some Primary	46.4	40.9	16.2	41.5	45.9	37.3	7.3	36.5	48.4	37.3	6.4	32.3
Completed primary	9.6	17.0	9.9	13.0	11.4	17.8	5.1	13.8	13.7	18.8	3.4	16.9
Some secondary	3.9	11.3	9.7	9.3	5.2	15.1	6.2	8.5	8.5	16.4	7.4	13.2
Completed secondary	1.3	9.6	16.2	6.8	2.1	6.9	9.0	8.6	2.8	8.5	8.6	7.0
Post secondary	0.5	8.1	43.6	9.0	1.6	10.5	69.6	17.0	1.7	9.2	70.7	16.4
Education missing					0.4	0.9	0.3	1.4	0.3	1.1	0.5	1.1
Economic sector:												
Crop agriculture	97.6	0.0	0.4	22.5	97.1	0.0	0.7	20.0	94.9	0.0	1.3	20.9
Non-crop agriculture	2.4	0.0	1.0	8.8	2.9	0.0	0.7	7.7	5.1	0.0	1.2	9.8
Mining & quarrying	0.0	1.2	0.0	0.1	0.0	3.7	0.1	0.3	0.0	0.7	0.0	0.6
Manufacturing	0.0	23.0	5.3	15.6	0.0	16.0	0.5	9.4	0.0	22.1	0.4	11.4
Public utilities	0.0	0.3	1.3	0.2	0.0	0.1	1.3	0.8	0.0	0.0	1.5	0.2
Construction	0.0	1.7	0.6	9.9	0.0	2.6	0.9	8.0	0.0	1.6	0.3	8.4
Trade	0.0	60.6	0.8	12.1	0.0	55.4	0.9	11.4	0.0	51.2	0.1	10.0
Hotels	0.0	4.5	0.6	1.8	0.0	8.0	0.4	5.1	0.0	10.2	0.1	3.8

(Contd...)

Transport/communication	0.0	3.2	3.3	7.7	0.0	3.7	2.8	10.5	0.0	4.9	1.9	8.1
Miscellaneous service	0.0	2.7	3.2	14.2	0.0	8.4	8.2	16.6	0.0	6.4	3.4	17.0
Public services	0.0	2.7	83.5	7.2	0.0	2.0	83.6	10.3	0.0	2.5	89.6	9.8
Place of residence:												
Rural	97.6	51.6	63.1	61.0	97.8	52.2	64.0	53.1	97.1	67.2	72.1	60.0
Urban	2.4	48.4	36.9	39.0	2.2	47.8	36.0	46.9	2.9	32.8	27.9	40.0
Region:												
Central	21.4	49.1	37.0	57.2	22.4	45.9	29.2	56.7	24.0	44.2	29.8	52.2
Eastern	32.1	24.0	29.3	14.2	27.2	24.3	30.3	15.6	33.1	22.4	23.0	15.8
Northern	19.3	9.5	14.1	5.3	21.9	11.8	16.6	6.4	19.3	8.4	14.1	6.4
Western	27.2	17.5	19.7	23.4	28.6	18.0	23.9	21.2	23.7	25.0	33.1	25.7

Source: Authors' calculations based on household surveys 1992, 1999 and 2002.
Notes: i) Estimates exclude the districts of Gulu, Pader, Kitgum, Kasese and Bundibugyo.
ii) Estimates based on main activity in the last 12 months prior to the surveys.

Employment rates for workers with less education and those working outside the working age fell throughout the period of analysis and this decline was higher for the self-employment in agriculture. By extension, share of urban employment in the private sector fell by nearly 7 percentage points between 1999 and 2002. Over time, the private sector is continuing to demand for more educated employees, for instance the demand for post secondary employees increased form its low level in 1992 of 9 percent to 16.4 percent in 2002.

Occupational Structure

The share of the workforce in different occupation by gender is presented in table 4. The occupations are classified into seven categories according to standard ILO classification – professionals and their associates; administrators including legislators, senior officials, managers and administrators; clerks and related workers; service including service workers, shop and market sales workers; agriculture including agriculture and fishery; production including craft & related workers, plant, machines operators and assemblers; and unskilled including elementary occupations. The share of professionals workers in total employment has increased from about 3 percent in 1992 to 5 percent in 2002; while that of administrators recorded a declining trend over the entire period. The increase in female professionals is worth noting, grew by 13 percent during the period 1999-2002. Such a significant growth might be attributed to the change in the level of human capital of the female workforce. It also suggests that the formal labour markets are becoming more competitive. As expected the agricultural workers make up the largest group, though the share is declining. There is evidence of growing female representation as service workers over time, with almost similar shares for males in 2002.

Yet, these jobs are traditionally associated with lower earnings and more insecure conditions. Generally speaking, the change in the occupational distribution by gender over the entire study period was relatively modest. There is evidence of changes in the female position within the occupation though the allocation across broad occupational aggregates remained limited.

Table 4: Share of Workforce by Occupation and Gender

	1992		*1999*		*2002*		*Annualized growth rates (%)*		
	Persons	*Share*	*Persons*	*Share*	*Persons*	*Share*	*92-99*	*99-02*	*92-02*
Uganda:									
Professionals & associated professionals	197,124	3.28	314,538	4.29	377,298	4.58	6.4	6.6	6.4
Legislators, senior officials, managers, & administrators	34,438	0.57	36,500	0.5	13,996	0.17	0.8	-34.8	-8.9
Clerks	68,483	1.14	40,708	0.56	38,283	0.46	-7.1	-2.2	-5.8
Service workers, shop & market sales	484,792	8.06	694,211	9.47	1,226,934	14.88	4.9	20.7	9.2
Agricultural & fishery	4,789,850	79.68	5,729,407	78.12	5,401,639	65.51	2.4	-2.1	1.2
Production	208,094	3.46	242,151	3.3	458,449	5.56	2.1	23.2	7.8
Unskilled	228,230	3.8	275,896	3.76	715,885	8.68	2.6	34.7	11.3
Not stated	565	0.01	541	0.01	12,685	0.15			
Females:									
Professionals & associated professionals	71,164	2.35	93,659	2.4	134,170	3.08	3.7	13.1	6.3
Legislators, senior officials, managers, & administrators	3,495	0.12	4,620	0.12	2,944	0.07	3.8	-16.4	-1.7
Clerks	26,468	0.87	18,284	0.47	22,765	0.52	-5.0	8.0	-1.5
Service workers, shop & market sales	166,104	5.48	335,116	8.58	612,795	14.09	9.6	21.9	12.9
Agricultural & fishery	2,682,512	88.51	3,332,089	85.34	3,305,001	75.98	3.0	-0.3	2.1
Production	59,839	1.97	54,010	1.38	106,501	2.45	-1.4	24.7	5.7
Unskilled	20,601	0.68	66,607	1.71	161,855	3.72	16.0	32.3	20.4
Not stated	565	0.02	48	0	3,566	0.08			
Males:									
Professionals & associated professionals	125,960	4.23	220,879	6.44	243,128	6.24	7.7	3.5	6.5
Legislators, senior officials, managers, & administrators	30,943	1.04	31,880	0.93	11,052	0.28	0.4	-38.5	-10.2
Clerks	42,015	1.41	22,424	0.65	15,518	0.4	-8.6	-13.4	-9.9
Service workers, shop & market sales	318,688	10.69	359,095	10.47	614,139	15.77	1.6	19.5	6.5

(Contd...)

Agricultural & fishery	2,107,338	70.7	2,397,318	69.9	2,096,638	53.82	1.8	-4.9	-0.1
Production	148,255	4.97	188,141	5.49	351,948	9.03	3.2	22.8	8.6
Unskilled	207,629	6.97	209,289	6.1	554,030	14.22	0.1	35.4	9.7
Not stated			493	0.01	9,119	0.23			

Source: Authors' calculations based on household surveys 1992, 1999 & 2002.
Notes: (i) Estimates exclude the districts of Gulu, Pader, Kitgum, Kasese and Bundibugyo.
(ii) Estimates based on main activity in the last 12 months prior to the surveys.

Wage Employment

The 'informal' sector remains a predominant employment sector. The share of formal paid employment in total employment declined from nearly 16 percent in 1992 to 14 percent in 1999 before rising again to about 15 percent in 2002. In other words, nearly a seventh of total employment is still accounted for by the 'formal' sector. In terms of annualized growth rates, the period 1992-99 experienced the lowest growth in wage employment of only 0.9 percent compared to 7.4 per cent over the period 1999-2002. In absolute numbers, formal paid employment grew from about 0.9 million persons in 1992 to nearly 1.2 million persons in 2002, representing a growth rate of 2.6 percent. Although this growth was lower than the overall growth in employment and particularly that of labour supply. The share of rural wage employment in total wage employment increased from 53.8 percent to 61.4 percent in 1999 and 2002 respectively. In terms of annualized growth rate, it grew by nearly 12 percent between 1999 and 2002, a growth rate well above that observed in the economy. This finding is largely attributed to recruitment of primary school teachers for the UPE program. The mushrooming Non-government Organizations (NGOs) might also explain this growth.

Wage employment has a marked regional dimension, with Northern Uganda recording the least share. It remained below 10 percent over the entire period (see table 5). The share of those employees with post secondary education increased from 22.3 percent in 1992 to 28.7 percent in 2002. In contrast, the share of employees with some primary declined from 32 percent to 26.8 percent in 1992 and 2002 respectively. There has been a marked increase in the participation of female employees in wage employment. The results reveal an increase of 9.3 percentage points, from 19.5 percent in 1992 to 28.8 percent in 2002. Worth noting is the share of wage employment in the manufacturing sector. It declined from 12.5 percent in 1992 to 7.8 percent in 1999 before rising to 9.8 percent in 2002. The patterns do mirror growth rates in the manufacturing sector at macro level.

Table 5: Wage Employment by Geographical Location

	1992/93		*1999/00*		*2002/03*		*Annualized growth rates (%)*		
	Persons	***Share***	***Persons***	***Share***	***Persons***	***Share***	***92-99***	***99-02***	***92-02***
Uganda:									
Public	331,642	35.4	247,882	24.9	283,194	23.2	-4.0	4.8	-1.6
Private	605,178	64.6	749,407	75.1	937,560	76.8	2.9	8.1	4.3
Rural:									
Public	209,220	36.2	158,692	28.5	204,231	26.6	-3.8	9.2	-0.2
Private	368,940	63.8	398,092	71.5	562,293	73.4	1.0	12.6	4.2
Urban:									

(Contd...)

Public	122,422	34.1	89,190	20.2	78,963	17.4	-4.3	-4.4	-4.3
Private	236,238	65.9	351,315	79.8	375,267	82.6	5.4	2.4	4.6
Central:									
Public	122,672	26.2	72,294	14.5	84,421	14.7	-7.2	5.6	-3.7
Private	346,023	73.8	425,094	85.5	489,195	85.3	2.8	5.1	3.4
Eastern:									
Public	97,111	53.1	75,099	39.1	65,247	30.6	-3.5	-5.1	-3.9
Private	85,763	46.9	117,008	60.9	147,878	69.4	4.2	8.5	5.4
Northern:									
Public	46,625	59.5	41,143	46.1	39,880	40	-1.7	-1.1	-1.5
Private	31,748	40.5	48,150	53.9	59,761	60	5.7	7.9	6.3
Western:									
Public	65,234	31.5	59,346	27.2	93,646	28	-1.3	16.6	3.6
Private	141,644	68.5	159,155	72.8	240,726	72	1.6	15.0	5.3
Total	936,820		997,289		1,220,754		0.9	7.4	2.6

Source: Authors' calculations based on household surveys 1992, 1999 and 2002.

Notes: (i) Estimates exclude the districts of Gulu, Pader, Kitgum, Kasese and Bundibugyo.

(ii) Estimates based on main activity in the last 12 months prior to the surveys.

Table 6 presents the shares of public and private sectors in wage employment. The results suggest that female participation in paid private sector employment has a positive trend rising from 54.5 per cent in 1992 to 74.7 percent in 2002 which may be explained increase in female human capital. Turning to age, younger individuals have a greater access to private sector while the older ones have a higher access to the public sector. Individuals with higher education are more likely to be employed in the public sector. However, the private sector has over time increased employment of individuals with higher education, from an average of 5 years of schooling in 1992 to nearly 7 years in 2002. The comparable figures for the public employment were about 10 to 12 years of schooling over the same time.

Table 6: Share of Paid Employment Across Sectors (%)

	1992		*1999*		*2002*	
	Public	***Private***	***Public***	***Private***	***Public***	***Private***
Age cohort:						
15 – 19	2.4	97.6	0.6	99.4	0.0	100.0
20 – 24	19.2	80.8	6.8	93.2	10.0	90.0
25 – 29	39.3	60.7	23.9	76.2	19.3	80.7
30 – 34	43.7	56.3	28.0	72.0	32.6	67.4
35 – 39	46.1	53.9	38.9	61.1	36.6	63.4
40 – 44	47.3	52.7	38.9	61.2	30.1	69.9
45 – 49	46.6	53.4	39.1	60.9	34.6	65.4
50 – 54	43.8	56.2	34.8	65.2	37.3	62.7

(Contd...)

50 – 54	43.8	56.2	34.8	65.2	37.3	62.7
55 – 59	41.3	58.7	29.2	70.8	39.4	60.6
60 – 64	30.5	69.5	21.6	78.4	27.8	72.3
Gender:						
Female	45.5	54.5	25.8	74.2	25.3	74.7
Male	32.7	67.3	24.6	75.4	22.4	77.6
Marital status:						
Female unmarried	33.3	66.7	13.6	86.5	13.0	87.0
Female married	55.5	44.5	38.8	61.3	38.1	61.9
Female divorced	39.5	60.5	16.0	84.0	19.6	80.4
Female widowed	59.8	40.2	22.7	77.3	28.9	71.1
Male	32.7	67.3	24.6	75.4	22.4	77.6
Education level:						
No formal education	10.5	89.5	5.6	94.4	6.4	93.6
Some Primary	17.6	82.4	6.2	93.8	5.7	94.4
Completed primary	29.4	70.6	10.9	89.1	5.8	94.2
Some secondary	36.5	63.5	19.6	80.4	14.4	85.6
Completed secondary	56.7	43.3	25.7	74.3	27.1	72.9
Post secondary	72.5	27.5	57.6	42.4	56.5	43.5
Education missing			6.5	93.5	12.2	87.8
Uganda	35.4	64.6	24.9	75.1	23.2	76.8

Source: Authors' calculations based on household surveys 1992, 1999 and 2002.
Notes: (i) Estimates exclude the districts of Gulu, Pader, Kitgum, Kasese and Bundibugyo.
(ii) Estimates based on main activity in the last 12 months prior to the surveys.

Conclusion

Using data from three nationally representative household surveys of 1992, 1999 and 2002, the study investigated the extent of female participation in the Ugandan labour market over the economic reform period. The analysis was restricted to the economically active population aged 15-64 years.

Evidence suggests that there has been a steady integration of female into the labour market. The indicators of this process are the increased participation of females in the labour market (mainly driven by their increased access to credit facilities and increased access to education); increased presence in self employment in non-agricultural activities; and increased share in professional occupations (for instance increased by 13 percent during 1999-2002, a rate higher than the national rate of 6 percent per annum). The findings suggest that there has been a narrowing gender gap in the level of participation in the labour market.

References

Bategeka, L., M. Ayoki and A. Mukungu (2004), *Financing Primary Education For All: Public Expenditure and Primary Education Outcomes in Uganda*. Institute of Development Studies, University of Sussex, Brighton.

Bigsten, A. and S.Kayizzi-Mugerwa (1999), *Crisis, Adjustment and Growth in Uganda*. Macmillan Press Ltd., London.

Deininger, K. and J. Okidi (2003), Growth and Poverty Reduction in Uganda. *Development Policy Review*, 21(4): 481-509.

Fallon, P.R. and L.A. Riveros (1989), *Adjustment and the Labour Market.* World Bank Policy Research Paper 214, Washington DC.

Lanot, C. and C. Muller (1997), *Dualistic Sector Choice and Female Labour Supply: Evidence from Formal and Informal Sectors in Cameroon*. Centre for the Study of African Economies, Working Paper Series 97-9, London.

Matshe, I and T. Young (2004), Off-farm Labour Allocation Decisions in Small-scale Rural Households in Zimbabwe. *Agricultural Economics*, 30: 175-186.

Okurut, F.N. (2005), *Credit Demand and Credit Rationing in the Informal Financial Sector in Uganda*. PhD Thesis, University of Stellenbosch.

Sharer, R.L., H.R. De Zoysa and C.A. McDonald (1995), *Uganda: Adjustment with Growth 1987-1994*. International Monetary Fund Occassional Paper 121,Washington DC.

Sudan, F.K (2006), Women in Watershed Development. *International Journal of Women, Social Justice and Human Rights*, 1 (1): 33-58.

Wambugu, A. (2003), *Essays on Earnings and Human Capital in Kenya*. Economic Studies, University of Goteborg.

8

Women Participation in Farming System

Barmon, B. K. *Hokkaido University*
Kondo, T. *Hokkaido University*
Osanami, F. *Hokkaido University*

Introduction

In general, women economically engage in producing goods and services for the family's own consumption, household production for sale and exchange in the market, and working for other source of income outside the home (Khandakar 1985). Rural women play not only an important role in agriculture in Asia (Kaur and Sharma 1991) but also in other developing countries in the world (Dey 1981). Women provide a significant share of both family and hired labour for farm activities (Dixon 1982). Nearly 84 percent of all economically active women are involved in agriculture in India with a positive correlation between agricultural growth rates and employment of female agricultural labour (World Bank 1991).

In Bangladesh, rural women are engaged in producing goods and services for the family's home consumption. Alone with household chores a large number of rural women Bangladesh play a pivotal role in agriculture. The rural women engage in various field operations of crops like transplanting and weeding of paddy, and vegetables and many harvest and post-harvest operations like harvesting, threshing, winnowing, and storage. Moreover, the rural women engage in rear dairy and poultry for home consumption. The women also clean the farmyard, collect cow dung as fuel for their daily meals or prepare manure for crop production.

In addition to this, a significant number of female workers also work in export-oriented industries, for example garments and shrimp/prawn industries. Mainly the illiterate and/or little educated poor and sheer poor girls and women are employed in the export-oriented garments and shrimp/prawn industries in Bangladesh. On the other hand, both the government organization and the non-government organizations (NGOs) have generated more employment opportunities for more educated female workers. However, the NGOs have generated more employment opportunities compared to the government sectors.

The female labour forces, as percentage of all workers, and as percentage of female population in Bangladesh from 1981 to 2001 are presented in Table 1. It is appeared from the table that the female labour force has increased significantly from 1985. The female labour force rose from 1.5 millions in 1981 to 22.8 millions in 2001. In other words, the female labourers have played a momentous role to contribute their household along with male labour participating in the agriculture, fisheries, livestock, and poultry sectors.

Table 1: Woman in the Civilian Labour Force, Selected Years from 1985 to 2000

Year	*Total Populations (millions)*	*Women Labour (millions)*	*Total Labour Force (millions)*	*As Percentage of all Workers*	*As Percentage of Total Population*
1981	87.1	1.5	25.9	5.8	1.7
1985	97.8*	3.2	30.6	10.5	3.3
1989	106.7*	21.0	50.1	41.9	19.6
1991	111.5	20.1	50.2	40.0	18.0
1996	121.7*	21.3	54.6	39.0	17.5
2001	129.2	22.8	58.1	39.2	17.6

Source: BBS [1996; 2001a and 2001b]

Note: * Indicate the projected population.

The agricultural system as well as cropping patterns have also changed since the development of export-oriented fresh water rice-prawn gher farming that have created the employment opportunities both for male and female workers in the southwest Bangladesh. There are few studies that focus on labour demand for male and female worker, daily wage rate, cost-benefit analysis of rice-prawn gher farming, the impact of shrimp gher farming on the environment and ecology in the coastal region in Bangladesh. The rice-prawn gher farming has positive impacts on both male and female labour market compared to MV *boro* and local *aman* paddy. The gher farming system has also increased daily labour wage rate for day labourers, landless, and marginal farmers compared to paddy farming (Barmon *et al.* 2004). The shrimp gher farming has negative impacts of environment in the coastal region in Bangladesh (Bhattacharya *et al.* 1999; Nabi *et al.* 1999), whereas the impacts of rice-prawn gher farming on environment are ambiguous. But the rice-prawn gher farming has negative impacts on ecology and a large number of indigenous species of fish have already disappeared (Datta 2001). However, women's participation in rice-prawn gher farming in the southwest Bangladesh has got less attention. Therefore, the present study evaluates the female labour participation in gher farming and examines income share of female workers to the total household income.

Methodology

Both primary and secondary data were used in the present study. The primary data were collected through a comprehensive cross-sectional field survey and the survey was conducted from November to December in 2003. The data for this study are from a farm household survey of two contrasting villages – Bilpabla and Kuloti, located in Khulna district. Khulna District is purposively selected for the study, as it is the leading rice-prawn producing district in Bangladesh, while Bilpabla village is selected as it is one of the typical villages in rice-prawn production in Khulna district. A total of 30 households were randomly selected from Bilpabla village.

Kuloti village is only 6 kilometers far from Bilpabla village and most of the farmers in this village cultivate MV *boro* and local *aman* paddy. Kuloti village is also chosen purposively with randomly selected 20 households. The altitude level of paddy field of Kuloti village is slightly higher than the land of gher farming in Bilpabla village. Therefore, the farmers in Kuloti village cannot convert their paddy field into gher farm.

The present study attempts to compare the female's income share of total household income and employment activities before and after the rice-prawn gher farming. However, the secondary data of before gher farming are not available. Moreover, cropping pattern of Kuloti village is similar to Bilpabla village prior to the gher farming system. Therefore, the present study used cross sectional field data of Kuloti village.

Rice-prawn Gher Farming System and Management

Gher is the physical construction used for freshwater prawn (*Macrobrachium rosenbergii*) farming. A gher is a modified rice field having high wide dikes and a canal inside the periphery of the dikes that retains water during the dry season. At the early stage of gher farming most of the farmers cultivated prawn in monoculture ponds, but recently the farmers commonly grow fish with prawn. In additions, rice, vegetables and fruit trees are also grown under the integrated gher farming system.

The gher cycle begins in May/June when the farmers release prawn post larvae (PL) into gher. Before this, farmers repair the gher dikes and trenches. This repair work is done almost every year. Farmers use lime during gher preparation to reduce soil acidity. During grow out period, the farmers give supplementary feeds to the prawn. Traditionally, only snail meat was used as a prawn feed, but nowadays farmers use wide range of homemade and commercial supplementary feeds.

Carp fish fingerlings are released into gher in May/June and cultured for nine months as long as sufficient water is retained in the gher. Usually, no specific supplementary feeds are provided for fish. Fish share the feeds that are supplied for prawn. Usually farmers grow vegetables in gher during both winter and summer seasons on the dikes. Some farmers grow vine-type vegetables up trellises inside the gher.

In the gher farming system, farmers usually grow *boro* rice on gher *chatal* (the land inside the gher) during the winter season between January and April. Farmers irrigate the paddy field from canal using indigenous handmade tools such as *Done,* and basket. Some large farmers use pump sets. Some times farmers do not irrigate to paddy field. Usually the gher farmers do not use any types of organic fertilizer for *boro* paddy production. Farmers give different types of feed in the gher unit during the prawn and carp fish production. But the prawn and carp fishes do not eat completely these supplied feeds. These remain unused feeds make the paddy field fertile and the paddy crop takes necessary nutrients from the fertile field. After *boro* paddy, the gher is used predominantly for prawn and fish cultivation.

Socio economic Characteristics

Status of Women in Bilpabla Village

Prior to the advent of rice-prawn gher farming in the study area, women were engaged in household chores and post harvest activities such as harvesting, threshing, winnowing, and storage of paddy and winter oilseeds and pulses. Sheer poverty had driven some of the poorest of the poor women to work in return for kind in the rich households. Of late a large number of women are involved in rice-prawn gher farming related activities.

Among the 401 households in Bilpabla village, 310 women are partly engaged in gher farming activities and mainly engaged in mud snail crushing for prawn feeding, and other home made feed preparation during prawn production period. In addition, these female are also engaged in unpaid economic household activities such as harvesting of paddy and winnowing of paddy. These women mainly work for their own purposes, for example, earning money from mud snail crushing that they buy ornamentals for their daughter and save surplus money they for their daughter's marriage as well as for their future. In addition, they bear their children's educational cost. Only a small portion of the total female working population in Bilpabla village engages in labour force for their livelihood. They mainly engage in uprooting of seedling, planting, weeding and harvesting of paddy during the paddy production and do repairing and maintenance the gher dike and weeding during the period of gher farming.

Women's Participation in Homestead Activities

The women in Bilpabla village have important role in homestead activities along with productive activities of gher farming and post harvest activities of paddy production. Table 2 summarizes the women's participation in homestead activities of Bilpabla village. It appears that the women of Bilpabla village are mainly engaged in washing utensils, clothes and cleaning the house, raising livestock and poultry, cooking for family members, making prawn feeding, purchasing and selling of livestock and poultry grow, vegetable at homestead, child rearing and caring, and collecting fuel. Almost similar patterns of rural women's participation in homestead activities are found in the other rural areas of Bangladesh (Paul and Saadullah 1991). The table also shows that women and daughters are more participating and helping in homestead activities compared to sons and husbands. Only the husband mainly involves in post harvest activities of paddy followed by women. The husband spent less time on homestead activities.

Table 2: Average Homestead Work Performed by Women in Bilpabla Village

Activities	*Per cent (%)*			
	Women	*Daughter*	*Son*	*Husband*
Washing, cleaning of utensils & homestead	82	16	1	1
Raising of livestock and poultry	64	33	2	1
Post harvest activities	60	12	6	22
Cooking	95	4	0	1
Making prawn feeding	72	12	3	13
Purchase and selling of livestock	77	10	3	10
and poultry				
Vegetable production at homestead	74	13	6	7
Child care	92	5	1	2
Fuel collection	79	15	2	4

Role of Women in Decision-making

Intensity of homestead activities and employments are the most important factors that could raise the status of women in the rural family as well as in the society in Bangladesh. The issue on women's decision-making in the family activities of this village cannot be separated from the problems of other rural areas in Bangladesh. In Bangladesh, in general male households are the main decision-makers in their daily activities. The role of women in decision-making in their family activities is presented in Table 3. It has estimated from the study that 70% of homestead cultivation, 45% of house making, 53% of sons' and daughters' marriage, 54% of participation in social acts/festival, 34% of prawn feed supply, 73% of selling vegetables, 17% of selling prawn, and 65% of selling livestock and poultry are performed by the women. In other words, from 45% to 73% of the decisions are taken by women except for prawn feed supply and prawn selling in the market. Both husband and wife execute most of the decisions of family activities. Sometimes son and daughter also help their parents to take proper decisions to their family activities. The gher farming system has slightly increased the decision making power of women compared to other rural areas in Bangladesh (Paul and Saadullah 1991).

Table 3: Role of Women in Decision Making in Bilpabla Village

Activities	*Per cent (%)*				
	Women	*Husband*	*Both*	*Son*	*Daughter*
Homestead cultivation	70	40	90	4	5
House making	45	75	86	4	0
Son and daughters' marriage	53	90	95	3	2
participation in social acts/ festival	54	64	96	4	6
Prawn feed supply	34	90	95	50	0
Selling vegetables	73	65	85	8	34
Selling prawn	17	85	90	14	0
Selling livestock and poultry	65	54	85	35	40

Status of Women in Kuloti Village

Kuloti is a non-gher farming village and most the people in this village cultivate paddy and winter oilseeds and pulses. They also depend mainly on paddy production and non-farm activities for their daily life. The farmers cultivate paddy and hire mainly male labourers during planting, weeding and harvesting times. In addition, the landless and marginal farmers supply their labourers in and around of the village. About 75 percent female workers are widow and they live with their children in father's house and/or brother's house or sometimes independently in motherland's village. In addition, they do not have land for agriculture as well as for living. Theses women work as day labour outside of the village especially in gher farming village. Women are engaged in gher farming activities such as gher dike repairing and maintenance, excavation of gher, uprooting of paddy seedling, planting of paddy, weeding and some post-harvest activities such as threshing and winnowing of paddy in gher farming villages. Usually the female workers come to local markets and the gher farmers hire themselves on daily or sometimes weekly basis. The female workers wake up very early in the morning and cook daily meals for their family members and her lunch. They start their work around 8.30 am and come back around 4.30 pm. During working hours they eat their lunch. The female workers usually engage in gher farming activities from 5 months to 8 months.

Table 4: General Characteristics of Women Involved in Rice-prawn Gher and Paddy Farming

Particulars	*Female*	*Male*
Gher farming (Bilpabla village)		
Education:		
Illiterate	18 (60)	16 (57)
Primary	12 (40)	14 (43)
Occupation:		
Main Occupation	Housewife (100)	Gher (60)
		Labor (40)
Subsidiary Occupation	Snail crashing (100)	NA
Average age (Years)	36	44
Family size	6.17	
Paddy farming (Kuloti village)		
Education	Illiterate (100)	Illiterate (100)
Occupation:		
Main	Labour (100)	Labour (100)
Subsidiary	Housewife (100)	-
Average age (Years)	37	42
Working place (farming)	Gher and paddy	Gher and paddy
Widow	7 (35)	NA
Family size	4.95	

The general socio-economic characteristics of the women of Bilpabla and Kuloti village are presented in Table 4. The sampled female in both villages is illiterate. The main occupation of the female of Bilpabla is housewife. Along with household chores the women are also engaged in gher farming activities. On the other hand, along with household chores the women of Kuloti village mainly sell their labour in gher farming for their daily meals. The sampled women of Kuloti village are almost widow. The average family size of Kuloti village (4.95) is larger than Bilpabla village (6.17).

Impacts of Rice-Prawn Gher Farming

The rice-prawn gher farming system has two direct impacts on employment for female labour market, and income share of total household income. The impacts of gher farming on the employment of female labour and income share are discussed below:

Impacts on Employment of Female Labour

The rice-prawn gher farming system has been created direct and indirect expansion on employment opportunities for male and female labour in the southwest Bangladesh since mid 1980's. Employment activities of male and female labour in rice-prawn gher farming are presented in Table 5.

Table 5: Employment Activities of Male and Female Labour in Rice-prawn Gher Farming

Activities	*Male*	*Female*
Direct:		
Prawn Production:	Excavation gher, repairing and maintenance of dike, weeding of gher, daily feeding of prawn, and harvesting of prawn.	Excavation of gher, repairing and maintenance of dike, weeding of gher, mud snail crashing for prawn feed, homemade feed, and harvesting of prawn.
Paddy Production:	Land preparation, uprooting and planting, weeding of paddy, irrigation, harvesting, threshing and carrying.	Uprooting and planting of paddy, weeding of paddy, irrigation, harvesting and threshing, drying, and winnowing of paddy.
Indirect:	Fry collection from sea/river, mud snail collection from swampland, farm gate market, local market (depot), intermediate markets, ice factory, commercial feed industry, grading of prawn, processing plant, and shipping for international markets.	Fry collection from sea/river, mud snail collection from swampland, de-heading and cleaning of prawn, grading of prawn, processing plants, and exporting plants.
Before gher farming: Direct:	Day labour, fishing from boatman, different activities of paddy farming.	Post-harvesting activities such as threshing, drying and winnowing of paddy.
Indirect:	NA	NA

Source: Field survey 2004
Note: NA indicates not applicable.

It is appeared from the Table 5 that the gher farming system has created more employment opportunities for female labour along with male labour. Before the gher farming had started, the farmers cultivated only local *aus* and *aman* paddy in the comparatively high land and only local *aman* paddy in the swampland in this area. The female labourers were mainly engaged in post-harvesting activities of paddy farming. Now the female labourers are engaged not only in post-harvesting in paddy but also in uprooting, planting, weeding and different types of gher farming activities.

Female Labour Utilization

The female labour utilization of different direct and indirect gher farming activities is depicted in flow diagram (Figure 1). It is appeared from the diagram that along with male workers female workers are mainly involved in gher preparation, fry collection from sea and river, cleaning of gher, weeding and feeding, icing, de-heading and cleaning, grading, processing of prawn and shipping. Mainly the widow and absolute poor women are engaged in gher excavation, rice plant uprooting, planting and weeding. These women mainly come from the outside of the gher-farming village.

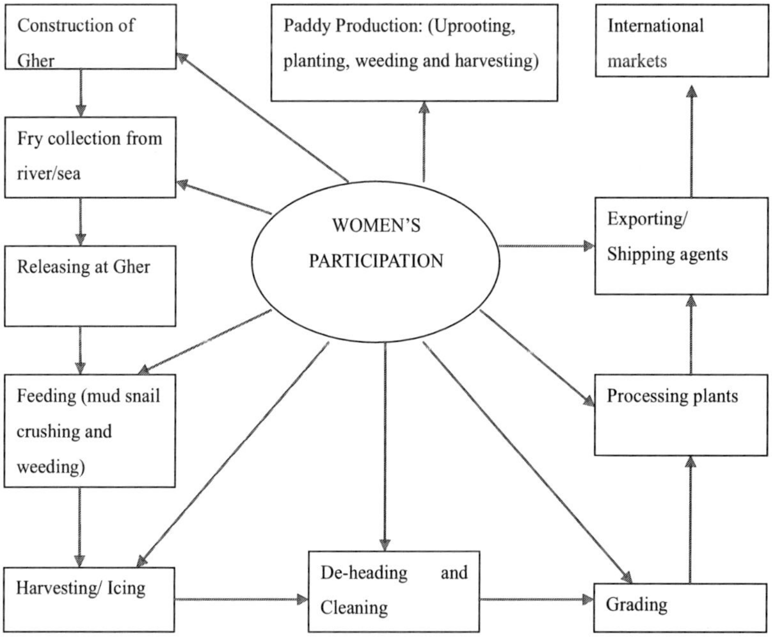

Source: Field survey 2004.

Figure 1: Flow Diagram of Rice-prawn Gher Farming and Women's Participation

The female labour demand is high during gher repairing and maintenance, and uprooting of paddy seedling and weeding in *boro* paddy production. The women of gher farming village mainly engaged in mud snail crushing and home made feed for prawn. The female children help their mother for mud snail crushing during end of July to November.

Impact of Female Labour Demand

Agricultural labour demand depends mainly on cropping pattern and cropping intensity. The cropping patterns and intensity have been changed after the introduction of rice-prawn gher farming technology in the southwest Bangladesh. Prior to gher farming, farmers cultivated local *aus* and *aman* paddy in the swampland, and the oil crops-rape, mustard and *til* (one kind of oil seed crop) were produced along with local *aus* and *aman* in the comparatively high land which is located in the small river side. Along with prawn and carp fish, the farmers can now cultivate *boro* paddy and vegetables in the same paddy fields. Total labour use per bigha for rice-prawn gher farming as well as MV *boro* and local varieties of paddy was estimated to assess the impact of rice-prawn gher farming on female labour.

Table 6: Per Bigha Female Labour Demand in Gher and Paddy Farming

Particulars	***Temporary hired labour (days)***		***Family labour (days)***	
	Male	***Female***	***Male***	***Female***
Gher farming (Bilpabla village)				
Gher farming	25	16	46	8
activities	(71)	(84)	(94)	(80)
	10	3	3	2
Paddy farming	(29)	(16)	(6)	(10)
	35	19	49	10
Total	(100)	(100)	(100)	(100)
Paddy farming (Kuloti village)				
MV *Boro*	10	5	13	4
	(59)	(72)	(45)	(50)
Local *aman*	7	2	16	4
	(41)	(28)	(55)	(50)
	17	7	29	8
Total	(100)	(100)	(100)	(100)

Source: Field survey 2003

Notes: (1) The figures in parentheses indicate percentage share of farm activities.
(2) One Bigha is equivalent to about 0.5 acres in the locality.
(3) Eight hours/day is equivalent to one man-day.

The rice-prawn gher farming system and the paddy production are completely different project. Therefore, per bigha labour use is also different in two types of agricultural system. Female labour per bigha use under rice-prawn gher farming system, and modern variety (MV) rice and local *aman* paddy production technology in Khulna district is shown in Table 6. The evident from the table shows that per bigha hired female labourers use in gher farming system was about three times higher than MV *boro* rice and local *aman* paddy production. However, per bigha family supplied female labourers use was almost same for the both types of agricultural system. On the other hand, per bigha hired male labour use in gher farming system was about two times higher than MV *boro* and local *aman* paddy production. Therefore, it can be concluded that rice-prawn gher farming has created more employment opportunity for female workers compared to MV *boro* rice and traditional rice.

Household Income

Income is one of the most important factors that could move up the status of women in the rural family as well as in the society. It gives them some kind of empowerment in the society. Most of the rural families keep one or more dairy animals and some poultry to supplement their income and fulfill the domestic demand for milk, milk products, eggs and meat. The diversity of women's duties makes it difficult to determine their contribution of total household income. Moreover, women frequently cultivate small vegetable gardens that provide subsistence food for home consumption. Even though the cash value of the products from these gardens may be negligible, it often represents an important source of income for rural women.

Table 7 delineates the household income of gher farmers in Bilpabla village, and landless and marginal farmers in Kuloti village and the contribution of income shares of female and male as labourers. The current estimate of income for female and male is calculated based on those activities by which the female and male labourers received direct economic benefits. Mainly the gher farming managements are controlled by men even though the women are usually responsible for homemade feeds, and sometimes mud snail crushing for prawn feed. Therefore, the study has considered that all gher farming income belongs to men. The evident from the table shows that on average, the sampled gher farmers earned taka 67,670 annually and gher-farming income is the main source of household income and its contribution to household income is about 43 percent. On the other hand, the sampled landless and marginal farmers earned taka 25,698 annually and daily labour wage (both male and female) is the main source of household income and its contribution to household income is about 85 percent. In other words, the household income of farmers in Bilpabla village is about three times higher than the household income of marginal and landless farmers in Kuloti village. The main reason is that the average farm size of the farmers of Bilpabla village (about 1.45 bigha) is higher than the farmers of Kuloti village (about only 0.5 bigha) and in addition, rice-prawn gher farming is more profitable enterprise compared to local varieties of paddy farming. The gher farmers in Bilpabla village earned about Tk 29,383 from gher farming whereas the farmers in Kuloti village earned only Tk 605 from paddy farming.

Table 7: Comparison of Household Income of Rice-prawn Gher Farmers and Paddy Farmers, and Income Share of Female Labour to Household Income

	Gher farmers	*Income share*	*Paddy farmers*	*Income share*
Sources of income	Taka	(%)	Taka	(%)
1. Profit/agricultural income	29,383	43	605	2
2. Family labours income				
(i) Male	9,210	14	404	2
(ii) Female	943	1	273	1

(Contd...)

3. Land income	3,450	5	1,002	4
4. Agricultural wage income (male)	12,500	19	11,565	45
5. Agricultural wage income (female)				
(i) Mud snail crashing	3,190	5	0	0
(ii) Paddy farming	460	1	6,205	24
(iii) Dike repair and weeding	493	1	4,195	16
6. Livestock and poultry	3,607	5	885	4
7. Off-farm income	2,967	4	0	0
8. Homestead gardening	1,467	2	564	2
Total household income	67,670	100	25,698	100

Source: Field survey 2003.

Notes: 1) 1US$=72.65 Taka, March 2006

2) Surveyed average gher and paddy farm size were 1.45 and 0.5 bigha.

3) Sample size of gher and paddy farmers were 30 and 20 respectively.

4) The household income is calculated based on the 30 gher and 20 paddy farmers.

Family supplied labour is common in agriculture in the developing countries especially in the South Asia. Both landless men and women, and family members work in agriculture as casual, daily and/or permanent labourers. Usually the male labour wage Tk 100 for the activities of paddy production and Tk 80-90 for the wage of various gher-farming activities. Both the family supplied male and female labourers of gher farmers are higher than the family supplied labourers of paddy farmers because rice-prawn gher farming is a labour intensive. The income from male agricultural labour wage (Taka 12,500) of gher farmers is slightly higher compared to the male agricultural wage income of paddy farmers. However, the contributing share of agricultural wage of male labourers to household income in Kuloti village is about 45% whereas this share is only 19% for male in Bilpabla village. In other words, agricultural wage is the main income source for daily life in Kuloti village.

The share of female workers in family household income is calculated and based on only snail crushing for prawn feed, paddy seedling uprooting, weeding and harvesting of paddy production, and dike repair and weeding of gher farming, which was only 7 percent of total household income. The female of Bilpabla village mainly engage in mud snail crushing for prawn feed as contract basis. The female workers usually crash two bags[1] of mud snail daily and get 20 taka per bag. Moreover, some poor and sheer poor female also engage in various activities of gher farming such as paddy seedling uprooting, weeding and harvesting of paddy and dike repair and weeding of gher farm in peak season. Usually the female labour wage taka 60 for the activities of paddy production and taka 70-80 for the wage of gher dike repair and weeding due to comparatively hard work. Even though it is not a significant amount of household income, it has significant impact on their family member's future because the household expenses particularly for children's education and daughter's marriage depend largely on this income.

However, the opposite pictures are seen in the other villages where the households are mainly engaged in other agricultural activities such as local paddy and various types of winter and summer vegetables. Females contribute a handsome portion of the total household incomes and sometimes they play role as a head of the households and are the main income earner of the family. It is appeared from the table that more than 40 percent household income comes from women's activities. The female workers of non-gher farming village are mainly work in gher farm as daily basis. In other words, the gher farming has created more employment sectors compared to paddy farming where the female workers of non-gher farming village works daily basis for their survival.

The shares of livestock and poultry income[2] (about 5%) is also higher for gher farm households of Bilpabla village compared to households (only 4%) of Kuloti village because the gher farm households have some own homestead land for living and rears more dairy and poultry farmers compared to the households of Kuloti village. Most of the surveyed households in Kuloti village have no own land for living and mainly they live in other's place and they only rear some poultry.

The surveyed landless and marginal farmers in Kuloti village mainly engage in daily agricultural wage whereas the farmers in Bilpabla village involve in other off-farm activities. The income from homestead gardening of Bilpabla village is also higher than from Kuloti village.

In general, both the male and female of Kuloti village mainly supply their labour in various activities of gher farming whole year for daily life and agricultural wage income is the main source of household income. On the other hand, agricultural income is the main source of household income for gher farming. Sometimes the agricultural wage income of women is the main source of daily life compared to Bilpabla village.

A Case Study

A case study is incorporated in this section to explain how the women are benefited from rice-prawn gher farming in the southwest Bangladesh.

Female Labour: The Case of Shahnaz Begum

Shahnaz Begum, 35, is a divorce woman, and has only one daughter. Shahnaz Begum got married with Zobair Ali of the same village before she was 20. After marriage, Shahnaz Begum started living with her husband at her father-in-law's residence. After few months of marriage, her mother-in-law and her husband started to dislike her. Torture of her mother-in-law and her husband reached to intolerable stage. Her husband divorced her after their daughter's birth and got married with another woman. After divorce she was in deep problem and passing a very hard time with her father's family. Always her family members misbehaved with her. One day she met with a gher farmer who lived in Bilpabla village and asked him to find any type job. Finally she moved to Bilpabla village for livelihood as well as her daughter's future. Now she is living on a gher's embankment and plays a role as watchman of the gher owner.

Shahnaz Begum is a very hard worker and she can do any types of agricultural activities like male worker. She works as planting, weeding, harvesting and winnowing in paddy production and as snail crushing, dike and canal repairing, gher maintaining, weeding etc. in prawn production. She earns, on an average, Tk 40 per day by selling her labour and fulfills their everyday need with this money. During the off-farm seasons, she also engages in vegetables business. She buys vegetables from village and sells it in town. Along with these types of works, she also rears poultry birds in her homestead and cultivates vegetables in the dikes of the gher. She is sending her daughter to school for education. At the beginning, the society did not accept her profession. Now a day, following the footstep of Shahnaz Begum many women are engaged in gher farming activities to support their family.

Conclusion

Rice-prawn gher farming is a new agricultural technology in the southwest Bangladesh since mid 1980s. Gher farming has created employment opportunity for female along with male compared to local paddy farming. Along with male the poor and sheer poor women of non-gher farming village are engaged in excavation of gher, weeding and cleaning of gher, harvesting of prawn, uprooting and transplanting of paddy, weeding, harvesting and winnowing of paddy. The women of gher farming village are mainly engaged in mud snail crushing and home made feed for prawn. However, some poor and sheer poor female workers also engage in uprooting, transplanting, weeding and harvesting of paddy production like the female worker of non-gher farming village. The gher farming system has increased the decision-making power of women compared to other rural areas of Bangladesh. The female workers of non-gher farming village earned more money (about six times higher) to supply their daily wage compared to the women of rice-prawn gher farming village. The women of gher farming village use their agricultural wage income for children's education, cloths, ornamental and their daughter's marriage, whereas the female workers use their agricultural wage income for daily life.

References

Barmon, B.K., Kondo, T., and F. Osanami (2004), Labour Demand for Rice-prawn Gher Farming in Bangladesh: A Case Study of Khulna District. *The Review of Agricultural Economics,* 60: 273-287.

BBS (1996), *Bangladesh Bureau of Statistics*. Statistical Yearbook of Bangladesh, Planning Division, Ministry of Planning, Government of the People's of Bangladesh.

BBS (2001a), *Bangladesh Bureau of Statistics*. Statistical Yearbook of Bangladesh, Planning Division, Ministry of Planning, Government of the People's of Bangladesh.

BBS (2001b), *Bangladesh Bureau of Statistics*. Government of the People's of Bangladesh, Ministry of Planning Statistics Wing, National Data Bank, Available at http://www.bbsgov.org

Bhattacharya, D., Rahman, M., and Khatun, F. (1999), *Environmental Impact of Structural Adjustment Policies: The Case Export Oriented Shrimp Culture in Bangladesh*. Centre for Policy Dialogue (CPD), Dhaka.

Datta, D. K. (2001), *Ecological Role of Fresh Water Apple Snail Pila Globosa and the Consequences of Its Over-harvesting from Beel Ecosystem of Bagerhat and Gopalgonj District*. A Study Report, Study Carried out Jointly by Khulna University and GOLDA Project of CARE Bangladesh, Funded through Department for International Development.

Dey, J. (1981), Gambian Women: Unequal Partners in Rice Development Projects. *Journal of Development Studies*, 17(3): 109-122.

Dixon, R.B. (1982), Women in Agriculture: Counting the Labour Force in Developing Countries. *Population and Development Review*, 8(3): 539-565.

Kaur, M., and Sharma, M.L. (1991), Role of Women in Rural Development. *Journal of Rural Studies*, 7: 11-16.

Khandaker, S. R. (1985), *Women's Role in Household Productive Activities and Fertility in Bangladesh*. Discussion Paper No. 488, Economic Growth Center, Yale University.

Nabi, S.M.N., Sarker, G., Alim, M.A., and Islam, M.T. (1999), *The Effect of Rice Cultivation on Growth of Freshwater Prawn (Macrobrachium rogenbergii) in Gher Farming Systems*. Greater Options for Local Development through Aquaculture (GOLDA) Project, CARE, Bangladesh.

Paul, D.C. and Saadullah (1991), Role of Women in Homestead of Small Farm Category in an Area of Jessore District, Bangladesh. *Livestock Research for Rural Development*, 3 (2): 23-29.

World Bank (1991), *Gender and Poverty in India*. World Bank, Washington DC.

Notes

1. Each bag contains about 20 Kgs of mud snail.
2. Dairy income is computed after deducting variable costs on green fodder, dry fodder, concentrates and veterinary expenses from gross income whereas, poultry income is computed after deducting variable costs on feed and veterinary costs.

9

Female household industry workers

Mustaquim, M. *Aligarh Muslim University*
Khan, J. H. *Aligarh Muslim University*

Introduction

Females constitute about fifty per cent of the total population not only in India but also in the entire world and they contribute in social, economic, cultural and political development. Women share abundant responsibilities and perform wide spectrum of duties both in the home and outside, but their participation is accepted as normal (Verma et al. 2006). Women in the several of the developed countries constitute a very active and important component in the changing evolution of labour market activity. In many families, they have become the major source of family income support (Sabhanayakam 1988). Women are distinguished from all other industrial workers by distinctive attitudes and actions of the modern society including employers, male workers and workers themselves. The female workers are generally regarded as a distinctive group in present day society (Mehrotra 2006).

Female employment is important from the point of view of their status and personal advancement. Females must enter into the workforce in all societies on an equal footing with males and get integrated into the world of the work. In developed countries females are equal partners but in the developing countries like India female participation in economic struggle is very low because males are thought to be sole earners of bread (Vohra and Sen 1985).

In India only 25.63 per cent of the total females are employed whereas, the male employment rate is more than double (51.68 per cent) in 2001 census. This low proportion of female employment in India may be caused by the patriarchal system of society, the age-old prejudice against female's mobility, the prejudice against their education, their relatively low status in the society, frequent child births, limited job opportunities for the females to avail themselves of these opportunities (Ramotra 1989).

The popular professions among the educated women are to work in the offices as assistants, steno-typists, etc. Only a small number of women are employed in manufacturing and ancillary units of heavy industries. In all these professions, women are always placed in a secondary or inferior position since they are lacking in self- confidence. The women are the co-ordinate and not the sub-ordinate half of the humanity. In general they are not ruled by law but are being ruled and controlled by costumes and traditions. Women everywhere has been still exploited because they are the worst exploited amongst the exploited. Harijans, Adivasis and women are treated on par and amongst the Harijans and Adivasis, the women is the lowest of the low (UNICEF 1978).

A society can change towards the better only when the women's out look, attitude and aptitude are changing favourably towards their participation in productive works. Training and mobilizing womanpower as a tremendous force is indispensable for development today (UNICEF 1978).

Thus, a comprehensive study requires to better understanding the relationship between female household industry workers and levels of socio-economic development in the state of West Bengal.

Objectives

The present study delineates the following objectives:

(i) To analyse the existing spatial distribution of female household industry workers,

(ii) To examine the levels of socio-economic development among the districts of the state,

(iii) To explain the relationship between female household industry workers and levels of socio-economic development,

(iv) To find out the linear relationship and test them to measure the significant levels of selected variables of socio-economic development influencing female household industry workers and

(v) To suggest a proposal to minimize the gap in the levels of socio-economic development and share of female household industry workers.

Data and Methodology

The present paper is entirely based on secondary sources of data obtained from Census of India publications, New Delhi and district wise indicators of socio-economic development collected from Bureau of Applied Economics and Statistics, Govt. of West Bengal, Kolkata for the year 2001. In the present work, a group of forty six (46) socio-economic indicators of various sectors have been taken into account to determine the levels of socio-economic development in the eighteen districts of West Bengal. These indicators fall into ten categories such as, population characteristics, literacy, educational facilities, agriculture, industry, health, power, transport and communication, per capita income and banking facilities. In the first step, the raw data for each variable which determines the geographical variations of socio-economic development have been computed into standard score. It is generally known as *Zi* value or *Z* score. The score measure the departure of individual observations, expressed in a comparable form. This means it becomes a linear transformation of the original data. It may be expressed as:

$$Z_{ij} = \frac{X_{ij} - \overline{X_i}}{\sigma X_i}$$

Where,

Z_{ij} = Standardized value of the variable *i* in district *j*

X_{ij} = Actual value of variable *i* in district *j*

X_i = Mean value of variable *i* in all districts.

σX_i = Standard deviation of variables *i* in all districts.

In the second step, the Z-scores of all variables have been added district wise and the average has taken out for these variables which may be called as composite score (CS) for each district and may be algebraically expressed as:

$$CS = \frac{\sum Z_{ij}}{N}$$

Where, *CS* is composite score, *N* refers to the number of variables, $\sum Z_{ij}$ indicates Z scores of all variables *i* in district *j*. The positive values relating to the districts Z score show high level of socio-economic development and negative values the low level of socio-economic development in the study area. The correlation co-efficient is computed between dependent variable (female household industry workers) and independent variables (selected variables of socio-economic development) and student t-test technique is applied to find out the determinants which are significant at 1 per cent and 5 per cent levels.

The correlation co-efficient has been computed on the basis of the Karl Pearson's correlation co-efficient (r) method which is as follows:

$$r = \frac{\Sigma xy - \Sigma x \Sigma y / n}{\sqrt{\Sigma x^2 - \frac{(\Sigma x^2)}{N}} \sqrt{\Sigma y^2 - \left(\frac{\Sigma y^2}{N}\right)}}$$

Where:

r is the co-efficient of correlation.

x,y are the two given variables.

n is the number of observation.

To find out the computed 't' value, student t-test technique is used which is given below:

$$t = r\sqrt{\frac{(n-2)}{1-r^2}}$$

Where:

t is the calculated value of 't' in the test of significance.

n is the number of observation.

r is the computed value of co-efficient of correlation.

Furthermore, advanced cartographic techniques and GIS-Arc View programmes (Version 3.2a) have been applied to show the regional disparities of female household industry workers and levels of socio-economic development among the districts of the state through maps.

Study Area

West Bengal has been chosen as a study area which is located between 21°25' to 26°50' north latitudes and 86°30' to 89°58' east longitudes with three international boundaries i.e., Bangladesh, Nepal and Bhutan. It occupies an area of about 88,752 sq. km. (2.70 per cent of the India's total geographical area) and stretching from the Himalayas in the north to the Bay of Bengal in the south. It is surrounded by Sikkim and Bhutan in the north, Assam and Bangladesh in the east, the Bay of Bengal in the south and Orissa, Jharkhand, Bihar and Nepal in the west. There are eighteen districts in the state (Fig.1). According to 2001 Census its total population is 80,176,197 (7.79 per cent of India's total population), density is 904 persons per sq. km. (In terms of population density West Bengal is on the top among the Indian states). Female literacy rate is 60.22 per cent (while in India as whole it is 54.70 per cent). Total female working population is 70,93,646 (18.32 per cent of West Bengal's total female population and 1.43 per cent of India's total female population). According to 2001 about 17.69 per cent of the total female workers are engaged in household industry in the state of West Bengal.

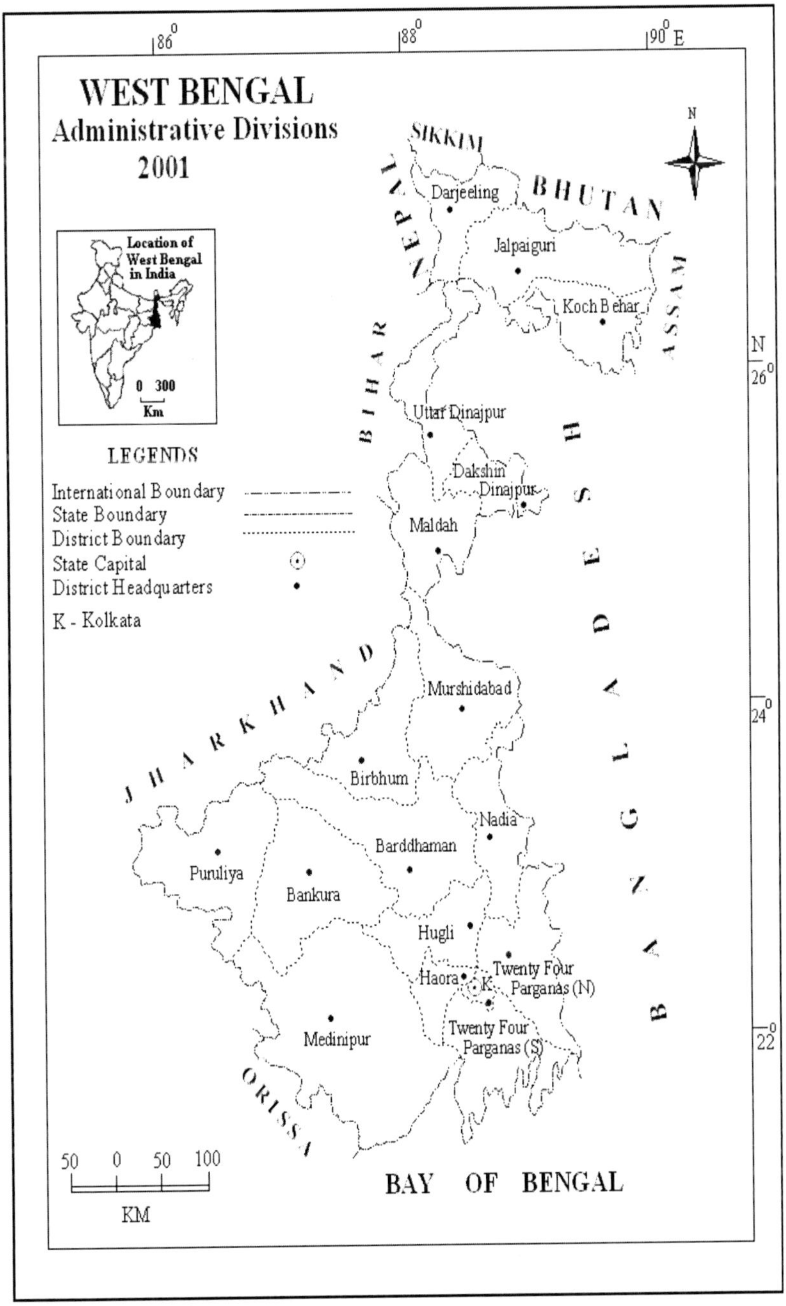
WEST BENGAL
Administrative Divisions
2001
Location of West Bengal in India
0 300
Km
LEGENDS
International Boundary
State Boundary
District Boundary
State Capital
District Headquarters
K - Kolkata
86°
88°
90° E
26°
24°
22°
N
SIKKIM
NEPAL
BHUTAN
ASSAM
BIHAR
JHARKHAND
BANGLADESH
ORISSA
Darjeeling
Jalpaiguri
Koch Behar
Uttar Dinajpur
Dakshin Dinajpur
Maldah
Murshidabad
Birbhum
Nadia
Barddhaman
Puruliya
Bankura
Hugli
Haora
K
Twenty Four Parganas (N)
Twenty Four Parganas (S)
Medinipur
50 0 50 100
KM
BAY OF BENGAL

Fig. 1

Regional Distribution of Total Female Household Industry Workers, 2001

Among the eighteen districts of the state of West Bengal the female household industry workers ranges from -0.92 score in Jalpaiguri district to 3.15 score in Murshidabad district (Table 1). These ranges of variations may

Table 1: District wise Distribution of Female Household Industry Workers and Levels of Socio-Economic Development in West Bengal, 2001

District	*Z score of Total Female Household Industry Workers*	*Composite Mean Z scores of Socio-Economic Development*
Darjeeling	-0.89	0.31
Jalpaiguri	-0.92	-0.12
Koch Behar	-0.59	0.19
Uttar Dinajpur	-0.55	-0.50
Dakshin Dinajpur	-0.48	0.04
Maldah	1.37	-0.36
Murshidabad	3.15	-0.58
Birbhum	-0.04	-0.03
Barddhaman	-0.31	-0.09
Nadia	0.95	-0.05
North Twenty Four Parganas	-0.18	-0.14
Hugli	-0.28	0.15
Bankura	-0.47	0.20
Puruliya	-0.44	-0.21
Medinipur	-0.01	0.23
Haora	0.69	-0.19
Kolkata	-0.83	1.44
South Twenty Four Parganas	-0.18	-0.28

Source: Census of India [2001]

be arranged into three categories i.e., Low (below -0.40 scores), Medium (-0.40 to 0.40 scores) and High (above 0.40 scores) (Table 2).

Figure 2 exhibits the regional distribution of female household industry workers among the districts of the state. Four districts of the state lie under the high grade (above 0.40 score) of female household industry workers and seventy five per cent of them constitute a perpendicular region in the central part of the study area and comprises the districts of Maldah, Murshidabad and Nadia. The medium score (-0.40 to 0.40 score) districts of female household industry workers are mainly concentrated in the southern part of the state and form a single prominent region in the study area. This region extents from

Table 2: Category wise Distribution of Total Female Household Industry Workers in West Bengal, 2001

Category	*Z score*	*No. of Districts*	*Percentage of total districts*	*Name of the Districts*
High	Above 0.40	4	22.22	Maldah, Murshidabad, Nadia and Haora.
Medium	-0.40 to 0.40	6	33.33	Birbhum, Hugli, Barddhaman, Medinipur, Twenty Four Parganas (North) and Twenty Four Parganas (South).
Low	Below -0.40	8	44.45	Darjeeling, Jalpaiguri, Koch Behar, Uttar Dinajpur, Dakshin Dinajpur, Kolkata, Bankura and Puruliya.
Total		18	100.00	

Source: Based on Table 1.

Birbhum district in the north to Medinipur and Twenty Four Parganas (South) districts in the south (Fig. 2). The low category of female household industry workers is found in eight districts of the state and nearly eighty eight per cent of them make two separate regions in the state of West Bengal. One, which is relatively large in size, lies in the northern part of the state including

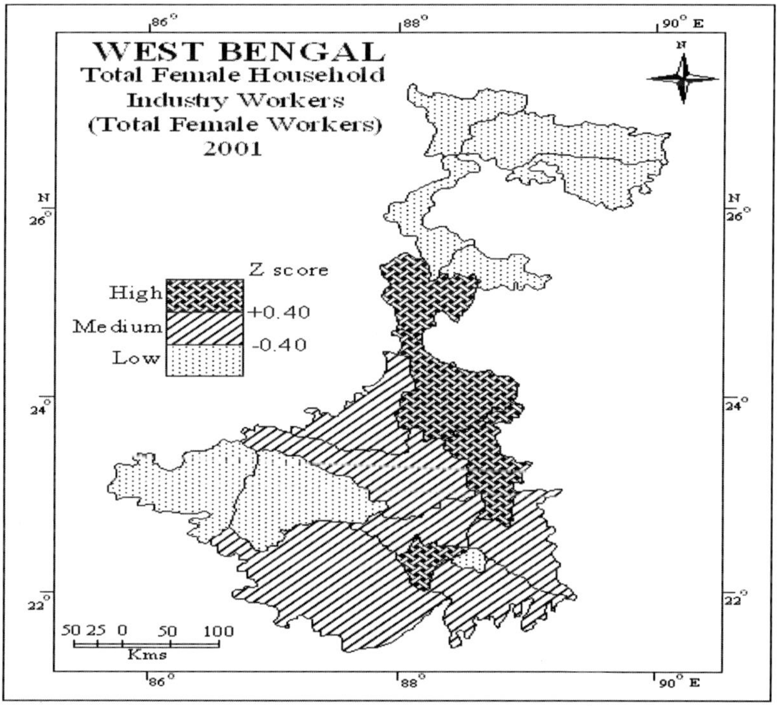

Fig. 2

the districts of Darjeeling, Jalpaiguri, Koch Behar, Uttar Dinajpur and Dakshin Dinajpur. And another region occurs in the southwestern part of the state, covering the districts of Purulia and Bankura.

Geographical Variation of Socio-Economic Development, 2001

The district wise composite score of socio-economic development among the districts of West Bengal is shown in Table 1. It varies from -0.58 to 1.44 scores among the districts of the state with a maximum score in Kolkata district and the minimum in Murshidabad district. All the districts may conveniently be arranged into three categories of socio-economic development (Table 3).

Table 3: Levels of Socio-Economic Development in West Bengal, 2001

Category	*Z-score*	*No. of Districts*	*Percentage of total districts*	*Name of the Districts*
High	Above 0.20	3	16.67	Kolkata, Darjeeling and Medinipur.
Medium	-0.20 to 0.20	10	55.55	Jalpaiguri, Koch Behar, Dakshin Dinajpur, Birbhum, Bankura, Nadia, Hugli, Haora, Barddhaman, and Twenty Four Parganas (North).
Low	Below -0.20	5	27.78	Uttar Dinajpur, Maldah, Murshidabad, Puruliya and Twenty Four Parganas (South)
Total		18	100.00	

Source: Based on Table 1.

The score of socio-economic development is marked with remarkable regional variation in its distribution among the districts of the study area. Only three districts share high score (above 0.20 score) of socio-economic development, they are Kolkata, Darjeeling and Medinipur, but failed to constitute any recognizable region in the state (Fig. 3).

About fifty six per cent districts of the state come under the medium category (-0.20 to 0.20 score) of socio-economic development and ninety per cent of them make two separate regions in the state (Fig. 3). The first region which is comparatively large in size locates in the southern part of the state, including the districts of Birbhum, Barddhaman, Nadia, Bankura, Hugli, Haora and Twenty Four Parganas (North). The other region of this grade lies in the northern part of the state comprising the districts of Jalpaiguri and Koch Behar. The low score (below -0.20 score) of socio-economic development is depicted in five districts of the study area and three of them form a longitudinal belt in the northern plain, they are Uttar Dinajpur, Maldah and Murshidabad districts. Remaining two districts of the same grade are located in the southern and western parts of the state (Fig. 3).

The present study, therefore, predicts the fact of regional disparities in the levels of socio-economic development among the districts of state of West Bengal. Levels of socio-economic development vary considerably across the districts of the state and such a variation is caused by the variation of social and economic determinants such as, literacy rate, educational facilities, health facilities, urbanization, agricultural development, industrial development and other infrastructural facilities.

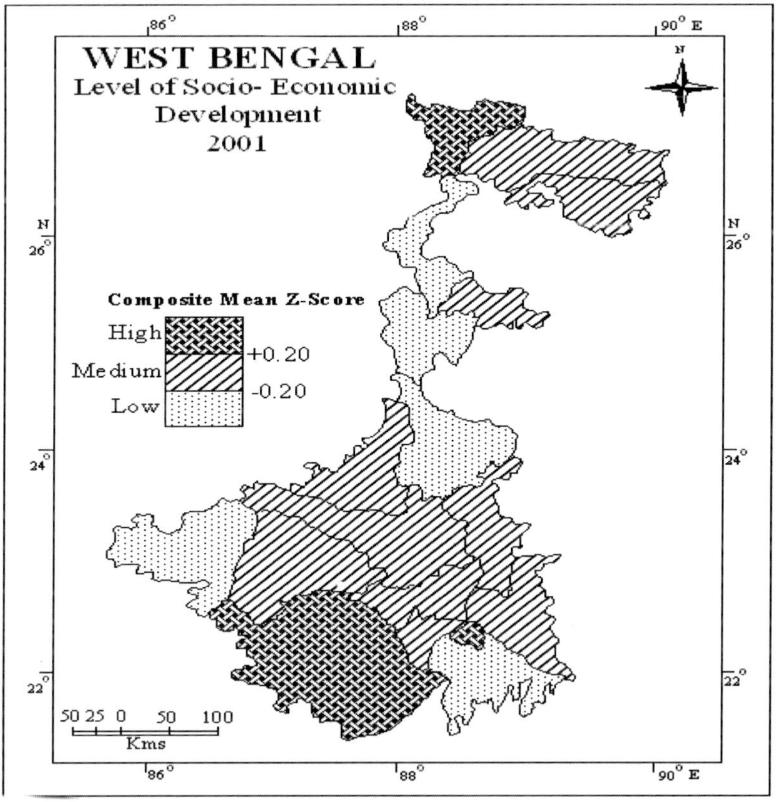

Fig. 3

Female Household Industry Workers vis-à-vis Socio-Economic Development

Figure 4 illustrates the diagrammatical representation of the relationship between the female household industry workers and levels of socio-economic development among the districts of the state of West Bengal. The figure 4 shows that four districts of the state come under the high category (above 0.40

score) of female household industry workers, among them, two districts have low level (below -0.20 score) of socio-economic development and remaining two districts have medium level (-0.20 to 0.20 score) of socio-economic development in the state. The districts of high grade of female household industry workers with low level of socio-economic development make a small region in the central part of the state, comprising the districts of Maldah and Murshidabad. One-third districts of the study area have medium level (-0.40 to 0.40 score) of female household industry workers, from which one district comes under the high level (above 0.20 score) of socio-economic development, four lie under the medium category (-0.20 to .020 score) of socio-economic development and last one in the low grade (below -0.20 score) of socio-economic development in the state of West Bengal (Fig. 4). A prominent region of medium level of female household industry workers versus medium grade of socio-economic development is depicted in the southern part of the state,

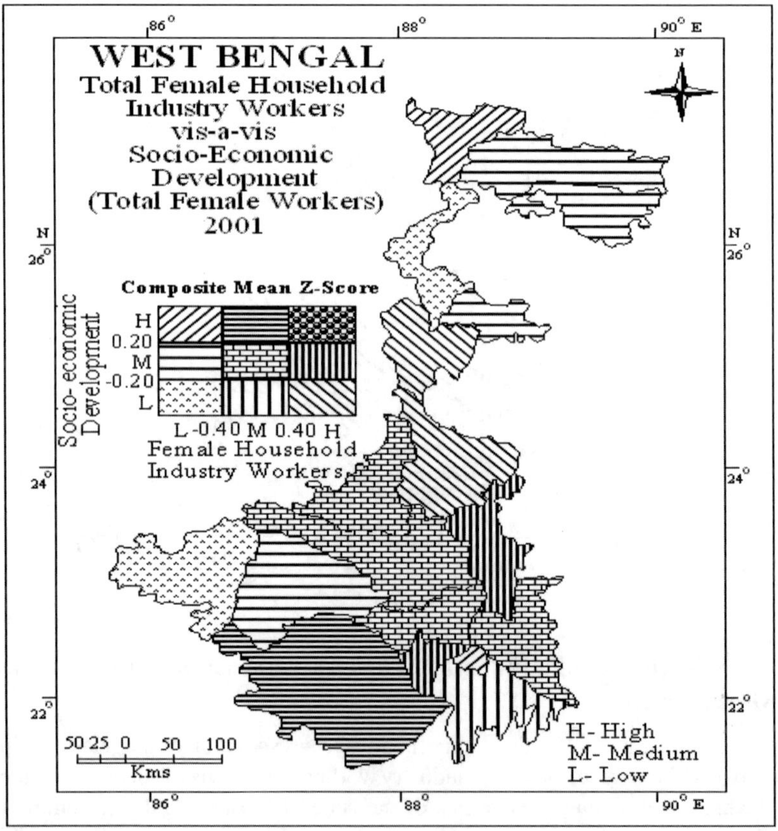

Fig. 4

including the districts of Birbhum, Barddhaman, Hugly and Twenty Four Parganas (North). As many as forty four per cent districts of the study area show the low grade (below -0.40 score) of female household industry workers, out of them, two districts have high score (above 0.20 score) of socio-economic development, another two districts have low grade (below -0.20 score) of socio-economic development and remaining four districts fall under the medium category (-0.20 to 0.20 score) of socio-economic development. Fifty per cent districts of the low grade of female household industry workers vis-à-vis medium score of socio-economic development constitute a small region in the northern part of the state, comprising the districts of Jalpaiguri and Koch Behar. Fig. 4 reveals that only two districts (Kolkata and Darjeeling districts) of the state come under the low level of female household industry workers but they fall under the high grade of socio-economic development. Another two districts of the study area namely, Uttar Dinajpur and Puruliya districts lie under the low grade of female household industry workers with low level of socio-economic development due to low female literacy rate, low urbanization, low agricultural development, low industrial development, and low infrastructural facilities. Not a single district of the state fall under the category of high level of female household industry workers versus high grade of socio-economic development in the study area (Fig. 4).

Correlation between Total Female Household Industry Workers and other Selected Variables of Socio-economic Development

Table 4 shows the causal relationship between female household industry workers and selected variables of socio-economic development. The table 4 depicts that out of forty-six variables; only six variables show the significant relationship with female household industry workers, but their magnitudes are different from each other. They are: X_6 (Percentage of Scheduled Caste and Scheduled Tribe Population to Total Population), X_7 (Literacy Rate), X_8 (Male Literacy Rate), X_{11} (Urban Literacy Rate), X_{30} (Urban Employment Rate) and X_{33} (Percentage of Total Workers in Households Industry). Among them $X_{7,}$ X_{11} and X_{33} are significant at 99 per cent level of confidence with female household industry workers, but first two variables (X_7 and X_{11}) are negatively and last one (X_{33}) is positively correlated with female household industry workers. Variables $X_{6,}$ X_8 and X_{30} are significant at 95 per cent level of confidence with female household industry workers, from them, variables X_6 and X_8 are negatively correlated and variable X_{30} is positively correlated with female household industry workers. It is observed that percentage of scheduled caste and scheduled tribe population to total population, literacy rate, male literacy rate, urban literacy rate, urban employment rate and percentage of total workers in households industry are closely associated with the regional variations of female household industry workers in the state of West Bengal.

Table 4: Result of Correlation (r) Between Female Household Industry Workers and other Selected Variables of Socio-economic Development in West Bengal, 2001

Variable	*Definition*	*Total Female Household Industry Workers(Y_f)*
X_1	Population Growth (1991-2001)	0.289
X_2	Population Density	-0.173
X_3	Sex -Ratio	0.217
X_4	Percentage of Rural Population to Total Population	0.212
X_5	Percentage of Urban Population to Total Population	-0.207
X_6	Percentage of Scheduled Caste and Scheduled Tribe Population to Total Population	-0.470**
X_7	Literacy Rate	-0.647*
X_8	Male Literacy Rate	-0.484**
X_9	Female Literacy Rate	-0.223
X_{10}	Rural Literacy Rate	0.055
X_{11}	Urban Literacy Rate	-0.641*
X_{12}	Number of Primary Schools per lakh of population	-0.209
X_{13}	Number of Primary Schools per 100 sq. km. of area	-0.167
X_{14}	Number of Middle Schools per lakh of population	-0.257
X_{15}	Number of Middle Schools per 100 sq. km. of area	-0.216
X_{16}	Number of High and High Secondary Schools per lakh of population	-0.321
X_{17}	Number of High and High Secondary Schools per 100 sq. km. of area	-0.192
X_{18}	Number of Colleges per lakh of population	-0.343
X_{19}	Number of Colleges per 100 sq. km. of area	-0.204
X_{20}	Number of Students per School	0.120
X_{21}	Number of Students per Teacher	0.363
X_{22}	Percentage of Net Area Sown to Total Reporting Area	0.276
X_{23}	Intensity of Cropping	0.465
X_{24}	Percentage of Irrigated Area to Net Sown Area	-0.094
X_{25}	Agricultural Productivity	0.073
X_{26}	Employment Rate	-0.282
X_{27}	Male Employment Rate	-0.164
X_{28}	Female Employment Rate	-0.199
X_{29}	Rural Employment Rate	0.031
X_{30}	Urban Employment Rate	0.534**
X_{31}	Percentage of Total Workers in Cultivation	-0.071
X_{32}	Percentage of Total Workers in Agricultural Labour	0.253
X_{33}	Percentage of Total Workers in Households Industry	0.952*
X_{34}	Percentage of Total Workers in Other Works	-0.273
X_{35}	Number of Registered Factories Workers per lakh of Population	-0.040
X_{36}	Number Registered Factories per 100 sq. km. of Area	-0.163
X_{37}	Numbers of Small Scale Industries per 100 sq. km. of Area	-0.189

X_{38}	Number of Hospitals & Primary Health Centres per lakh of population	-0.052
X_{39}	Number of Beds in Hospitals per lakh of population	-0.287
X_{40}	Percentage of Electrified Village to Total Villages	0.226
X_{41}	Density of Surface Road per sq. km. of Area	-0.187
X_{42}	Number of Motor Vehicles on Road per lakh of Population	-0.273
X_{43}	Number of Post &Telegraph Offices per lakh of Population	-0.231
X_{44}	Per capita Income (in Rs.)	-0.017
X_{45}	Number of Commercial Banks per lakh of Population	-0.259
X_{46}	Number of Credit Societies per lakh of Population	-0.153

* Significance at 1 per cent level, ** Significance at 5 per cent level

Source: Calculation is based on district level published data, Census of India [2001] and Statistical Abstract, Govt. of West Bengal [2002-2003]

Conclusion

The above mentioned study noticeably reveals that there are ample regional variations of female household industry workers, levels of socio-economic development, and in the relationship of female household industry workers with the levels of socio-economic development among the districts of the state. The concentration of female household industry workers is high in the central and southern parts and comparatively low in the northern part of the state. The level of socio-economic development is relatively high in the southern districts and low in the northern and central plain districts of the state. The districts of high level of female household industry workers versus medium grade of socio-economic development are mainly located in the southern part of the state. On the other hand the region of high grade of female household industry workers with low level of socio-economic development is found in the central part of the study area. A dominant region of medium level of female household industry workers versus medium grade of socio-economic development is depicted in the southern part of the state. Two districts i.e. Kolkata and Darjeeling districts of the state appear under the low level of female household industry workers but they fall under the high grade of socio-economic development. Another two districts of the study area namely Uttar Dinajpur and Puruliya districts lie under the low grade of female household industry workers with low level of socio-economic development due to low female literacy rate, low urbanization, low agricultural development, low industrial development and low infrastructural facilities. Not a single district of the state fall under the category of high level of female household industry workers versus high grade of socio-economic development in the study area. It reveals that the regional distribution of female household industry workers and levels of socio-economic development do not follow any particular pattern in the study area. Percentage of scheduled caste and scheduled tribe population to total population, literacy rate, male literacy rate, urban literacy rate, urban employment rate and percentage of total workers in households industry are closely associated with the regional variations of female household industry workers in the state of West Bengal.

The following remedial measures may be adopted to develop the household industries and to minimize the regional variations in the distribution of female household industry workers and levels of socio-economic development in the state of West Bengal.

- Beside general education, job-oriented educational and training programmes should be introduced for women both in rural as well as urban sectors.
- Employment opportunities have to be extended for females in the field of household industry.
- Large number of household industries should be established both in the rural and urban areas of the state, because these allow the people to work at their residence with the help of each and every family members including women.
- There are great prospects of the development of agro, forest and mineral based industries in the state. The especial emphasis has to be given to develop the agro-based household industries in the plain districts, mineral and forest based in the south-western plateau region, forest and horticulture based in the northern mountainous area and forest and marine based household industries in the southern delta region of the state.
- Financial assistance should be easily provided to females to run the household industries, because these industries consume the large volume of human resources in general and female resources in particular.
- The state and central governments have to provide various incentives to household industries especially run by females to produce qualitative goods, and efficient mechanism has to be developed to purchase the finished products of these industries at standard rates.
- For improving the status of females in the society, radical transformations have to be made in the society by changing the roles played by males and females in the society.

References

Census of India (2001), *Primary Census Abstract, Total Population*, Series 1, Table A-5, Government of India, New Delhi.

Government of West Bengal (2003), *Statistical Abstract, 2002-2003*, Bureau of Applied Economic and Statistics, Kolkata.

Mehrotra, S.N. (2006), Women Labour in India, In: Sharama, U. (ed.), *Female Labour in India*, Mittal Publications, New Delhi.

Ramotra, K.C. (1989), Female Work Participation: A Geographical Perspective with Special Reference to Marathwada, *Indian Geographical Journal*, 64(1): 80-87.

UNICEF (1978), *Women's Development: Some Critical Issues*, Marwan Publications, New Delhi.

Sabhanayakam, S. (1988), *Human Resources: Development and Utilization*, Renaissance Publishing House, Delhi.

Verma, S. B., Joloka, S. K. and Kushwas, K. J. (eds.) (2006), *Rural Women Empowerment*, Deep & Deep Publications, New Delhi.

Vohra, R. and Sen, A.K. (1985), *Status, Education and Problems of Indian Women*, Delhi.

10

Gender Differences in Microenterprises

Boohene, R. *University of Cape Coast*
Kotey, B. *University of New England*

Introduction

In recent years extensive attention has been given to the role of small businesses in facilitating global economic development (Verheul and Thurik 2002). The small business sector is seen as an important contributor to the transition to a market economy, through the processes of innovation, job creation, income generation and provision of competitive environment (Hisrich and Ozturk 1999). Thus, the World Bank and other international funding agencies have linked grants to transitional economies to policies and programs aimed at creating stable macro-economic environments conducive to private investment, particularly, to developing the small and medium enterprise (SME) sector. However, in the majority of cases these programs have failed to achieve the desired outcomes because they are not tailored to the specific needs of the recipient countries (Baffoe 2005). In Ghana, for example, sources indicate that the small business sector accounted for 15.5 percent of the labour force and 6 percent of the Gross Domestic Product (GDP) in 1998 (Kayanula and Quartey 2000). Despite efforts to improve this sector, the growth and performance of these enterprises in terms of their contribution to income, innovation and employment generation remains unsatisfactory (Bani 2003). The contribution of the small enterprise sector to overall economic development is dependent on its performance and performance of the individual firms that comprise the sector. In addition, performance can be explained by the strategies small firms adopt. Since in small firms strategies derive from the owner-managers' personality and demographic characteristics, gender differences in performance can be traced back to differences in socialisation, training and experiences men and women encounter before entry into business (Carter, Williams and Reynolds 1997; Sexton and Bowman-Upton 1990).

Despite the attention given to gender issues in Africa in the popular press and in other published materials the issues have limited coverage in the academic literature, in particular the small firm literature with few research papers providing critical analyses of the problem and its causes. In this paper we adopt the liberal and social feminist theory, developed in the West, to examine African women's performance as small business owners vis-à-vis their male counterparts. In Ghana, women form the majority of operators in the small business sector. However, their educational levels and managerial experiences are lower than those of their male counterparts (Boohene, Kotey and Folker 2005). This paper investigates the influence of gender on the owner-manager's psychological and demographic characteristics and how they influence business strategies and performance.

The paper comprises five sections. The theoretical framework and accompanying hypotheses are developed in the next section. This is followed by the research methodology. Data analysis and results are discussed in the fourth section. The fifth section presents implications of the study to policy makers and business owners as well as limitations of the study.

Research Framework and Hypotheses Development

Small Business Performance, Strategy, Owner-manager Personal Values and Demographics of the Firm

The overall contribution of the small enterprise sector to economic development is dependent on the performance of the individual firms that comprise the sector. Performance at the individual firm level is in turn determined by the strategies realised by the firms (Blackman 2003; Gray 1997; Kotey and Meredith 1997). According to the strategic adaptation theory (Child 1997; Papadakis and Dimitris 1998), the key to business success lies in the decisions of the owner-manager who identifies opportunities, develops strategies, assembles resources and takes the initiative to effectively implement the strategies (Lerner and Almor 2002).

For small businesses, strategies implemented are not necessarily those planned, but generally emerge from a series of incremental adjustments to the opportunities and threats confronted by the firm over-time. Business strategies can thus be deduced from activities in the major functional areas of planning, finance, human resource management, marketing, operations and information and communications technology (Galbraith and Schendel 1983). The literature presents numerous types of strategies and their impact on performance. Popular among these are Miles and Snow's (1978) four strategy-types and Porter's (1980) five competitive strategies. In the small business literature, strategy-types are generally uni-dimensional, ranging from entrepreneurial to conservative or proactive to reactive (Caughey and Chetty 1994; Covin and Slevin 1989; Julien *et al.* 1997). Proactive strategies are portrayed as associated with innovation, industry leadership and risk taking. Firms with this strategic orientation continually search for new products, services and technologies

(Covin, Green and Slevin 2006; Morgan and Strong 2003), improve existing products (Lumpkin and Dess 1997), emphasise customer service, brand-name development and use effective promotion strategies.

Various streams of research suggest that the owner-manager's demographic and psychological characteristics have important influences on organisational outcomes. These influences may be both direct and indirect (Nonis and Swift 2001). In small businesses the direct influence is seen as the most important force driving organisational outcomes, whereas, indirect influence is evident in the impact on a number of variables which in turn determine firm performance (Papadakis and Dimitris 1998). Drawing from the sociological and psychological literatures some researchers favour demographic characteristics because of their objectivity and because they seem likely to influence organisational outcomes through various variables (Da Silva 2000; Nonis and Swift 2001). Others argue that demographic characteristics despite their objectivity and ease of measurement are unlikely to influence outcomes (Papadakis and Dimitris 1998). These authors view psychological characteristics as better predictors of decision-making behaviour. In addition, several studies have provided sufficient evidence to confirm that psychological characteristics are especially useful in predicting business strategies (Da Silva 2000; Oshagbemi 2004). The present study examines both psychological and demographic characteristics as sources of influence on firm performance, because the study of either stream in isolation provides partial rather than a holistic explanation of the owner-manager's behaviour (Papadakis and Dimitris 1998).

Fagenson (1993) presented that values exert strong influence on an individual's vocational behaviour. The specific behaviour of interest in this study is the behaviour of owner-managers in small firms. Accordingly, a key factor in the creation and implementation of strategy in small business is the determining influence of the owner-manager's values (Walker and Brown 2004). The values of owner-managers are, therefore, essential to explaining firm strategy. Owner-managers' values determine the goals pursued by the business and influence their management style, problem solving and decision making behaviour as well as the structure of the business and strategies employed (Olson and Currie 1992; Verheul, Risseeuw and Bartelse 2002). Thompson and Strickland (1984: 49) wrote:

> Strategy formulation is rarely so objective an analytical process that the personal values and aspirations of managers are excluded…There is a natural human tendency for managers to draw upon their own personal values, background experiences, preferences, and ambitions when choosing among alternative strategies and when interpreting the strategic plan.

The literature indicates that owner-managers with entrepreneurial values who adopt proactive strategies exhibit stronger performance than those with less entrepreneurial values who tend to be reactive in strategic orientation (Blackman 2003). The personal values associated with proactive strategies often referred to as entrepreneurial values cover creativity, risk taking, innovation, achievement orientation, ambition and independence (Hodgetts and Kuratko 2001; Kickul and Gundry 2002; Verheul, Uhlaner, and Thurik 2002). In contrast, values such as equity, affection, social protection and compassion are described as conservative and associated with reactive type strategies (Kotey 1994).

In addition to the personal values of owner-managers the literature indicates that owner-managers' demographics such as business experience, education and age, impact on their firm's performance because the owner-manager is typically the locus of decision-making in small firms (Begley and Boyd 1986; Blackwood and Mowl 2000; Bosma *et al.* 2004; Bruderl, Preisendorfer, and Ziegler 1992; Da Silva 2000; Hambrick and Mason 1984).

The literature suggests that owner-managers who start businesses in areas closely related to their previous employment acquire repertoires of pertinent expertise or appropriate problem solving abilities needed to develop contacts with potential customers and suppliers (Cooper, Gimeno-Gascon, and Woo 1994; Edelman, Brush, and Manolova 2002). Similarly, Bird (1989) argued that industrial experience provide awareness of industry norms for pricing, employment and supplier relations. Furthermore, previous experience increases the managers' credibility.

Education increases knowledge, skills, problem-solving ability, discipline, motivation and self-confidence (Bird, Sapp and Lee 2001). These qualities enable owner-managers to cope with the day-to-day activities and problems associated with managing their businesses (Cooper, Gimeno-Gascon, and Woo 1994). Blackman (2003), Bosma *et al.* (2004) and Da Silva (2000) highlighted the importance of the owner-manager's education in small firms where stakeholders evaluate firms based on observable characteristics such as education, which they presume to be correlated with the unobserved quality of the firm and its founder. Education also contributes to owner-managers' ability to innovate and to marshal and manage the firm's resources (Bird 1989). Before granting loans, banks often resort to evaluation schemes, which take into account the level of education of the owner-manager, since educated owner-managers may have the skills to present financial information and communicate more effectively with lending officers (Coleman 2000).

The importance of owner-manager's age to business performance stems from the fact that age along with time dimensions has a powerful effect in shaping attitudes and hence behaviour of owner-managers (Kabacoff and Stoffey 2001; Oshagbemi 2004). Owner-managers' age provides an indication of their business experiences, and years in business stand for expertise (Hambrick and Mason 1984). Experience in turn affects efficiency in organising and managing the production process, ability to attract customers and to obtain new capital from investors (Bruderl, Preisendorfer and Ziegler 1992; Coleman 2000; Hambrick and Mason 1984). Furthermore, age influences access to finance and the business strategies of owner-managers (Coleman 2000; Hambrick and Mason 1984).

Gender, Performance, Owner-manager Personal Values, Demographics and Business Strategies

A generally accepted premise in the small business literature is that female owner-managers behave differently from male owner-managers and that several factors unique to women influence the strategies they adopt and ultimately performance of their business. Downing (1990) suggested that personal values and objectives of females differ from those of males. This is because men and women undergo different socialisation processes, where each sex acquires specific sex-related personal values and learns sex-appropriate behaviours (Bird, Sapp and Lee 2001; Eagly 1987). Men have been traditionally socialised to be materialistic, achievement-oriented and pleasure seeking. This is demonstrated by their value for innovation, risk-taking, independence, capability, courage, ambition, logic, a comfortable life, a sense of accomplishment, freedom and family security (Dio *et al.* 1996; Fagenson 1993; Rokeach 1973). The majority of these values are consistent with those presented in the literature as entrepreneurial. On the other hand, women are socialised to be care givers, oriented towards religious values with less emphasises on the things valued by men (Kalleberg and Leicht 1991). These gender differences in behaviour are consistent with the social feminist theory which contends that women and men have different experiential backgrounds and ways of thinking that derive from differences in educational and socialisation patterns (Johnsen and McMahon 2005; Watson 2001).

Carter, Williams and Reynolds (1997) and Carter, Anderson and Shaw (2001) argued that if the execution of business strategy is influenced by the owner-manager's values, experiences, motivations and belief structures, then male and female owner-managers should differ in the performance of their businesses. This is because their different socialization patterns means men and women will exhibit different personality characteristics (Bird, Sapp and Lee 2001). Compared to men, women have been found to be more cautious (Jianakoplos and Bernasek 1998), less confident, less aggressive, easier to persuade, and have lower problem solving abilities when making decisions under risk conditions (Johnson and Powell 1994; Sonfield *et al.* 2001). Powell and Ansic (1997), for instance, noted that women have been stereotyped as being conservative and risk averse, whereas males are viewed as more entrepreneurial and risk taking.

Similar to the developed economies, there is evidence in the literature that supports differences in the socialisation of boys and girls in Africa. With no formal social security system, males in the African society are perceived to be a form of security for their families so they have to be well socialised to perform this role (Boohene, Kotey and Folker 2005). They are socialised to become heads of households and breadwinners with responsibility for the welfare of all household members including women. In the process they are given control over the resources necessary for discharging these responsibilities (Amu 2005; Dolphyne 2000). An African male is encouraged to be aggressive, and to display 'machismo'. These qualities assist in building their self-esteem and confidence (Bortey and Dodoo 2005). Thus, the key developmental areas in the values of boys in African societies are assertiveness, risk taking, independence, innovativeness, and achievement orientation. What the African male achieves through intimate connection with others, he must manage as a man by disconnecting, by separating himself and asserting his right to be distinct (Bortey and Dodoo 2005).

African women, on the other hand, are not encouraged to display the same degree of assuredness in their abilities (Dolphyne 2000). They bear the primary responsibility for child nurturing, cooking, washing and collecting fuel-wood and water (Boohene, Kotey and Folker 2005; Nikoi 1993). They are socialised to be gentle, to put the needs of others before theirs but never to be winners. Girls in the African social context become unattractive when they demonstrate male behaviours. Hence, it is appropriate for women to be quiet, to hang back, and to accept what life doles out to them (Amu 2005; Boohene, Kotey and Folker 2005).

In addition, women are increasingly channelled into secondary jobs, mainly as a result of limited access to education and training (Akuffo 1996; Greenstreet 1981; Nikoi 1993). It is explained that in traditional societies, the major role of a woman is to ensure the continuity of the family lineage. She is therefore, expected to marry soon after puberty and does not need formal education to perform this role. Moreover, a man is expected to provide for his wife and children. Since education is a means to highly paid jobs in the formal sector, it is considered more important for boys to have formal education to enable the execution of their roles as breadwinners in the family (Dolphyne 2000; Tsikata 2001). In addition, the education of African females is hindered by the overall cost of education, customary fostering, puberty rites, early marriages, and the perception of parents that educating girls is not as rewarding as educating boys (Amu 2005; Dolphyne 2000; Republic of Ghana 2004).

Differences in the socialisation of boys and girls in African society imply that they will exhibit different values, experiences, motivations and belief structures. These in turn will affect the business strategies they make as owner-managers and ultimately performance of their businesses. In employing the liberal and social feminist theory in this paper, we assume that there are direct differences in performance, personal values and demographics between the genders due to differences in their socialisation patterns. We also contend that gender differences in personal values and demographics of owner-managers influence business strategies, which ultimately influence business performance. The theoretical relationships among gender, owner-manager personal values and demographics, business strategies and enterprise performance are depicted in Figure 1 below.

Figure 1 depicts the research framework adopted in this study. It shows the effect of gender on performance through owner-manager characteristics and business strategies. Owner-manager's characteristics determine the strategies pursued and ultimately performance of the firm.

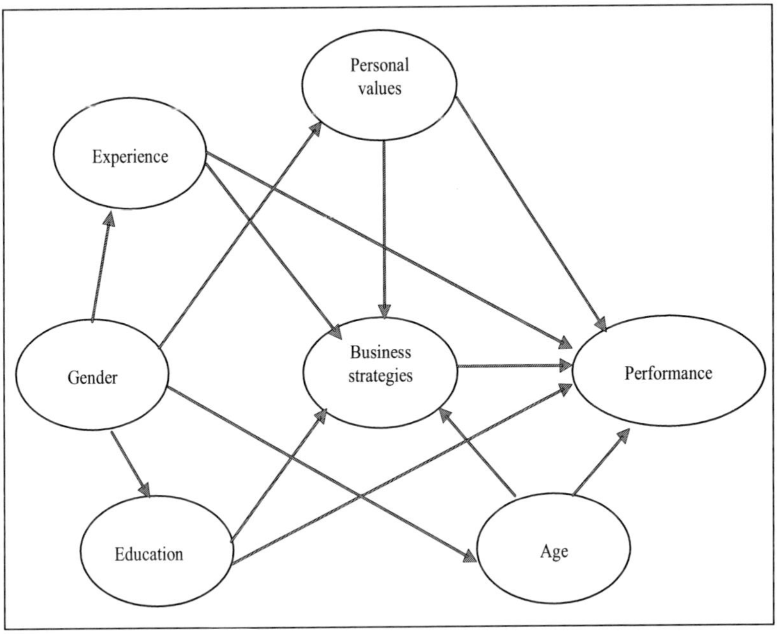

Figure 1: Relationships among Gender, Owner-Managers Characteristics, Business Strategies and Firm Performance

From the theoretical framework depicted in Figure 1, the following hypotheses are drawn to be tested:

Hypothesis 1: Small businesses operated by Ghanaian female owner-managers achieve lower performance than those operated by Ghanaian male owner-managers

Hypothesis 2a: Ghanaian female owner-managers exhibit entrepreneurial values to a lesser degree than Ghanaian male owner-managers.

Hypothesis 2b: Ghanaian female owner-managers display entrepreneurial values to a lesser degree and hence exhibit lower performance than Ghanaian male owner-managers.

Hypothesis 2c: Gender differences in the personal values of Ghanaian owner-managers influence their business strategies and ultimately their performance.

Hypothesis 3a: Ghanaian female owner-managers have less business experience than Ghanaian male owner-managers.

Hypothesis 3b: Ghanaian female owner-managers have less business experience and therefore exhibit lower performance than Ghanaian male owner-managers.

Hypothesis 3c: Gender differences in business experience of Ghanaian owner-managers' influence their business strategies, and ultimately performance of their businesses.

Hypothesis 4a: Ghanaian female owner-managers have lower levels of education than Ghanaian male owner-managers.

Hypothesis 4b: Ghanaian female owner-managers have lower levels of education and therefore will exhibit lower business performance than Ghanaian male owner-managers.

Hypothesis 4c: Gender differences in educational levels of Ghanaian owner-managers' will influence their business strategies, and ultimately performance of their businesses.

Hypothesis 5a: There are gender differences in the ages of owner-managers in Ghana.

Hypothesis 5b: Gender differences in the ages of Ghanaian owner-managers will influence the performance of their businesses.

Hypothesis 5c: Gender differences in the ages of Ghanaian owner-managers influence their business strategies, and ultimately performance of their businesses.

Research Method

Population, Sample Selection and Data Collection Methods

Owner-managers of small firms in Ghana formed the population from which the sample was drawn for the study. In order to control for the myriad of confounding factors that may impact on the results from a cross-sectional survey and also improve internal validity of the instruments employed, the study was restricted to a single sector and location. Thus, retailers in the Accra Metropolis were selected as the population for the study. Area sampling was then used to select six hundred and seventy four respondents for the study.

Face-to-face interviews using structured questionnaires were employed for data collection. Mail and telephone surveys are less reliable because of the inefficient and erratic nature of Ghana's telecommunication systems. Listwise deletion of missing cases resulted in a final sample of six hundred respondents.

Measurement of Variables

The latent constructs used in this study were measured using multi-item indicators. For most constructs, the indicators were generated from previous research and modified to fit the current research context.

The gender of the owner-manager or major decision maker was measured on a categorical scale using 0 for men and 1 for women.

Kotey's (1999) performance indicators were modified to include other performance indicators in the literature. Kotey (1999) argued that because research and government interest in small firms are associated with macro economic objectives such as job creation, innovation and increased productivity, enterprise performance should be measured in terms of respondents' desire to meet and their levels of satisfaction in achieving these and other business objectives. Respondents were first asked to indicate the importance they attach to ten performance goals on a six point Likert scale, ranging from 5 = extremely important to 0 = not at all important. Secondly, the respondents were asked to indicate on a seven point Likert scale the extent to which they are satisfied with the firm's performance on the same indicators with 7 being highly satisfied and 1 being highly dissatisfied. Ratings of importance were multiplied by the levels of satisfaction to compute a performance index for each firm (Miles, Covin, and Heeley 2000). Dess and Robinson (1984) found that performance measured in this way has high validity and reliability values and is consistent with the objective measures of performance.

Hulland (1999) suggests that when a construct is multi-dimensional, it is appropriate to separately present each dimension in the statistical model. Following this suggestion respondents were provided a list of strategic activities generated from the literature for the various functional areas. Kotey and Meredith's (1997) strategy instrument was modified to include activities in the area of information technology and to reflect the unique characteristics of the sample studied. Thus, strategy was measured as comprising activities in the functional areas of planning, finance, human resource management, operations, marketing and information and communications technology. Respondents were asked to rate the extent to which they perform the various activities in these functional areas on a six point Likert scale, ranging from always = 5 to never = 0.

Rokeach's (1973) personal value survey and personal value concepts drawn from a review of existing literature formed the majority of items used to measure personal values in this research. Rokeach's (1973) personal value survey was used because his taxonomy remains the most popular conceptual structure in organisational research (McDonald and Gandz 1991). It is easy and simple to design, and economical to administer, provides reasonably reliable and valid measures, is reported by participants to be interesting, thought provoking, and ego-involving, and produces responses directly expressed in quantitative terms (Rokeach 1973: 87). Lenartowicz and Johnson (2002) further argued that Rokeach's (1973) value survey also plays a central role in the conceptualisation of behaviour in organisations. It can differentiate the value orientations of men from those of women (Munso and McIntyre 1979). Furthermore, it has been validated for the international setting and its psychometric properties well documented (Schwartz and Bilsky 1990). Thus, the personal value items adopted in this research cover innovation, risk taking, a need for achievement and ambition, responsibility, broadmindedness, aggressiveness, family security and trust.

Bosma et al. (2004) and Bruderl, Preisendorfer and Ziegler (1992) provided a measure of experience that incorporates both general and specific experience. General experience encompasses a person's prior work experience while specific experience is made up of industry-specific and entrepreneurial-specific components (Dyke, Fischer and Reuber 1992; Firkin 2001; Lerner and Almor 2002). Industry specific experience refers to familiarity with a particular industry or sector whereas entrepreneurial specific experience includes a person's previous experience and family background in entrepreneurship (Indarti and Langenberg 2004; Lerner and Almor 2002; Sirmon and Hitt 2003). Because the respondents for the study are from the service sector and are expected to have gained experience in various fields, work experience was operationalised by asking respondents to indicate whether they had any general experience, which incorporate experience in management and entrepreneurship prior to commencing their businesses. This was measured on a nominal scale 0 (no) and 1 (yes) (Dyke, Fischer and Reuber 1992; Indarti and Langenberg 2004; Saffu *et al.* 2006).

In measuring the level of education, the survey participants in this study were asked to indicate the highest level of education they had attained, from a set of alternatives on an ordinal scale ranging from 'never been to school' to 'postgraduate degree'.

In most research, the age of owner-managers is measured by simply asking respondents to indicate their age (Coleman 2004). In this study, respondents were given a set of age ranges using an ordinal scale based on the classification method employed by the Ghana Statistical Service for its population and housing census (Ghana Statistical Service 2002). Respondents were thus asked to tick or indicate their age category.

Analytical Techniques

The partial least squares (PLS) approach to structural equation modelling (using PLS graph version 3) was used in this study. PLS is a component-based technique that simultaneously examines theory (structural model) and measurement of the constructs in the study (measurement model). The advantage of using this technique is its ability to handle multiple exogenous and endogenous constructs at the same time. The model is also able to deal with multicollinearity among endogenous constructs and to create latent construct scores directly from the cross products of the multi-item indicators. Although PLS estimates parameters simultaneously for the measurement and structural models the two models are analysed and interpreted separately (Hulland 1999).

Analyses of Results

Descriptive Statistics

Of the 600 responses used in the analyses 50.6 percent were from males and 49.3 percent from females. The majority of the respondents (69.8 percent) were married and 30.2 percent had never been married, were separated or divorced. Marital status did not differ between the sexes. The most common age category of respondents (20.5 percent) was the 30-34 age group. The chi square test did not show any significant differences in age between men and women owner-managers ($x2$=14.06: p> 0.05). However, disparities in education were evident ($x2$=62.870: p< 0.05) with females' respondents presenting lower educational qualifications than the male respondents. More male owner-managers (55.1 percent) had more previous work experience than females (44.9 percent). This is evidenced by a significant chi square statistic ($x2$= 9.630: p<0.01) and confirms findings in the literature that males have more previous entrepreneurial and managerial experiences than females.

The firms in the study were small with an average of 2.21 full-time employees and 0.44 part-timers or casuals for male employers and 1.58 and 0.35 full-timers and part-timers respectively for female-owned firms. The chi-square test revealed significant differences between men and women owner-managers for the number of full time employees (x^2=34.17: p<0.05) but not for part-timers or casuals. The results are consistent with data on the informal sector in Ghana, which indicates that a larger proportion of females (62.6 per cent) than males (41.6 per cent) are self-employed without employees (Republic of Ghana 2005).

The Measurement Model

The measurement model evaluates the relationships between constructs and their indicators by assessing the reliability and validity of the instruments used. The tests commonly used for these assessments include individual item reliabilities (factor loadings), composite reliabilities (internal consistency), average variance extracted from the indicators associated with individual constructs (convergent validity), and discriminant validity. Consistent with Hulland's (1999) suggestion that indicators with low loadings are not generalisable across settings and that they may bias the estimates of the parameters associated with the construct, all indicators with loadings below 0.5 were discarded. The composite reliabilities for the constructs in the study range from 0.8 to 0.92, all higher than the 0.70 level suggested by Nunally (1978).

Convergent validity was used to measure the amount of variance that the latent variables captured from their indicators relative to the amount due to measurement error. This was assessed by using the average variance extracted (AVE). AVE of 0.5 or more demonstrates adequate convergent validity (Chin 1998). However, Magner, Welker and Campbell (1996) argued that AVEs of 0.4 are also indicative of adequate validity. As shown in Tables 1 to 4, the AVEs of all the constructs are 0.4 and above providing evidence of adequate convergent validity. The factor loadings, composite reliabilities, and convergent validity are presented in the tables below for the final measurement models of the constructs used in the study.

Table 1 indicates that respondents considered profit levels, sales revenue, income to look after family, and business stability as performance indicators important to them and/or were satisfied with their firms' performance on these indicators. However, industry leadership, job creation, organizational growth and business stability are indicators with the highest loadings for the performance construct. These indicators are consistent with those for SME contribution to economic development in the literature (Friar and Meyer 2003).

Table 1: Factor Loadings, Composite Reliability and Convergent Validity (AVE) for Performance

Latent Variable	*Mean*	*Std. Deviation*	*Factor Loadings*
Performance (PF) (Composite Reliability = 0.86; AVE = 0.42)			
Sales revenue	20.90	8.36	0.55
Creating jobs	14.51	9.01	0.70
Business stability	20.04	8.12	0.68
Profit levels	21.53	8.34	0.59
Contribution to community development	16.17	8.99	0.61
Organisational growth	18.31	8.17	0.70
Industry leadership	14.29	9.10	0.77
Income to look after family	20.79	8.52	0.54
Lower cost of operations	15.98	9.01	0.64

All indicators for strategic planning have high factor loadings whilst record-keeping and inter-firm comparisons feature prominently on the financial strategy dimension of the strategy construct. HRM is well represented by the activities in that functional area. Important indicators for operations centre on management of stock and equipment as well as employee remuneration. Concern for quality features highly on the marketing strategy and ICT is represented by the use of a range of applications.

Table 2: Factor Loadings, Composite Reliability & Convergent Validity (AVE) for Strategy

Latent Variable	*Mean*	*Std. Deviation*	*Factor Loadings*
Strategic Planning (PL) (Composite Reliability = 0.92; AVE = 0.75)			
Develop plans	3.45	1.55	0.88
Set goals for business	3.47	1.46	0.93
Make decisions on how to achieve goals	3.39	1.50	0.91
Make changes to initial plans for managing the business	2.67	1.45	0.71
Compare actual performance with business goals	2.71	1.61	0.89
Financial Strategy (FIN) (Composite Reliability = 0.80; AVE = 0.51)			
Keep records on actual performance	2.95	1.70	0.84
Keep strict check on cost	3.49	1.44	0.50
Compare business performance (profit and sales) with that of competitors	2.08	1.65	0.56
Compare business performance (profit and sales) with that of industry averages	1.10	1.52	0.89
Human Resource Strategy (HR) (Composite Reliability = 0.90; AVE = 0.63)			
Use various sources to recruit staff	0.91	0.73	0.66
Employ a number of techniques to select staff	0.88	0.86	0.77
Offer various training programmes for employees	1.27	0.73	0.76
Utilise various methods to appraise staff	1.20	0.71	0.88
Use a variety of incentives to motivate workers	1.20	0.71	0.88
Operations Strategy (OP) (Composite Reliability = 0.81; AVE = 0.58)			
Pay employees exactly minimum wages	1.59	1.90	0.55
Pay employees above competitive wages	2.10	1.97	0.62
Maintain equipment/furniture regularly	2.71	1.87	0.64
Check stock of goods regularly	3.49	1.52	0.73
Keep high levels of stock	3.25	1.52	0.74
Marketing Strategy (MKT) (Composite Reliability = 0.81; AVE = 0.60)			
Knowing what your competitors are doing	2.78	1.67	0.59
Inform manufacturers of how they can improve the product	2.40	2.03	0.85
Look for ways to improve products	2.40	2.03	0.85
Sell on wholesale basis	1.92	1.95	0.52
Information and Communications Technology Strategy (IT) (Composite Reliability = 0.92; AVE = 0.68)			
Use IT for accounting based applications	0.33	1.03	0.87
Use IT for database systems	0.31	1.02	0.89
Use IT for office support systems	0.55	1.37	0.85
Use IT for local area networks	0.17	0.75	0.77
Use IT for external networks	0.16	0.71	0.74

It must be noted that because gender, education, business experience and age were measured as categorical variables their factor loadings, composite reliabilities and AVE's were all 1 respectively.

Discriminant validity (the ability of some indicators to have low correlation with indicators of dissimilar concepts) was evaluated by comparing the square roots of the AVEs to the correlation between constructs (Table 3). The correlations among constructs are in the off-diagonal cells and the square root of the AVEs in the diagonal cells. The diagonal values are all greater than their respective off-diagonal values, indicating adequate discriminant validity. It can be concluded from the assessment that the measurement models for the constructs are reliable and valid.

Table 3: Discriminant Validity for Overall Measurement Model

	MKT	FIN	HR	IT	PL	OPS	PER	EDU	AGE	PV	EXP	GEN
MKT	0.77											
FIN	0.38	0.71										
HR	0.26	0.23	0.79									
IT	0.08	0.32	0.35	0.82								
PL	0.54	0.51	0.27	0.09	0.87							
OPS	0.51	0.40	0.49	0.21	0.48	0.76						
PER	0.31	0.34	0.29	0.14	0.52	0.35	0.65					
EDU	0.27	0.31	0.34	0.33	0.33	0.37	0.14	1.00				
AGE	-0.01	-0.05	-0.11	-0.14	-0.07	-0.12	-0.02	-0.17	1.00			
PV	0.39	0.27	0.21	0.12	0.55	0.39	0.37	0.31	-0.12	0.64		
EXP	-0.11	0.14	0.064	0.06	0.04	-0.01	0.09	0.08	0.02	0.02	1.00	
GEN	-0.07	-0.15	-0.14	-0.15	-0.19	-0.17	-0.03	-0.21	0.01	-0.14	-0.11	1.00

Discriminant Validity for Overall Measurement Model

Diagonal elements = square root of AVE; off-diagonal elements = correlation between constructs

Results of the Structural Model

Business performance and strategies, personal values, business experience, education and age were analysed simultaneously in the PLS model to assess the influence of gender, modelled as the sex of the owner- manager on these variables. Figure 2 illustrates the PLS graph with the path coefficients and significant levels included. The R^2s from the PLS bootstrapping procedure

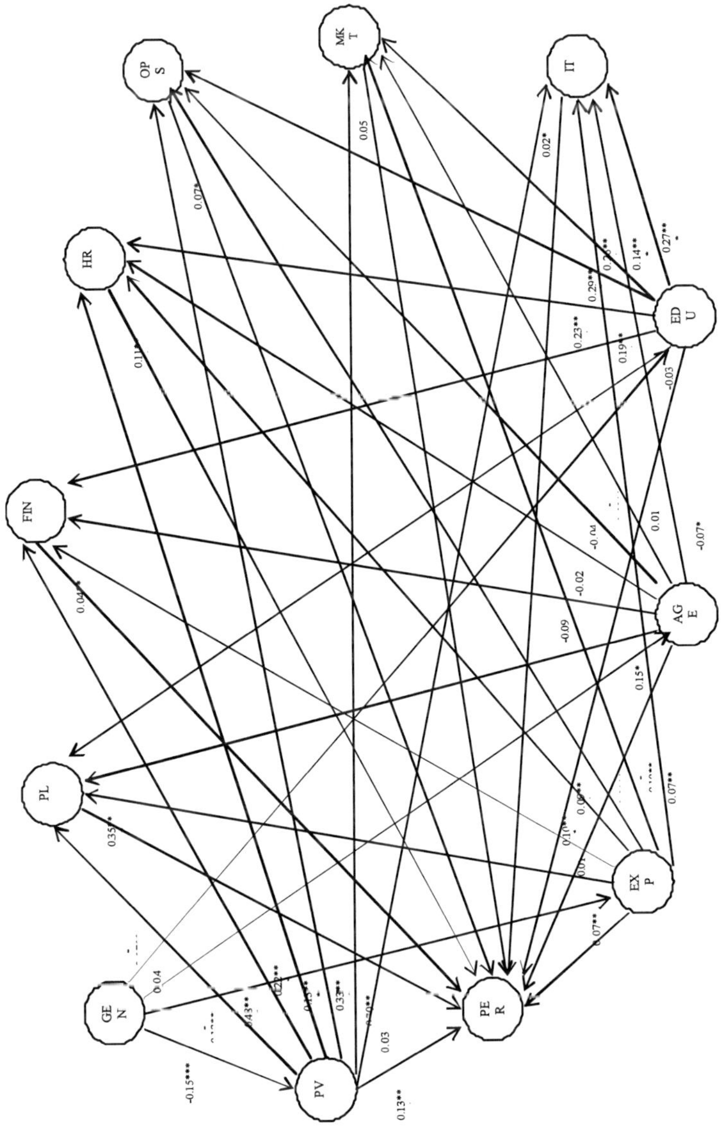

Figure 2: PLS Graph: Relationships between Owner-managers Characteristics, Gender and Firm Performance

suggest that business performance, strategic planning, finance, human resource management, operations, marketing, information and communications technology strategy, personal values, experience, education and age contributed 33 per cent, 31 per cent, 15 per cent, 14 per cent, 23 per cent, 13 per cent, 9 per cent, 2 per cent, 1 per cent, 3 per cent, and 0.01 per cent of the variance in the model respectively. The AVA for the R^2s was 12 per cent, and greater than the benchmark of the recommended 10 per cent (Falk and Miller 1992). The path coefficients and significant levels for performance, business strategies and personal values, experience, education and age are discussed individually.

Gender and Performance

Consistent with hypothesis 1, in comparison with their male counterparts, female owner-managers in the retail sector of Ghana were less confident in and less satisfied with their ability to influence business outcomes and thereby contribute to economic growth.

Table 4: Gender Differences in Performance

Gender Path to:	*Hypotheses*	*Path Co-efficient*	*t value*
PER	1	-0.1239	1.28*

***$p \leq 0.01$, ** $p \leq 0.05$, * $p \leq 0.10$

Women's rating on the performance construct comprising importance attached to and satisfaction with achievement on increasing sales revenue and profits, creating jobs, contributing to community development, seeking organisational growth and industry leadership, and operating more efficiently, was lower than that of Ghanaian male owner-managers. This finding mirrors research based in the West, where it is reported that businesses operated by women are smaller than those operated by men (Bird and Sapp 2004; Cliff 1998; Kalleberg and Leicht 1991; Verheul, Risseeuw and Bartelse 2002) and that women are less likely to pursue growth-oriented goals than men (Brush and Hisrich 2000; Verheul, Risseeuw and Bartelse 2002). Despite the predominance of Ghanaian women in the self-employment sector and in particular retail trade, the self-assessments indicate that female owner-managers perform lower compared to male owner-managers.

Personal Values and Gender

For hypothesis 2a, it was predicted that Ghanaian female owner-managers would exhibit entrepreneurial personal values to a lesser degree than Ghanaian male owner-managers. The findings confirmed this position. As shown in Table 5, the PLS result was significant and negative for the path from gender to personal values.

Table 5: Gender, Personal Values, Business Strategies and Performance

Gender Path to:	*Hypotheses*	*Path Co-efficient*	*t value*
PV	2a	-0.1470	4.11***
Sobel's Test of Indirect Effects			
PV*PER	2b	-0.0194	2.48***
PV*PL*PER	2c	-0.0159	3.43***
PV*FIN*PER	2c	-0.0017	1.68**
PV*HR*PER	2c	-0.0013	1.88**
PV*OPS*PER	2c	0.0043	1.38*
PV*MKT*PER	2c	0.0005	0.77
PV*IT*PER	2c	-0.0002	0.69

****pd*"0.01, ** *pd*"0.05, * *pd*"0.10

Social structures influence how individuals interact, how they perceive their environment, what they value, and ultimately their behaviour. In the Ghanaian society, women's and men's self-perceptions are shaped by the traditions and cultures in which they are raised. Women perceive themselves as more feminine while men describe themselves as more masculine (Bortey and Dodoo n.d.). The self-perceptions of Ghanaian men follow from a socio-cultural environment in which they are expected to develop high levels of self-assertion, self-esteem, achievement-orientedness and dominance. In contrast, women's feminine self-perceptions arise from society's expectation that they possess high levels of communal qualities such as selflessness, a concern for others, and interpersonal sensitivity. Females are likely to incur social disapproval for straying from these socially accepted gendered normative patterns of behaviour. This reduces their self-confidence and assertiveness, and often produces a hostile environment for ambitious women. Males on the other hand, receive praise and encouragement from engaging in innovative play and non-conformist behaviour. Thus, female owner-managers may perceive themselves as being less entrepreneurial than male owner-managers because of a lack of confidence in their own abilities. The findings support the social feminist theory, which posits that men and women undergo different socialisation processes, and as a result develop different value systems and expectations (Bird and Sapp 2004; Manolova *et al.* 2006). In addition, the results provide empirical validation for the propositions of Chaganti (1986), Kalleberg and Leicht (1991), Olson and Currie (1992) and Verheul, Risseeuw and Bartelse (2002) that women entrepreneurs are generally oriented towards conservatism and risk aversion.

A strong association between performance and entrepreneurial values from the results for hypothesis 2b implies that owner-managers who rate high on entrepreneurial personal values perform better than those with lower ratings on these values. It therefore follows that, since Ghanaian female owner-managers rate lower than their male counterparts on entrepreneurial values, their contribution to economic growth will also be lower than those of men.

Risk-taking behaviour, achievement-orientedness, innovativeness, self-confidence, and dependability are values that push men to strive for the economic goals by which society judges their worth. In contrast, as a consequence of their socialisation and the socio-cultural environment in which they operate, women feel less confident about pursuing the economic goals expected of Ghanaian men, and when they do so they are less confident in their ability to attain such goals. Ghanaian men are praised for their success in achieving these economic goals, but women who strive for and achieve similar goals are shunned and looked down on with suspicion. Again in consonance with social feminist theory it could be argued that, having been socialised to be nurturing and expected to care for their families Ghanaian women in business have to divide their time and efforts between business and family commitments. It is considered an embarrassment for a Ghanaian woman not to cook or look after her family or for her spouse to be seen performing these chores. Thus, while Ghanaian men are afforded more time to pursue economic goals, Ghanaian women are hampered by their socially bestowed family responsibilities from pursuing similar economic goals.

The findings for hypothesis 2c confirm the contention that the personal values of owner-managers influence their decisions and the way they operate their businesses (Olson and Currie 1992). Also consistent with literature largely from the West (Blackman 2003;Kotey and Meredith 1997), the entrepreneurial values of Ghanaian owner-managers were found to be associated with a proactive orientation towards management. Entrepreneurial values positively influence activities in the functional areas of human resource management, operations, financial and marketing management as well as strategic planning. Although the association between entrepreneurial values on one hand and information technology and communication management on the other is also positive, it is not significant. In addition, when male and female owner-managers are compared, the results indicate that their entrepreneurial orientations encourage Ghanaian men to aspire to higher economic goals and to seek to achieve these through proactive management practices. Entrepreneurial values positively influence strategic planning and financial and human resource management. Activities in these functional areas in turn affect performance positively Thus, Ghanaian male owner-managers are able to perform better than Ghanaian female owner-managers because of their higher ratings on entrepreneurial values. While entrepreneurial values also influence activities in the marketing area, the higher ratings of women owner-managers in this area do not translate to higher performance because marketing activities have no significant influence on performance in the Ghanaian retail industry. Nevertheless, efficient management of resources provides women owner-managers with a competitive advantage over their male counterparts in spite of their lower ratings on entrepreneurial values. The findings concur with liberal feminist theories, which propose that, for socio-cultural reasons, there will be gender differences in business strategies and performance (Kutanis and Bayraktaroglu 2003).

Experience and Gender

The results of the relationships between gender, experience and performance from the PLS procedure are reported in Table 6.

Table 6: Gender, Experience, Business Strategies and Performance

Gender Path to:	*Hypotheses*	*Path Co-efficient*	*t value*
EXP	3a	-0.1270	3.54***
Sobel's Test of Indirect Effects			
EXP*PER	3b	-0.0090	1.64**
EXP*PL*PER	3c	-0.0002	0.18
EXP*FIN*PER	3c	-0.0007	1.48*
EXP*HR*PER	3c	-0.0008	1.56*
EXP*OPS*PER	3c	-0.0001	0.26
EXP*MKT*PER	3c	-0.0001	0.75
EXP*IT*PER	3c	-0.0004	1.14

***$p \leq 0.01$, ** $p \leq 0.05$, * $p \leq 0.10$.

The results from testing hypothesis 3a reveal that female owner-managers in Ghana have less previous work experience than Ghanaian male owner-managers. The gendered nature of work organisations in Ghana and the existence of a glass ceiling for women in formal employment positions constitute major barriers to women's acquisition of experiences in upper management positions and in the formal labour market. In keeping with their traditional roles as bread winners, there is a general feeling Ghana that a man should have a source of income and must therefore be given priority over a Ghanaian woman in job-seeking and promotion in the workplace (Amu 2005). This perception often leads to employment discrimination against women, especially when it comes to promotion or appointment to very senior administrative or management positions. The lower educational qualifications of Ghanaian women and their areas of specialisation such as in arts and vocational education also prevent them from gaining access to positions that will enable them to build the management experience needed to function effectively in business. These findings are compatible with liberal feminist theory which asserts that gendered socialisation practices and institutionalised gender biases shape human capital investments such that women develop less of the work experience conducive to the successful management of businesses (Bird and Sapp 2004). They also reflect those of Verheul, Risseeuw and Bartelse (2002), who reported that female owner-managers in the real estate industry in the Netherlands have less business experience than their male counterparts.

Previous experience has a positive influence on performance, thus the lower rating of women owner-mangers on experience also explains their lower performance, supporting hypothesis 3b. These findings concur with suggestions by Bird (1989) and Bosma *et al.* (2004) and with the work of Saffu *et al.* (2006), who established the importance of previous work experience for firm performance. Previous experience enables owner-managers to develop skills relevant to the effective conduct of various managerial functions. Previous experience in the same or similar industry to the one in which the owner-manager operates is able to enhance knowledge of industry variables, the key success factors, major players, and competitive dynamics. Industry knowledge from previous experience is therefore useful for carving out a competitive position.

For hypothesis 3c, previous experience has a positive influence on financial and human resource management but a negative influence on marketing and on information and communications technology management. Along the lines of the discussion in the preceding paragraphs, previous experience creates access to the resources necessary for functioning effectively in the areas of financial and human resource management. However, it is not surprising that previous experience should relate negatively to marketing and to information and communications technology management. The majority of management and supervisory positions usually occupied by men are provided with secretaries who handle all business communications and thus deal with issues relevant to information and communications technology. This means that any advantages that Ghanaian male owner-managers demonstrate over female owner-managers in the area of information and communications technology would have been developed on the job as business owners. In addition, the marketing skills relevant to business operations are usually developed on the job through hawking, petty trading or working as sales assistants in other businesses. These are positions usually occupied by women and this explains why women owner-managers have an advantage over their male counterparts in the area of marketing (see Section 8.2.2). Ghanaian male owner-managers are able to gain a performance advantage over their female counterparts through previous experience that provides them with an upper hand in developing skills and networks relevant to effective financial and human resource management. Ghanaian women's superior skills in marketing management do not provide a performance advantage because marketing does not significantly influence performance in the retail industry.

Education and Gender

Table 7 provides a breakdown of the relationship between gender education and firm performance.

Table 7: Gender, Education, Business Strategies and Performance

Gender Path to:	*Hypotheses*	*Path Co-efficient*	*t value*
EDU	4a	-0.1740	4.62***
Sobel's Test of Indirect Effects			
EDU*PER	4b	0.0054	0.71
EDU*PL*PER	4c	-0.0078	3.10***
EDU*FIN*PER	4c	-0.0022	1.74**
EDU*HR*PER	4c	-0.0035	2.16**
EDU*OPS*PER	4c	0.0040	1.38*
EDU*MKT*PER	4c	0.0003	0.76
EDU*IT*PER	4c	-0.0020	1.39*

***$p \leq 0.01$, ** $p \leq 0.05$, * $p \leq 0.10$.

As expected the survey results for hypothesis 4a present lower levels of education for Ghanaian female owner-managers than for Ghanaian male owner-managers. The fact that female owner-managers have lower educational levels compared to male owner-managers is supported by the results of a survey of the social characteristics of the population of the Accra Metropolis, which was carried out by the government of Ghana in the year 2000. The survey reported that for the district of Accra, the proportions of males in senior secondary schools, vocational/technical schools, and tertiary education are higher than for females. However, the percentages of women with non-tertiary post-secondary training in teaching and nursing exceed those for men (Republic of Ghana 2005). As suggested above, these differences are attributable to the acculturation and socialisation processes that give males priority access to education when there are insufficient funds to finance the education of children. Further, whilst the educational qualifications of owner-managers in the retail sector in Ghana are generally low, male operators in the sector were found to have higher educational qualifications than females. This finding is compatible with the outcome of a previous study conducted in British Columbia, Canada by Collins-Dodd, Gordon and Smart (2004), they found that men tend to have higher levels of education than women.

From the PLS results for hypothesis 4b, education has no direct impact on performance in the retail sector of Ghana, thus, there is no direct performance advantage for male owner-managers due to their higher educational level. Whereas the literature underscores the importance of higher education for operating in professional sectors such as medicine, accounting, law, consulting, and engineering, one does not need a degree to aim for and achieve economic success in the retail sector of Ghana. Some of the illiterate or semi-literate traders in this sector have been able to grow their businesses into successful wholesale and import businesses. It may be difficult to change parents' attitudes to female education in Ghana, if it is held that formal education is not crucial to achieving economic prosperity, especially for retailers in the urban centres

(Amu 2005). Nevertheless, as explained below performance advantages can ensue from education through more effective management practices.

Education is positively associated with all functional area activities. The findings from the PLS procedure shows that strategic planning, human resource management, financial management, and information technology management positively influence performance in the retail sector in Ghana. Since male owner-managers in this sector have higher educational qualifications, they are able to achieve performance advantages over female owner-managers through effective practices in financial, human resource, and information technology management as well as through strategic planning, thereby supporting hypothesis 4c. Again women's strength in marketing management does not translate into performance advantages because of the lack of association between marketing management and performance. Nevertheless, women owner-managers are able to achieve some performance advantage over their male counterparts by reason of efficient management of their scarce resources, and in spite of their relatively low educational levels.

Age and Gender

The relationships between gender, owner-manager's age, and firm performance are depicted in Table 8 below.

Table 8: Gender, Age, Business Strategies and Performance

Gender Path to:	*Hypotheses*	*Path Co-efficient*	*t value*
AGE	5a	0.0360	0.8927
Sobel's Test of Indirect Effects			
AGE*PER	5b	0.0018	0.77
AGE*PL*PER	5c	-0.0003	0.72
AGE*FIN*PER	5c	-0.0001	0.43
AGE*HR*PER	5c	-0.0001	0.66
AGE*OPS*PER	5c	0.0003	0.73
AGE*MKT*PER	5c	-0.0001	0.22
AGE*IT*PER	5c	-0.0001	0.69

***$p \leq 0.01$, ** $p \leq 0.05$, * $p \leq 0.10$.

The results from testing hypothesis 5a indicated no differences in the ages of male and female owner-managers in the retail sector in Ghana. Traditionally Ghanaian women have dominated the sector for much longer periods than men due to their lower educational qualifications and lack of access to formal employment. However, since the Structural Adjustment Programme (SAP) was introduced in Ghana, the informal sector, particularly the retail sector, has become one of the main sources of employment for re-deployees both young and old. Furthermore, low barriers to entry encourage

Ghanaians from all walks of life and all ages to set up small retail shops in any location, provided they have the basic start-up resources.

The results for hypothesis 5b show that age has a positive influence on performance. That is, older owner-managers rate higher on the performance construct than younger owner-managers. Older owner-manager have more work experience and the networks relevant to effective operation in the sector. Older owner-managers are thus likely to have the resources and skills necessary to back their aspirations and the ability to achieve goals that contribute to economic development. The absence of age differences between male and female owner-managers means neither one nor the other has a performance advantage by reason of age.

Not surprisingly, younger owner-managers rate higher on information technology management than older managers. In addition, younger owner-managers have higher ratings on operations activities such as maintenance of high stock, regular maintenance of equipment, and frequent checking of stock. Since there are no age differences between the sexes, the associations between age and activities in these functional areas do not result in a performance advantage for any of the sexes.

Conclusion and Implication of Finding for Policy and Practice

The results of this research have several implications for small business development in transitional economies, particularly Ghana. Differences in performance between the sexes do not, on their own, justify government intervention. However, as these differences result from inequitable distribution of resources, skills, and information such that women are placed in a disadvantaged position in relation to men, it can be concluded that these institutional failures call for government intervention. Since Ghanaian women have limited access to the resources, education, skills and experience required for business growth, and are discouraged by socio-cultural practices from building on their entrepreneurial values to enable them aspire to and achieve the same economic goals as Ghanaian men, affirmative action is clearly justified. The study shows that, for many Ghanaian female owner-managers the context within which they establish and seek to grow their businesses differ greatly from that of their male counterparts. This suggests that the socially constructed nature of gender poses significant challenges to women's enterprises (Shaw *et al.* 2006). Since economic development is associated with pursuit of growth and profitability by private enterprises (Friar and Meyer 2003), the Ghanaian government can spur on economic development by encouraging more entrepreneurs. Since the study demonstrates that female owner-managers are under-represented in this group, attention to inequities in this area should yield positive overall results for the economy.

The study confirms that entrepreneurial values are associated with proactive strategies and proactive strategies in turn with high performance. As such on the basis of their lower ratings on entrepreneurial values, Ghanaian women are less proactive in strategic orientation than Ghanaian men, leading to lower performance for women's businesses. Differences in value orientations between the sexes are attributable to differences in their socialisation processes. This imbalance requires the systematic education of Ghanaian parents about the potential of their female children, as well as training and mentoring programmes for women that encourage the pursuit of growth goals and equip them with the skills to successfully realise these goals. Whilst a cautious or conservative approach to business operation may have merits in terms of sustainability, businesses that merely survive add little to economic development (Acs and Storey 2004).

It is important that women are not discouraged from pursuing their child bearing and rearing roles while raising their economic profiles. Thus government intervention should include assistance programmes that enable women to achieve their economic goals while meeting their family commitments. Experiences from the West indicate that encouraging women to participate in formal employment including business operation can result in adverse social effects if these are not anticipated and addressed alongside programmes and policies that enhance the economic wellbeing of women. Currently in Ghana, women who are actively engaged in the workforce employ other women to assume their household chores. These house helps are paid meagre wages and deprived of the opportunity to develop their full potential (Tsikata 2001). Policies to address the gender imbalance in performance should include social programmes such as child care centres, maternity leave, and paid time off work to care for children and loved ones. Programmes are also required to encourage men's participation in domestic duties.

The findings from this research do not preclude the ongoing need for academics and policy makers to investigate and remedy barriers to realising the full potential of female-owned businesses. The government and its agencies can address the causes of women's lower performance directly through tailored training programmes and support services that assist them with improving their business management skills. Following a liberal and social feminist approach, programmes that improve access to resources, education and managerial experiences should equip Ghanaian women with the managerial and technical skills required to compete on an equal footing with male owner-managers. For instance, in order to ensure access to resources particularly credit, financial institutions can provide credit to female-owned small firms by lending to a group of women rather than to individual women. In this way, the group can use peer pressure, responsive disbursement mechanisms, and group savings as cash collateral to guarantee and ensure repayments of amounts loaned to them (Amu 2005). These strategies could help ensure high loan repayments from clients and also secure the financial institution's portfolio. In addition, as women also lack access to skills there is a need to provide skills training for female entrepreneurs and retraining to enhance their managerial abilities so that their earning power can be improved. It is paramount to enhance the efforts by all stakeholders; government and government agencies, women advocacy groups, other civil society groups, and international development partners to promote training for women at all levels and in all spheres of economic endeavour.

Finally, given the potential contribution of profitable small businesses to economic growth, greater attention should be paid to both encouraging their development and identifying the factors that help them ascend beyond the small level to that of growing firms. While a great deal of attention is given to encouraging the establishment of small enterprises as a means of poverty alleviation, encouraging the growth of these firms should ultimately help alleviate poverty specifically through job creation and income generation. Since women dominate the small business sector in Ghana, policies and programmes that aim at ensuring equitable access to resources and a level playing field for both sexes should in part encourage growth of small businesses.

The government could help champion female empowerment by incorporating, as part of its policy framework, gender equality in all spheres (economic, social and political) of the Ghanaian environment (Amu 2005; Tsikata 2001). This can be in the form of actions aimed at shaping or influencing decisions on start-ups and management of businesses. It could also involve creating frameworks for affirmative action legislation, governmental programmes and budgets that provide equal access to resources for all business owners. The principles and guidelines enunciated and proposed in these policy documents should be drawn directly from a consultative process. However, this can be effective only if there is a strong representation of women in the national, provincial and local legislative branches of government. Thus, it is only when there is a critical mass of women in both appointed and elected decision-making positions that gender issues could be addressed effectively in the policy agenda (Tsikata 2001). However, as noted by Taylor-Carter, Doverspike and Cook (1995) developing an appropriate gender policy through affirmative action needs to be threaded with caution because it requires a sound understanding of the effects of the programmes on the individual and cultural environment in question. The experience from Western countries suggests that such legislative actions are often resisted and can cause a backlash from the community concerned.

In addition, women's advocacy groups could be encouraged to participate in consultative forums in key policy and legislative processes. For example, they could become involved in law commissions, making representations to government departments responsible for policies in the areas of equal opportunities such as customary law, domestic violence and child maintenance, all of which have direct bearing on the quality of women's lives. The female advocacy group can also make submissions to public hearings, and campaign for awareness of gender inequalities in the various communities (Amu 2005). Advocates can help shape the development of policies and legislation through these strategies. They are also in a position to identify possible weaknesses in the approaches of government, public agencies and society that may hinder the governments' ability to implement specific equal opportunity rights and obligations (Stevenson 2006).

Successful women could also act as role models to girls. These require these successful women to be visible and vocal in society. Presentations at forums in schools and at community activities should ensure their visibility. In addition, female business owners could be connected to successful business owners through various networking strategies. Links with community-based small business organisations, national and trade associations, and corporate bodies should also improve access to resources for Ghanaian women (Stevenson 2006). Other mentorship programmes include peer-to-peer networking programmes that bring women entrepreneurs together to discuss how to move their businesses forward (National Women's Business Council 2006). New female entrepreneurs could be mentored by successful entrepreneurs with substantial business experience, who can provide contacts, services, and suggestions to assist the new entrepreneurs. However, it must be emphasised that these suggestions need full commitment on the part of stakeholders, and adequate funding if their proper implementation is to be ensured (Nikoi 1993).

The above suggestions for government intervention need to occur in a larger policy context. The government of Ghana must first formulate and implement a clear and detailed small business policy to address the imbalance in business performance between the genders. In terms of developing the private sector, Ghana can learn from other transitional economies such as Kenya, which has not only accepted the informal sector as a vital part of its economy but has since 1986 implemented systematic national policies and plans for small business development (King 1996). While Ghana has, since 1983, adopted a monetarist approach to economic development, and was once hailed by the World Bank as the 'success story' of how neo-liberal policies can help achieve business growth, the so-called success was a myth (Arthur 2001). Thus, despite the belief among policy makers that government have 'no business doing business', creating a conducive environment for businesses to thrive and also enhancing the ability of small firms to contribute to economic development is a major government responsibility.

However, the results need to be interpreted subject to the usual limitation of survey research. In particular, the focus on the retail sector and in only one locality limits the extent to which the results could be generalized across other sectors and localities. We also acknowledge the limitations posed by not considering the influence of the owner-manager's skills and resources on strategy and business performance and propose this as an area for future research. From a policy-making perspective, these factors would need to be considered if the goal of enhancing women's contribution to economic development is to be achieved.

References

Acs, Z. J, and Storey, D. J. (2004), Introduction: Entrepreneurship and Economic Development, *Regional Studies,* 38 (8): 871-877.

Amu, J. N. (2006), *The Role of Women in Ghana's Economy*, Available at www.library.fes.de/pdf-files/bueros/ghana/02990.pdf

Arthur, P. K. (2001), *Promoting Small-scale Industries in Ghana: Development Institutions, Culture and Politics*, Department of Political Studies, Queen's University, Ontario.

Baffoe, N. (2005), The IMF and the World Bank, Available at www.nipissingu.ca/business/media-imf.html

Bani, R. J. (2003), *Micro Enterprise Development in Ghana*, Accra.

Bauerschmidt, A. and Hofer, C. W. (2004), The Determinants of New Venture Performance: An Extended Model, Available at www.web2.infotrac.galegroup.com.ezproxy.une.edu.au/itw/infomark/914/860/5

Beasley, C. (1999), *What is Feminism Anyway?* South Wind Production Limited, Singapore.

Bird, S. R., and Sapp, S. G. (2004), Understanding the Gender Gap in Small Business Success, *Gender and Society,* 18 (1): 5-28.

Bird, S. R, Sapp, S. G. and Lee, M. Y. (2001), Small Business Success in Rural Communities: Explaining the Sex Gap, *Rural Sociology,* 66 (4): 507-531.

Blackman, A. J. (2003), *Entrepreneurs: Interrelationships between their Characteristics, Values, Expectations, Management Practices and SME Performance*, School of Business, Griffith University, Gold Coast Campus, Gold Coast.

Boohene, R, Kotey, B. and Folker, C. A. (2005), *Explaining Gender Differences in Performance among Small and Medium Enterprise Owners in Ghana,* Paper Presented at 51st World Conference of the International Council of Small Business, June 2005 at Washington DC.

Bortey, C. A, and Dodoo, F. (2005), *Adolescent Attitudes regarding Gender Roles in Ghana*, Available at www.forms.gradsch.psu.edu/ equity/sroppapers/204/BorteyChristiana A. pdf

Bruderl, J, Preisendorfer, P. and Ziegler, R. (1992), Survival Chances of Newly Founded Business Organisations, *American Sociological Review,* 57 (2): 227-242.

Brush, C G, and Hisrich, R.D (2004), *Women-owned Businesses: An Exploratory Study Comparing Factors Affecting Performance*, Available at www.riseb.org/finalbrush.pdf

Carter, N. M, Brush, C. G., Greene, P. G., Gatewood, E. and Hart, M. M. (2003), Women Entrepreneurs who Break through Equity Financing: The Influence of Human, Social and Financial Capital, *Venture Capital,* 1 (1): 1-28.

Carter, N. M, Williams, M. and Reynolds, P. D. (1997), Discontinuance among New Firms in Retail: The Influence of Initial Resources, Strategy and Gender, *Journal of Business Venturing,* 12:125-145.

Carter, S. (2000), Improving the Numbers and Performance of Women-owned Businesses: Some Implications for Training and Advisory Services, *Education and Training,* 42 (5/5): 326-333.

Carter, S., Anderson, S. and Shaw, E. (2004), *Women's Business Ownership: A Review of the Academic, Popular and Internet Literature*, Available at www.celcee.edu/abstracts/c20021209.html

Caughey, M. and Chetty, S. (1994), Pre-export Behaviour of Small Manufacturing Firms in New Zealand, *International Small Business Journal,* 12 (3): 62-68.

Chaganti, R. (1986), Management in Women-owned Enterprises, *Journal of Small Business Management,* 24 (4): 18-29.

Child, J. (1997), Strategic Choice in the Analysis of Action, Structure, Organisations and Environment: Retrospect and Prospect, *Organisation Studies,* 18:43-76.

Coleman, S. (2004), Access to Debt Capital for Women- and Minority-owned Small Firms: Does Educational Attainment have an Impact, *Journal of Developmental Entrepreneurship,* 9 (2): 127-143.

Collins-Dodd, C., Gordon, I. M. and Smart, C. (2004), Further Evidence of the Role of Gender in Financial Performance, *Journal of Small Business Management,* 42 (4): 395-417.

Covin, G. J., Green, K. M. and Slevin, D. P. (2006), Strategic Process Effects on the Entrepreneurial Orientation-sales Growth Rate Relationship, *Entrepreneurship Theory and Practice,* 3 (1): 57-81.

Covin, J.G. and D.P.Slevin, (1989), Strategic Management of Small Firms in Hostile and Benign Environments, *Strategic Management Journal,* 10 (1): 75-87.

Da Silva, N. (2000), *An Examination of Owner Characteristics and Entrepreneurial Management Strategy in Predicting Small Firm Performance*, The Faculty of the Department of Psychology, University of Houston, Houston.

Dess, G. G., and Robinson, R.B. (1984), Measuring Organisational Performance in the Absence of Objective Measures: The Case of Privately held Firms, *Strategic Management Journal,* 5 (3): 265-273.

Dio, D., Saragovi, L. C., Koestner, R. and J. Aube (1996), *Linking Personal Values to Gender*, *Sex Roles,* 34 (9/10): 621-636.

Downing, J. (1990), Gender and the Growth Dynamics of Microenterprises, In: GEMNI Working Papers, Wasington, DC.

Du Reitz, A., and Henrekson, M. (2000), Testing the Female Underperformance Hypothesis, *Small Business Economics,* 14 (1): 1-10.

Dyke, L. S., Fischer, E. M. and Reuber, A. R. (1992), An Inter-industry Examination of the Impact of Owner Experience on Firm Performance, *Journal of Small Business Management,* 30 (4): 72-87.

Eagly, A. H. (1987), *Sex Differences in Social Behaviour: A Social Role Interpretation*, Lawrence Erlbaum Associates, Hillsdale, New Jersey.

Fagenson, E. (1993), Personal Value Systems of Men and Women Entrepreneurs versus Managers, *Journal of Business Venturing,* 8:409-430.

Friar, J. H., and Meyer, M. H. (2003), Entrepreneurship and Start-ups in the Boston Region: Factors Differentiating High-growth Ventures from Micro-ventures, *Small Business Economics,* 21 (2): 145-152.

Galbraith, C., and Schendel, D. (1983), An Empirical Analysis of Strategy Types, *Strategic Management Journal,* 4 (2): 153-173.

Ghana Statistical Service (2002), *2002 Population and Housing Census*, Summary Report of Final Results, Accra.

Gibcus, P. and Kemp, R.G.M. (2003), *Strategy and Small Firm Performance*, Zoetermeer, The Netherlands.

Gray, J. (1997), Small Business Strategy in Australia, *Academy of Entrepreneurship Journal,* 2 (2): 44-58.

Greene, P. G., Hart, M. M., Gatewood, E., Brush, C.G. and Carter, N. M. (2004), *Women Entrepreneurs: Moving Front and Centre: An Overview of Research and Theory*, Available at www.usabe.org/knowledge/whitepapers/greene2003.pdf

Gundry, K L., and Welsh, H. P. (2001), The Ambitious Entrepreneur: High Growth Strategies of Women-owned Enterprises, *Journal of Business Venturing,* 16 (5): 453-470.

Hall, B. P. (2001), Values Development and Learning Organisations, *Journal of Knowledge Management,* 5 (1): 19-32.

Hall, G. (1995), *Surviving and Prospering in the Small Firm Sector*, London, Routledge.

Hisrich, R. D., and Ozturk, S. A. (1999), Women Entrepreneurs in a Developing Economy, *The Journal of Management Development,* 18 (2): 114-124.

Hodgetts, R. M., and Kuratko, D. F. (2001), *Effective Small Business Management*, Harcourt College Publishers, Orlando, Fla.

Hulland, J. (1999), Use of Partial Least Squares in Strategic Management Research: A Review of Four Recent Studies, *Strategic Management Journal,* 20 (2): 195-204.

Indarti, N., and Langenberg, M. (2004), Factors Affecting Business Success: Empirical Evidence from Indonesia, Paper Presented at 12th Annual High Technology Small Firms Conference at Netherlands.

Jianakoplos, N. A., and Bernasek, A. (1998), Are Women More Risk Averse, *Economic Inquiry,* 36 (4): 620-630.

Johnsen, G. J., and McMahon, R. G. P. (2005), Owner-manager Gender, Financial Performance and Business Growth amongst SMEs from Australia's Business Longitudinal Survey, *International Small Business Journal,* 23 (2): 115-140.

Johnson, J., and P. Powell (1994), Decision Making, Risk and Gender: Are Managers Different? *British Journal of Management,* 5:123-138.

Julien, P., Joyal, A., Deshaies, L. and Ramangalahy, C. (1997), A Typology of Strategic Behaviour among Small and Medium-sized Exporting Businesses. A Case Study, *International Small Business Journal,* 15 (2): 32-49.

Kabacoff, R. I., and Stoffey, R. W. (2001), *Age Differences in Organisational Leadership*, Paper Presented at 16th Annual Conference of the Society of Industrial and Organisational Psychology at San Diego, CA.

Kalleberg, A. L., and Leicht, K. T. (1991), Gender and Organisational Performance: Determinants of Small Business Survival and Success, *Academy of Management Journal,* 34 (1): 136-161.

Kayanula, D., and Quartey, P. (2000), The Policy Environment for Promoting Small and Medium-Sized Enterprises in Ghana and Malawi, In: *Finance and Development*

Research Programme Working Paper Series, Paper No. 15, World Bank, Washington DC.

Kickul, J., and Gundry, K. L. (2002), Prospecting for Strategic Advantage: The Proactive Entrepreneurial Personality and Small Firm Innovation, *Journal of Small Business Management,* 40 (2): 85-97.

King, K. (1996), *Jua Kali Kenya: Change and Development in an Informal Economy: 1970-1995*, James Currey, London.

Koch, C. and Kok, J. (1999), *A Human-resource-based Theory of the Small Firm,* EIM Small Business Research and Consultancy, Zoetermeer.

Kotey, B. (1994), *Personal Values of Owner/mangers, Business Strategies and Enterprise Performance,* The Southern Cross University, New South Wales.

Kotey, B. (1999), Debt Financing and Factors Internal to the Business, *Incorporating European Small Business Journal,* 17 (3): 11-29.

Kotey, B. and Meredith, G. G. (1997), Relationship among Owner-manager Personal Values, Business Strategies and Enterprise Performance, *Journal of Small Business Management,* 32 (2): 37-64.

Kutanis, R. and Bayraktaroglu, O. (2004), *Female Entrepreneurs: Social Feminist Insights for Overcoming Barriers*, Available at www.mngt.waikato.ac.nz/research/ejrot/cmconference/203/proceedings/gender/kuntanis.pdf

Lenartowicz, T. and Johnson, J. P. (2002), Comparing Managerial Values in Twelve Latin American Countries: An Exploratory Study, *Management International Review,* 42 (3): 279-307.

Lerner, M., and Almor, T. (2002), Relationship among Strategic Capabilities and Performance of Women-owned Small Ventures, *Journal of Small Business Management,* 40 (2):109-125.

Liou, N. and Aldrich, H. E. (1995), *Women Entrepreneurs: Is there a Gender-based Relational Competence?* Paper Presented at American Sociological Association Meeting at Washington, DC.

Litz, R. A. and Folker, C. A. (2002), When He and She Sell Seashells: Exploring the Relationship between Management Team Gender-balance and Small Firm Performance, *Journal of Developmental Entrepreneurship,* 7 (4): 341-359.

Lumpkin, G. T. and Dess, G. G. (1997), Clarifying the Entrepreneurial Orientation Construct and Linking it to Performance, *Academy of Management Review,* 21 (1): 135-172.

Magner, N., Welker, R. B. and Campbell, T. L. (1996), Testing a Model of Cognitive Budgetary Participation Processes in Latent Variable Structural Equation Framework, *Accounting and Business Research,* 27 (1): 41-50.

Manolova, T. S., Manev, I. V., Carter, N. M. and Gyoshev, B. S. (2006), Breaking the Family and Friend's Circle: Predictors of External Financing Usage among Men and Women Entrepreneurs in a Transitional Economy, *Venture Capital,* 8 (2): 109-132.

Manuh, T. (2006), *Women in Africa's Development*, Available at www.un.org/ecosocdev/geninfo/afrec/bpaper/maineng.htm

Markman, G. D., and R. A. Baron, (2003), Person-entrepreneurship fit: why some people are more successful as entrepreneurs than others, *Human Resource Management Review,* 13:281-301.

McDonald, P. and Gandz, J. (1991), Identification of Values Relevant to Business Research, *Human Resource Management,* 30 (2): 217-236.

Miles, M. P., Covin, G. J. and Heeley, M. B. (2000), The Relationship between Environmental Dynamism and Small Firm Structure, Strategy and Performance, *Journal of Marketing Theory and Practice,* 8 (2): 63-74.

Miles, R. and Snow, C. (1978), *Organisational Structure and Process*, McGraw Hill, New York.

Moore, M. (2005), Towards a Confirmatory Model of Retail Strategy Types: An Empirical Test of Miles and Snow, *Journal of Business Research,* 58 (5): 696-704.

Morgan, R. E. and Strong, C. A. (2003), Business Performance and Dimensions of Strategic Orientation, *Journal of Business Research,* 56 (3): 163-176.

Munso, J. M., and McIntyre, S. H. (1979), Developing Practical Procedures for the Measurement of Personal Values in Cross-cultural Marketing, *Journal of Marketing Research,* 16:48-52.

National Women's Business Council (2006), *Formal Business Mentoring Programs*, Available at www.nwbc.gov/Mentoring/programs.html

Nikoi, G. (1993), *Gender and Development,* Buck Press Limited, Accra.

Nonis, S., and C. O. Swift, (2001), Personal Value Profiles and Ethical Business Decisions, *Journal of Education for Business,* 76 (5): 251 256.

Nunnally, J. C. (1978), *Psychometric Theory*, McGraw-Hill, New York.

Olson, S. F. and Currie, H. M. (1992), Female Entrepreneurs: Personal Value Systems and Business Strategies in a Male-dominated Industry, *Journal of Small Business Management*, 30 (1): 49-57.

Oshagbemi, T. (2004), Age Influences on the Leadership Styles and Behaviour of Managers, *Employee Relations,* 26 (1/2): 14-29.

Papadakis, V. and Dimitris, B. (1998), The Chief Executive Officer as Corporate Champion of Technological Innovation: An Empirical Investigation, *Technology Analysis & Strategic Management,* 10 (1): 89-109.

Porter, M. (1980), *Competitive Strategy,* Free Press, New York.

Powell, M. and Ansic, D. (1997), Gender Differences in Risk Behaviour in Financial Decision-making: An Experimental Analysis, *Journal of Economic Psychology,* 18:605-628.

Republic of Ghana (2005), *Ghana Districts*, Available at www.ghanadistricts.com/reg-info.asp?RegionID=1.

Rokeach, M. (1973), *The Nature of Human Values*, The Free Press, New York.

Saffu, K., Aporih, S., Elijah-Mensah,A. and Ahumata, J. (2006), *A Study of the Performance Factors of Small Tourism Ventures*, Paper Presented at 51st World Conference of the International Council for Small Business, 18th - 22nd June at Melbourne.

Schmidt, R. A. and Parker, C. (2003), Diversity in Independent Retailing: Barriers and Benefits - the Impact of Gender, *International Journal of Retail and Distribution,* 31 (8): 396-407.

Schwartz, S. H. and Bilsky, W. (1990), Toward a Theory of the Universal Content and Structure of Values: Extensions and Cross-cultural Replications, *Journal of Personality and Social Psychology*, 58:878-891.

Sexton, D. and Bowman-Upton, N. (1990), Female and Male Entrepreneurs: Psychological Characteristics and their Role in Gender Related Discrimination, *Journal of Business Venturing,* 5 (1): 29-36.

Shane, S. and Venkataraman, S. (2000), The Promise of Entrepreneurship as a Field of Research, *Academy of Management Review,* 25 (1): 217-226.

Shaw, E., Lam, W., Carter, S. and Wilson, F. (2006), *Theory, Practice and Policy: An Integrated View on Gender, Networks and Social Capital,* Paper Presented at 51st World Conference of the International Council for Small Business, 18th-22nd June at Melbourne.

Sirmon, D. G. and Hitt, M. A. (2003), Managing Resources: Linking Unique Resources, Management, and Wealth Creation in Family Firms, *Entrepreneurship Theory and Practice,* 27 (4): 339-358.

Sonfield, M., Lussier, R., Corman, J. and M. McKinney, (2001), Gender Comparisons in Strategic Decision-making: An Empirical Analysis of the Entrepreneurial Strategic Mix, *Journal of Small Business Management,* 39 (2): 165-173.

Stevenson, L. (2006), *Women Entrepreneurship: Really Making a Difference*, Paper Presented at 51st World Conference of the International Council for Small Business at Melbourne.

Taylor-Carter, M. A., Doverspike, D. and Cook, K. (1995), Understanding Resistance to Sex and Race-based Affirmative Action: A Review of Research Findings, *Human Resource Management Review,* 5 (2): 129-157.

Thompson, A., and Strickland, J. (1984), *Strategic Management: Concepts and Case*, Business Publications Inc., Texas.

Tsikata, D., (ed.) (2001), *Gender Training in Ghana: Politics, Issues and Tools*, Woeli Publishing Services, Accra.

Verheul, I., Risseeuw, P. and Bartelse, G. (2002), Gender Differences in Strategy and Human Resource Management, *International Small Business Journal*, 20 (4): 443-476.

Verheul, I., Uhlaner, L. and Thurik, A. R. (2002), What is an Entrepreneur? Self-image, Activities and Gender, Paper Presented at International Council for Small Business, 47th World Conference, June 16th-19th 2002 at San Juan, Puerto Rico.

Walker, E., and Brown, A. (2004), What Success Factors are Important to Small Business Owners? *International Small Business Journal,* 22 (6):577-594.

Watson, J. (2001), Examining the Impact on Performance of Demographic Differences between Male and Female Controlled SMEs, *Journal of SEAANZ,* 9 (2): 55-71.

11

Accessibility of Credit to Rural women

Wawire, N.H.W. *Kenyatta University*

Introduction

The Kenya government recognizes the role of women as primary players in the agricultural and informal sectors. It has therefore heeded to the call by women for greater economic empowerment and has formulated policies to mainstream them alongside men in the overall development of the nation (Republic of Kenya 1994a, 1996). Income-generating projects for women's groups are, and will continue in the foreseeable future, to be one of the most important instruments through which individuals and their families are economically empowered. The groups aim at building capacity to help themselves by undertaking programs that have a direct impact on their welfare. These programs have had a new orientation of income-generation as opposed to original aim of group work and merry-go-round. This has culminated in the rapid growth of small-scale businesses run and managed by women groups. UNICEF (1992) study reinforced this point by asserting that women groups play a significant role in the effort to reduce maternal deaths, child deaths and poverty. But central to the success and sustainability of women's groups' projects in the rural areas, are issues related to access, affordability and availability of credit.

Justification of the Study

The adoption of World Bank and the International Monetary Fund led Structural Adjustment Programs by Kenya in the early 1980's placed additional burden to Kenyans. Employment opportunities dwindled with time and subsidies on social services were removed. People's standards of living were adversely affected especially for the majority who live in the rural areas. It is believed that the worst hit group economically is women in the rural areas where more women than men live (United Nations Fund for Population Activities/Women's Bureau 1996:18). The woman with an independent source of income has dignity, is less likely to be a victim of domestic violence and has more say in the household decision making process.

To economically empower these people, there is a need to enhance their level of participation in productive activities. Therefore, mechanisms need to be put in place that will ensure provision of basic economic assets through availing affordable credit to them. Affordable credit will lead to increased returns, economic independence, and material provision for the family and improved social welfare for the society as a whole.

Objective

The objective of the paper is to highlight the challenges that face women groups regarding access to affordable credit and opportunities that are available. It addresses the emerging credit policy issues so as to ensure financial adequacy, success and sustainability of the groups' income-generating activities.

Study Area, Sampling Technique and Sample Size

The study area was Kakamega district, which is in western province of Kenya. According to Kenya (Republic of Kenya 1999: 105) report on poverty, Kakamega district had, on the overall, 50.6 per cent poor people, with males and females making up to 51 per cent and 49 per cent respectively. In the district, cultural biases against women, especially on rights to land ownership and other resources are still a major concern (Republic of Kenya 1994b, 1997). Difficulties in land inheritance, obtaining title deed and loans, are common problems.

Systematic Random Sampling method was used to obtain the sample size that fulfilled the requirement of efficiency, representation, reliability and flexibility as recommended by Kothari (1985: 88). Fourteen per cent sample was desired hence the first women's group in each source list per division was selected randomly from the first seven groups and thereafter every seventh group was automatically included in the sample. Informants for each woman's group in the sample consisted of group leaders, members, and representatives of the government, micro-finance institutions, commercial banks and international agencies. Primary data on sources of funds were collected for 171 women's groups' income generating activities by way of observation, personal interviews, focussed group discussions and administration of questionnaires.

Empirical Result and Discussion

The survival of the women's groups' income generating activities entirely rests on the availability of funds. Availability of affordable credit creates opportunities for the groups to get funds so as to embark on income-generating activities. It was therefore hypothesized that the presence of money lending institutions especially commercial banks and micro-finance institutions would encourage the groups to borrow the much-needed funds. The commercial banks that operate in the study area are Barclays Bank, Kenya Commercial Bank, Standard Chartered Bank, National Bank and Post Bank. The major money lending Non-bank institutions in the area include Improve Your Business; K-REP; Kenya Women Finance Trust; PRIDE- Kenya; Partnership for Productivity Service Foundation (PFP) -Kenya and Women Enterprise Development Company. The religious organizations involved in credit provision include ADRA; the Catholic Church; National Council of Churches of Kenya and Young Women Christian Associa-tion (YWCA). The government is also involved in providing credit through the Rural Enterprise Fund; Community Development Trust Fund (CDTF); Kenya Industrial Estate; and the Lake Basin Development Authority. Embassies of Japan, America, Britain and the Netherlands also provide financial assistance to the groups. Other agencies/authorities that provide financial assistance include Kenya Finland Cooperation, KENAFYA (A primary health care program carried out by Kenya and Finland), Danish International Development Agency, Swedish International Development Authority and Finish International Development Agency.

It can be seen from the foregoing that credit is actually available in the study area to those who can meet the lending conditions of various credit-offering institutions. However, it appears that women groups do not take loans from these credit-offering institutions as depicted in the table 1.

Table 1: Sources of Funds for the Women's Groups Projects

Source	*Number of projects*	*Percentage*
Members Contributions	55	32
Funds Drives	44	25
Kenya Government	29	17
International Agencies	21	12
Micro finance Institutions	18	10
Commercial Banks	3	2
Religious Organizations	3	2
Individual Donations/loans	0	0
Total	171	100

Source: Field Data.

Thirty two percent of the projects sampled were funded from members' contributions. This is in line with the Makoffu (1995) finding that 95 per cent of funds used by the groups come from member's contributions. This phenomenon explains why groups lack enough funds for their activities. This is because members often default on their contributions. Twenty five percent of the projects that were sampled had been funded through funds drives

(*Harambee*). In the researcher's view, this is a potential source of funds given the Kenya's long tradition of self-help. However, the groups must be well organized and pursue economically viable projects if they have to attract funds through this method.

Seventeen percent of the projects in the sample had received financial assistance from the Government. Most of them had been funded from the Presidential Women's Development Funds drive of 1997. However, the funds were inadequate to the extent that some groups only managed to open bank accounts. Furthermore, the funds were received only once and most groups, which benefited, registered for just that purpose and have since ceased to exist. These funds also generated a lot of misunderstanding between members that split the groups instead of uniting them. Moreover, a few groups had shared the money among members.

International donor agencies and embassies had funded only twelve percent of the sampled projects. Moreover, these agencies and embassies do not directly target Women's Groups' projects but instead fund specific activities that are related to their programmes. Only ten percent of the projects sampled had been funded through credit from micro-finance institutions. These institutions therefore play a minimal role as far as financing of the women's groups activities are concerned. Only two percent of the sampled projects were financed by credit from commercial banks despite several banks operating in the area as listed in the section dealing with availability of credit. Ironically, Kenya Commercial Bank operates a fund for small and micro-enterprises in the area. The recent closure of some of the sub-branches of commercial banks has made access to credit by those operating in the rural areas even more elusive. Ninety six per cent of the sampled groups operated bank accounts while four per cent did not. Seventy one per cent of the groups that operated bank accounts indicated that their accounts had minimum balances most of the time. They also complained of paying high bank charges. However, they were forced to maintain the account because it is one of the requirements for registration and existence of the group.

There are several religious organizations and churches that give credit to women's groups. These organizations give modest loans to their members and groups. Some of them charge interest rates as low as seven percent. However, this source of credit is not open to everybody and this may explain why only two percent of the sampled projects were funded from this source. Another source of credit that was investigated was loans from individuals. On a priori basis, it was postulated that progressive and prominent members in the community could donate and /or lend funds or materials towards the groups' activities. Unfortunately, none of the sampled activities had been funded from this source.

Challenges

Appropriate Collateral

Credit offering institutions demand collateral in form of land title deed, houses and share certificates. While women groups do not own valuable properties, have no share certificates, and the land they access do not belong to them. In fact most groups did not have enough land on which to carry out their project despite the hypothesis that land is available and cheap in the rural areas. The factors that are observed to be contributing to lack of own land or inadequacy of it are: cultural practices that do not allow women to own land through inheritance (Republic of Kenya 1994b: 101) and low economic empowerment of rural women (Republic of Kenya 1986 and 1992).

Lending Condition

Credit offering institutions have stringent lending conditions. They require groups to have registered, paid registration fees, able to file certain statements of accounts, prepare and show cash flow analysis, business plans and project proposals. However, these groups operate with no business plans, keep their records poorly and some do not keep records at all. They cannot therefore file proper statements of accounts and provide correct up to date information on their activities, which is one of the requirements that must be made for them to qualify for a loan. Furthermore, Credit offering institutions dictate to the groups the type of businesses to be undertaken. For example, those dealing with second hand clothes do not qualify for credit. Some groups complain of short grace and repayment periods.

Interest Rates and Bank Charges

Most groups sampled indicated that they do not borrow from commercial banks and micro-finance institutions due to high interest rates and bank charges. In fact, only ten percent and three percent of the project sample were funded through loans taken from the micro-finance and commercial banks respectively. This is a major challenge because interest rates must be charged at the market rates to sustain the credit scheme. Moreover, it has not been proved that groups that borrow at market rates of interest do not make profit and are therefore unable to repay their loans. In fact, according to Ehigiamusoe (1995), Malcolm, Esipisu and Rao (1998), the poor are capable of borrowing at commercial of interest rates and repay their loans. Other reasons given by Ehigiamusoe (1995) for charging commercial rates of interest include high transaction costs due to many applicants, promotion of discipline, protection of the loan fund against losses through bad debts and inflation, and expansion of the size and value of the loan fund. United Nations (1994) also argued that financial institutions should charge interest rates that cover operating costs and risk provision. This paper therefore argues that the idea of high interest rates and bank charges prohibiting taking of credit is a perceived one developed due to wrong attitude of the groups. This is a challenge that must be content with.

Drive, Inadequate Information and Experience in Taking Loans

According to Republic of Kenya (1992), Oketch (1999), Ekpenyong and Nyong (1992), and Oketch and Dondo (1994), lack of drive among the groups to seek institutional credit, inadequate information about credit availability, lack of experience in taking credit and inability of the groups to understand the complexity of credit transactions, hinder the groups from taking loans. Commercial banks and micro-finance institutions are partly to blame because of their restricted network and outreach activities. The argument that low level of numeracy and literacy among the group members hinder them from taking loans is unfounded because studies have shown that they are good borrowers because they remember facts and figures more often than the literate ones who rely on records (Malcolm, Esipisu, Mohanty and Rao 1998, United Nations 1994).

General Fear of Taking Loans

The general fear of taking loans was cited as a challenge. The fear emanates from the experience of seeing individuals in the community being prosecuted in case of defaulting on loan repayment and their properties being taken away (Malcolm, Esipisu, Mohanty and Rao 1998).

Outreach Programs and Poor Network

Most banks and micro-finance institutions have limited network and outreach programs. They concentrate their activities in urban areas and target successful businesspersons and progressive farmers. According to Oketch (1999:49) the outreach programs of micro- finance institutions like K-REP, KWFT, PRIDE-Kenya, FAULU and CARE-Kenya are limited due to shortage of resources and lack of legal capacity to provide a wide range of financial services. Most of them depend on grants and to require them to effectively expand their outreach activities is a big challenge.

Reluctance by Formal Financial Institutions to Lend to the Groups

Formal financial institutions are reluctant to lend to the groups due to high administrative overheads relative to the size of loans (Ekpenyong, and Nyong 1992, Oketch 1999, Republic of Kenya 1992). This is the case notwith standing the government's policies contained in Session papers No. 2 of 1992 and No.1 of 1986 that identifies financial institutions to be important agents in the delivery of credit and finance to micro and small-scale enterprises (Republic of Kenya 1992, 1986). The challenge is to appropriately assess beneficiaries and deal with high levels of bad and doubtful debts in the banking sector.

Insurance Cover

Insurance is an important ingredient in business. It ensures the continuity of business after the risk has happened even though it adds to the cost of doing business. Furthermore, the insurance cover could be used as collateral for obtaining loan. It is against this background that some financial institutions require groups to have taken insurance covers for their businesses before applying for a loan. However, since most groups do not take insurance covers for their business, this poses a major challenge to them.

Taxation

The groups pay tax to the government. Sixty four per cent of those who pay tax argue that taxation adversely affect their operations by reducing their working capital, thereby hindering expansion of their businesses. They were of the view that the government should consider exempting them from paying taxes. Furthermore, some credit offering institutions pay taxes to the government, which reduces the funds available for lending.

Conclusion

Opportunities are enormous that could be explored to improve the situation. Unexplored potential (opportunities) range from goodwill on the part of the present coalition government and the donor community in eradicating poverty, the working nation ethics, zero tolerance of corruption, availability of resources especially raw materials, possibility of establishing collaboration with the government, NGOs, and financial institutions in areas of training, and emotional management counselling, to the availability of credit and the extra hardworking women groups in the rural areas of Kenya. The groups need to effectively tap these opportunities that are available and put in place measures that will repel possible threats like the dwindling financial resources, liberation that has increased poverty among members and the effects of HIV/AIDS pandemic on their productivity. The paper therefore makes the following recommendations.

Credit offering institutions should:

- Give credit to the group relying on ability to pay and not land as collateral. The institutions may consider the characteristics of the group, peer pressure, type and profitability of the projects to be funded before granting credit.
- Lessen their lending conditions regarding business insurance covers, cash flow analysis, and type of collateral, type of project that they accept to fund and prosecution in case of default, and consider increasing the grace and repayment periods.
- Hire technical officers to advice the groups; evaluate performance of the groups' projects, and assist in writing business plans, record keeping and follow up visits.

- Extend their outreach programs and network to the interior rural areas and avoid concentrating their activities in urban places.
- Organize training on loan management, leadership and governance before loan disbursement.
- Repackage their lending conditions and tailor their products taking in mind the shortcomings of the formal banking practices that hinder the groups' access to credit.
- Encourage popular participation and involvement of the target groups in designing and implementing the credit scheme, loan application, processing, evaluation and approval.
- Apply instalment repayment procedures for the groups that are involved in petty trades and dairy animal rearing due to low frequent earnings. While bulk repayment procedure should be applied to those groups that are involved in crop farming since they receive income once annually after harvesting.

The Government should:

- Set policies and legal framework that will remove barriers in credit provision by the commercial banks and micro-finance institutions.
- Consider exempting small-scale businesses owned by the groups in rural areas from paying taxes so as to increase their working capital.
- Exempt micro-finance institutions that give credit to groups in the rural areas from paying taxes and duties so as to extend more credit to the groups.

The groups and other stakeholders should:

- Be sensitized about credit availability.
- Undertake business counselling and emotional management training in order to manage credit properly and have positive attitudes about taking loans.
- Be made aware of alternative possible sources of funds through outreach programs and public awareness.
- Undertake business activities that are within the scope of funding from commercial Banks and micro-finance institutions.

References

Ehigiamusoe, G. (1995), *Women Credit and Empowerment*, LAPO Development Series No. L, Uri Publishing, LAP-Lift above Poverty Organization, Benin.

Ekpenyong, B. D. and Nyong, M.O. (1992), *Small and Medium Scale Enterprises in Nigeria: Their Characteristics, Problems and Source of Finance*, AERC Research Paper No. 16, AERC, Nairobi.

Kothari, C. R. (1985), *Research Methodology: Methods and Techniques*, New Age International Pvt. Ltd., New Delhi.

Makoffu, M. (1995), *Organization of the Self-employment: Productive Employment and Equity in the Rural and Informal Sectors in Kenya*, A Report on the National Policy Workshop on Optimal Forms of Assistance to Women's Employment in the Rural and Informal Sectors, Nyeri, Kenya.

Malcolm, H., Esipisu, E., Mohanty, A.K. and Rao, D.S.K. (1998), *The New Middle Women Profitable Banking through On-Lending Groups*, Intermediate Technology Publications, London.

Oketch, H. (1999), Credit and Finance, In: A. Mullei and C. Bokea (eds.), *Micro and Small Enterprises in Kenya: Agenda for Improving the Policy Environment*, The Intentional Center for Economic Growth/USAID, Nairobi.

Oketch, H.O. and Dondo, C.A. (1994), *Causes and Consequences of Defaulting among Micro-enterprises in Kenya*, Research Paper No. 16, Kenya Rural Enterprise Program, Nairobi.

Republic of Kenya (1986), *Economic Management for Renewed Growth*, Session Paper No. 1, Government Printer, Nairobi.

Republic of Kenya (1992), *Small Enterprises and Jua Kali Development in Kenya*, Session Paper No. 2, Government Printer, Nairobi.

Republic of Kenya (1994a), *Recovery and Sustainability Development to the Year 2010*, Session Paper No. 1, Government Printer, Nairobi.

Republic of Kenya (1994b), *Kakamega District Development Plan: 1994-1996*, Government Printer, Nairobi.

Republic of Kenya (1996), *Industrial Transformation to the Year 2020,* Session Paper No.2, Government Printer, Nairobi.

Republic of Kenya (1997), *Kakamega District Development Plan*, Government Printer, Nairobi.

Republic of Kenya (1999), *National Poverty Eradication Plan 1999-2015*, Government Printer, Nairobi.

UNICEF (1992), *Children and Women in Kenya: A Situation Analysis 1992*, Regal Press Ltd., Nairobi.

United Nations (1994), *United Nations Expert Group on Women and Finance*, Women's World Banking, United Nations, New York.

United Nations Fund for Population Activities/Women's Bureau (1996), *Women and Men in Kenya: Facts and Figures 1995*, UNFPA/Women's Bureau, Nairobi.

12

Joint Liability Borrowing and Livelihood Asset for Rural Poor

Kiiru, J. *University of Nairobi*
Mburu, J. *University of Bonn*

Introduction

In the recent times we have witnessed much enthusiasm for micro-finance as a poverty reduction tool. Many governments and non-governmental organizations hold the view that by availing credit to the poor it would be possible to enhance their incomes and thereby bring about an improvement in welfare. Microfinance programmes are therefore assumed to initiate a series of virtuous spirals of economic empowerment thereby leading to increased well being for the poor. Given this assumption, there have been many deliberate attempts, to avail credit to as many poor people as possible.

Issue of costs to borrowers especially those at the lower socio-economic category who use the group borrowing method have not been widely researched. User costs are defined as sum of price costs and transactions costs (Schreiner 2003). Price costs to users are revenues for lenders. Transaction costs arise mainly in three phases, the first is search and information costs. These are costs such as those incurred in determining whether a prospective group is willing to accept a new group member and at what conditions. The second are the bargaining costs, which basically include the costs incurred until both the prospective member and the pre-existing members are in agreement thereby enabling the drawing up of a contract. And finally policing and enforcement costs, which include the costs of making sure that all the solidarity group members stick to the terms of the contract, and taking appropriate action in case of default. Solidariy groups are supposed to use peer pressuring to ensure that every member repays their loans and therefore it is the responsibility of all the members to police one another.

For any given household, user costs will be affected by several factors. These include the specific economic characteristics of the household, the type of business enterprise they are involved in, and the characteristics of the solidarity group setting within which the individual is operating. These costs will also be affected by the individual's personal knowledge, personal network, transaction skills, and location of business in terms of town centre or rural village setting. Even if contractual terms are the same for all borrowers from the same solidarity group, the user costs and therefore welfare outcome of engaging in the joint liability borrowing is likely to vary substantially across households.

The question that this paper poses is what are the user costs of joint liability borrowing and how do they affect household livelihood assets. Our main hypothesis is that given different household characteristics, user costs are likely to vary for different households, and therefore we expect differences in net welfare after a microfinance intervention.

To begin with, we found that it is not just peer pressure passé that is used to ensure loan repayments by joint liability borrowers. This finding is similar to other findings by IFRI in a study that focused on the Malawi Rural Finance Corporation (MRFC); the results of the study were contrasting to conventional wisdom and assumptions regarding the informal advantage of the joint liability and its implications for incentives for peer selection, peer monitoring and peer pressure with respect to loan repayment. The findings did not support the widely held presumption that joint liability is responsible of the high repayment rates of the successful group lending programs. In particular the study found that no effective peer monitoring was taking place in the credit groups because of the social costs associated with it (Diagne 2000).

Given the high social costs associated with peer monitoring, joint liability borrowers are devising ways to ensure that there is limited peer monitoring, while at the same time upholding high repayment rates. One of these innovations includes the use of basic household assets to act as collateral for individual loans within the group. What this means is that, the group will still be jointly liable for all the loans as far as the financing institution is concerned. However every member must pledge some collateral at the group level. Solidarity groups use basic household assets as collaterals for individual loans, complimented by an acceptable[1] guarantor for the loans, to further minimize limited liability for borrowers. If default by a member(s) does occur, the solidarity group will first repay the loan to the microfinance institution, and then attach personal assets belonging to the defaulter in an attempt to recover their money. In case the defaulter does not have enough personal assets to cover the debt then they attach property belonging to the guarantor. This has led to a depletion of pre-existing livelihood assets for some poor households, thereby leading to vulnerability and poverty.

We also found that for many users with no other source of income, the only rational way for them to keep up with regular loan repayments and forced savings is to engage in short-term small over exploited business ventures with supposedly marginal but quick returns; however the competition in these ventures is rising, leading to an over-supplied market. Women caught up in such scenarios are not able to meet their tight financial obligations but unfortunately they have no other option but to repay. They then result to unsustainable debt coping mechanism like voluntary or involuntary liquidation of assets or incurring other debts.

The study also established that there exists a selection bias whereby the most vulnerable of the society are automatically excluded from the solidarity groups for fear of their eminent default. This coincides with the findings of Amin *et al.* (2002) that where as microfinance is successful at reaching the poor it is less successful at reaching the vulnerable. In line with similar studies we found that microfinance is likely to have better welfare effects for already better off households while the poorer households became more vulnerable in the current contractual arrangements where a household does not have limited liability and could be forced to deplete pre-existing livelihood assets in the course of loan repayments.

The rest of this paper is organized as follows. Part two is some interesting information on how the current intra-group insurance works on the basis of the Kenyan experience, part three is a theoretical analysis of how the solidarity group as an institution works within the framework of transactions costs. Part four explains the research design, methodology and data sources. Part five is the results and discussions, while the last section concludes the study.

Intra Group Insurance and Access to Credit by Rural Households: The Kenyan Experience

The original Grameen model, which Yunus and his colleagues developed from the late 1970s to late 1980s, involved: credit (as opposed to savings or other financial services). It was still based on joint liability borrowing, in which clients insure each others loans. Group lending shifts some classic banking tasks onto borrowers, such as judging who is credit worthy. It also shifts the burden of debt collection to the peers in a borrowing group. The group lending approach as developed by Yunus is hailed to be pro poor mainly because it over come the challenge of lack of collateral by the poor, thereby encouraging the poor to access credit. Most importantly, the original Grameen borrowers operated on pure trust and those who did well in business assisted those who did not make it to repay their loans. What research should find out is to what extent cultural context played a role in the success of the repayment arrangements by borrowers and how easy it is to replicate the same model for other communities. Researchers as well as policy makers agree that at least the Grameen if not necessarily other micro lenders is a worthwhile social investment. This is so given that surplus for Grameen products users exceed subsidy by non-users (Schreiner 2003).

Many modifications have been made to the original Grameen banking model, even Grameen Bank itself since 2001 is no longer having joint responsibility lending for all its clients. Many other modifications have also been incorporated to the joint responsibility-lending model by other microfinance lending institutions and borrowers. During fieldwork and participant observation for this study we realized that joint responsibility borrowing in Kenya today does not necessarily mean zero collateral loans. Peers no longer agree to guarantee each others loans without any guarantee of repayment by the borrower. As a pre-condition to join a solidarity group, a prospective member will have to formally sign a contract with her peers guaranteeing her future loans, the assets used for this kind of transaction are basic livelihood assets like livestock, household furniture and cutlery. Capital assets like sawing machines, and electronics among other assets, are also accepted.

Amongst all solidarity groups there exists a rigorous administrative structure to ensure that every loan is repaid on time. For example, In order to minimize the risk of non-repayment by some poorer borrowers, solidarity groups advise their weaker members to start submitting their loan instalments to the group's treasurer on a weekly basis. Further there is a forced minimum monthly saving of Kshs 400 (US$ 5.56) by every borrower that acts as a partial guarantee to loans taken by the individual as well as those taken by other group members. The Microfinance institution will only release this money to the individual if he/she is quitting the group and has been cleared by all her peers. The institution also has the right to freeze all forced savings for all group members in case of default by even one member. Further research should help us understand the extent to which forced savings and weekly loan repayments lead to under capitalization of small enterprises and to what extent does this under capitalization compromise returns.

Micro-finance lending institutions impose financial penalties on groups that delay the remittance of a loan instalment. These penalties are borne equally by all group members. An incentive is therefore created to exclude very poor households or colleagues who have a bad debt repayment record in order to minimize penalties in case of default. It is also an incentive for peers to be extremely aggressive when dealing with a colleague who is not in a position to meet her immediate financial obligations. Such instances usually lead to strained relations in social networks. Again there is an opportunity for future research to shed light on extend to which strained relations in rural poor communities undermine the social capital for households.

Theoretical Framework

User costs include all expenses and opportunity costs, fixed and variable, which arise due to being a member of a joint liability-borrowing group. In

New Development Economics, user costs are considered to be of substantial interest for development finance (Fiebig *et al.* 1999).

There are three main assumptions underlying transactions cost theory. The first assumption is that Individuals behave in an opportunistic manner. This is so because there is an asymmetry of information between business-partners in a way that information may be passed on incompletely or not at all. This scenario allows that in case of goal conflicts individuals adopt opportunistic behaviours. The second assumption is that Individuals are characterized by bounded rationality. Bounded rationality is due to lack of competence, knowledge and information processing capabilities in all necessarily areas and as such human individuals are not always able to act in a rational manner even if they plan to do so. Due to bounded rationality it is impossible to write complete contracts that take care of every possible environmental state or action of transaction partners. And thirdly, uncertainty and specificity of investments necessary to carry out transactions are relevant factors. Investment specificity refers to possible alternate use of investments made. For highly specific investments such an alternate use is hardly possible.

Microfinance borrowers within a joint liability group are the decision makers and are assumed to behave in a way consistent with bounded rationality, in that they consider a restricted range of alternatives but in a rational way. They also may behave opportunistically in some situations. However when making such a decision, they weigh the costs and benefits of defaulting from the expected behaviour. Finally, solidarity group members may have varying preference for risk. As with opportunism, one need not assume a single preference for risk among all actors.

Transactions within the solidarity group operations may be affected by uncertainty and opportunities for opportunistic behaviour among members. The source of this uncertainty may be either opportunistic behaviour of the individuals or an uncertain environment. Information may not be distributed equally among all individual group members. Where one member has more or better information than the other, again the possibility of opportunistic behaviour presents itself. Information problems are clearly more acute when the members involved have low trust for each other.

The central question is: How is solidarity group operations shaped by the attributes of actors and transactions? Rationally, the group as an institution works towards minimizing the financial costs of dealing with an uncertain future given possible opportunistic tendencies of members. To achieve this, contractual agreements to guarantee repayment are entered with all individual members. This will indeed raise the efficiency in loan repayment to the lending institution.

Research Design, Data and Methodology

Research Design and Data

This research is a case study of Makueni district, Kenya. We used a random sample of 200 microfinance borrowers from different solidarity groups, who were just taking or had just taken their first loans. Each household was followed and observed for a period of eighteen months. Three structured interviews were carried out with the household every six months. The main focus of the study was the operations of the solidarity group in the context of microfinance and the welfare impacts to the borrowers. Apart from the structured interviews, other methods of data collection used include participant observation, and focus group discussions.

Wealth Ranking Data

In this study wealth ranking as an indicator of socio-economic well being plays a central role. We realized that assets[2] in this particular study context were very significant for the household if the household was to become a member in a microfinance programme. Assets were closely associated with intra group insurance activities in that microfinance users were not willing to insure each others loans based on trust alone. Group members demanded to be shown what assets could be liquidated by the group in case of default. To be able to compile a legitimate[3] list of assets, which could be used for wealth ranking, we asked borrowers to write down all the assets that are available among members and could be used to secure their loans. What we learned from this exercise is that the poor don't have many assets and virtually every asset they had apart from land was eligible to act as collateral depending on its condition. These assets included kitchenware, simple electronics, clothing, furniture and livestock.

During focus group discussions we asked the participants to rate the worth of every asset relative to another. The ranks given by members indicated the value attached to each asset and gave an indication of magnitude of the index assigned to the different assets in this study. It is true that these weights are very subjective, but the good thing about them is that they were informed by how the society attaches value to assets in terms of well being of a household. A much more complete list of the assets used is given at the annex section of this paper. The other advantage about this kind of exercise is that in case a household has problems of repayment of their loans the same assets would be liquidated in most cases. On the other hand, if a household became better off, there is an incentive to invest in more assets since they could be used to guarantee larger loan amounts in the future, as much as they would serve to place the household in the upper class in the community. Vandell *et al.* (1993), observes that there is a strong case that assets are particularly useful indicator of impact because their level does not fluctuate as greatly as other economic indicators and it is not simply based on annual estimates. Zeller and Meyer (2002), Argues that subjective measures of relative poverty or well being are very important since to be poor is relative; it is therefore the relativity in poverty that is important to the policy maker (Zeller and Meyer 2002).

Apart from ownership of assets focus group discussions revealed that the general condition of a homestead is also a strong indication of the social economic status of that particular household. In light of this we included variables like walls, roofing and floor of main house to explain household socio-economic status. Each was ranked differently depending on how the community viewed the worth of such construction materials.

Survey Area

The study was conducted at the Eastern province of Kenya. The exact villages studied are at the South Western part of the province and border Kajiado district that is in the Rift valley Province. In normal circumstances many household in the rural setting would depend mainly on rain fed agriculture. However, the area had been hit by a severe drought since previous 5 years prior to the study. Only few better off households had dug wells and were involved in irrigated garden farming. Majority of the other households had taken in to non-agricultural income generating activities like micro enterprising to earn a living. Little wonder that 88% of the respondents said that micro-business was their primary occupation even though they were in a rural setting. During the time of the survey the drought condition was so bad that majority of the households were receiving food aid from the government. Many of the economic activities included micro enterprising, casual labour; bicycle taxiing commonly known as '*boda boda*'. No cash crops had been grown in the area for the last 5 years due to the drought.

However micro-finance is thriving in the area, this could be influenced by the fact that the main highway Mombasa-Nairobi, passes through the study area cris-crossing shopping centres like Makindu, Emali and Simba which were part of the research area. The area is served by three major microfinance institutions KWFT (Kenya Women Finance Trust) that served 60% of the households studied, KRep 20% and Kadet (Kenya Agency to Development of Enterprise and Technology) 20%. KWFT only gives loans to women entrepreneurs.

Research Methodology

Sustainable livelihood approaches have focused on assets to measure poverty and vulnerability to poverty (Dercon, 2000). Quantitative work has also found that access to assets is an important determinant of poverty and of the ability to cope with hardship. Depending on the conceptual framework, the relationship between possessions and the condition of poverty can be either a poverty profile or an attempt to understand the determinants of poverty (Escobal *et al.* 2000).

In this study our first main task is to develop an analytical framework to determine when a household could be said to have become poorer based on ownership of assets. Let the vulnerability of household h, be vh, and the welfare measure be y which for this case is the wealth index, This defines the vulnerability of household h_i as $vh_i = f(yh_i, z, ph_i)$ where z is a benchmark welfare indicator and p is the probability of falling below this bench mark. Z is a relative benchmarking which for all households it is less than the initial wealth index.

Therefore vulnerability or decrease in welfare (Z_i) after a microfinance intervention can be defined as follows $E(Z_i) = P_i(Z_i) = f(\alpha X_i)$

Where Z_i denotes vulnerability as a discrete variable, and X_i denotes variables that can be hypothesized to affect vulnerability. Some of these variables could be defined as per the table 1.

Table 1: Variables Used in the Model

Variable	Abbreviation	Definition
Own food	fod	How long in months home grown food lasts in the previous 3 growing seasons.
Age of head of household	agehead	In years
Gender of household head of household	headhseld	Dummy variable, 1= male, 0 other wise
Wealth index	wea	Average Calculated index (the bigger the index the wealthier the household)
Level of education of head of household	edu	Number of years spent in formal schooling of head of household
House hold size	hhsize	Number of people who live together and eat from the same kitchen in a particular household
KADET	kadetdum	1 if household receives loan from Kadet, 0 otherwise
KWF	kwftdum	1 if household receives loan from KWFT, 0 otherwise
KREP	krepdum	1 if household receives loan from KREP, 0 otherwise

By employing the model as specified above, the logit model can be applied to provide information about the determinants of welfare outcome (better or worse) after microfinance intervention for different households. The Logit model is usually specified as follows:

$$E(Z_i) = P(Z_i) = \frac{e^{\alpha X_i}}{1 + e^{\alpha X_i}}$$

Where α is the coefficient to be estimated and $E(Z_i) = P(Z_i) = 1$, if the individual becomes worse off after microfinance intervention 0 otherwise.

Results and Discussion

Table 2: Descriptive Statistics

	Minimum	*Maximum*	*Mean*	*Std. Deviation*
Number of years of formal education (Borrower)	1.00	14.00	9.9802	2.92010
size of the household	2.00	13.00	4.5000	1.93223
Age of borrower	23.00	61.00	36.0660	9.13341
Total wealth index	10.00	85.50	43.6263	17.56711

Source: Field data.

Fourteen years of formal education means that the borrower has at least finished secondary education and has had vocational training for two years. Primary education in Kenya requires eight years to complete. Seventy two percent of all the borrowers were female, while 46 % of all the households were female headed. From a social welfare point of view, it is believed that lending to women will bring a bigger impact on household spending on children's education, household nutrition and health; also for practical and operational reasons it is more efficient to lend to women, since women are culturally more sensitive to protecting the reputations of their families, and therefore very keen to repay their debts to avoid any embarrassments Roodman and Qureshi (2006), Coleman (2006). This explains why many joint liability borrowing groups have women as the majority and why many microfinance institutions targeting the poor prefer lending to women.

Price Costs

We find that admission in to a joint liability-borrowing group is purely a function of ability to repay loans. And this ability to repay is judged depending on two criteria; the first is ownership of assets that act as collateral, and the second is the ability to provide the group with a guarantor in case one is not able to meet their liabilities for any other reason other than death.

Once a prospective borrower has passed the first two hurdles, the next hurdles are purely financial. There is a group member ship fee, ranging from a minimum of Ksh 500 (US$ 7) to 1000 (US$ 14) depending on the prospective group. Another charge is the passbook fee about Kshs 65 (US$1) to 200 (US$ 2.7) depending on the lending institution. A charge of about 1% is also to be paid to the bank as insurance fee just in case of death of the borrower, plus another 150 Ksh (2 US$) as membership fee with the microfinance institution. The prospective member must also join the rotating credit arrangement of the solidarity group and pay the contribution for the current recipient. Different solidarity groups have got different contributions for each recipient per month that range from between Ksh 500 (US$ 7) to 1000 (US$ 14). Once the foregoing conditions are fulfilled the member is asked to make an advance one month instalment of the loan they intent to take. This advance payment depends on the loan amount, the repayment duration and the interest charged by the bank. Usually the interest rates by the microfinance institutions that were involved ranged from 24% to 30 %. Roodman and Qureshi (2006) write that much about how microfinance is delivered can be understood as responses to business imperatives, and that the power of commercial imperatives to explain so many product design choices weakens the explanation that microfinance is primarily meant to help the clients.

About 90% of the households surveyed were not able to raise the initial financial price from their own sources. Borrowers who were not able to meet the initial financial cost acquired bridge loans from friends and relatives to be repaid when the new larger loan from the microfinance institution comes through. Dynamic incentives by microfinance institutions offer opportunities for larger loan amounts if a borrower repays the current loan. As such households would often get bridge loans to offset microfinance loans and get new larger ones. The loan amount left for entrepreneurship is too small since borrowers would first repay all debts, to the extent that micro- enterprises still remain undercapitalised and unable to make substantial profits to meets all financial liabilities of micro-entrepreneur. The end result is that households get in to a debt cycle, concealing, deferring and finally the ultimate confrontation with trouble when there is no way out but to liquidate households property, given that the chances of default and getting away with it are very minimal.

Opportunity Costs

Micro-finance recipients open accounts with other banks, since microfinance institution do not offer saving facilities. However compulsory savings must be deposited with the lending institution. The banks usually serve

Table 3: Summary Statistics for Three Opportunity Costs

	Minimum	*Maximum*	*Mean*	*Std. Deviation*
Distance to the bank in KM	35	175	70	10.11
Length of meetings in hours (per week)	1	5	2	0.53
Round ticket fare to the bank (in Ksh)	150	600	460	57.33

Source: Field data.

as the pay points for the cheques drawn by microfinance institutions, as well as households could use them for their own savings. Some of the major activities of solidarity group meetings can be described as follows.

Some of the biggest challenges facing rural entrepreneurship are low incomes leading to low demand for goods and services, there by leading to limited markets. There is also the challenge of competing basic needs like health care, food, and education for children. Micro entrepreneurs often have the dilemma of investing given the risks, or meeting the basic needs with the loan money. This means that loan money will be used for different purposes; focus group discussions revealed that whereas the official reason stated for acquiring loans is business oriented, usually to boost or start one, in reality borrowers used the money for various reasons.

Table 4: Loan Uses

% of borrowers	*% of loan money used for domestic purposes*
1	100
5	75
37	25
20	< 25
37	~0

Source: Field data.

The other loan uses includes basic household necessities, like school stationery for children, health care, food and at times school fees. It is not necessarily bad that households would borrow to smooth consumption, however savings would offer more viable alternative since it equips poor households to manage income volatility without the stress of debt.

We also sought to understand the experiences of micro entrepreneurs concerning their business growth over the period.

Table 5: Micro Enterprises Growth

Business growth rate	*Percentage of businesses*
Some growth	24
Stunted 40	
Worsened (Depletion of stock)	36

Source: Field data

This scenario could be a function of many aspects that cannot all be directly linked to saving and repayment of microfinance. Six months after the first cross-sectional survey, 23 % of the initial microfinance recipients had dropped out of the borrowing groups, citing repayment problems as the main cause of their dropping out. However no group had been unable to repay loans. The poor have already proved that they can borrow and repay at very high interest rates. What should instead worry the policy maker is the cost at which these loans are being repaid.

Respondents shared their experiences on loan repayment with the following result,

Table 6: Loan Repayment

Method of Loan repayment	*% of poor borrowers affected*
Duress	60
Property confiscation by peers	4
Sale of pre-existing property	17
Incur other debts	2
Business Proceeds	17

Source: Field data

Payment by duress in this context means repayment merely due to excessive peer pressure, and not because the borrowers′ financial position allows for voluntary repayment. Domestic animals, house furniture, and electronic goods and sometimes clothing were some of the major assets sold or confiscated to repay the loans. Within eighteen months, 33 % of the initial respondents had dropped out of microfinance schemes. Majority of the dropouts cited difficulties in loan repayment as the main causes of their dropping out. Interestingly many more new borrowing groups had been formed and were still forming at the time.

Wealth ranking before and after eighteen months revealed different welfare outcomes. Some households had thrived; others remained unchanged in terms of their social economic welfare while others had slipped backwards. The

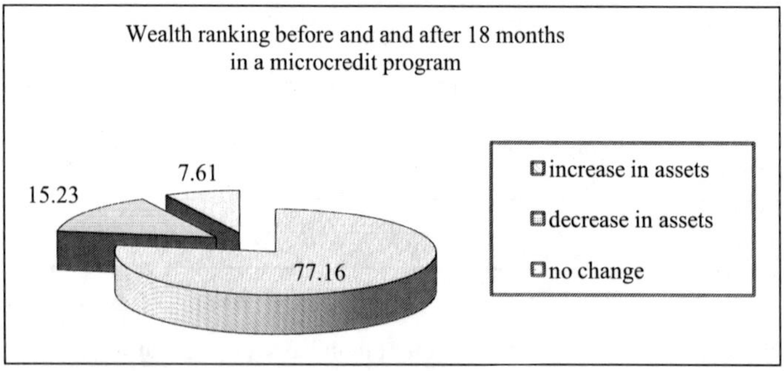

Source: Field data

Figure 1: Micro-finance Recipients Wealth Ranking

decrease in assets in this study is directly linked to microfinance repayment. There is an incentive also for households to acquire more assets since they could be used to guarantee larger amounts of loans in the future. Therefore households, whose incomes improve in the process, are willing to invest in more household assets.

Regression Results

A probit was used to determine the probability that a household in microfinance was going to fall in to more poverty, as indicated by a depletion of household assets. The results of the regression are shown in Table 7.

Table 7: Regression Results

Variable	*Coefficient*	*Std. error*	*P Value*	*Mean of X*
Constant	-.81616288	1.23826944	.5098	
wea	-.02768702	.00839209	.0010***	42.7623762
fod	-.27085159	.25484010	.2879	.50495050
hhsize	.06738075	.06961234	.3331	4.41089109
headhseld	-.70364182	.28975303	0152**	.52970297
Edu	-.00322728	.04709062	.9454	9.98019802
Agehead	.01779930	.01594885	.2644	34.40559406
k-rep dum	.23846750	.78133825	.7602	.19801980
kwftdum	.01074530	.75545375	.9887	.58515842
kadetdum	-.69689990	.80940690	.3892	.19306931

Source: Field data.
Note: ** Significance at 5 percent, *** Significance at 1 percent.

Only two variables are significant, one at 1% the other at 5%. Total wealth, which is a proxy of a socio economic well being of a household, is significant at 1 % level. The negative sigh means that wealthier households have increased chances of not being worse off after accessing microfinance. Other writers have also come to similar conclusion, in a paper measuring impact Coleman (2006) also found that wealthier households receiving microfinance had significant positive impact while the impact on less well off household was insignificant. The results in this study generally stretch one step further than Coleman (2006) to show that indeed the impact is insignificant to some households while it is also negative for others. The other significant variable is the gender of the household head, which is significant at 5%. We find that female-headed households are also likely to get worse off on accessing microfinance. Empirical studies have found that female-headed households were more vulnerable in terms of poverty, yet it is this vulnerability that makes microfinance institutions to be able to impose strict regulations on their borrowers. According to Roodman and Qureshi (2006), poor borrowers have no options of other better financial services and have no option but to adhere to the strict regulations of microfinance institution. Kiriti-Nganga (2007) also had a similar finding that where as microfinance was really assisting the less poor women to improve their welfare, the poorer women became worse off.

Conclusion

Many micro-finance institutions have posted high repayment rates. In many cases repayment rates by the poorer in society have hit 90-99% mark. This is possible because micro-finance institutions have innovatively shifted two classic banking obligations to the borrowers. First, it is the borrowers who decide who is credit worthy and second; it is still the same borrowers who impose debt collection. Currently, at least in the study region there is no limited liability for micro-finance joint liability borrowers, unless every one in the group decides to default, but then the costs are too high for such an occurrence. We seek to argue that the shifting of costs from a legal institution to an informal group setting that is tightly bound to the extent that it would give no room for limited liability for borrowers has ensured the very high loan repayment rates. Roodman and Qureshi (2006), observe that through an interaction of human ingenuity and evolutionary dynamics micro-finance leaders have found a suite of techniques in product design and management that solve the fundamental micro-finance problems of controlling costs, building volume, keeping repayment high, and preventing internal fraud, all while operating in a poor country.

Currently loan repayment by the poor is not a big worry to the policy maker; the poor have already proved that they can repay. What should instead worry the policy maker is the cost at which these loans are being repaid. It is generally accepted that many poor people borrow from moneylenders at even higher interest rates for their consumption, so willingness or ability to repay should not be assumed to demonstrate the profitability of investments. As long as there are bridge loans to repay current loans, the end result is that households get in to a debt cycle, concealing, deferring and finally the ultimate confrontation with trouble when there is no way out but to liquidate household's property either voluntary or involuntary. This result could be conceptualised in figure 2.

What many readers could be asking right now is whether the study concludes that micro-finance is unsuitable for poverty reduction. What we intend to highlight in this paper is that the success of micro-finance depends on individual household characteristics that affect user costs, and these household characteristics are very much influenced by cultural and socioeconomic context of the recipients. Once this possibility has been considered then the result of mixed welfare outcome is expected. This not withstanding, micro-finance can be a good source of liquidity to 'unlock' labour that has been locked up due to liquidity constraints, thereby increasing productivity for the household.

On the practical side of things, it has been easy for rural households to acquire capital for micro enterprises through micro-finance. However one major challenge that still remains unsolved is the issue of effective demand for the products. For example it is easy to start a small home based bakery or start a vegetable stall, but if there is no effective demand for the products, then there cannot be an improvement in welfare. The questions that need to be addressed are; first, how do we get the rural poor micro entrepreneurs linked up to vibrant markets for their products. Better still we could start talking on how to create those markets in the rural areas, by increasing the demand for goods and services for rural communities.

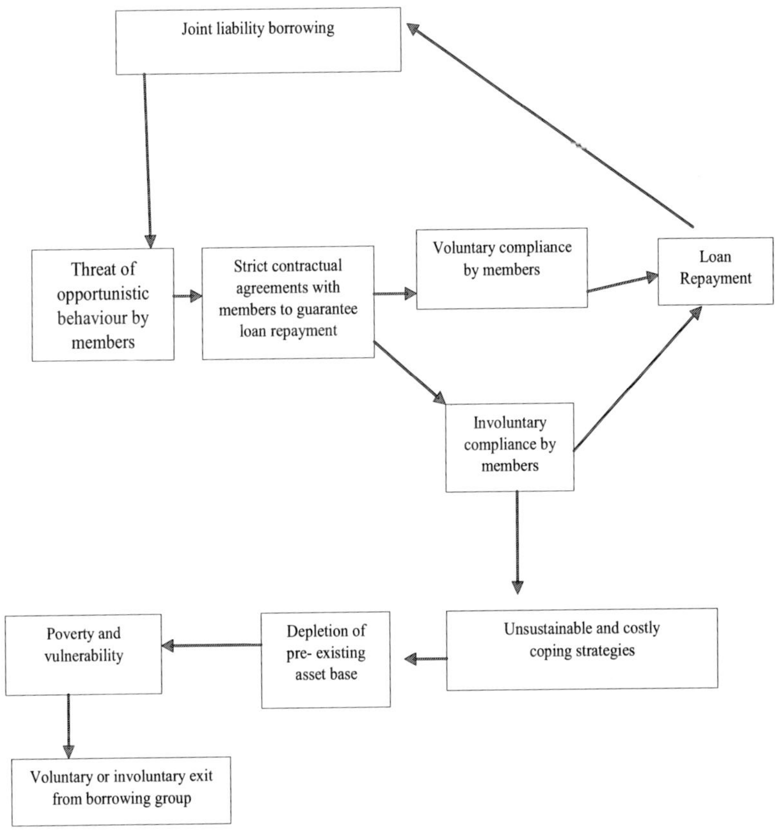

Figure 2: Joint Liability Borrowing and Repayment Process

Since the shift towards commercialised micro-finance, the poor are expected to pay commercial rates for their loans. The options for lenders have been a sharp business approach in dealing with poor borrowers, disregarding the fact that excess debt can have serious consequences. Excess debt can deplete household capital assets and other basic livelihood assets, thereby leaving the household exposed and vulnerable and definitely worse off than before. Excess debt can also increase the propensity for financial crises and it can have poor households locked up in vicious debt cycles as they seek more debts to repay other debts.

There is currently a receptive attitude in the national and international community towards new micro-finance instruments, and by and large the micro-finance institution still has the 'polite and respectable image' among many donors and governments. It is also true that there is no major apparent crisis or emergency in the institution but signs are beginning to show that all might not be very well if the current trend of business like innovations continues in the sector. This study is timely because policies implemented in tranquil times can help prevent major problems in the future.

We come to the conclusion that governments and donor organization who are major stockholders in the micro-finance practice can leverage the benefits of micro-finance, while minimizing vulnerability to crisis by improving debt management capacities of the poor, setting clear regulations in the micro-finance sector and creating policies that create demand for goods and services in the rural areas.

Annotation

Assets used for wealth ranking are electronics (mobile phones, radios and televisions); domestic animals (goats, sheep, cows, oxen, donkey and hen); household dwelling (floor of main house, roofing of main house and walls of main house, presence of a toilet and bathroom facility, ownership of borehole and type of fuel used by household) and capital assets (ownership of donkey cart, sawing machines, plough, rental houses and oxcart, household cutlery like china ware and aluminium cooking pots and furniture such as sofa chairs, tables, stools, beds, clothing such as 'good' bed linen, and 'good' clothing fabrics).

Notes

1. Acceptable depending on their wealth and willingness to formally accept liability in case the borrower is unable to repay.
2. The list of assets used in this study includes only assets that households use to measure household well being and could also be used to guarantee their joint liability loans.
3. A list of assets that is relevant in the study context.

References

Amin, S., Rai, A. and Topa, G. (2003), Does Microcredit Reach the Poor and Vulnerable? Evidence from Northern Bangladesh. *Journal of Development Economics*, 70 (1): 59-82.

Coleman, E. (2006), Micro-finance in North East Thailand: Who Benefits and How Much. *World Development*, 34(9): 1612-1638.

Dercon, S. (2000), *Income Risk, Coping Strategies and Safety Nets.* Working Paper No. 136, Centre for the Study of African Economies, Oxford University, London.

Diagne, A. (2000), *Design and Sustainability Issues of Rural Credit and Savings Programs: Findings From Malawi.* IFRI Policy Brief No. 12, Washington DC.

Escobal, J., Saavedra, J. and Torero, M. (2000), *The Assets of the Poor in Peru.* Grupo de Analisis para el Desarrollo, GRADE 2000, Working Paper No. 261, Lima.

Fiebig, M., Hannig, A., and S. Wisniwski (1999), Saving in Context of Micro-finance: State of Knowledge. In Rainer Schliwa (ed.). *Challenges of Micro-savings Mobilization.* GTZ, Eschborn.

Kiriti-Nganga, T. W. (2007), Micro-Finance and Poverty Alleviation: How Effective is it in Alleviating Gender Based Poverty? In Clem Tisdell (ed.). *Poverty, Poverty Alleviation and Social Disadvantage: Analysis, Case Studies and Policies.* Serials Publications, New Delhi.

Roodman, D. and Qureshi, U. (2006), *Microfiance as Business.* Centre for Global Development, Working Paper No. 101, Washington DC.

Schreiner, M. (2003), A Cost-Effectiveness Analysis of the Grammen Bank of Banglandesh. *Development Policy Review,* 21 (3): 357-382.

Vandell, K.D., Barnes, W., Hartzell, D., Kraft, D. and Wendt, W. (1993), Commercial Mortgage Default: Proportional Hazards Estimation Using Individual Loan Histories. *Journal of Real Estate Economics*, 21 (4): 451-480.

13

Finance for Women Microenterprises

Okurut, F. N. *University of Botswana*

Introduction

Microenterprises in Uganda are defined as urban and rural small scale, self-employed activities, with or without hired labour, employing five or less persons. They operate with low level of organization, low capital, low technology and often on temporary premises, with their income usually below a threshold. In most cases they are not supported by formal financial institutions, and are not usually registered in government. The microenterprise sector comprises of household enterprises and small-scale establishments (Uganda Bureau of Statistics 2002).

The microenterprise sector is argued to be an engine of employment creation and economic growth in most developing countries (Centeno 2001). It is argued that the development of the microenterprise sector will favour the development of the private sector and economic empowerment of women, with potential implications of contributing to poverty reduction and a fairer income distribution.

Given this important role played by microenterprises in economic development, it is therefore critical to have an understanding of the constraints faced by microenterprises with a view of to formulation of appropriate policy framework to enhance their growth. This study therefore investigated the financing constraints faced by microenterprises in Uganda, with specific reference to those solely owned by women.

Data Source and Methodology

The study used data from the Uganda national household survey for 2002-2003 collected Uganda Bureau of Statistics based on the informal sector module. The informal sector module captured the following specific information on microenterprises: category, ownership, constraints in starting the business, main financing sources for the running of the business and main constraints for expansion of the business. The microenterprises were classified under five broad categories: (i) Livestock, poultry, bee-keeping and fishing; (ii) Forestry; (iii) Mining, quarrying and manufacturing; (iv) Hotels, lodges, bars, restaurants, and eating places; (v) Trade and services. The analysis method involved cross tabulations of the key variables of interest.

Finding

Female represents microenterprises owned by women as sole proprietors, while male denotes microenterprises owned by men as sole proprietors, and partnership are those microenterprises owned in form of a partnership between either men or women. The statistics in tables are basically column percentages computed within each category of ownership, with the total number of observations within each category denoted as N. By implication, the reported statistics are percentages of N for each ownership category.

Distribution of Microenterprises by Sector

Out of a total of 6,371 microenterprises surveyed, the highest proportion (44.4%) was engaged in the trade and services sector, followed by mining, quarrying and manufacturing sector (26.6%), and least in the forestry sector (3.5%) (Table 1). The conclusion from these results is that the majority of microentreprenuers derive their livelihood from the trade and services sector. This finding is reinforced by the researcher's observation of the rapid expansion of small markets in both the rural and urban places. For example, in the urban area of Kampala, the rapidly expanding markets include Owino, Nakawa, Kalerwe and Bwaise. In the rural areas, there are mobile markets held on different days of the week for the various locations. For example in Kumi district in eastern Uganda, the main market days are arranged as follows: Mondays in Bukedea and Kumi; Thursdays in Ngora and Mukura. On these main market days, the traders take to the markets products ranging from agricultural output to household consumer goods for purchase by the clients. A variety of other services are also provided in these mobile markets such as make shift restaurants for food, repairs of various items. A visit to these mobile markets testifies to the beehive type of microenterprise trading activities.

The sole proprietorship is the major mode of ownership of micro-enterprises. Of the sampled microenterprises, 96.4% were sole proprietorship while only 3.6% were partnerships. The decomposition of ownership by gender suggests that female sole proprietors accounted for 34.7% of the sampled microenterprises. This is indicative of significant women empowerment in terms of participation in income earning microenterprises, which is a departure from their traditional domestic roles. The greatest participation of women sole proprietors was in the mining, quarrying and manufacturing (41.1%), followed by trade and services (30.9%).

Table 1: Distribution of Microenterprises by Sector and Ownership

Type	*Ownership by Gender*			
	Female	*Male*	*Partnership*	*Total*
Livestock, Poultry, Bee-keeping and Fishing	6.9	15.5	22.4	12.7
Forestry	4.0	3.3	1.8	3.5
Hotels, Lodges, Bars and Restaurants	17.2	10.1	14.9	12.7
Mining, Quarrying and Manufacturing	41.1	18.3	30.3	26.6
Trade and Services	30.9	52.8	30.7	44.4
Total	100.0	100.0	100.0	100.0
N	2,213	3,930	228	6,371

Acquisition of Microenterprises by Gender

The main mode in which the microenterprises were acquired was through the ingenuous initiative of the proprietors (Table 2). For the entire sample, over 95% were started by the proprietors themselves with the exception of the livestock, poultry, bee-keeping and fishing sub sector which accounted for 76.7%. The implication here is that the creation of microenterprises is a direct response of rational agents to their economic conditions. There is embodied technical know how of the management of the microenterprise within the sole proprietor, hence the micoenterprises tend to collapse with the demise of the owners. This may partly explain why acquisition of microenterprises through inheritance tends to be marginal (in most cases below 2.5%), with the exception of livestock, which was relatively higher (approximately 9.1%). Among the women sole proprietors, the majority of microenterprises (over 94%) were started by the women themselves, with the exception of livestock sub sector, which was 71.7%. The conclusion from these results is that it is own initiative that drives the creation of microenterprises as a means of survival to cope with the prevailing economic challenges.

Table 2: Acquisition of Microenterprises by Gender

(a) Livestock, Poultry, Bee-keeping and Fishing				
Method of Acquisition	*Ownership by Gender*			
	Female	*Male*	*Partnership*	*Total*
Started it	71.7	79.3	60.8	76.7
Inherited	7.2	8.7	19.6	9.1
Bought	5.9	4.8	2.0	4.8
Received as a gift	10.5	5.9	9.8	7.0
Other	4.6	1.3	7.8	2.3
Total	100.0	100.0	100.0	100.0
N	152	609	51	812

(Contd...)

(b) Forestry				
Method of Acquisition		***Ownership by Gender***		
	Female	***Male***	***Partnership***	***Total***
Started it	100	93.0	100.0	95.9
Inherited	0	2.3	0	1.4
Bought	0	4.7	0	2.7
Total	100	100.0	100.0	100.0
N	89	129	4	222
(c) Hotels, Lodges, Bars, Restaurants and Eating Places				
Method of Acquisition		***Ownership by Gender***		
	Female	***Male***	***Partnership***	***Total***
Started it	96.3	97.0	94.1	96.5
Inherited	1.3	1.5	2.9	1.5
Bought	0.3	0.8	2.9	0.6
Received as a gift	1.8	0.8	0.0	1.2
Other	0.3	0.0	0.0	0.1
Total	100.0	100.0	100.0	100.0
N	380	397	34	811
(d) Mining, Quarrying and Manufacturing				
Method of Acquisition		***Ownership by Gender***		
	Female	***Male***	***Partnership***	***Total***
Started it	97.8	97.5	92.8	97.5
Inherited	0.9	1.4	5.8	1.3
Bought	0.1	0.7	1.4	0.4
Received as a gift	1.2	0.4	0.0	0.8
Total	100.0	100.0	100.0	100.0
N	909	717	69	1,695
(e) Trade and Services				
Method of Acquisition		***Ownership by Gender***		
	Female	***Male***	***Partnership***	***Total***
Started it	94.7	95.8	92.9	95.4
Inherited	2.3	2.0	4.3	2.2
Bought	0.3	1.3	0.0	1.0
Received as a gift	2.0	0.7	2.9	1.1
Other	0.6	0.2	0.0	0.3
Total	100.0	100.0	100.0	100.0
N	683	2,077	70	2,830

Constraints in Starting Microenterprises

The binding constraint in the start up of most of womens' microenterprises was obtaining the start up capital, with the exception of the forestry sub sector that was finding a market for the products (Table 3). It should be noted that within the various microenterprise sub sectors, the women sole proprietors had a greater constraint in accessing start up capital as compared to men. For example in the livestock sub sector, while 46% of women sole proprietors experienced a constraint in accessing start up capital, only 44.4% of the male sole proprietors experienced the same constraint. In the hotels sector, 72.3% of the women sole proprietors were constrained in access to start up capital as opposed to 71.4% of the male sole proprietors in the same sector. A similar inequality in access to start up capital is observed in the mining sector where 53.4% of women sole proprietors were constrained in access to start up capital as compared to 48.7% of the men sole proprietors. The main conclusion from these results is that there is inequality in access to start up capital, with the women being the most disadvantaged. These results conform to earlier empirical evidence that women have constrained access to credit markets (Okurut *et al.* 2005, Okurut 2007).

Table 3: Main Problem in Starting Microenterprise

(a) Livestock, Poultry, Bee-keeping and Fishing				
Main Problem		***Ownership by Gender***		
	Female	***Male***	***Partnership***	***Total***
No problem	21.2	18.5	14.3	18.7
Obtaining Start-up Capital	46.0	44.4	38.1	44.4
Technical Know-how and Skills	11.7	10.3	11.9	10.6
Accessing Raw Materials	6.6	7.5	7.1	7.3
Finding Market	2.9	3.3	0.0	3.1
Government Regulations	0.0	1.2	0.0	0.9
Utilities (Water/Electricity/transport)	2.9	6.1	4.8	5.4
Other	8.8	8.7	23.8	9.6
Total	100.0	100.0	100.0	100.0
N	137	574	42	753

(b) Forestry				
Main Problem		***Ownership by Gender***		
	Female	***Male***	***Partnership***	***Total***
No problem	17.0	22.0	25.0	20.1
Obtaining Start-up Capital	2.3	25.2	0.0	15.5
Technical Know-how and Skills	0.0	7.9	0.0	4.6
Accessing Raw Materials	10.2	11.0	25.0	11.0
Finding Market	67.0	3.1	50.0	29.7
Government Regulations	0.0	2.4	0.0	1.4

(Contd...)

Utilities (Water/Electricity/transport)	0.0	4.7	0.0	2.7
Other	3.4	23.6	0.0	15.1
Total	100.0	100.0	100.0	100.0
N	88	127	4	219
(c) Hotels, Lodges, Bars, Restaurants and Eating Places				
Main Problem		***Ownership by Gender***		
	Female	***Male***	***Partnership***	***Total***
No problem	11.5	12.2	15.2	12.0
Obtaining Start-up Capital	72.3	71.4	69.7	71.7
Technical Know-how and Skills	0.8	1.5	0.0	1.1
Accessing Raw Materials	2.7	1.5	3.0	2.1
Finding Market	9.6	8.9	9.1	9.2
Government Regulations	0.8	1.0	3.0	1.0
Utilities (Water/Electricity/transport)	0.3	0.5	0.0	0.4
Other	2.1	3.0	0.0	2.5
Total	100.0	100.0	100.0	100.0
N	375	395	33	803
(d) Mining, Quarrying and Manufacturing				
Main Problem		***Ownership by Gender***		
	Female	***Male***	***Partnership***	***Total***
No problem	15.0	10.3	10.4	12.9
Obtaining Start-up Capital	53.4	48.7	61.2	51.7
Technical Know-how and Skills	5.6	9.9	9.0	7.6
Accessing Raw Materials	11.4	13.8	3.0	12.1
Finding Market	11.1	9.8	11.9	10.6
Government Regulations	0.1	1.1	0.0	0.5
Utilities (Water/Electricity/transport)	0.7	3.6	4.5	2.1
Other	2.6	2.7	0.0	2.5
Total	100.0	100.0	100.0	100.0
N	906	715	67	1,688
(e) Trade and Services				
Main Problem		***Ownership by Gender***		
	Female	***Male***	***Partnership***	***Total***
No problem	12.9	9.7	5.9	10.4
Obtaining Start-up Capital	64.3	69.1	72.1	68.0
Technical Know-how and Skills	2.7	2.6	4.4	2.6
Accessing Raw Materials	2.5	1.7	0.0	1.9
Finding Market	12.8	9.7	7.4	10.4
Government Regulations	0.9	2.5	1.5	2.1
Utilities (Water/Electricity/transport)	1.2	1.9	5.9	1.9
Other	2.7	2.8	2.9	2.8
Total	100.0	100.0	100.0	100.0
N	672	2,056	68	2,796

Sources of Finance for Microenterprises

Own savings is the most important source of finance (over 83%) for womens' sole owned microenterprises in all the sectors (Table 4). Womens' reliance on own savings for financing microenterprises is highest in the livestock sector (92.7%) and followed by mining sector (91.7%). Bank credit clearly plays an insignificant role in financing womens' microenterprises, which accounts for less than 2.5% in all sectors. The marginal role played by bank credit in financing womens' microenterprises may be explained by the fact that banks consider small businesses to be risky as they hardly have any attractive collateral to offer as security. In addition, the loan requirements for microenterprises are small which entail high operational costs for the banks (in terms collection of information for assessment and recovery of loans) as opposed to the small interest income from such small loans. This therefore raises the probability of microenterprises being rationed out of formal credit markets (Atieno 1998,Okurut *et al.* 2005). It is also interesting to observe that own savings also stands out as the most important source of finance for the microenterprises owned by men.

These results show that savings are important for financing micro-enterprises and so there is a need for financial institutions to create appropriate savings instruments to enable the low-income women to save. This includes the easing of the bank account opening requirements, locating branch networks in areas accessible to the low-income earners. The licensing of deposit-taking microfinance institutions by the Bank of Uganda is a step in the right direction to offer flexible savings instruments to microenterprise operators (Government of Uganda 2003).

Table 4: Main Source of Financing Microenterprises

(a) Livestock, Poultry, Bee-keeping and Fishing				
Source of Finance		***Ownership by Gender***		
	Female	***Male***	***Partnership***	***Total***
Own Savings	92.7	96.5	94.1	95.7
Loan from Friends	2.6	2.6	2.0	2.6
Loan from Money Lender	1.3	0.2	0.0	0.4
Loan from Bank	2.0	0.7	2.0	1.0
Other	1.3	0.0	2.0	0.4
Total	100.0	100.0	100.0	100.0
N	151	607	51	809
(b) Forestry				
Source of Finance		***Ownership by Gender***		
	Female	***Male***	***Partnership***	***Total***
Own Savings	83.7	94.6	75.0	90.0
Loan from Friends	0.0	2.3	0.0	1.4

(Contd...)

Other	16.3	3.1	25.0	8.7
Total	100.0	100.0	100.0	100.0
N	86	129	4	219
(c) Hotels, Lodges, Bars, Restaurants and Eating Places				
Source of Finance	***Ownership by Gender***			
	Female	***Male***	***Partnership***	***Total***
Own Savings	87.6	91.7	85.3	89.5
Loan from Friends	10.6	4.5	8.8	7.5
Loan from Money Lender	0.3	1.0	2.9	0.7
Loan from Bank	0.3	2.0	0.0	1.1
Other	1.3	0.8	2.9	1.1
Total	100.0	100.0	100.0	100.0
N	379	397	34	810
(d) Mining, Quarrying and Manufacturing				
Source of Finance	***Ownership by Gender***			
	Female	***Male***	***Partnership***	***Total***
Own Savings	91.7	94.3	87.0	92.6
Loan from Friends	5.4	3.6	5.8	4.7
Loan from Money Lender	1.1	0.3	2.9	0.8
Loan from Bank	0.6	0.6	1.4	0.6
Other	1.2	1.3	2.9	1.3
Total	100.0	100.0	100.0	100.0
N	908	717	69	1,694
(e) Trade and Services				
Source of Finance	***Ownership by Gender***			
	Female	***Male***	***Partnership***	***Total***
Own Savings	88.2	92.6	90.0	91.4
Loan from Friends	6.3	3.6	1.4	4.2
Loan from Money Lender	1.5	0.9	1.4	1.0
Loan from Bank	2.5	2.0	2.9	2.2
Other	1.5	1.0	4.3	1.2
Total	100.0	100.0	100.0	100.0
N	680	2,068	70	2,818

Main Problems in Expansion of Microenterprises

The main crosscutting constraint that was experienced by women sole proprietors with regard to expansion of microenterprises in the various sectors was access to external finance (Table 5). It should be noted that access to external finance is critical in enhancing microenterprise expansion. As already pointed out, the formal banking sector regards the microenterprise sector to be risky, and so the only light in the tunnel in overcoming credit constraints to women are the microfinance institutions (Morduch 1999,Wamasembe 2001).

Table 5: Main Problem in Expanding Microenterprises

Main Problem	Ownership by Gender			
	Female	Male	Partnership	Total
(a) Livestock, Poultry, Bee-keeping and Fishing				
No problem	5.3	6.8	5.9	6.4
Finance	40.0	39.4	35.3	39.3
Supply of inputs	9.3	9.4	11.8	9.5
Demand for output	4.7	2.6	3.9	3.1
Profitability	4.7	5.4	5.9	5.3
Technical	0.7	1.0	0.0	0.9
Labour	14.0	11.4	5.9	11.5
Government Regulations	0.7	1.3	0.0	1.1
Outlets	0.7	1.7	0.0	1.4
Competition	0.7	2.0	3.9	1.9
Others	19.3	19.0	27.5	19.6
Total	100.0	100.0	100.0	100.0
N	150	606	51	807
(b) Forestry				
Main Problem	Female	Male	Partnership	Total
No problem	4.5	12.4	25.0	9.5
Finance	4.5	18.6	25.0	13.1
Supply of inputs	0.0	0.8	0.0	0.5
Demand for output	24.7	12.4	0.0	17.1
Profitability	6.7	3.9	0.0	5.0
Labour	16.9	20.9	25.0	19.4
Government Regulations	0.0	3.1	0.0	1.8
Outlets	9.0	4.7	0.0	6.3
Competition	21.3	3.1	25.0	10.8
Others	12.4	20.2	0.0	16.7
Total	100.0	100.0	100.0	100.0
N	89	129	4	222
(c) Hotels, Lodges, Bars, Restaurants and Eating Places				
Main Problem	Female	Male	Partnership	Total
No problem	3.7	4.8	2.9	4.2
Finance	51.1	59.7	67.6	56.0
Supply of inputs	1.9	2.8	2.9	2.3
Demand for output	12.4	6.8	5.9	9.4
Profitability	12.4	11.3	8.8	11.7
Technical	0.0	0.3	0.0	0.1
Labour	2.1	1.5	2.9	1.9
Government Regulations	1.9	0.3	0.0	1.0

(Contd...)

Outlets	0.5	0.5	0.0	0.5
Competition	5.6	3.3	2.9	4.3
Others	8.5	8.8	5.9	8.5
Total	100.0	100.0	100.0	100.0
N	378	397	34	809

(d) Mining, Quarrying and Manufacturing

Main Problem	***Ownership by Gender***			
	Female	***Male***	***Partnership***	***Total***
No problem	4.5	2.9	0.0	3.7
Finance	45.1	42.2	46.4	43.9
Supply of inputs	7.0	7.9	5.8	7.4
Demand for output	13.3	10.7	14.5	12.3
Profitability	8.4	9.2	11.6	8.8
Technical	0.9	3.9	2.9	2.2
Labour	5.5	10.9	2.9	7.7
Government Regulations	0.8	1.1	0.0	0.9
Outlets	2.4	2.1	0.0	2.2
Competition	7.8	4.7	8.7	6.5
Others	4.3	4.3	7.2	4.4
Total	100.0	100.0	100.0	100.0
N	909	718	69	1,696

(e) Trade and Services

Main Problem	***Ownership by Gender***			
	Female	***Male***	***Partnership***	***Total***
No problem	5.1	4.9	4.3	4.9
Finance	52.6	52.6	48.6	52.5
Supply of inputs	2.8	2.2	1.4	2.3
Demand for output	9.8	7.7	4.3	8.1
Profitability	11.9	11.5	17.1	11.8
Technical	0.4	2.9	1.4	2.3
Labour	1.9	1.8	2.9	1.9
Government Regulations	2.5	2.6	0.0	2.5
Outlets	1.0	0.8	1.4	0.9
Competition	4.8	5.2	7.1	5.1
Others	7.0	7.8	11.4	7.7
Total	100.0	100.0	100.0	100.0
N	681	2072	70	2,823

Conclusion

The study findings reveal active participation of women in the microenterprise sector, which is indicative of economic empowerment of women. However the greatest challenge faced by these women is access to external finance for start up, running and expansion of their businesses. For this reasons the women primarily rely on their own savings for financing enterprises. Given the well-known positive relationship between income and savings, by implication the low earnings of microenterprises will dictate low savings, which may constraint their future expansion. To enable the microenterprise sector to become an engine of growth in terms of employment creation and poverty reduction in Uganda, it is recommended that financial institutions should create appropriate savings instruments to enable the small savers to accumulate funds for financing microenterprises. In addition, access to both formal and microfinance credit by women needs to be improved to enhance microenterprise expansion.

References

Atieno, R. (1998), Credit Rationing and Access to Credit: A study of Formal and Informal Credit Institutions in Kenya, *African Journal of Economic Policy*, 5 (2): 29 - 53.

Centeno, V.C. (2001), *The Role of the Microenterprises as Engine of Economic Development: The Peruvian Case*, Paper Presented at the IFUP 4th International Conference in October 16-19, Morocco.

Government of Uganda (2003), *Micro Finance Deposit-Taking Institutions Act, 2003*, The Uganda Gazette XCVI (20), Uganda Printing and Publishing Corporation, Entebbe.

Morduch, J. (1999), The Microfinance Promise, *Journal of Economic Literature*, XXXVII: 1569-1614.

Okurut, F.N., Schoombee, A. and van der Berg, S. (2005), Credit Demand and Credit Rationing in the Informal Financial Sector in Uganda, *South African Journal of Economics*, 73(3): 482-497.

Okurut, F.N. (2007), Access to Credit by the poor in South Africa: Evidence from Household Survey Data 1995 and 2000, *Applied Economics and Policy Analysis*, 1 (1): 25-42

Uganda Bureau of Statistics (2002), *Uganda National Household Survey 2002/03 Manual of Instructions*, Kampala

Wamasembe, W. (2001), Microfinance in Uganda: The State of the Practice, *The Microfinance Banker*, 1 (3): 14-15.

14

Microfinance and Women Empowerment

Rena, R. *Eritrea Institute of Technology*

Introduction

The microfinance has been playing an important role in many developing countries of the world. The microfinance refers to small-scale financial services (primarily credit and savings) provided to people who engage in the farming, fishing and operate micro-enterprises to gain subsistence income from these activities and subsequently support the rural economy. Many of these households have multiple sources of income and carry out several small-scale income-generating activities (IGA). Above all, microfinance services help low income people to reduce risk, improve business management, raise productivity, obtain higher returns on investments, increase their incomes, and thus increase the quality of their lives (Vonderlack et al. 2001; Gema 2002; Rena 2006b).

The Microfinance is relatively a new tool used in the development process but one that is widely discussed in literature, as well as by development theoreticians and practitioners. Can microfinance solve problems that were unsuccessfully addressed with various other development tools? An attempt is made in this paper to discuss the impact of microfinance to reduce poverty of women entrepreneurs in Eritrea. Microfinance has proved to be a successful tool in supporting the economically active poor to improve their businesses and livelihoods. Theoreticians though have not yet reached a consensus about the effectiveness of the tool for poverty alleviation. Therefore, it is interesting to study the microfinance sector in an extremely poor country like Eritrea that has encouraged women through microfinance to set up or enhance business enterprises (Wright 2000; Gema 2002; Spring 2002).

Country Profile

Eritrea is located in the Horn of Africa shares borders with Sudan, Ethiopia, Djibouti, and the Red Sea. It has an estimated population of 4.5 million and a total land area of 12.2 million hectares. Its annual population growth is estimated at 2.9 percent. There are nine ethnic groups[1] and six administrative *zobas* (provinces/regions).[2] It has the per capita income of less than $250. The economy is primarily based on agriculture including fishing, light industry, and services, including tourism. The majority of the population is involved in agriculture, but the sector contributes only 16 percent to the GDP and provides less than a third of Eritrea's merchandise exports. In the years after the war for independence, Eritrea enjoyed an average annual growth rate of 7 percent, one of the highest in Africa. Eritrea was in a de facto currency union with Ethiopia from 1993-1997, and the Ethiopian Birr was the official tender. In 1997, the Bank of Eritrea established the Nakfa, [3] and by early 1998, the government had managed to stabilize the economy. The outbreak of the new conflict with Ethiopia in 1998 brought this progress to a halt (Rena 2006a; Rena 2006b).

Eritrea has a long history of armed conflicts and devastating natural catastrophes. After a short time of economic development, the 1998 border conflict with Ethiopia and two years of war destabilised the efforts towards development. Furthermore, the no-war no-peace situation from 1998 to present deteriorates the economic lives of the people. To make things worse, agricultural production in 2003 and 2004 was low due to drought. In such economic and disaster contexts, it is important to assess the impact of microfinance programs on livelihoods.

Information about the microfinance in Eritrea is scarce. Studies include: Spring (2002); Stillhardt, Brigitta, Ghebru, Bissrat, Mehari Haile, Abraham (2003); NUEW (2003); CARE (2003); Savings and Micro Credit Program (2005) mainly dealt with the women entrepreneurs and their role in the economy. The studies also highlight the problems of women in accessing the credit and provide the information about the microfinance institutions and their impact on the rural people of Eritrea.

The paper has been divided into five parts. Section two discuses the women enterprise development. And section three deals with the challenges of microfinance in Eritrea. Section four provides information on the microfinance institutions in the country. The final section provides concluding remarks.

Women and Development

A comprehensive countrywide study of micro, small, and medium-sized enterprises (MSMEs) was carried out in Eritrea in 1995-1996. For the primary study, 17,030 enterprises, employing 34,773 people, were surveyed as were 3,419 enterprises for a secondary study in Asmara; major, small, and rural towns, rural localities, and large, medium, and small-villages. These data, much disaggregated by gender, are seven to eight years old but still provide a baseline for project design and implementation of new enterprises (Spring 2002:26).

The study estimated that women comprised 42 percent of the total labour force, while 45 percent of enterprises had no women workers and 35 percent consisted of female workers only. As the size of the enterprise increased, the proportion of women owners and workers decreased. A relatively high proportion of women were owners (81 percent), and 42 percent of all Eritrean medium and small-scale enterprises (MSMEs) were owned by women; only 1-2 percent were operated jointly by a man and woman. The rate of launching enterprises since liberation was equal for men and women. Female dominance in the manufacturing sector (66 per cent) of enterprises was "due to smaller activities such as brewing of traditional drinks, baskets and traditional broom-making, mat-weaving, and producing different kinds of snacks and juices," all mainly in the informal sector. At the industrial level, female-owned MSMEs were less prominent, except for hair salons and rental services, while in trade, "female-owned MSMEs accounted for greater than half of hotels and guest houses, restaurants and bars, tea houses, traditional drink saloons, vending food and non-food items, and retailing edibles (poultry, spices, baskets, juices, and vegetables)." More women than men owners were unmarried, and women more often were taking care of families and dependents. Two-thirds of women had no formal business training but acquired their skills through their own work experience (Spring 2002:27).

Constraints to Women Development

The number of poor households in Eritrea is high. Many are women-headed households, whose husbands died during the conflicts or who are now serving in the National Service. Women-headed households are particularly vulnerable and have to deal with additional workload and social constraints, especially in the male-dominated agricultural businesses. It is reported that women share about 50 percent of the farm tasks, whereas men's share in the domestic work is minimal (Tronvoll 1998; Rena 2005). In contrast the majority of Sub-Saharan Africa, practices home-based agriculture, putting the women in a dominant position within the production system. Absence of male labor therefore has great impact on women–headed households.

Most households in the highlands practice subsistence farming, with crops such as sorghum, barley, maize, wheat, *teff* and *dagusha.* Animal husbandry and small-scale trading are also conducted. The most common animals besides drought oxen are sheep and goats. Households also keep chicken for food and egg production and some also have a donkey for transport, carrying water, grain, firewood and goods from the market. Some cows and mules are also found, while camels are mainly seen in the lowlands (Rena 2006a). In this regard, MFIs can provide credit for the rural farmers particularly women to develop poultry, floriculture, bee-making, and horticulture enterprises.

It can be said that for poor farmers with small plots, the potential of increasing the agricultural output is limited. Investment in an off-farm activity would for many peasant households be more lucrative (Spring 2002; Rena 2005). Those with the fewest agricultural assets and income are typically also least able to make up this deficiency through non-farm earnings. It should be considered as well that non-farm activities often also signify an additional burden on the already heavy workload that women do in the household (Rena 2006a). Households with more or high quality assets have good opportunities to develop their businesses. Important assets could be the educational level, the access to more arable land or a stand at the local market to sell grain or vegetables (Cheston and Lisa 2002; Sebstad and Monique 2001).

The following summarizes the problems women face in developing enterprises and entering businesses at all levels (Spring 2002; Cheston and Lisa 2002; Sebstad and Monique 2001).

1. There is a tendency to associate women with micro-level enterprises and with certain sectors (stereotypic enterprises like backyard poultry) rather than realizing that woman may be found in almost all types and at all levels (small, medium-sized, and large scale) of enterprises. There are few entrepreneurial role models for Eritrean women that are not stereotypes.
2. In planning enterprise development for women, there may be certain constraints in terms of level and sources of capitalization. Women may be fearful of credit and loans.
3. Women in all levels of business may be reluctant to discuss business practices or to mentor others. They may not admit to having few business skills and may act uninterested in business development services.
4. Fewer women are found in the agricultural and agro-business sectors, although some are in sectors that deal with agricultural commodities.

Objectives and Methodology

The objective of this study is to assess the possible impact of this development tool on the livelihoods of poor Eritreans. The study is based on both primary and secondary data. The primary data were collected through in-depth interviews of microfinance recipients in selected areas of Eritrea. The secondary data were collected from the journals, books, reports and publications of government and microfinance institutions (MFIs), as well as from the Internet.

This study was conducted in Anseba province of Eritrea in July 2006. The village of Hagaz and the town of Keren (capital of Anseba) were selected. Hagaz is located 25 kilometers from Keren. Altogether sixteen participants – 6 women and 10 men were studied. A Participatory Rural Appraisal (PRA) method was adopted to carry out the study.[4] Chambers, in his definition, described PRA as a growing techniques of Anthropological techniques which use indigenously available means and measures that exude locally available wisdom in a given set of circumstances with almost cent percent societal participation. The essential of complete participation of people in a given time and in a given circumstances ensures not only the people's participation but also in capturing the wisdom of people. However, the task is not as simple as its definition. It matters most in regard to human values and motivation. Chambers emphasized that motivate the people's participation by giving top priority to people with their own knowledge and perception in their own locality and the activities that are being undertaken by them which means, giving top priority to indigenous knowledge and wisdom, for a wise devolution of development programs (Chambers 1999). In line with this, we motivate the beneficiaries to share their experiences with us. We persuade the local thinking i.e., knowledge, sharing and attitudes towards the microfinance program.

Challenges of Microfinance in Eritrea

The Agency for Co-operation in Research and Development (ACORD) has introduced the microfinance programme in 1994. By 2002, about 30,000 people use the services provided by Small and Micro Credit Program (SMCP). In addition, another 5,000 clients used to be involved in a scheme but have exited programs in the middle due to their socio-economic problems after paying back their respective loans adjusted with their relatives. Since the cessation of hostilities with Ethiopia in June 2000, local and international NGOs have started to provide financial services. Nevertheless, the microfinance has been dominated in Eritrea by two organizations i.e. SMCP and ACORD (CGAP 2002:7).

The Political Uncertainty:

(a) Increased security risks to staff, clients, and assets;

(b) Human resource constraints including the loss of management staff or members of support groups who fled their country; and employees who left for better jobs or educational opportunities

(c) Increased expenses incurred to maintain a high quality portfolio that include higher administrative cost to contact and monitor clients, additional security costs, higher labor costs for training, and other costs for risk mitigating measures (CGAP 2002:5)

On the one hand, the presence of armed conflicts is a limiting factor, and on the other hand, is an opportunity for microfinance programs. Indeed, the Ethio-Eritrean border conflict has contributed to develop new clients for microfinance including: refugees and returnees, internally displaced people (IDP), landmine survivors, war widows, rape victims, and others. Also entrepreneurs who previously had access to the formal banking system can no longer afford large loans to rebuild their businesses. In the case of Eritrea some entrepreneurs have found financial support from the MFIs while the formal banking system was being re-established. In general, MFIs must understand the new market situation and assess and modify services and procedures to correspond to the new characteristics and the transformed client base (CGAP 2002).

Currency and Legal Frameworks

A high inflation rate of over 25 percent in Eritrea puts restrictions on the business endeavors of the MFIs and their clients. For clients, the problem of a high inflation rate emerges and is even more accentuated when program is based on recycling funds. The legal framework that regulates the microfinance sector is not yet developed, thereby restricting MFIs, as well as clients.

Eritrea Landscape of Microfinance Institutions

There are nine microfinance institutions and one "meso-finance" institution active in Eritrea. These ten organizations target different groups and have different approaches. The "meso-finance" program: The goal of "meso-finance" is to enhance macro-economic growth through assisting private small and medium enterprises. Therefore the amounts of loans disbursed are by far higher than from MFIs. The details of this program discussed in the later part of this article.

REIP: A Program to Enhance Economic Development

The Rural Enterprise Investment Partnership (REIP) is a governmental program to restore agricultural capacity. REIP focuses on strengthening the development of agriculture and agribusiness as the basis for improving rural income and food security. It finances enterprises in the southwest and along the Red Sea littoral that are suitable for irrigation, as well as for extensive rain-fed agriculture. The Rural Enterprise Unit (REU) is REIP's program planning and administration center, and is responsible for coordinating assistance to rural enterprises and facilitating linkages with the Commercial Bank of Eritrea that manages the credit component of the program.

ACORD and SMCP are the two largest microfinance programs that encompasses about 90 percent of all microfinance clients. Both work with a village-bank approach to build sustainable long-term financial institutions in the villages. They have a wide range of clients from poor peasants to petty traders to businesspeople who could take loans from formal banks.

SMCP: The Largest MFI in Eritrea

The Savings and Micro-credit Program (SMCP) was established as a component of the Eritrea Community Development Fund (ECDF) in 1996 and has been independently operating since 2002. SMCP is the largest microfinance program in Eritrea; and in 2006, there were 33,167 clients[5] (13,267 women clients) from all *zobas* (provinces). From 1996 to December

2006, the village bank savings captured Nakfa 72.34 million (USD 4.8 million) (SMCP 2006). The main objective of the SMCP is the creation of new income and employment in poor communities through the promotion of micro-scale activities.

The Tier-I loan targets clients deemed to be poor or very poor. This includes women and women led households. Under this Tier -I loan, voluntarily organized solidarity groups of 3–7 persons of at least 35 clients set up a community bank but the maximum number of clients does not exceed 105 in the village bank. In any case, if the client's number exceeds 105, they split into two or more village banks and thus develop the customers and banks. It is to be noted that the Group members (solidarity groups)[6] guarantee each other's loans. Clients under this particular program can access loans ranging from Nakfa 3,000 (USD 200) to 40,000 (USD 2,667) disbursed in ten progressive loan cycles. Like all Micro Finance Institute loans, SMCP loans are short term. For the first four cycles, the loan term ranges from 3 – 12 months, while loans in the next six cycles can be paid within 3 – 24 months. Indeed, the clients are required to pay the loan in monthly installments. It is observed that an off-shoot of this particular loan program (Tier-one B) SMCP introduced as an incentive to encourage clients to pay on time allows clients to borrow individually after demonstrating perfect loan repayment records in four consecutive loan cycles.

Tier-I loans range from US$100 to US$1,000. The second tier loan is an individual loan program. Clients eligible under this loan program can access loans ranging from Nakfa 40,000(USD 2,667) to 150,000 (USD10, 000) disbursed in six different loan cycles. Each loan is granted based on best performance and full repayment of previous loans. Loan term under this program ranges from 3 – 36 months. Most loans under this program are given to people owning small enterprises and persons with some exploitable skills for working capital and investment capital needs. Unlike in the group loan (Tier–I), for any one to be eligible under this loan program, collateral/cosigners are a requirement. The second tier loan program has a unique advantage of creating job opportunities (Rena, 2006b). Tier-II clients receive larger amounts (US$1,000 to US$10,000) to invest in business development (CGAP 2002). Tier-II clients do not have to have a business plan or collateral. However, a loan is only handed out after SMCP's staff has checked the economic performance of a business (SMCP report 2005).

Table 1 explains the women clients in Tier-I and Tier-II during the period 1996-2006. It is important to note that the women clients have consistently increased both in total and percentage over a decade. In 1996, under the Tier-I, 30 percent of women clients were extended credit, which then increased to 40 percent in 2006. Under Tier-II, no one was extended credit in 1996, but in 1997, female clients were 14 percent that then increased to 42 percent in 2004 and then declined to 35 percent in 2006. It may because of the escalating situation with Ethiopia over the border conflict.

Table 1: Women Clients Covered under SMCP 1996-2006 (numbers and percent).

Year	*Tier I*		*Tier II*	
	Number	*Percent*	*Number*	*Percent*
1996	441	30	0	None
1997	718	30	1	14
1998	1,513	28	2	6
1999	1,711	30	5	14
2000	1,793	30	71	29
2001	3,812	37	333	36
2002	4,597	40	529	36
2003	5,506	40	636	39
2004	6,646	43	700	42
2005	8,211	41	857	38
2006	10,176	40	1,109	35

Source: SMCP Annual Report[2007]

Field Study in Hagaz and Kerern

In 2006, the SMCP has 4,807 clients in Anseba province out of which 1,406 are women. Almost half of the clients (about 2,500) are from Keren town. They lacked collateral and business licenses that constrained small trading and agribusiness. In Anseba province the loan recovery rate was 86 percent. Several case studies from the interviews provide data on the successes and problems of the program.

One client who is 37 years has four children and a husband who works in national service for $30 per month. She received a SMCP loan, and states the following. "We never had an idea of such a service, but there was a meeting in our village, and then they gave us five days training and distributed the money. I took Nakfa 5,000 (USD 333) and invested in handcrafts manufacturing pottery (traditional *zebena* used for coffee ceremony). I employed four girls to help me to design and manufacture. I now have a good business, and I sell most of my goods in Asmara with the help of one employee. The market in Asmara is better than Keren. I repaid the loan now and am planning to take a Tier-II loan and enlarge my business."

Another women client is 43 years and has five children; her husband is an employee in an office in Keren and earns Nakfa 1,000 (USD 67) per month. She is a grain-trader and highlights the quick distribution of money: "I am happy because after applying, they gave me the money quickly; it was a nice startup capital." The small entrepreneurs of Keren are typical Tier I clients, have to start with a loan of about US$ 100, and after timely repayment they successively receive higher amount of loans up to US$1,000. In addition to the limited amount of money, she also stated: "Everything is fine. But I want more money. Unfortunately I am torn by the regulation that the loan amount is on increasing basis. It would be better if they had a longer repayment period of 6 months or more. You have to buy and sell the items first, before you can generate an income." She mentioned the loan amount as her only criticism of SMCP: "When I started business it was adapted to my capacities, but now I need more money."

The risk-averse strategy and the focus on savings the SMCP applies constitute some restrictions for the members of the credit association. Clients who have taken loans are not happy with the short repayment period since they do not encourage members to invest in income generating activities with longer gestation times. Moreover, the fact that the operating cycle of a savings group does not exceed one year also discourages long-term investment.

The majority of interviewees as part of the SMC program put more than a thousand Nakfa in their savings account. These figures prove that the savings service is highly valued. One 31 year old woman noted: "I can easily withdraw money; it is like I am taking it from home." She has two children and her husband is in national service 400 Km away. She was living in a poor condition before she acquired the loan. Now, she is a tailor and has a good income; she bought three more machines and employed three people.

Farmers in the program strongly criticized the interest rate (16%) as high, while women entrepreneurs in Hagaz and Keren, said that neither the interest rate nor the repayment rate was a problem. One said: "The interest rate is okay. I do not feel it. The accesses to the money are good and also that I can pay back the money on much extended time." Concerning the interest rate as well as the repayment period small entrepreneurs seem to differ significantly from local farmers who are now participants.

A woman from Hagaz who received a Tier II loan is 33 year old and has three children. In 2005, she was given Nakfa 25,000(USD 1,667) to expand her grocery business. The activity generated good income, so within a year she repaid the entire loan amount. She then applied for Nakfa 40,000(USD 2,667) as second cycle loan to expand her business. She earns average Nakfa 5,000 (USD 333) per month.

Another woman from Hagaz who is 39 years old with one child and a husband who is in the military and her new group has only three women, all taking Tier-I loans. Along with the group members, she was allowed Nakfa 3,000(USD 200) in 2005.With this amount she started a sheep and goat rearing business. But due to family problems, she could not manage them properly. As a result, she could not do the business well or repay her loan. She asked a relative, who lives in abroad to help her repay the loan. She noted that she was not interested in taking future loans because the interest was high.

A 48-year widow with 6 children lives in the Keren town. Facing severe poverty, she had a small plot of land where she started a poultry business. In 2003, she heard about the SMCP, and. without any capital of her own, obtained a loan of Nakfa 3,000(USD 200) from the SMCP. With this money she opened a small shop, and within a year paid back the loan on time. After two years, in 2005 she received another loan of Nakfa 5,000 (USD 333) to sell vegetables and employed her daughter. Her profits were Nakfa 45- 75 ($3-5) per day. As a result, her standard of living started to change, and three years later constructed a two-room house. Before she got the microcredit from the SMCP, she said, "my life was pathetic and incomparable; I didn't have a cent, and hardly any clothes. It's like heaven and hell."

SMCP data shows that the repayment rate among the women is as high as 90 percent in both the Tier-I and Tier-II where as in the case of men; the rate is less than 70 percent. There is a client drop out rate of less than eight percent.

Men Beneficiaries in the Field Study

Six men beneficiaries were selected from Hagaz. They have taken the Tier-I loan and complain that they do not get the money in time, which can have bad consequences in agriculture, where timing is very crucial.

A man from Hagaz village, who is 52 years old with five children and a wife. He is a farmer and all the family assists him in the farming. He has less than 2 hectares of land. He said that "The money should be at hand at the right time. Farmers are seasonal producers. You need to receive the money in time, because if a field is not weeded at the right time, the production will be lower. Last year (2005) we received the money in August that was too late" He further stated that "I did not take loans from the bank because I did not have a business to invest the money and to pay back the money would have been difficult because of the remoteness of the Hagaz village. The best thing is the possibility to receive money, because this is not easy in this remote area. They gave us money with the simple confidence that we can repay it. I suggest everybody to repay the loans in time. If they do so, there would be more money in our village bank."

The other farmer who is 47 years old and has three children with wife said that "they understood the crop failure and didn't give us a hard time, they didn't push us to repay and it become a big problem for other potential farmers who take loan from the SMCP" He also revealed that "the money given was not sufficient to buy the agricultural seeds and other equipments."

Another client 49 years old who has two children and wife said that "In SMCP the interest rate is a bit high (16 percent) and the repayment period is just one year that is a bit too short. I like the group collateral (solidarity group) system. If I am not present at a monthly meeting, the other group members can pay my share" He was not happy because the amount taken was not paid by him and depends on his group and they insist him to pay the money.

Another client who is 47 years old and has three children and wife said that "the interest rate is high. I spend all my money for the repayment of the loan. Because I'm the head of the family I would have to attend the monthly meetings. In fact, I am afraid to go there, because last year agriculture was very bad they should extend our repayment period for a year or so"

Another man who is 45 years old has one child taken the loan and purchased sheep and goats and he graze them for few weeks or months and sell them for higher prices He is happy that he paid the loan back without any problem.

Another farmer client who is 55 years and has four children and wife he expressed the concern "The program doesn't include all of the poorest but parts of them. Working labor is the most important asset. The poorest with labor force are included. Excluded are old people, disabled people and women-headed households with children" He invested the money in agriculture but struggling to repay the money due to the poor harvest.

The other four men beneficiaries were selected from Keren. A man who is 47 years old married but no children. He started barber saloon and gets good money for his family maintenance and paid the entire loan.

Another man who is 46 years old has two children and wife started a small bakery where he prepares the *Ambesha* (local big -bread) and sells in the shops and thus make good money and repaid the loan.

Another client who is 48 years old has five children and wife has started a small shop. But he was not happy because the money was not sufficient for his shop needs. He drinks the money that he earns was misused and could not pay the loan. His group members are forcing him and took some belongings from his home.

Another client who is 53 years old has three children started a small shop in the grain market in the town. He said that "I was expelled from Ethiopia in 1999 and I came empty -handed. But now I look like a citizen who has been here for the last 25 years. I have a good standard of living". "The SMCP helped me to cope with the crises. After displacement I took the third loan of Nakfa 10,000(USD 667). This money helped me to reach my former level of business that I was doing while I was in Ethiopia". He makes the profit of Nakfa 75-100(USD 6-7) and trying to other business with the help of his family members. It is to note that most of the wives in village areas do not have jobs except helping their husbands in the farming activities and taking care of the houses.

Table 2: The Performance Indicators of Savings and Micro Credit Program (July 1, 1996-December 31, 2004)

	1996	1997	1998	1999	2000	2001	2002	2003	2004
Total Number of Village Banks (VBs)	25	39	76	85	88	146	162	191	207
No. New VBs established	25	14	37	9	3	58	16	29	16
No. of Cumulative village Clusters	81	107	246	285	290	519	552	561	595
Avg.No. of Active Clients per VB.	59	61	72	68	68	71	71	72	73
Balance of Loans Outstanding Tier I	1,316,100	3,778,367	8,902,521	9,184,808	9,259,712	17,617,584	23,037,580	34,043,292	35,888,089
Balance of Loans Outstanding Tier II	0	66,107	515,625	582,108	2,658,224	14,052,734	29,961,806	35,403,875	34,481,746
No. of active loans (Tier I&II)	1470	2380	5504	5815	6187	11229	12,961	15396	17267
Effective Interest Rate (Tier I)	16	16	16	16	16	16	16	16	16
Inflation(during the period) (Tier I)	-	3.7	9.5	9.0	14.6	14.6	14.6	25	25
Real effective interest rate (Tier I)	16	0.120	0.060	0.06	0.01	0.01	0.01	-0.07	-0.07
Effective Interest Rate (Tier II)	14	14	14	14	14	14	14	14	14
Inflation (during the period) (Tier II)	-	3.7	9.5	9.0	14.6	14.6	14.6	25	25
Real effective interest rate (Tier II)	14	0.099	0.041	0.046	-0.005	-0.005	-0.01	-0.09	-0.09

(Contd...)

TIER I									
No. of Active Clients	1470	2373	5477	5779	5942	10304	11492	13765	15602
No of Loans Disbursed (Tier I)	1685	3808	9005	4391	2744	9206	11520	11588	10728
TIER II									
No.of Active Clients	-	7	27	36	245	925	1469	1631	1665
No.Loans Disbursed (Tier II)	-	7	33	46	259	1040	1016	721	658
Total No. of Women Beneficiaries;% (Tier I)	30	30.26	27.62	29.6	30.18	37	40	40	42.6
Total No. Women Beneficiaries; % (Tier II)	-	14.29	6.45	14.29	29	36	36	39	42.04
Portfolio in Arrears over 30 days	0.00	1.15	2.04	7.12	5.96	2.71	7.5	21.55	20.58
Portfolio in arrears over 1 day	0.00	1.28	2.09	7.48	6.33	3.37	9.36	26.47	24.34

Source: SMCP Annual Report [2005]

Table 2 provides the overall activities and performance of SMCP in all the six regions of Eritrea. As of December 31, 2004 it had 43 percent of women in Tier-I and 42 percent in Tier-II. The active clients under the first tier loan program spread over 207 village banks. It can be noticed that the number of cumulative village clusters increased from 81 in 1996 to 595 in 2004. The table further explains that the SMCP has outstanding balance loans of Nakfa 35.88 million in the Tier-I and Nakfa 34.48 million in the Tier-II during the period 1996-2004. The number of active clients has also increased considerably from 1,470 to 15,602 during the same period. According to the SMCP the number of clients increased to over 35,000 by the end of 2007. This indicates that the SMCP has extended its operations in all the six regions of the country. The rate of interest charged by SMCP is found to be constant i.e. 16 during the eight year period. The inflation in Eritrea has sharply increased from 3.7 to 25 percent during 1997-2004. However, the SMCP did not make any steps to reduce the rate of interest to encourage its clients. Therefore, many clients expressed their concern that the interest rate in SMCP is very high, which will even deter the involvement of some potential clients in the program.

The Agency for Cooperation in Research and Development (ACORD)

ACORD, established in 1976, is a consortium of international NGOs in the North, as well as by other NGOs and UN organizations like United Nations Development Program (UNDP) and World Food Program (WFP) and to provide its members with operational capacity to address poverty issues resulting from the drought in sub-Saharan Africa.

The ACORD[7] mainly functions in the areas such as micro credit, HIV/AIDS awareness campaign, and livelihood and conflict management. It works in 526 villages (out of 979) of zoba Debub (southern province) i.e. it covers 54 percent of the villages in the zoba. It enables the poor people to improve their livelihood through credit facilities. In 2002, it is reported that it has 8,795 clients, out of which 43 percent are women. The numbers of loans were 2,840 out which 49 percent were disbursed to women (ACORD 2004).

The first loan of any member cannot exceed Nakfa 5,000(USD 333). The savings have to equal at least 5 percent of the amount of the loan requested. After successful repayment of the loan a member can get further loans and higher amounts of money. Loans can be used for any economic investment from fattening sheep to digging a well. The interest rate for loans is 14% per year, on declining bases. This system favors early repayment, because the interest rate is significantly below 14% if the loan is repaid after a shorter period than a year.

The Microfinance Programs of Vision Eritrea and HABEN

The Community-based Savings and Credit Association (CSCA) was originally based on a program design of the British CARE Internationals.

CARE International-Eritrea is funded by USAID. It proposed an 18-month pilot program to build up the capacities of two Eritrean NGOs, VISION ERITREA and HABEN, to establish viable community-managed savings and credit associations (CSCAs). The program supported the two local NGOs to work in several communities in each of there *zobas*: the Gash Barka, Northern Red Sea and Maekel (central province), HABEN was only responsible for the latter. CARE International-Eritrea trains VISION ERITREA and HABEN staff to implement all aspects of the project. Before the training, CARE arranged a visit of these two NGOs to a CSCA program in Uganda(CARE 2003: 1). It has the total customers of 248 out of which 233 are women. The operations are mainly conducted in the zoba Gash Barka and Northern Red Sea areas. The amount of loan disbursed was Nakfa 466,537.50(USD 31,102).

Manitese: Microfinance as Complementary Service

The Manitese development program assists women to improve their skills in handicraft production. The microfinance section of Manitese only provides loans to the participants of their business creation. During 2000 and 2003, Manitese started projects for women in Gash Barka and Northern Red Sea that focus on the specialization and improvement of local handicrafts production. Manitese also organizes start-up programs on the specialization and improvement of local handicrafts that can serve as a source of income for the trained women, most of whom are illiterate. Manitese provides these women with a center where they can work and benefit from the daily exchange of personal knowledge and ongoing training. In addition, Manitese supports the women clients by purchasing raw materials, establishing a central store near the center, and helping clients to find markets to sell finished products (Manitese 2003).

The microfinance component is one part of this holistic approach. The women are provided with an interest-free credit. The repayment period for the loans is 10 to 12 months but the repayment rate was less than 75 percent. Manitese does not make any profit because the money is paid into a revolving fund and does not have any interest (Manitese 2003). Since Manitese does not have manpower and infrastructure to run the microfinance program, it works with the National Union of Eritrean Women (NUEW). After a year, the clients left the program, and they are supported by the NUEW. The Manitese project mainly aimed at women entrepreneurs because of which it has been amalgamated with the NUEW.

MOA: The Microfinance Component of an Agricultural Project

The Ministry of Agriculture (MoA) operates an agricultural development (microfinance) project in the Emni Haili of zoba Debub (southern region). One component provides microcredit to farmers. The project area is characterized by mixed farming systems, but crop and livestock yields are low. The main constraints on productivity are land degradation (poor soil fertility), high population density, and lack of inputs (e.g. good-quality seeds, fertilizers, and pesticides). Irrigation activities have not been introduced and there is a lack of adequate drinking water. In a process of trying to identify the needs of the local people, men and women farmers were approached to identify major problems. Irrigation and drinking water were identified, as well as crop input supply and training.

The MoA formulated the main objectives that included strengthening consciousness on gender issues and empowering women in various income-generating activities. To achieve these objectives, a women's program that included a training and credit service was implemented, Most of the women in the project area do not own any resources except of their labor. There is an acute shortage of credit especially for those women wanting to undertake various food production activities, such as sheep or goat breeding and poultry rearing.

Every year about 45-60 women are trained for 20 days in home economics (food and nutrition, health and sanitation, mother and child care), gardening, and animal husbandry. Immediately after the training, the loan is given to those who want to start or enlarge their businesses. Another 30 women who request a loan from the project also get credit after receiving a three day orientation and training about the aim and objectives of the credit and related subjects. The primary beneficiaries are 300 women who are directly provided with credit. The money then circulates as a revolving fund that contains a total of Nakfa 900,000(USD 6,000) and distributed among the clients.

National Union of Eritrean Women (NUEW): A Credit and Savings Program

The NUEW was established in 1979 during Eritrea's liberation struggle. The NUEW is administered by its Headquarters in Asmara (national capital), as well as by regional offices in all six zones. It has membership of over 200,000 and gets income from monthly membership fees, grants and projects and fund-raising activities by members. Since 1999, NUEW has continued to enhance the role of women by raising their political consciousness through literacy campaigns, credit programs, English lessons, and other skills training. (NUEW 2003).

In 1995, the NUEW initiated a microfinance program, but after the 1998 war, there were problems. Most of the members were located in Gash Barka and Debub that were badly affected due to which the program has been stopped until now. In 2000, it started a new program with the United Nations Development Project (UNDP) in Maekel where 400 clients (mostly rural) were involved. The budget was about US$150,000. Its objectives are to encourage women economic self-reliance, to improve their business knowledge, and to provide credit for income generating activities. All mentally and physically able women between 18 and 60 are potential clients, but there is a focus on poor women headed households, displaced women, and women who live in remote areas (NUEW 2002). The improved standard of living of families, that includes food security, health care, access to education, and safe and secure housing.

Originally the program planned to provide its services in four sub-zobas in Maekel province with 87 clients in each sub-zoba. Participants are organized into groups of four to six women, all from the same village. The groups are self-organized and function as collateral groups through trust and agreed upon amounts for regular. All the members must be the breadwinners in their households (NUEW 2002). Beneficiaries of the program are engaged in different income generating activities.

The loan size ranges between Nakfa 500(USD 33) and 5000 (USD 333) with an interest rate of 12 percent. In the second round an amount up to Nakfa 5,000(USD 333) is possible. The repayment rate is 12 months, but for agricultural activities, the period can be extended to 18 months.

International Medical Corps (IMC): The Microfinance and Community Health Program

The IMC microfinance program is small and closely linked to its Mobile Clinics and Community Health Programs. The Eritrean refugees, who come from Sudan and residents of host communities gain access to microcredit. Eventually, they establish and promote small income generating activities and receive other related support. Village Credit Committees were formed in the sites of Aklalat, Dressa and Ali Gider. The local communities formed the credit groups (IMC 2003).

The individual loan size ranges between 3,500 and 5,000 Nakfa, The group loan instead goes up to Nakfa 15,000 (USD1,000). In June 2003 the IMC disbursed a total amount of Nakfa 269,500 (USD 17,967). One quarter of this amount was handed out to women (25 percent). The interest rate for loans with less than six months repayment period is 8 percent, for loans of more than six months duration the interest rate is 12 percent. The IMC has disbursed 297 loans, 49 group loans and 248 individual loans. The IMC is satisfied with the repayment rate. By the end of March 2003 the overall repayment percentage for the three sites was calculated as 94 percent. The 6 percent default represents businesses that were rescheduled because of market changes. For these clients the repayment period was extended so that the business cash flow was not affected and a business collapse could be avoided (IMC 2003).

HABEN: Small-scale Microfinance Programs for the Extreme Poor

HABEN, one of two local NGOs is involved in microfinance, as well as emergency relief, helping people affected by the war in the Southern zone (Debub) and Gash Barka. In the Southern Zone, the program is based in Senafe, a small town, about 40 kilometers from the Ethiopian border. Because of its geographical location, the town and the surrounding villages were very badly affected by the war. Besides the severe bombing, a lot of households were looted and subjected to violence. Women especially were victims of sexual and gender-based violence. In the religious and traditional society of rural Eritrea, women who were abused by these crimes are excluded from the community and were divorced from their husbands. With the loss of their social network, they became vulnerable and struggle to survive. HABEN [8] started the "Emergency Response to Sexual and Gender-Based Violence Program". The original goal was to help victimized women, but this was difficult because the social and religious background hindered women from talking about the crimes committed by the Ethiopian soldiers. These circumstances led to the present design in which the most vulnerable women (usually household heads) are targeted.

HABEN runs a similar program in Ali Gider, close to Tessenei where many refugees from Sudan live, and where HABEN, UNHCR and the International Medical Corps try to secure their survival. The HABEN programs are limited for example, in 2003; there were only 231 women clients.

The Impact of Microfinance on Secure and Insecure Poor Microfinance Members

Loan money is invested in the business-related spheres like livestock and production, whereas the potential surplus is invested in the other related spheres of action such as: housing, education, medicines, as well as in also in family and social networks (expenses for weddings and funerals) (Tronvoll 1998; Seep Network 2000). That the loan money is strictly invested in business-related activities can mainly be explained with the programs interests that their clients invest money in integrated business development activities. The pressure of MFIs is probably not necessary because the clients understand that the loan has to be repaid and that only the surplus should be invested more freely. This procedure functions without serious problems for small entrepreneurs. The problem with the farmers is that they all invest in livestock. In contrast to their confidence in these investments the study shows that investing in livestock is risky! Generally, it is observed that investment in agriculture is insecure and poor smallholder households find it difficult to improve their income through agriculture. Most of the farmers interviewed invested the loan money in livestock; few clients purchased agricultural inputs. The example of one villager in Hagaz is the only MFI member interviewed who succeeded in improving her standard of living through constant investment in agriculture.

Conclusion

Currently, microfinance is a highly accepted and recognized development tool. While microenterprises are an important source of income for many poor households particularly women entrepreneurs, they are only one part of their overall livelihood systems. Microfinance is, as this study has shown, more than just credit and can play an important role beyond enterprise development in supporting the livelihoods of the poor. The concept of livelihoods is a broader one than that of enterprise development. It considers a mixture of resources, activities and capabilities that enable individuals and households to pursue their economic goals. In reality, resources within households are fungible and it is important to recognize, that clients will use microfinance services for a variety of purposes. The women clients in Eritrea invest in enterprises or find new businesses. By providing money when it is needed, microfinance helps the women clients to reduce their vulnerability and expand their business options. The study indicates that there are mixed feelings over the functioning and SMCP system as a whole. Some women have benefited while others are still not. Microfinance in Eritrea has not been able to help very poor women people climb out of poverty, although it may reduce their vulnerability. Most of the microfinance institutions including the SMCP provide training to their clients for proper management of the credit, but are less successful in providing business skills and markets.

To conclude, the role of microfinance in reducing vulnerability for the women clients and their households point to continued donor investments in microfinance programs. Microfinance services contribute to building assets, diversifying income sources, and strengthening coping mechanisms for the women clients. Thus, microfinance has potential to assist has both poor women and small-scale women entrepreneurs.

Notes

1. Eritrea has nine ethnic groups. They are: Tigrigna, Tigre, Saho, Afar, Bilein, Hidareb, Kunama, Nara and Rashaida. All these ethnic groups have their own languages and cultures.
2. In 1996, Eritrea was restructured from ten administrative regions into six. The new political map is now divided in 6 regions, 55 sub-regions and 651 villages/area administrations. The six Administrative regions in Eritrea are: Anseba (Keren capital), Debub (Mendefera), Gash Barka (Berentu), Maakel (Asmara), Northern Red Rea (Massawa), and Southern Red Sea (Asseb).
3. Eritrean currency Nakfa was introduced on 8 November 1997. The present exchange rate for 1 USD is 15 Nakfa.
4. The author visited these two areas with the help of SMCP staff. The staff provided all the necessary information and help in conducting this study.
5. In addition to the Tier-I and Tier-II, SMCP has started 'instant loan program' in 2006 for the government and private employees. The total clients were 4,874. It is included in the total figure of 33,167.

6. Solidarity groups are the 3-7 group of people, who cooperate among themselves by giving guarantee for each other members' loans.
7. Due to the Government policy, the ACORD closed its operations in 2006. The microcredit programs of the ACORD are merged with the SMCP in April 2007.
8. Donors support HABEN, the Bureau for Population, Refugee and Migration (BPRM), Norwegian Church Aid (NCA) and CORDAID. These programs started in 2001 and were designed for two years. But in summer 2003, HABEN decided to keep both programs running. Due to the Government policy, HABEN was also closed its operations in 2006.

References

ACORD (2004), *Annual Report*, Available at www.acord.org.uk/b-aboutacord.htm

CARE (2002), *Community-based Savings and Credit Association Program: Gash Barka, North Red Sea and Maekel Zones*, CARE International, Eritrea.

CARE (2003), *Evaluation Report on Community-based Savings and Credit Association Project*, CARE International, Eritrea.

CGAP (2002), *Micro-credit, a Modality of Intervention to Face Emergency and Development*, Washington DC.

Chambers, Robert (1999), *Whose Reality Counts? Putting the First Last*, Intermediate Technology Publications, London.

Cheston, Susy, Kuhn Lisa (2002), *Empowering Women Through Microfinance*, Available at www.microcreditsummit.org/papers/+5cheston_kuhn.pdf

CIA (2003), Available at *www.cia.gov/cia/publications/factbook/geos/er.html*

Gema PKM Indonesia. (2002), *Poverty and Microfinance*, Gema PKM Indonesia, Jakarta.

IMC (2003), *Summary Sheet: BPRM Funded Sites for Micro Credit Activities*, In: Internal Report.

Manitese (2003), *Quarterly Report*, April - June 2003, Eritrea, In: Internal Report.

NUEW (2002), *Credit and Saving Program*, In: Internal Report.

NUEW (2003), *Micro-saving Report*, In: Internal Report.

Rena, Ravinder (2005), Challenges for Food Security in Eritrea: A Descriptive and Qualitative Analysis, *African Development Review*, 17(2), 193-212.

Rena, Ravinder (2006a), *Handbook on the Eritrean Economy: Problems and Prospects for Development*, New Africa Press, Dar Es Salaam.

Rena, Ravinder (2006b), *Financial Institutions in Eritrea*, New Africa Press, Dar Es Salaam.

Savings and Micro Credit Program (2005), *Annual Report*, Savings and Micro Credit Program Asmara, Eritrea.

Savings and Micro Credit Program (2007), *Annual Report*, Savings and Micro Credit Program Asmara, Eritrea.

Sebstad, Jennefer, Cohen, Monique (2001), *Microfinance, Risk Management and Poverty*, The Consultative Group to Assist the Poor (CGAP), Washington DC.

Seep Network (2000), *Learning from Clients: Assessment Tool for Microfinance Practitioners*, Available at www.mip.org/pdfs/aims/Tools%20Manual%20(English).pdf

Spring, Anita. (2002), *A Gender Assessment of Health Parameters and Delivery Systems, Agricultural and Enterprise Development, and Women's Participation in Eritrea*,

A Women in Development, Technical Assistance Project Funded by the USAID, Development Alternatives, Inc.

Stillhardt, Brigitta, Ghebru, Bissrat, Mehari Haile, Abraham (2003), *Small-scale Micro Irrigation in Eritrea, A Feasibility Study on the Introduction of Affordable Micro Irrigation Technology in Eritrea*, Available at www.cde.unibe.ch/pubmedia/pdf/micro_drip.pdf

Tronvoll, Kjetil. (1998), *Mai Weini: A Highland Village in Eritrea - A Study of the People, their Livelihood, and Land Tenure during Times of Turbulence*, The Red Sea Press, Trenton N J.

Vonderlack, Rebecca M., Schreiner, Mark (2001), *Women, Microfinance, and Savings*, Available at www.econwpa.wustl.edu/eps/dev/papers/0108/0108004.pdf

Wright, Graham (2000), *Microfinance Systems: Designing Quality Financial Services for the Poor*, Vedams Books, Dhaka.

15

Trade Liberalisation on Female-led Households

Tsheko, B.O. *University of Botswana*

Introduction

A major policy question facing Botswana's policy makers is whether and to what extent they should pursue trade liberalisation to conform to the World Trade Organisation (WTO) rules while at the same time addressing sustainable economic diversification and reducing abject poverty. While a carefully formulated program on trade liberalisation, at aggregate level, can have positive impact on the economy (trade creation, growth in Gross Domestic Product (GDP), improvement in welfare, industrialization and increase in foreign investment), it is also likely to have very different effects on different sectors of the economy and population. The majority of poor households in Botswana are female-headed.

Given that Botswana's agriculture and textile industries currently enjoy substantial protection and special dispensation through European Union/Africa, Caribbean and Pacific (EU/ACP) agreement and African Growth and Opportunity Act (AGOA), additional broad-based trade liberalisation may have a detrimental impact on small-scale activities, informal sector as well as other enterprises facing low productivity. These activities employ several households especially in the rural areas where poverty is concentrated, as this exposes these sectors and people to more international competition. Limited skills, economies of scale, technological base and imperfect factor and product markets, generally disadvantage small developing countries like Botswana and impact adversely on the poor especially females.

The Relationship between Overall Trade Policy and Poverty Reduction

Trade liberalization can affect the welfare of the poor through a number of channels: (I) by changing the prices of tradable goods (i.e., lowering prices of imports for poor consumers and producers, increasing prices of exports for poor producers), and improving access to new products; (ii) by changing the relative prices of factors (skilled and unskilled labour and capital) used in the production of tradable goods and affecting the income and employment of the poor; (iii) by affecting government revenue from trade taxes and thus the government's ability to finance programs for the poor; (iv) by changing incentives for investment and innovation and affecting economic growth; and (v) by affecting the vulnerability of an economy (or subgroups within the economy) to negative external shocks that could affect the poor

The empirical evidence confirms the theoretical prediction that poverty effects of reform vary from case to case and, within a country, from group to group One possible generalisation seems to be that the net effect on poverty is more likely to be positive where agriculture is more egalitarian and dynamic, but even there those that lose may include many of the poorest. A highly productive agricultural sector assuming other complimentary policies like credit, land reform, infrastructure, etc, are there can contribute to poverty alleviation through direct and indirect income and demand linkages (Delgado *et al.* 1998).

However the link between trade and poverty is a new area of study. Although the recent emphasis on poverty has spurred some initial research (Winters 2000a), this is still mostly theoretical and few empirical investigations have been undertaken. There is consensus, however, that the essential precondition for sustained poverty alleviation is rapid economic growth. By providing incentives for an efficient allocation of resources, an open and transparent trade regime is an important precondition for broad-based and sustained growth. Thus, in the medium term, trade reform has an important role in poverty alleviation through its effects on the rate and sectoral pattern of growth.

In the short run, trade reform could have re-distributive effects on income that can hurt the rich and the poor alike. Trade theory has generally assumed that lump sum transfers are possible from winners to compensate the losers (Deacon 2000). However, lump sum redistribution of the gains from trade is hardly ever practical, let alone politically feasible. Thus, although trade reforms may raise average incomes in the medium term, in the short term some segments of society may suffer losses. Because the poor or near poor have fewer assets to protect them during economic hard times, they are less able to absorb adjustment costs than other segments of society. This justifies looking more carefully at the effects of trade liberalization on the poor.

Who are the poor? The simplest definition is that of income/consumption poverty, which defines people as poor if their access to economic resources is insufficient to acquire enough commodities to meet basic needs (World Bank 2000). This definition implicitly relies on the establishment of a level of income/

expenditure that is necessary to acquire a basket of goods that satisfies basic needs (i.e., the poverty line). This traditional definition ignores many of the social and participatory aspects of poverty. Under this definition trade reform will increase poverty if it results in a greater number of individuals or households with income falling below the poverty line.

There are other attributes of poverty that are important to consider in relation to the effects of trade reform. First, the poor lack physical, financial, or human capital and are therefore much more vulnerable to economic fluctuations or sudden changes in the economic environment (such as might come from trade reform). Second, there is evidence of considerable rotation of households into and out of poverty. To the extent that trade policy affects the determinants of these movements, it will have an effect on the number of poor (Winters 2000b). More important, severe shocks can turn transitory poverty into a permanent phenomenon. Even a transitory loss of income can cause the poor to lose opportunities to acquire human capital through education,

Third, the poor are not tightly linked to the formal economy. They generally subsist on the urban informal sector or rural subsistence agriculture. Thus for a trade policy reform that seeks to improve the welfare of the poor, it is necessary that the effects on these sectors are not ignored.

To capture the potential effects of trade liberalization on the poor this paper uses the 1996/97 Social Accounting Matrix (SAM)-based model for Botswana which provides a complete, consistent and comprehensive record of the interactions between actors in an economy. That is, to analyse the effects of changes in export earnings in different industries on poverty, we use the fixed- price income Social Accounting Matrix (SAM) multipliers based on the 1996/97 SAM updated using 2005 household, income and expenditure survey (HIES) report . The fixed-price income multiplier assumes that prices do not change when income varies. As indicated earlier some accounts are treated as exogenous while others are endogenous. Conventionally, government, capital and the rest of the world (international trade) are treated as exogenous accounts or variables while factors (labour and capital), households and other institutions and activities are endogenous accounts. This means the change in income or export earnings is introduced as a shock into endogenous accounts while prices are kept constant. The external policy shock here is the rest of the world. The results of the shocks are discussed later on.

Furthermore, the SAM multipliers are used to identify the sources of income of the various households in both rural and urban areas and examine their links to traded sectors and the rest of the world/international trade. Opportunities for and threats to improved income/poverty-reduction and sustainable environment will be explored following global trade liberalization.

Social Accounting Matrix (SAM)

In a SAM framework it is important to address the question of which accounts should be considered exogenous and which endogenous. For this research, it is logical to consider the government, the rest of the world, and the capital account as exogenous and the factors, households and activities accounts as endogenous. Table 1 shows this partitioning.If a certain number of conditions are met-in particular, the existence of excess capacity and unemployed labour resources the SAM can be used to estimate the effects of exogenous changes and injections, such as an increase in the demand for a given production activity, government expenditures or exports on the whole system. As long as excess capacity prevails, any exogenous change in demand can be satisfied through a corresponding increase in output without having any effect on prices.

Table 1: The Partition of the SAM to Get a Model Structure

Receipts	*Expenditures*		
	Endogenous Accounts	*Exogenous Accounts*	*Totals*
Endogenous Accounts	$N = A_n\hat{y}_n$ (1)	X	$y_n = n + x$ $= A_n y_n + x$ (3)
Exogenous Accounts	$L = A_l\hat{y}_n$ (2)	R	$y_x = l + Ri$ $= A_l y_n + Ri$ (4)
Totals	$y'_n = (i'A_n + i'A_l)\hat{y}_n$	$y'_x = i'X + i'R$ (9)	
	$\therefore i' = i'A_n + i'A_l$ (8)	$\therefore A_l y_n - X'i = (R - R')i$ (10)	$\lambda' a y_n = x'i$ (11)

Source: Pyatt and Round [1979]

$A_n = N\hat{y}_n^{-1}$= Matrix of average endogenous expenditure propensities; i.e., the square matrix of the coefficients of the endogenous accounts.

$A_l = L\hat{y}_n^{-1}$= Matrix of average propensities to leak; That is, the coefficients in the rows of the exogenous accounts. These leakages are, for example, the induced demand for imports, government revenues, and savings.

$Ni = n$= Vector of row sums of $N = A_n\hat{y}_n \rightarrow n = A_n y_n$;

$Xi = x$= Vector of row sums of X;

$Li = l$ = Vector of row sums of $L = A_l\hat{y}_n \rightarrow l = A_l y_n$;

$\lambda'_a = i'A_l$= Vector of column sums of A_l, i.e., the vector of aggregate average propensities to leak;

N = the matrix of SAM transactions between endogenous accounts;

X= the matrix of injections from exogenous into endogenous accounts;

L= the matrix of leakages from endogenous into exogenous accounts;

R= the matrix of SAM transactions between exogenous accounts.

Thus, for any given injection anywhere in the SAM, its influence is transmitted through the interdependent SAM system. The total direct and indirect effects of the injection on the endogenous accounts, i.e., the total outputs of the different activities and the incomes of the various factors and socio-economic groups, are estimated through the multiplier process.

By definition (the materials balance relationship) and from (3) we get a matrix of SAM multipliers

$$\begin{aligned} y_n &= A_n y_n + x \\ y_n - A_n y_n &= x \\ (I - A_n) &= x \\ y_n &= (I - A_n)^{-1} x \\ y_n &= M_a x \end{aligned} \tag{12}$$

This can also be applied to leakages

$$\begin{aligned} l &= A_l y_n \\ &= A_l (I - A_n)^{-1} x \\ &= A_l M_a x \end{aligned} \tag{13}$$

And the equilibrium condition of Keynesian macroeconomics, 'injection equal to withdrawals', is given by

$$[\, i'A_n + i'A_l)\hat{y}_n]'i = y_n' i = i'(A_n y_n + x\,)$$

Note that to derive and illustrate the underlying logic of this methodology, we maintain the previous assumption that the only three accounts that are endogenously determined are activities, factors and households, while Government, capital and the rest of the world are exogenous (Pyatt and Round 1979).

The Results of the SAM- income Multipliers

While it is true that the poor do not have resources to benefit from improved market access generally, in Botswana they have limited livestock (cattle and goats) that they could export as meat subject to improved management, skills, productivity and access to infrastructure. For instance, in Botswana the poor especially females, usually harvest veldt products such a mophane worm, which is exported, to several countries including South Africa as food and livestock feed. Thus an improved marketing and environmentally benign harvesting system coupled with better packaging and distribution could enhance the incomes of several households in the Central district where most phane is harvested. Of course prevailing sanitary and phyto-sanitary (SPS) measures should be observed to regulate the trade. Further through direct employment in tourism and textiles some of the poor households, especially those headed by females, can benefit if they are also empowered with knowledge and skills.

Effects of Improved Beef Export Earnings on Poor Households

In the 1996/97 SAM there are seven types of households of which six are citizen while the last type is for non-citizen. Among the six citizen-type households there are three in urban areas based on, wage-income, self-employment and transfers. In the rural areas we also have the same three types of households based on wage-income, self-employment and transfers. Households whose income is based on transfers are considered poor in this paper simply because from the SAM, it is clear that these households are overly dependent on Government transfers and transfers from urban households for their livelihoods. Households whose income is based on transfers in both rural and urban areas altogether account for just 7 percent of total household income while the waged-based families in both areas (urban and rural) received about 59 percent of total income (Figure 1).

Further poor households spent at least 30 percent of their income on food and clothing the bulk of which is imported hence the critical role of global trade liberalization to improve income and food security for the poor. In this paper special interest was paid to how trade liberalization affects households whose income is based on transfers in both urban and rural areas. Furthermore, poor households are characterized by low levels of formal education and skills.

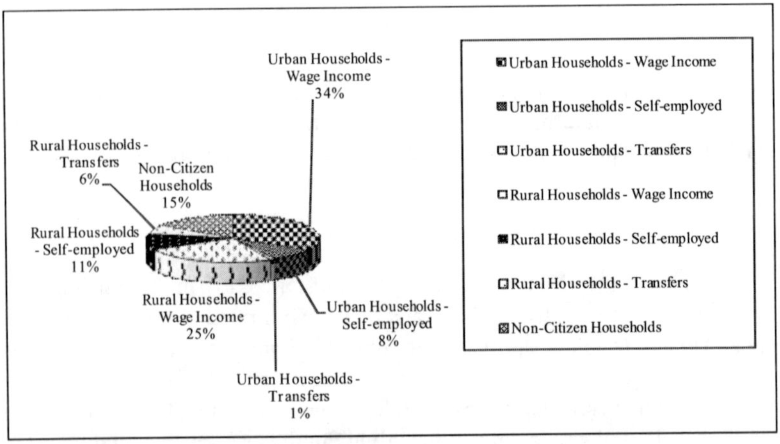

Figure 1: Share of Total Household Income by Household Type

When beef export earnings increased by 10 percent due to improved market access globally, we identified the following effects at factor, household and activity levels.

Factor Level

Except for mixed income which registered a 2 percent increase in income after a 10 percent increase in beef export earnings; all other factors recorded less than 1 percent increase in income. Mixed income represents factor income for households that depend on informal sector income in this particular case .all employed workers including gross operating surplus or return to owners of capital only witnessed less than 1 percent increase in income after a 10 percent increase in beef export earnings.

Household Level

Among households, it was only the self-employed female-headed households based in both urban and rural areas that experienced about 1per cent each increase in their income after a 10 percent increase in beef export earnings. Other households gained less than 1 percent increase in income after an increase in beef export earnings. Self-employed households own cattle and therefore it is not surprising that an increase in beef export earnings also affects them significantly. Poor citizen households in both urban and rural areas whose income is from transfers did not benefit from improved beef export earnings, as they do not own cattle. About 45 percent of rural households do not own cattle in Botswana (Central Statistics Office, 2001). This means poverty alleviation in Botswana will not necessarily benefit from improved beef market access.

Activity Level

Following the 10 percent increase in beef export earnings; there are activities whose output/income increases. As expected meat processing witnesses a 5.7 percent increase in output/income after beef earnings have improved while cattle rearing in both traditional and free-hold area record each about 2.7 percent increase in income or output after an increase in beef export earnings. Other farming activities as well as, dairy production, gathering and hunting just gain about 1 percent in income. The increase in income or output of livestock- related activities including meat-processing following in improvements in beef export earnings shows income and demand linkages in the economy. Other several activities witness an increase in income or output but the gain is less than 1 percent. As the SAM captures the circular flow of income and expenditure in an economy, an increase in beef export earnings positively affects several activities in the economy even though some experience output/income increase less than 1 percent.

Improved Tourism Export Earnings on Poor Households

Government has identified tourism as an important sector for economic diversification and employment creation especially in the rural areas, which could possibly contribute to improving incomes of the poor if unskilled personnel are employed. Some communities in Botswana have entered into agreement with tourist operators to view game in their areas at negotiated fees. The fees are to be used by the community for development. Further, tourism export earnings are among the top four sources of foreign exchange in Botswana. We now examine the effects of a 10 percent increase in tourism export earnings on factors, households and activities in Botswana.

Factor Level

Among factors, both employees and gross operating surplus witness less than 1 percent increase in income after a 10 percent increase in tourism export earnings. This means very limited income and demand linkages with tourism sector and that the sector may not contribute significantly to reducing unemployment among the unskilled.

Household Level

All households experienced less than 1 percent increase in income following a 10 percent increase in tourism export earnings. This once again shows very limited income and demand linkages between the tourism sector and household welfare. The poor households are therefore not likely to benefit from a booming tourism industry despite the government commitment to this sector. As a relatively as a superior good, tourism requires higher disposable income for households to benefit hence the limited participation by households based on income transfers.

Government has come up with financial assistance schemes such as Citizen Entrepreneurial Development Agency (CEDA) to empower citizens to participate in sectors like tourism. However, given the relatively capital intensive nature of tourism it is unlikely that poor female headed households will benefit from the expansion of this export led industry.

Activity Level

Among activities, hotel and restaurants, trade, transport and business services benefit from an increased tourism export income. As expected hotels and restaurants witness at 6.2 percent increase in their income after a 10 percent increase in tourism export income. Other activities only witness less than 1 percent increase in output/income. This also shows very limited inter-industry income and demand linkages in the tourism sector.

Effects of Improved Textiles Export Earnings on Poor Households

The textiles industry in Botswana is currently benefiting under the preferential US-Africa trade initiative through which exporters are exempted from duty. This is the main industry in Botswana where female workforce is in the majority. Thus an improvement in market access in this industry is more likely to benefit women. Further, the industry has over the years been identified as one of the important manufacturing activities for economic diversification, and as a result the sector has benefited from public financial support. In addition, the industry is considered as a possible source of employment especially among unskilled and semi-skilled persons who constitute the largest number of the unemployed people in the country. We examine the effects of a 10 percent increase in textiles export earnings on poor household welfare. It is assumed that as the textiles industry is likely to employ unskilled persons, possibly the poor households could benefit.

Factor Level

Among workers, an increase in textiles export earnings all witnessed very insignificant income improvements (less than 1 percent). Textiles are expected to generate additional employment opportunities especially for the unskilled members of the labour force. This result shows very limited positive effect on employment including unskilled workers. And the results clear show that female-headed poor households will be adversely affected.

Household Level

All households witness less than 1 percent increase in income after a 10 percent increase in textiles export revenue. For the households whose income is based on transfers once again, as the poorest families, who are predominantly female they do not benefit from global export market access primarily because they lack resources and skills. As wage income is very important among households, improved acccss to skills and resources could enable members from poor households to benefit from sectors such as textiles.

Activity Level

While the textiles industry records a 9 percent increase in income after a 10 percent increase in export earnings, other activities only register less than 1 percent increase in output/income. It is evident that in general, the textiles industry has relatively weak linkages with several sectors in the domestic economy. Assuming the industry is globally competitive, it is possible to generate more income-demand linkages if existing trade distortions and technical barriers are reduced/removed while productivity is enhanced. As a result public goods like education, infrastructure, health, technology/research, etc will need to be developed for the textiles industry to be competitive and for the poor households to benefit.

Conclusion

Trade liberalization through tariff liberalization in general has more potential benefits to the poor than improved export market access. Tariff reduction in food products like beef, dairy etc benefit the poor very significantly while increase in export earnings has limited effects.

The results also point to the limitation of trade liberalization in addressing poverty alleviation. More specifically there is a need for the development and implementation of complimentary policies to reduce market failures and poor price transmission normally caused by inadequate institutional and legal support systems. Further, poor households will also need to be empowered with skills, education, financial resources, negotiation skills and be effectively involved in policies and programmes designed for their welfare.

It is therefore difficult to see how Botswana would be able to overcome all the economic and social challenges it would face at the end of a preferential trade arrangement with the EU and AGOA with the USA. Botswana has one of the highest HIV/AIDS infection rate in the world. This poses a threat to continued economic growth in Botswana, mostly because of its impact on the labour force, but also because of its possible impacts on savings and investment.

References

Deacon, B. (2000), *Globalisation and Social Policy: The Threat to Equitable Wefare*. United Nations Research Institute for Social Development Occasional Paper No. 5, Geneva.

Delgado, C., Hopkins, J. and Kelly, V. (1998), *Agricultural Growth Linkages in Sub-Saharan Africa*. Research Report No. 107, International Food Policy Research Institute (IFPRI), Washington D C.

Pyatt, G. and Round, J.I. (1979), Accounting and Fixed Price Multipliers in a Social Accounting Matrix Framework. *The Economic Journal,* 89 (December): 850-873.

Winters, L.A. (2000a), *Trade, Trade Policy and Poverty: What are the Links?* Discussion Paper No. 2382, Centre for Economic Policy Research, London.

Winters, L.A. (2000b), *Trade Liberalisation and Poverty*. Discussion Paper No.7, Poverty Research Unit, University of Sussex, Brighton.

World Bank (2000), *World Development Report 2000*. Washington DC.

Index

M

N

Y

Z